Intersections of Multiple Identities

Counseling and Psychotherapy
Investigating Practice From Scientific, Historical, and Cultural Perspectives

A Routledge book series

Editor, Bruce E. Wampold, University of Wisconsin

This innovative new series is devoted to grasping the vast complexities of the practice of counseling and psychotherapy. As a set of healing practices delivered in a context shaped by health delivery systems and the attitudes and values of consumers, practitioners, and researchers, counseling and psychotherapy must be examined critically. By understanding the historical and cultural context of counseling and psychotherapy and by examining the extant research, these critical inquiries seek a deeper, richer understanding of what is a remarkably effective endeavor.

Published

Beyond Evidence-Based Psychotherapy: Fostering the Eight Sources of Change in Child and Adolescent Treatment
George W. Rosenfeld

Cognitive Behavioral Therapy for Deaf and Hearing Persons with Language and Learning Challenges
Neil Glickman

Counseling and Therapy with Clients Who Abuse Alcohol or Other Drugs
Cynthia E. Glidden-Tracy

The Great Psychotherapy Debate
Bruce Wampold

*The Psychology of Working:
Implications for Career Development, Counseling, and Public Policy*
David Blustein

Neuropsychotherapy: How the Neurosciences Inform Effective Psychotherapy
Klaus Grawe

Principles of Multicultural Counseling
Uwe P. Gielen, Juris G. Draguns, Jefferson M. Fish

Forthcoming

The Pharmacology and Treatment of Substance Abuse: Evidence and Outcomes Based Perspective
Lee Cohen, Frank Collins, Alice Young, Dennis McChargue

Making Treatment Count: Using Outcomes to Inform and Manage Therapy
Michael Lambert, Jeb Brown, Scott Miller, Bruce Wampold

The Handbook of Therapeutic Assessment
Stephen E. Finn

IDM Supervision: An Integrated Developmental Model for Supervising Counselors and Therapists, Third Edition
Cal Stoltenberg and Brian McNeill

The Great Psychotherapy Debate, Revised Edition
Bruce Wampold

Culture and the Therapeutic Process: A Guide for Mental Health Professionals
Mark M. Leach and Jamie Aten

Intersections of
Multiple
Identities

**A CASEBOOK
OF EVIDENCE-BASED
PRACTICES WITH
DIVERSE POPULATIONS**

Miguel E. Gallardo & Brian W. McNeill, Editors

Routledge
Taylor & Francis Group
New York   London

Routledge
Taylor & Francis Group
270 Madison Avenue
New York, NY 10016

Routledge
Taylor & Francis Group
2 Park Square
Milton Park, Abingdon
Oxon OX14 4RN

© 2009 by Taylor & Francis Group, LLC
Routledge is an imprint of Taylor & Francis Group, an Informa business

International Standard Book Number-13: 978-0-8058-6190-7 (Softcover) 978-0-8058-6189-1 (Hardcover)

Library of Congress Cataloging-in-Publication Data

Intersections of multiple identities : a casebook of evidence-based practices with
    diverse populations / [edited by] Miguel E. Gallardo & Brian W. McNeill.
        p. ; cm. -- (Counseling and psychotherapy : investigating practice from
        scientific, historical, and cultural perspectives)
    Includes bibliographical references.
        ISBN 978-0-8058-6189-1 (hardcover : alk. paper) -- ISBN 978-0-8058-6190-7 (pbk.
        : alk. paper)
    1. Psychiatry, Transcultural--Case studies. 2. Evidence-based psychotherapy--Case
studies. I. Gallardo, Miguel E. II. McNeill, Brian, 1955- III. Series: Counseling and
psychotherapy.
        [DNLM: 1. Psychotherapy--methods--Case Reports. 2. Adolescent. 3. Cultural
Characteristics--Case Reports. 4. Cultural Competency--Case Reports. 5. Ethnic
Groups--psychology--Case Reports. 6. Evidence-Based Medicine--methods--Case
Reports. 7. Mental Disorders--ethnology--Case Reports. WS 163 I61 2009]

RC455.4.E8I72 2009
616.89--dc22   2008039913

Visit the Taylor & Francis Web site at
http://www.taylorandfrancis.com

and the Routledge Web site at
http://www.routledge.com

To my parents,
for giving everything they had
so I could achieve.

Miguel E. Gallardo

For my precious daughters,
Kimi and Mari,
whose multiple dimensions and
intersections of identity and diversity
represent the future.

Brian W. McNeill

Contents

Series Editor Preface

This innovative new series is devoted to grasping the vast complexities of the practice of counseling and psychotherapy. As a set of healing practices delivered in a context shaped by health delivery systems and the attitudes and values of consumers, practitioners, and researchers, counseling and psychotherapy must be examined critically. By understanding the historical and cultural context of counseling and psychotherapy, and by examining the extant research, these critical inquiries seek a deeper, richer understanding of what is a remarkably effective endeavor.

There are two major guiding movements in mental health treatments currently. The first is evidence-based practice. The adjective "evidence-based" seems to be used to modify many terms in our field to give them the imprinteur of science. The second is multiculturalism. Many have noted that racial and ethnic minorities underutilize mental health services despite profound need for those services. As a consequence, there have been concerted efforts to provide culturally competent services. These movements are quite ambiguous—terms are used in various ways, concepts are general, inferences are many and often contradictory, and dogma is often the final result. Moreover, the intersections of these two movements are sparse. The field has desperately needed an integration of these movements, one which carefully examines each and then draws the implications for practice. This integration is accomplished by Miguel Gallardo & Brian McNeill in their edited volume *Intersections of Multiple Identities: A Casebook of Evidence-Based Practices with Diverse Populations*. The premise of this volume, which is presented in the introductory chapter, is that evidence-based multicultural practice is needed to deliver acceptable and effective mental health services. Each of the authors then presents cases that illustrate how this notion translates into clinical practice. The cases are fascinating, bringing to life the principles inherent in the integration.

Bruce E. Wampold, Ph.D., ABPP, Series Editor
University of Wisconsin - Madison

Contributors

Joseph M. Cervantes, PhD, is an associate professor of counseling at California State University, Fullerton, and a practicing psychologist at Affiliated Professional Psychologists in Orange, California. Dr. Cervantes integrates modern psychotherapy with traditional spiritual healing approaches in his work with Latino populations.

Melissa J. Corpus is a doctoral student in the counseling psychology program at Teachers College, Columbia University. Her research interests include the intersections of identity—race, gender, and sexual orientation. In addition, Melissa is an academic advisor and adjunct instructor at Kingsborough Community College in Brooklyn, New York.

Matt Englar-Carlson, PhD, is an associate professor of counseling at California State University, Fullerton. He has published in the area of men and masculinity, child counseling, and social justice/multicultural counseling. Recently he is the coeditor of the books *In the Room With Men: A Casebook of Therapeutic Change* (APA, 2006) and *Counseling Troubled Boys* (Routledge, 2008).

Miguel E. Gallardo, PsyD, is a licensed clinical psychologist and currently serves as an associate professor of psychology at Pepperdine University's Graduate School of Education and Psychology. He maintains an independent/consultation practice where he conducts therapy with individual adolescents and adults.

Jennifer Gibson, PhD, is on staff at the University of California, Davis. She received her PhD in clinical psychology with an emphasis on community and multicultural psychology from the California School of Professional Psychology. Dr. Gibson is a writer, researcher, consultant, and trainer in the area of clinical competency and disability.

Carol D. Goodheart, EdD, is in independent practice in Princeton, New Jersey, and a clinical supervisor at the Graduate School of Applied and Professional Psychology, Rutgers University. She served as chair for the 2005 American Psychological Association (APA) Presidential Task Force on Evidence-Based Practice, which developed the policy recommendation adopted by the APA. She is a fellow of the APA and a distinguished practitioner in the National Academy of Psychology.

Jeff King, PhD, is an associate professor at Western Washington University's Department of Psychology, where he is also director for the Center for Cross-Cultural Research. He is a licensed clinical psychologist and has provided clinical services to primarily American Indian populations for the past 20 years. He was the director of Native American Counseling in Denver, Colorado for 13 years. Before coming to Western Washington University, Dr. King worked for 2 years among the Taos and Picuris Pueblo through Indian Health Service. He is currently the president of the First Nations Behavioral Health Association and an active board member of the National Alliance of Multi-Ethnic Behavioral Health. Dr. King is a tribally enrolled member of the Muscogee (Creek) Nation of Oklahoma.

Laurie "Lali" McCubbin, PhD, is an assistant professor of counseling psychology at Washington State University and has worked extensively with Native Hawaiian populations in issues of education and ethnic identity.

Brian W. McNeill, PhD, is a professor and director of training for the Counseling Psychology Program at Washington State University. He is the coeditor of *The Handbook of Chicana and Chicano Psychology and Mental Health* (2004) and *Latina/o Healing Practices: Mestizo and Indigenous Perspectives* (2008) and is a licensed psychologist in the states of Washington and Idaho, where he practices and consults.

Olga L. Mejía, PhD, is an assistant professor at California State University, Fullerton, in the Department of Counseling and is a licensed psychologist. Her research interests include immigration, Latino families, acculturation, and women's issues. Dr. Mejía conducts individual, couple, group, and family psychotherapy in English and Spanish. Most recently she provided psychotherapy in a community program for Latina/o youth and their families. The program is field-based and offers comprehensive bilingual and bicultural clinical and case management services. Dr. Mejía also has extensive experience with college students, focusing on multicultural counseling, in major universities in Texas and California.

Marie L. Miville, PhD, is the director of training, program coordinator, and associate professor of psychology and education at Teachers College, Columbia University. Her areas of research and practice include multicultural counseling, Latino/a mental health issues, universal-diverse orientation, social attitudes and identity development, intersections of identities, supervision, training, consultation, and professional and student development.

Fernando Ortiz, PhD, is currently an assistant professor at Alliant International University, California School of Professional Psychology, San Diego campus, where he specializes in personality assessment, multicultural competencies, and clinical skills. He received his PhD in counseling psychology from Washington State University, specializing in cross-cultural research and Mexican ethnopsychology. He completed a postdoctoral internship at the University of California, Santa Barbara Counseling Center with a specialization in multicultural clinical training. His research interests include minority personality assessment and cross-cultural issues, Mexican ethnopsychology, and indigenous healing modalities. He has worked extensively with ethnic minorities in the California mental health system.

Thomas Parham, PhD, is the assistant vice chancellor for Counseling and Health Services and director of the Counseling Center at the University of California, Irvine. As the past president of both the National Association of Black Psychologists and the Association for Multicultural Counseling and Development, he is recognized as the architect of the "Rites of Passage" program for the 100's "Passport to the Future" program and for the Los Angeles-based "College Bound" program.

Sophia Rath, M.S., is a doctoral student in counseling psychology in the Department of Counselor Education and Counseling Psychology at Western Michigan University. She is a second-generation Cambodian American; her family emigrated from Cambodia during the 1970s.

LeLaina Romero is a doctoral student in counseling psychology at Teachers College, Columbia University. Her research and applied work center on creating partnerships with people of color from low-income communities to enhance well-being. She also works with college students, particularly first generation, in teaching and advising roles.

Daryl M. Rowe, PhD, is a professor of psychology in the Graduate School of Education and Psychology at Pepperdine University. His research and teaching interests include both cross-cultural and culturally specific mental health issues. In addition to alcohol and other substance abuse prevention and treatment theories and techniques of counseling, psychotherapy, and clinical supervision, he conducts research, consults, trains, and publishes on psychological issues affecting African Americans. He holds a national position in the Association of Black Psychologists and sits on the board of several community agencies. Dr. Rowe is a licensed psychologist with a private practice emphasizing couples and marital therapy in the Los Angeles area.

Sandra Lyons Rowe, PhD, is a licensed clinical psychologist with many years of experience working with children and adults in a variety of settings. She is currently the coordinator of Psychological Services at Santa Monica College in Santa Monica, California. In her position she is responsible for planning and overseeing the delivery of psychological services to the college community. Her previous position was as director of Community Services at Hollygrove Children and Family Services located in Hollywood, where she was responsible for all of the agency's mental health and child welfare programs. She is a child advocate and has consulted with child welfare agencies around the country as a master trainer for the Child Welfare League of America. Dr. Rowe has held staff psychologist positions and taught at Loyola Marymount University and the California School of Professional Psychology. She also maintains a private practice in Los Angeles with her husband, Dr. Daryl Rowe, where they specialize in working with couples.

Maryam Sayyedi, PhD, is the founder and clinical director of Omid Multicultural Institute for Development (O.M.I.D.) in Irvine, California. She is a licensed clinical child psychologist and an adjunct faculty in the department of counseling at California State University Fullerton. She obtained her PhD from Washington State University in clinical psychology with concentrations in child development and neuropsychology. Dr. Sayyedi is bilingual and fluent in Farsi and she has devoted her practice and research to addressing the mental health needs of the Middle Eastern-American adolescents, children and their families.

Foreword

Carol D. Goodheart

Intersections of Multiple Identities: A Casebook of Evidence-Based Practices With Diverse Populations is a pioneering effort to take the essential hallmarks of Evidence-Based Practice in Psychology (EBPP) and apply them in a very diverse world. It represents a large step forward in the development of psychological services that are culturally appropriate, derived from sound evidence, and reasonable to implement in fluid and demanding practice environments. This is no small task. Editors Miguel E. Gallardo and Brian W. McNeill have chosen to emphasize a contextual approach to practice, one based on common factors in well-established therapies. They have assembled courageous authors to provide demonstrations of EBPP within circumstances that contain complex group identities and processes. Why are they courageous? Because they are willing to risk showing the kind of innovative and synthesizing work that is still in progress (in some cases), that is still being refined, and that proceeds despite gaps in the clinical research literature that can be filled in only over time.

What is meant by the term EBPP? As defined by the American Psychological Association (APA, 2006), it is an overarching conceptual approach to practice: "Evidence-Based Practice in Psychology (EBPP) is the integration of the best available research with clinical expertise in the context of patient characteristics, culture and preferences" (p. 273).

As chair of the task force that created the language adopted by APA, I can attest to the fact that there are many different opinions and points of view about what EBPP should comprise and what should be emphasized. Having listened carefully to many discussions among clinicians and researchers on the topic, I think it is fair to say there are five important elements to take into consideration for EBPP: the individual therapist, the therapeutic relationship, the treatment method, the active engaged patient, and the principles of change

(Goodheart, Kazdin, & Sternberg, 2006; Norcross, Beutler, & Levant, 2005). Any and all of these elements may be especially germane, depending on particular clinical circumstances. In the chapters to follow, the salience of these factors is aligned with the multiple intersecting identities of those involved in the therapeutic endeavor, such as ethnicity/race, religion/spirituality, disability, and sexual orientation. Taken individually and as a whole, the authors contribute to a better understanding of multiculturalism and the aspects of identity that must be taken into account in EBPP.

What counts as "evidence"? A clarification and elaboration about evidence is offered in a commentary on EBPP (Wampold, Goodheart, & Levant, 2007) that seems particularly relevant to the aims of the casebook:

> Evidence is not data nor is it truth. Evidence can be thought of as inferences that flow from data. These data may be of various types but are derived from observations, in the generic sense of the word (e.g., they may be "observed" by a machine and transformed before being processed by the human brain or they may be sensory experience transformed during self-observation). The data become evidence when they are considered with regard to the phenomena being studied, the model used to generate the data, previous knowledge, theory, the methodologies employed, and the human actors. (p. 617)

The treatment examples in the casebook are heuristic and contribute to a blueprint for better tailoring services to patients' characteristics, sociocultural and family contexts, and preferences. The reader must keep an open mind and recognize that some of the modifications may be in their early stages, as applied to specific populations, and it will take time for research developments to further support them. It is important to realize how little research, relatively, has been done on ethnic minority patients or those who identify themselves as disabled or lesbian, gay, bisexual, or transgendered. For example, from 1986 to 2005, about 10,000 participants were included in randomized clinical trials evaluating the efficacy of targeted psychological treatments; no information on race or ethnicity was provided for nearly half of them (4,991 of the 10,000); and not one study analyzed the efficacy of the treatment by ethnicity or race (Zane, 2005).

Editors Gallardo and McNeill have structured the consistent format of the chapters to show how evidence can be used to benefit patients with diverse backgrounds and can provide multilayered contexts for their lives. Culturally specific treatments are considered evidence-based when they are demonstrated to be both acceptable to patients and effective. However, practitioners must make use of their clinical expertise and the available knowledge to make inferences when such demonstrations are not available. The consistent use of case formulation in the casebook is an excellent example of a well-defined core component of clinical expertise. Furthermore, a careful process of monitoring patient progress and adjustment of treatment as needed allows professionals to offer tailored approaches and innovative methods or creative combinations of methods, while ensuring that interventions are safe and effective. After all, the goal of EBPP is to "promote effective psychological practice and enhance public health, by applying empirically supported principles of assessment, case formulation, therapeutic relationship, and intervention" (APA, 2006, p. 280).

It takes a sense of social justice to forge effective psychological treatment approaches for all people in need, not just for the majority patients on whom clinical research has most often been focused. The editors and contributors bring determination and a strong commitment to social justice in their attempt to improve the lives of patients through the explorations in this casebook. Clinicians and counselors who want to practice in culturally proficient effective ways will be enriched by the case examples and heartened by the recommendations for the provision of culturally appropriate services that are consistent with the principles of EBPP. It is possible to see now the shape of what is to come: a world in which evidence-based practice in psychology is broadly defined and specifically applicable to meet the diverse needs of people in evolving complex societies.

References

American Psychological Association. (2006). Evidence-Based Practice in Psychology. *American Psychologist, 61*, 271–285.

Goodheart, C. D., Kazdin, A. E., & Sternberg, R. J (Eds.). (2006). *Evidence-based psychotherapy: Where practice and research meet.* Washington, DC: American Psychological Association.

Norcross, J. C., Beutler, L. E., & Levant, R. F. (Eds.). (2005). *Evidence-based practices in mental health: Debate and dialogue on the fundamental questions.* Washington, DC: American Psychological Association.

Wampold, B., Goodheart, C. D., & Levant, R. F. (2007). Clarification and elaboration on evidence-based practice in psychology. *American Psychologist, 62*, 616–618.

Zane, N. (2005). *Patient's characteristics, preferences and context in EPPP.* Paper presented at the Presidential Symposium, annual convention of the American Psychological Association, Washington, DC.

Introduction

Psychotherapy as Healing Practice
Multiple Identities, Common Factors, and Evidence-Based Practice

Brian W. McNeill
Miguel E. Gallardo

In the past two decades, the need to prepare and train mental health personnel in working with diverse populations has been addressed through an ever-increasing theoretical and empirical literature. As a result, the so-called Multicultural Movement has been referred to as the "fourth force" in psychology (Pedersen, 1998). As a consequence of this increased awareness, traditional training programs in professional psychology spend the majority of their time attempting to increase students' cultural responsiveness in terms of knowledge, skills, and awareness of biases and stereotypes as they relate to underrepresented and underserved populations. Toward this end, many excellent preparatory textbooks exist for the purposes of increasing trainees' understanding in each of these three domains (e.g., Pedersen, Draguns, Lonner, & Trimble, 2006; Sue & Sue, 2008). In addition, many of these programs implement a single semester course that attempts to impart a stronger theoretical base about a specific cultural group's characteristics. However, in our view, the missing links in these courses are the specific skill development recommendations for applied practice with diverse populations. Consequently, the purpose of this casebook is to bridge this gap between practitioner self-awareness, knowledge of diverse groups, and the practice of psychology based on solid theory and research.

A key component to this casebook is the history of work pointing to the common factors responsible for the effectiveness of psychotherapy as a healing practice. In 1972, E. Fuller Torrey first published *The Mind Game* (1983), in which he studied *curanderismo*, a Mexican American healing practice, in Santa Clara County, California, as well as healing traditions in other cultures, including Ethiopia and Borneo. He concluded that the differences between psychiatrists and so-called witch doctors may not be so great, citing common components in all healing traditions. These components include a shared world view, the personal qualities of the therapist, patient expectations, and use of techniques. Over a number of years, Jerome Frank (Frank, 1961; Frank & Frank, 1991) have argued that all healing practices share (a) an emotionally charged, confiding relationship with a healer; (b) a healing context in which the therapist has the power and expertise to help, along with a socially sanctioned role to provide services; (c) a rationale or conceptual schema to explain problems; and (d) a ritual or procedure consistent with the treatment rationale.

More recently, Fischer, Jome, and Atkinson (1998) expanded upon and reviewed the evidence supporting what they term "universal healing conditions" in a culturally specific context, which includes four common components. First, it is now widely accepted across all therapeutic orientations or approaches to psychotherapy that the therapeutic relationship serves as a base for all therapeutic intervention across cultures. Second, a shared world view, conceptual schema, or rationale for explaining symptoms provides the common framework by which both the healer and client work together. Third, the client's expectation in the form of faith or hope in the process of healing exists across all cultures. These three factors set the stage for the therapeutic ritual or intervention that all healing shares. This therapeutic ritual or intervention is in the form of a procedure that requires the active participation of both the client and the therapist, and the procedure is believed by both to be the means of restoring the client's health.

Recent research in common factors associated with psychotherapy effectiveness by Wampold (2001a, 2001b) supports the view that all healing traditions share common healing factors responsible for effectiveness. In his impressive review and analysis of the research on the efficacy of psychotherapy, Wampold (2001b) presented a strong case for the lack of evidence supporting the medical model of psychotherapy where specific therapeutic treatments or "ingredients" (e.g., empirically supported treatments) are assumed to be primarily responsible for the effectiveness of psychotherapy. Consequently, Wampold concluded that all treatments intended to be therapeutic are equally efficacious, as attempts to identify specific effects have not produced consistent findings. In contrast, the therapeutic relationship or working alliance has consistently been demonstrated to be related to outcome across various treatments. Interestingly, allegiance to the specific therapy investigated has also been shown to be related to outcome, as therapeutic allegiance results in effects larger than treatment effects. Moreover, treatments delivered with manuals are not superior to treatments delivered without manuals. Finally, therapist effects in the form of the personal qualities of the therapist account for about 9% of the variance in outcome, and the typical research design that ignores therapist effects results in an overestimation of treatment effects.

These findings demonstrate some of the most important concepts for consideration in the context of culture and therapy. What Wampold highlighted and the cases included in this volume underscore is the importance of the therapeutic relationship or working alliance. In addition, Norcross (2001) reported that empirically supported treatments (ESTs) fail to include several important variables in psychotherapy: (a) the therapist as a person, (b) the therapy relationship, and (c) the patient's nondiagnostic characteristics. Goodheart (2006) further stated that a clinician's reluctance to implement ESTs is the result of narrowly defined treatments tested in controlled laboratories that have very little real-world application. Goodheart's statement is particularly relevant when you review the complexities of the cases presented in this casebook. The narrow application of ESTs in applied clinical settings provides an avenue for the exploration of variables not accounted for in laboratory settings.

Similar to Wampold (2001b), Norcross (2002) found that therapeutic variance was attributed to only 8% for treatment methods used, whereas 10% could be attributed to the therapeutic relationship, 25% attributed to patient contributions, and 45% attributed to unexplained variance in therapeutic factors. These findings provide solid evidence for reexamining the nature in which we investigate and implement research methodologies within a global multicultural context. For example, Townsend and McWhirter (2005) conducted a literature review over a span of 19 years and found that connectedness continues to remain the essence of psychologically healthy relationships and personal functioning. Townsend and McWhirter used a definition of connectedness that highlights relatedness or one's involvement with another as a way to promote well-being. The authors further stated that counselors serve their clients well when counselors "embrace a connected-oriented psychotherapy" (p. 196). In essence, our connection with clients becomes one of the most important therapeutic interventions we can implement in the course of therapy (Lambert & Barley, 2001). The authors in this casebook describe their experiences in building therapeutic relationships as a first step in treating their culturally diverse clients. As a result, the approaches developed in working with these cases are the results of the clinical experiences these authors have with specific cultural groups.

The work of these researchers has strongly influenced the 2006 report of the American Psychological Association (APA) Presidential Task Force on Evidence-Based Practice. The task force defined Evidence-Based Practice in Psychology (EBPP) as "the integration of the best available research with clinical expertise in the context of patient characteristics, culture, and preferences" (APA, 2006, p. 273). As such, EBPP reflects a movement away from narrowly defined ESTs, which in most cases have not been empirically tested for their application to diverse populations (Atkinson, Bui, & Mori, 2001). The APA report (2006) further stated that broader considerations are needed for the inclusion of not only the best research evidence, but also clinical expertise and client characteristics as indicators of good outcomes in therapy. Best research evidence includes not only traditional experimental design methodologies, but also clinical observation, qualitative research, case studies, and ethnographic investigations (APA, 2006). According to the task force report, clinical expertise is conceptualized as the competence attained by psychologists through education, training, and experience, which results in effective practice. Consequently, clinical expertise includes assessment; diagnostic judgment; clinical decision making; interpersonal expertise; continual self-reflection and acquisition of skills; evaluation and use of research evidence; culturally relevant interventions in understanding the influence of individual, cultural, and contextual differences on treatment; seeking available resources as needed; and a cogent rationale for clinical strategies. EBPP also "involves consideration of the client's values, religious beliefs, world views, goals, and preferences for treatment with the psychologist's experiences and understanding of the available research" (APA, 2006, p. 278), including individual client characteristics such as gender, gender identity, culture, ethnicity, race, age, family context, religious beliefs, and sexual orientation, as well as the impact of these variables on the treatment process, relationship, and outcome (APA, 2000, 2003).

In making a strong case for the complementary nature of culturally relevant or competent treatment and EBPP, Whaley and Davis (2007) defined cultural competence as a set of problem-solving skills that includes (a) the ability to recognize and understand the dynamic interplay between the heritage and adaptation dimensions of culture in shaping human behavior; (b) the ability to use the knowledge acquired about an individual's heritage and adaptational challenges to maximize the effectiveness of assessment, diagnosis, and treatment; and (c) internalization, diagnosis, and treatment; and (d) internalization (i.e., incorporation into one's clinical problem-solving repertoire) of this process of recognition, acquisition, and use of cultural dynamics so that it can be routinely applied to diverse groups. (p. 565)

In addition, Vasquez (2007) and Comas-Díaz (2006) examined the cultural variation in the therapist–client relationship within an EBPP perspective. The authors addressed cultural variations by examining the differences across cultures in the expression of affect, hierarchical relationships, and personal attributes leading to the development and enhancement of cultural empathy. Ridley and Lingle (1996) defined cultural empathy as "a learned ability of counselors to accurately gain an understanding of the self-experience of clients from other cultures—an understanding informed by counselors' interpretations of cultural data" (p. 32). Most recently, Sue and Sue (2008) presented a variety of traditional and contemporary treatment approaches and interventions in a culturally relevant EBPP context.

Thus, our intention in this casebook is to provide demonstrations of culturally responsive EBPP with diverse populations. In addition, primary themes across the case presentations are the multiple dimensions and intersections of identity and diversity throughout each chapter. As demonstrated by the constantly changing demographics of our multicultural society, and most prominently by Barack Obama, the first multiracial President of the United States, it is no longer enough to simply understand diverse groups of individuals as identifying only with a single ethnic or cultural background. Consequently, it has become essential that to truly understand individuals who make up the multicultural world in which we live, we must begin to examine, conceptualize, and treat according to the multiple ways in which individuals identify themselves. In addition to ethnicity or racial background, these multiple identifications include religion/spirituality, disability, and sexual orientation, to name a few. Hands-on practical recommendations from the perspective of EBPP and culture have not been well documented to date. Thus, the case examples serve to inform both trainees and practitioners via examples of EBPP, with methods of culturally responsive intervention, while addressing various dimensions of diversity in the healing encounter.

The format for the case presentations includes an introduction to the treatment of each author's respective client, a defined theoretical orientation from a traditional perspective, and an explanation of the ways in which each author has modified the orientation to provide more culturally appropriate EBPP treatment. The authors also provide a clinical case example and discuss the treatment process through a session analysis of each case. In addition, a case conceptualization section addressing common healing factors and EBPP, an additional section on clinical considerations, and a section addressing how each author's own dimensions of diversity and world view enhance or potentially impede the therapeutic endeavor are incorporated. A final section including cultural references and recommended readings, media references, and organizations is also provided. Finally, the authors provide their conclusions based on their work with each case and include discussion questions at the end of their chapters to stimulate educational dialogue with other colleagues or in the classroom setting.

The cases we included provide examples of the multiple intersections of identity within the context of EBPP and common factors important to the healing process. Thus, we have drawn on the clinical expertise of a number of practicing clinicians/healers whose varied experiences with multicultural populations provide examples of EBPP within a culturally responsive framework. The case described by Joseph M. Cervantes in "In Search of a Biethnic Identity: Clinical and Ethical Issues in the Treatment of a Latino/African American Adolescent Boy" reflects the changing demographics in our multicultural society in terms of the increasing populations of multiracial identity people and the challenge for identity formation, including the impact of racism and discrimination. Similar themes are explored within a family therapy setting by Olga L. Mejía in "Struggling With Research and Practice With a Mexican American Family: The Case of Robert."

Indigenous psychologies have used common factors in the healing process for centuries and illustrate the importance of understanding diverse world views in particular. In "Conversations in Marriage ©: An African-Centered Marital Intervention," Daryl M. Rowe and Sandra Lyons Rowe demonstrate the importance of converging world views through a program designed to empower African American couples grounded in a culture-specific African psychology context. Similarly, the Native Hawaiian conceptions of mental health, well-being, and identity determine the course of therapeutic intervention in "Intersecting Multiple Identities: The Case of Lehua" by Laurie "Lali" McCubbin. Jeff King demonstrates the Native American Indian world view and impact on the therapeutic process rooted in a native psychology in "Psychotherapy Within an American Indian Perspective" and also illustrates the important role of traditional spiritual activities as part of the healing process.

Although religion and spirituality have always encompassed the American Indian world view, the undervalued role of religion and traditional spirituality has been increasingly acknowledged in the formation of identity and psychological health (e.g., McNeill & Cervantes, 2008). The complex intersection of spirituality and sexual identity and the integration of spirituality in the psychotherapeutic setting are illustrated by the work of Fernando Ortiz in "Spirituality and Psychotherapy: A Gay Latino Client." The array of social status conflicts for a gay man of color are further explored and conceptualized in an innovative yet practical manner by Marie L. Miville, LeLaina Romero, and Melissa J. Corpus in "Incorporating Affirming, Feminist, and Relational Perspectives: The Case of Juan."

Emerging populations and the unique perspectives and issues reflected in their experiences are addressed by Matt Englar-Carlson and Sophia Rath in "The Conflict of Navigating Cultural Expectations: The Case of Sam" and by Maryam Sayyedi in "Psychotherapy With a 17-Year-Old Iranian American Female: Therapeutic Guidelines." Finally, the important intersection of disability and ethnicity are explored by Jennifer Gibson in "Clinical Competency and Culturally Diverse Clients With Disabilities: The Case of Linda."

Our hope is that this casebook contributes to the evolving area of multicultural psychology by serving as an example of what the future holds in working with culturally diverse individuals with multiple identities and world views while utilizing the common factors central to the healing process within the EBPP perspective.

References

American Psychological Association. (2006). Evidence-Based Practice in Psychology. *American Psychologist, 61,* 271–285.

Atkinson, D. R., Bui, U., & Mori, S. (2001). Multiculturally sensitive empirically supported treatment--an oxymoron? In J. G. Ponterotto, J. M Casas, L. A., Suzuki, & C. M. Alexander (Eds.). *Handbook of multicultural Counseling* (pp. 542–574). Thousand Oaks, CA: Sage.

Comas-Díaz, L. (2006). Cultural variation in the therapeutic relationship. In C. D. Goodheart, A. E. Kazdin, & R. J. Sternberg (Eds.), *Evidence-based psychotherapy: Where practice and research meet* (pp. 81–105). Washington, DC: American Psychological Association.

Fischer, A. R., Jome, L. M., & Atkinson, D. R. (1998). Reconceptualizing multi-cultural counseling: Universal healing conditions in a culturally specific context. *Journal of Counseling Psychology, 26,* 525–588.

Frank, J. D. (1961). *Persuasion and healing: A comparative study of psychotherapy.* New York: Schocken Books.

Frank, J. D., & Frank, J. B. (1991). *Persuasion and healing: A comparative study of psychotherapy* (3rd ed.). Baltimore: Johns Hopkins University Press.

Goodheart, C. D. (2006). Evidence, endeavor, and expertise in psychology practice. In C. D. Goodheart, A. E. Kazdin, & R. J. Sternberg (Eds.). *Evidence-based psychotherapy: Where practice and research meet* (pp. 37–61). Washington, D.C.: American Psychological Association.

Lambert, M. J., & Barley, D. E. (2001). Research summary on the therapeutic relationship and psychotherapy outcome. *Psychotherapy: Theory, Research, Practice, Training, 38*(4), 357–361.

McNeill, B. W., & Cervantes, J. M. (2008). Latina/o healing traditions: Mestizo and indigenous perspectives. New York: Routledge.

Norcross, J. C. (2001). Purposes, products, and products of the task force on empirically supported therapy relationships. *Psychotherapy: Theory, Research, Practice, Training, 38*(4), 345–356.

Norcross, J. C. (2002). (Ed.). *Psychotherapy relationships that work: Therapist contributions and responsiveness to patients.* New York: Oxford University Press.

Pedersen, P. B. (1998). *Multiculturalism as a fourth force.* Philadelphia: Bruner-Mazel.

Pedersen, P. B., Draguns, J. G., Lonner, W. J., & Trimble, J. E. (2008). *Counseling across cultures* (6th ed.). Thousand Oaks, CA: Sage.

Ridley, C., & Lingle, D. W. (1996). Cultural empathy in multicultural counseling: A multidimensional process model. In P. B. Pedersen, J. G. Draguns, W. J. Lonner, & J. E. Trimble (Eds.), *Counseling across cultures* (4th ed., pp. 21–46). Thousand Oaks, CA: Sage.

Sue, D. W., & Sue, D. (2008). *Counseling the culturally diverse* (5th ed.). Hoboken, NJ: John Wiley & Sons.

Torrey, E. F. (1983). *The mind game: Witchdoctors and psychiatrists.* New York: Jason Aronson.

Townsend, K. C., & McWhirter, B. T. (2005). Connectedness: A review of the literature with implications for counseling, assessment and research. *Journal of Counseling and Development, 83,* 191–201.

Vasquez, M. J. T. (2007). Cultural difference and the therapeutic alliance: An evidence-based analysis. *American Psychologist, 62,* 875–885.

Wampold, B. E. (2001a). Contextualizing psychotherapy as a healing practice: Culture, history, and methods. *Applied & Preventive Psychology, 10,* 69–86.

Wampold, B. E. (2001b). *The great psychotherapy debate: Models, methods, and findings.* Mahwah, NJ: Lawrence Erlbaum.

Whaley, A. L., & Davis, K. E. (2007). Cultural competence and evidence-based practice in mental health services: A complementary perspective. *American Psychologist, 62,* 563–574.

In Search of a Biethnic Identity
Clinical and Ethical Issues in the Treatment of a Latino/African American Adolescent Boy

Joseph M. Cervantes

Contents

Introduction

An understanding of ethnic minority adolescents, now referred to as adolescents of color (AOC), has had limited attention in the literature, and even less as applied to evidence-based treatments (EBTs) (Chambless et al., 1996; Hall, 2001). Recent writing by Lau (2006) and Barrera and Castro (2006) highlight the task of providing EBTs for children of color that have appropriate application and efficacy in real-world service settings. Comprehensive, but more general, attention to the assessment of children and adolescents has been provided by Achenbach and Rescorla (2007). Issues related to several contextual dimensions such as low socioeconomic level, language barriers, cultural variance, and so forth tend to undermine the social validity of interventions. In addition, issues related to oppression, discrimination, racism, and related social justice factors also are viewed to play a role in the validation of appropriately applied professional care to ethnic minority communities (Trimble & Fisher, 2005). Nevertheless, the challenge remains in the service provision of these communities to provide a standard of care that is acceptable and consistent with culturally appropriate intervention. Consequently, empirical support for customizing therapeutic processes and the measurement of effective outcomes for people of color and other disempowered groups remains elusive (Lam & Sue, 2001).

This writing acknowledges the lack of knowledge that is evident when addressing the mental health needs of communities of color, especially with AOC. Ethnic identity plays a salient role in this understanding (Cokley, 2005; Fuligni, Witcow, & Garcia, 2005; Phinney, 1990), one that will be articulated within the context of a clinical case discussed as the foundation to this chapter. Although dated, Phinney's (1990) review of relevant issues in ethnic identity for AOC indicates that this dimension is especially salient to personal knowledge about oneself as a result of the stereotypes and images that are characteristically based on phenotype. These features typically include skin color, primary language use, last name, cultural values, and any other unique characteristics that may bring attention to AOC. Furthermore, this population of youth can be often subject to cultural oppression and racism, which adds another level of challenge for adolescents, especially those from immigrant families (Falicov, 1998). There is another layer of stress that this growing subgroup must deal with in relation to the realities of learning a new language, establishing a new peer group, and transacting the complexity of urban youth culture from one cultural venue to another. How does one integrate ethnic identity when there is more than one?

The issue of ethnic identity for AOC becomes significantly more complex when there is more than one identity that an individual must incorporate (O'Hearn, 1998; Robinson, 2005; Root, 1992). This writing will focus directly on a brief literature review specific to biethnicity and particular to the ethnic dynamics of the presented case, Latino/African American. An initial discussion of the author's theoretical perspective will be provided to set a conceptual foundation for the understanding of the case, followed by a description and discussion of the presented adolescent. Case analysis and conceptualization will be described next, with additional clinical considerations provided. An overview of this writer's perspective on cultural/ethnic diversity will proceed. Conclusions will be made, and specific clinical recommendations for practice will be given.

Theoretical Orientation

My professional outlook has been influenced by three distinct arenas: three decades of professional practice, exposure to a wide range of ethnically and culturally diverse individuals and families, and my own biethnic identification as both Chicano–Latino and my indigenous background. My history of professional practice was initiated following my formal training with professional employment as an Air Force psychologist, which provided the seeds for working with several different populations. After a 3-year military commitment as a commissioned officer, I had the opportunity to be the director of a child guidance center for several years, followed by a combination of independent practice and graduate-level instruction at various universities.

A continuous theme that was interwoven throughout all of my years as a practicing psychologist has been the opportunity to consult with a wide range of individuals, developmental ages, and family situations. Consequently, there has been a gradual seasoning of my professional outlook that has shaped humility about the human condition. Second, the exposure to a culturally diverse range of individuals and families, inclusive of the wide range of socioeconomic status, has provided me confidence in knowing my own limitations while still yet having the ability to manage a broad landscape of emotional and psychological concerns and being able to admit weaknesses when they arise. Last, my history as an indigenous person has given me a unique perspective with regard to the theoretical foundation for how I view human experience. Some of these primary theoretical influences I wrote about in a prior publication (Cervantes, 2008); however, I will provide a brief overview of those particular tenets now.

I have learned to embrace a strong transpersonal framework in my thinking about life and my relationship with others. This framework incorporates the principle of interconnectedness of all living things, which affirms that as humans we share a responsibility to protect one another and the environment. Furthermore, I view the world as a place of magic and wonder that is embraced in the arms of Mother Earth, the protectress of all living things. In this context, the icon and archetype, Our Lady of Guadalupe, has become a prominent fixture in my psyche as well as on the shelf in my respective home (Castillo, 1996; Rodriquez, 1994). I have been influenced by the writings from the medicine man Black Elk, as communicated through his biographer Neihardt (1961), who wrote about this man's life, mission, and mystical visions that alert and protect his people. I have also been influenced by numerous other indigenous writers such as Lame Deer (Lame Deer & Erdoes, 1972), a holy man of the Lakota Sioux tribe who reported about his own story of manhood as it was experienced through oppression, discrimination, and protection of his ancestral land.

Theoretically, some of the basic tenets that I ascribe to include the interconnectedness of the Earth and living things, communities and systems, and the intricate roles and responsibilities that interplay with one another. The dimension of spiritual beingness and how it influences one's day-to-day interactions with self and others is an intimate aspect of this belief system (Cervantes, 2008). In addition, there is a strong humanistic component to my therapeutic posture that places emphasis on the deep regard for human experience and unique respect for individual and group differences. Last, I am influenced by the now several decades of multicultural literature that provides the framework for understanding diversity in relationship to clinical competency and ethics (i.e., Hoshmand, 2006; Ivey, D'Andrea, Ivey, & Simek-Morgan, 2007; Sue & Sue, 2007; Thomas & Schwarzbaum, 2006; Trimble & Fisher, 2005).

Case Description and Analysis

Psychological Treatment of Donny Ruiz

Adolescence has been framed as a turbulent time, a continued pattern of episodic mishaps that have been attributed to physiological, psychological, family life stage issues, and a search for identity. These issues become even more complex as AOC struggle to find their place in the larger collective (Cokley, 2005; Phinney, 1990). There is limited information in the professional literature about this particular population, and even less with regard to adolescents who share biethnic identities (Root, 1992). A current article (Choi, Harachi, Gillmore, & Catalano, 2006) suggested that there are significant relationships between ethnic identity and racial discrimination within selected problem behaviors. The adolescent in this case study, Donny Ruiz, whose name has been changed to protect his identity, was chosen for several reasons.

Donny is a 15-year-old boy who was referred for counseling as a result of several emotional, familial, and social environmental concerns. Along with being groomed to be a gang member of "The Loopers" in his urban environment, he did not share the characteristics of many "gang bangers" that are often typical of adolescent boys. For example, Donny came from a two-parent family, with his parents highly committed to the well-being of their children. This demonstration of their concern was noted in their desire for a higher education for Donny as the oldest of four children, in their vigilant monitoring of his social peer group, and in their involvement with his teachers, school activities, and community sports where he participated.

A second reason Donny was selected as the case for this writing is that Donny demonstrated himself to be a very bright boy who wanted to achieve yet felt pulled by the influence of other peers who were intent on not doing well in school and prone toward impulsivity in their activities and interactions with others. Finally, and primarily, this case was selected because of Donny's biethnic identity of Latino and African American background. With his father as Latino (Mexican American) and his mother as African American, Donny demonstrated a uniqueness to active participation in both ethnic groups. He further showed a curious understanding to the various challenges posed by this heritage that had been bestowed on him and his younger brothers and sister by their parents. It is this last dimension that contributed to an interesting qualitative understanding of this boy, his unique perspective, his understanding of race and ethnicity, and his resolution of many of the push-and-pull forces that were defining his life.

Kitahara Kich (1992) provided a brief overview of the developmental stages in the integration of a biracial, bicultural identity. The feeling of differentness and discrepancy, a desire for self-acceptance and a push toward bi-cultural identity, and, last, the acknowledgment of this process as a lifelong task are a brief overview to some of the initial areas relative to a bicultural identification process.

This adolescent boy was seen over a period of 2 years with a combination of primarily individual with some family therapy work. Donny was seen on a weekly basis, and his parents and younger brothers and sister were included as needed both to provide support and to clarify family issues that were brought up by Donny. In addition, there were several ethical issues that were presented in this case that have direct implication not just for dealing with the specifics of counseling with Donny, but also for having a broader focus on psychotherapy practice with individuals of color. These ethical issues will be highlighted toward the end of this chapter.

This case discussion will introduce this adolescent boy, provide the initial description of each of the three treatment phases, and outline the specific psychological challenges in each phase.

Introduction to the Case Donny Ruiz is a 14-6-year-old adolescent male of Latino and African American background who was brought into psychotherapy by his mother, herself African American, who was very concerned about two areas. Donny had been failing the eighth grade and was starting his freshman year in high school with poor motivation and minimal interest in wanting to do well academically. This behavior is in contrast to prior years before he entered the eighth grade where he was in an accelerated academic program and had spoken often about wanting to attend a university. Second, the mother reported that her son had been involved in a peer group that she characterized as a gang, and she was fearful that he would get himself into trouble eventually. Already, she indicated that Donny had been staying out beyond curfew, was becoming increasingly disrespectful toward her and her husband, and was inclined toward not participating in many family activities. Donny is the oldest of four children, with a younger brother who immediately follows him and was entering the eighth grade, a younger brother entering the fifth grade, and a little sister who, at age 9, was also academically very gifted and was starting an accelerated academic program. Both parents have been gainfully employed, the mother as a third-grade teacher at a public elementary school, and the father as a diesel mechanic for a large trucking company, where he has been employed for the past 10 years.

Phase I Donny's entry into counseling was prompted by the combination of his poor academic performance in middle school, his involvement with potential gang influence, and the increased disrespect that he was demonstrating toward his parents. This young boy was found to be very bright, alert, yet negative in his outlook and highly sensitive to the subtleties of relationships and his interactions with people. For example, it was noted immediately that Donny would comment on his peers as "best buddies" and highlight particular characteristics that were evident with several of these friends. He also described his various interactions with them, the activities that he participated in with many of these peers, and the areas of concerns that he described as problematic for him. Some of these areas included staying out beyond his 8:00 p.m. curfew on school nights, engaging in shoplifting episodes, and smoking marijuana occasionally with his friends.

This boy's initial reaction to me, the treating therapist, was that of resistance coupled with some curiosity about who I was and why his parents would bring him to see me. An obvious intellectual brightness was noted immediately in his vocabulary use, method of verbal expression, and in the stories he told about himself, his family, and those peers who he felt close to him. His telling of stories proved to be very helpful in coming to understand who this boy was and personal reactions relative to a variety of social situations, and general arenas in his life.

Donny was by no means a reticent boy, but rather one who displayed an oppositional attitude and a quiet anger that seemed to characterize his style of coping with life. At the same time, he recognized that his intellectual talents and abilities far surpassed many of those peers whom he had been socializing with. It was this initial hook, namely, Donny's intellectual talents, that allowed the present writer to make an inroad into a meaningful therapeutic relationship along with the sincere attempt to understand this boy's general feelings and personal struggles that became evident during each visit.

Early on, Donny commented on the difficulty he has had in struggling with his dual ethnic background. "They make fun of me if I see myself as Black, and at the same time I can't hang with my homeboys because I can't speak Spanish as well … so I usually hang with the White kids, or I hang by myself." With these insightful comments, Donny came to highlight the particular issues related to the core of his identity, his discomfort with the complexity of his ethic identity and the difficulties he has had establishing stable and enduring relationships with either side of his cultural inheritance. This is an issue that he reported identifying even in his elementary school years but felt that it was becoming increasingly more critical as he was learning to manage the everyday interactions and more advanced sophistication of his developing social awareness. There is a growing literature base that reports that having ethnic minority status may indicate risk for a variety of stresses and psychosocial stressors, including low self-esteem, drug and alcohol abuse, feelings of alienation and marginality, and adverse outcomes (Anderson, 1995; Bowles, 1993; Gibbs, 1998; Phinney, 1991).

The first few visits in my introduction to this adolescent boy found him to be initially oppositional yet not defiant, moderately closed to self-disclosure yet curious, and anxious yet emotionally present. The first several visits with Donny were spent primarily in helping him to feel comfortable with the counseling process and in identifying particular themes and issues that were most relevant to his well-being. This last aspect was difficult, due to both his lack of willingness to disclose information and the fact that he had entered a new dimension in his education as a freshman in high school that prompted some imbalance and work to the benefit of the therapeutic process. He felt more self-conscious about his involvement in counseling and whether his peers would find out.

Phase II The subsequent phase to the counseling of Donny merged with the theme of not being comfortable with his mixed Latino–African American identity. This issue played out dramatically in his freshman year in high school, as he was prompted to choose sides between each of these respective ethnic groups (O'Hearn, 1998). This boy's physical appearance could easily define him as being African American, although there was a behavioral posture evident in his relating and in his bilingual ability that also marked him as underscoring his Latino heritage. It was interesting that although Donny appeared more African American in physical features, he felt more comfortable with his Latino peers. This concern became highlighted during the late fall semester in school when he was cornered by a group of African American youth and asked why he was a "sell out." Donny reported being intimidated and taunted by this group, and at the same time felt conflicted about his own ethic affiliation and uncertainty about how to respond to these aggressive comments. This incident was reported to have ended peacefully, but caused Donny to be physically shaken over how he was being made to choose.

A family visit with the parents and Donny over this very concern caused significant dismay with each of the parents, who themselves had not resolved how to support their son on this matter. Each took a position that he should choose on his own how to integrate a pluralistic identity, yet both admitted that they were unclear about how he might do this. Nevertheless, this dialogue proved to be helpful to Donny in feeling supported being both, although he did not have the necessary behavior modeling about how to integrate his biethnic inheritance. Consequently, some of the outcomes that occurred as a result of this issue of unresolved identity prompted an involvement in the use of illegal drugs (marijuana and experimentation with methamphetamines) and led to significant disruption in his relationship with his parents. The last half of Donny's ninth-grade year was spent on academic probation and characterized continued involvement with his Latino peer group that appeared non-supportive of his academic abilities, as well as aggressive confrontation with his parents. This latter event brought more involvement in family therapy for Donny and his family, resulting in some temporary resolutions and a continual restabilizing of Donny's behavior.

Two principal life events resulted in a significant opportunity for Donny to reflect on the course of his developmental trajectory. These events co-occurred within the same time frame of the summer following the completion of his freshman year. The first event concerned his involvement with a girlfriend who was 2 years older and caused him to question his own sexuality. This issue became prominent as he attempted to initiate sexual contact and found himself unable to perform, and as a result the girl taunted him over his "lack of manliness." This relationship resulted in Donny starting to doubt whether he truly was attracted to women and to question if perhaps he was either bisexual or homosexual. The next several weeks of consultation with this boy were focused on his sexuality, which became intertwined with the theme of his biethnicity and subsequent confusion over his ethnic identity while questioning his sexual orientation. This resolution was primarily solved by the termination of this girlfriend relationship and his desire to casually see other young girls in his age range whom he felt supported him and whom he was drawn to romantically. However, it was also at this point that a traumatic event occurred in Donny's family life. The unexpected loss of a younger brother, who was tragically killed in an automobile accident as he was riding with a classmate and his family, proved to be an existential crisis that shifted emotional priorities and unexpectedly prompted a working solution to his identity problem.

Donny's 10-year-old brother, Harold, apparently was not wearing his seatbelt when the car in which he was riding flipped over, and he was ejected. All of the riders in the car survived the accident except for Harold. It is unfortunate that this tragedy occurred right after summer school let out and close to Donny's home, as he had missed the bus and instead walked by the commotion at the intersection where the accident occurred. Donny was the first in his family to identify his brother, who was already surrounded by paramedics and was declared brain dead on site. This event set in motion a significant anger at the family who had driven this car, at his parents for allowing his brother to be in this class excursion, and at God for allowing this to happen to his family.

Donny's own religious socialization was Catholic, although his family did not participate in religious services on a regular basis. Nevertheless, Donny had spent some of his initial years in a parochial elementary school and had been taught the significance of belief in a Creator and all the related expectations and socialization with practicing Catholicism. With this tragedy came a direct anger at God and questions about why this event was allowed to occur in his family. Although Donny's illegal drug use continued, particularly marijuana with his peer groups, the tragedy of losing his brother also caused a deeper level of personal reflection and unexpected quietness to settle in. Donny reported that some of his anger was specific not to God, but, more importantly, to himself for the angry episode he had had with his brother the day before and the lack of resolution over it. He blamed himself and felt significant guilt over the inability to have an opportunity to say he was sorry and to say good-bye to Harold on the morning that he was killed.

Counseling focused particularly on releasing the guilt and blame as well as on saying good-bye to his brother and to accept that it was not his fault that his brother had died. Just as important, the issue of Donny's biethnicity again became apparent as he revealed that his brother had always viewed himself as being fortunate that he was able to take pleasure in his cultural inheritance and felt enriched with his ability to speak Spanish. This skill afforded him many opportunities to relate to a wide variety of friends in various ethnic groups. It was this awareness that allowed Donny to make the connection between his brother's tragic death and the gift of self-acceptance that had been bestowed on him following the tragic circumstances. That gift was being able to accept himself and the cultural inheritance he had been given and to recognize that the most direct way in which to remember his brother was to acknowledge the cultural richness of his family background. It is from this point on that Donny stopped his use of marijuana and began to transition to a more responsible position in his behavior and attitudes.

Phase III   Following the end of Donny's first semester of his sophomore year in high school, the tragedy of losing his younger brother and the realization of his heterosexual comfortableness allowed a level of stability to enter. In this regard, a new phase of learning appeared to be evident with this young adolescent male, as he began taking more responsibility, was more kind to himself and to his parents, and stopped using illegal drugs to manage his confused feelings.

A prominent therapeutic issue that became increasingly important in counseling was his asking the question, "Who is my reference group?" With this question came a significant undertone of conflict yet revelation at being able to make this relevant comment about himself, allowing a more direct path of therapeutic inquiry to take place. It was in the context of this question that Donny began relating the various cultural messages about himself that he had received initially from his parents and subsequently from his peer groups throughout middle school and through his entry into high school. Donny recalled the large family gatherings that would happen on both sides of the family when he was growing up, with his mother's side and the various relatives that would sometimes visit from Tennessee, where she was originally from. These family members liked to gather and tell stories about their respective communities. These stories were also filled with commentary about dealing with racism and oppression and having to cope with poverty yet always feeling there was "enough to go around." He reported being especially close to his maternal grandfather, who passed away when Donny was just entering middle school, but who had spent significant time with him growing up. This grandparent provided him constancy in their relationship and strong feelings of affection for both him and his younger brothers and sister.

Donny's recollection of the Latino side of his family through his father was also filled with numerous family gatherings, although they were less frequent than those with his mother's side. These gatherings were typically kept separate, although it was never explained why this was the case. In those recollections, Donny reminded himself of the border crossing of his paternal grandfather from Juarez, Mexico in the late 1940s to be part of a newly developed Bracero program that had been initiated through the U.S. government. This program allowed his grandfather to move freely between the United States and Mexico while he was providing a needed work resource for the ranchers and farmers in the United States. The Bracero program allowed his grandfather to eventually settle in the United States, marry, and subsequently bring his family from the state of Aguascalientes, Mexico, where he was from.

The review of family and extended family history and dynamics proved to be relevant to the psychological understanding that Donny was starting to grasp about why his parents came together. A significant family therapy meeting that took place during this time resulted in his parents disclosing to Donny and their other children that their marital union was initiated in their high school acquaintance and fostered through their 1 year of study at a junior college. It was at that point that they elected to marry at the disapproval of both sides of the family. This disapproval eventually resulted in a cooperation between both sides of the family to support a new marriage and the children who were to come. Although there was no apparent aggression and hostility evident from anyone, the choice not to intermingle these extended families nevertheless occurred over the next several years, such that each of their families would have separate celebrations without integrating both sides. This knowledge provided a significant movement for Donny to become aware of some of the potential reasons for why the mixed heritage of his background was not more integrated. In addition, this knowledge also resulted in Donny's taking increased responsibility for himself and coming to realize the uniqueness that characterized his personality development as well as his ability to navigate between African American and Latino peer groups.

By the close of Donny's second year of high school, his academic performance had significantly improved and the intellectual brightness that had always characterized this young boy became increasingly more apparent again. Donny had an interesting request regarding his 16th birthday in the beginning of summer. Donny asked the present writer to attend his birthday celebration in which a ritual of manhood was being planned by both sides of his extended family. After some consultation with peers about this request, I elected to participate, and I was introduced not only as Donny's therapist but also as a significant influence in this boy's behavioral changes and emotional stability. The manhood ritual, which involved a brief coming-of-age speech to his extended family, was complemented by stories that were recited to him by his maternal grandmother and paternal grandparents about their recollections of his development. Donny was then expected to comment about the stories and the impact those experiences had had on him. This 2-hour experience proved to be enriching and extremely powerful in the galvanizing of Donny's sense of who he was becoming and in the integration of his mixed heritage background. This event was also one of the few of which both sides of his extended family were present. The next several visits with this boy were spent primarily in reflecting back on the experiences that he had for his birthday celebration, as well as his reactions to the present writer being involved in this process.

It became apparent that after approximately 2 years of a therapeutic relationship with Donny, some permanent and gratifying changes were starting to take place for this young man. Initially, he had crossed over from a sense of being a boy to being a more responsible individual and taking his life more seriously. The experience of having lost his young brother and receiving clarity on his role as a heterosexual male also produced a significant boost of confidence in who he was becoming. With the start of his third year in high school, Donny was beginning to take a leadership role in school and was feeling increasingly more at ease not only in navigating his Latino and African American peer groups but also in crossing lines with other ethnic groups toward building a larger sense of community for himself.

The therapeutic relationship with Donny moved further away from a traditional therapeutic role to that of a mentoring relationship in which my involvement was less as a problem solver and resolver of family difficulties and more as one who was providing direction and goal-setting activities. The next several months of professional involvement were seen as Donny's "checking in" to provide feedback about his relationships, his involvement in school activities, and his future goals.

This boy's third year in high school proved to be his best, as he was starting to win awards both for his academics and for his involvement in leadership activities. Toward this end, Donny's desire to have the present writer involved in those award ceremonies increased. He was feeling that because the present writer had played such a significant role in his evolution, he had become increasingly comfortable about the shift in relationship ties that had now solidified into a clear mentor–mentee relationship. Furthermore, Donny became less invested in whether he was one ethnic group or the other, but stating, "I belong to the world," which was his way to indicate that the internal struggle of whom he should affiliate with and who he should be was moving toward resolution. Donny reported having limited interest in wanting to segregate or isolate one ethnic group from the other, and he was playing a more integral role in his high school. This included being an effective mediator between various ethnic groups and not feeling pulled by ethnic exclusivity or being told that he should be part of one group and not the other.

Donny was seen minimally during his last year of high school other than for him to continue checking in on his accomplishments. He successfully completed an academic track that routed him directly toward opportunities to apply to various distinguished universities. Donny was subsequently accepted in a university that complemented his academic goals and that brought increased distinction to the emotional and psychological changes that he had made over the past several years. Donny continues to maintain contact with the present writer, and he has used me as a reference point and advisor. This young man has continued to evolve a strong sense of responsibility toward helping others, learning how to bridge conflict and bring a social justice perspective to his broadening interests and attitudes.

Case Conceptualization: Evidence-Based Practice in Psychology (EBPP) and Common Factors

The treatment of Donny Ruiz is a characteristic example of how I work with individuals, particularly teenagers. I view my role as setting a primary environment of trust and being prepared, especially with adolescents, for any shock value messages that are often part of work with this population (Martin, 2003). In Donny's case, there was less an issue of shock and manipulation than the presence of behavioral instability, the use of marijuana with his friends, and the significant discomfort relative to his biethnicity. Although all three played a role in the understanding of this case, the last dimension was especially critical toward the resolution of his confusion and the stabilization of his self-perceptions. Writing by Kitahara Kich (1992) provides a limited but organized developmental stage model for understanding biethnic identity. This stage model was a useful backdrop to conceptualizing Donny's emotional discomfort regarding his identity as both African American and Latino, and allowed for some direction in the outcome of this resolution. It is interesting to note that toward the end of psychotherapy with this boy, his comment related as "I belong to the world" spoke volumes about his increased comfort and ability to navigate his integration of biethnicity and to utilize that knowledge in balancing his relationships with several other ethnic groups in his high school environment.

A recent article by Shih, Bonam, Sanchez, and Peck (2007) addressed the issue that multiracial individuals typically have no reference point relative to identification within a specific ethnic category. Consequently, in the absence of U.S Census labeling and other related ethnic categorization, these populations will frequently rely less on ethnic labels and more on viewing race as a socially constructed label (Gaskins, 1999). Donny's commentary of his belonging to the world was understood as a statement that he had limited use for an ethnic identity, as it may have felt too constraining.

The combination of both a family psychology perspective and an understanding of the process from a multicultural perspective provided the backdrop to understanding this case. My conceptual lens, as noted previously, has been strongly influenced by my integration of indigenous philosophy, which indicates that all living beings are related and that, as the famous medicine man Chief Seattle commented a century and a half ago, "whatever we do to the web of life, we do to ourselves." From my standpoint, this translates into at least three assumptions: we must learn to be kind and loving to each other in spite of the eventual conflict that is part of human nature; there are consequences for our lack of respect toward others in nature; and service to the community is the natural outcome to human growth (Cervantes, 2008a). These tenets were prominent in my working with Donny as they translated in the context of this boy's initial anger and discomfort with his sense of being. I felt that a resolution of his biethnic identity crisis would result in an integration that could have a significant effect on his ability to help others. It was toward this goal that I elected to focus in this arena and to provide a needed foundation to help him discover those elements that were impacting him and causing emotional distress.

As with most treatment cases, I am aware that life moves forward and that no psychological problem is static but is always in transition or dynamic. Consequently, the unexpected outcome of Donny's conflict over feeling he may be bisexual initially blurred some of the work that was being done relative to his biethnicity. Furthermore, the tragic loss of his brother in the midst of psychotherapy proved to be a significant stressor for him yet promoted an internal push for Donny to elevate the level of anger he was already feeling. Interestingly, the later resolution of Donny's relationship with his brother proved to be a galvanizing force that assisted in his healing process.

Some of the common factors that played out in this treatment include the characteristics of genuine warmth and accurate empathy that are part of my therapeutic style. In addition, recognizing the value of a strong therapeutic relationship, especially with teenage boys, also proved to be a significant process in recognizing Donny's need to belong, find a reference group, and not feel odd. These issues are typical in working with adolescents and formed the backdrop toward effective work with this population (Martin, 2003).

Relative to EBPP factors, a recently published article on EBPP by the APA Presidential Task Force (2006) provides the following working definition: "Evidence–Based Practice in Psychology is the integration of the best available research with clinical expertise in the context of patient characteristics, culture, and preferences" (p. 273). The definition and the language utilized in this article are broad enough to include qualitative research, systematic case studies, and clinical observations of individual counseling. The need for broadness in this definition of EBPP is particularly important when working with people of color since there are a variety of factors that impact the conceptualization and clinical intervention of effective consultation and the counseling process. Nagayama Hall (2001) writes in his commentary about the lack of empirically supported evidence for treatment effectiveness with ethnic minority populations. His article provides several distinct steps toward developing the appropriate cultural sensitivity and identification of relevant outcomes and treatment effectiveness. However, the point of Nagayama Hall's article and that of the APA Presidential Task Force on Evidence-Based Practice is that some accommodations must be made for the various dimensions that are involved in the effective conceptualization and treatment of people of color.

The case presented in this chapter is an example of a single case study that is examined in detail relative to case conceptualization, cultural sensitivity, and treatment outcome. An in-depth description of this kind of case that includes a detailed exploration of various psycho-social, cultural, and ethnic identity issues is critical in the evolution of a working theory for biethnic or multiethnic individuals. Just as important, however, is the accumulation of these kinds of cases that would allow for a synthesis and integration of appropriate treatment protocols. Laying the foundation for this level of case study will assist greatly in providing an analysis of several single case studies that can increase insight and a more qualitative approach toward effective treatment with people of color.

Identification of Author's Personal Dimensions of Diversity and World View

This writer's perspective on diversity has been derived by my own biethnic background, as well as my being influenced by the multicultural literature of the past 30 years. Sue's classic text (1981) was one of the first initial writings that provided a comprehensive view of the impact of culture in counseling, but even prior to this resource, there were writings that explored the counseling and psychotherapy process for people of color populations, particularly Latino and African American groups. Those early writings compared the counseling process for ethnic minority clients with White therapists. The outcome of that research almost exclusively resulted in negative findings relative to minority clients remaining in counseling no more than a session or two. Consequently, a revolving door of conflicting results prevailed in the counseling and psychotherapy literature relative to the usefulness of psychological intervention with people of color. As a result, my sense of equity and social justice was a significant parameter in disproving those assumptions and at least intuitively knowing that some combination of design error and analog research did not accurately portray the realities of counseling for disempowered ethnic minority populations (Hall, 1997; Sue, 2003).

There has been an explosion of literature in the multicultural arena over the past 10 years. These writings have explored select themes in the multicultural perspective: the role of privilege, oppression, and diversity (Anderson & Middleton, 2005); a life-span approach to multicultural counseling (Baruth & Manning, 2007); a critical overview of culture and psychotherapy (Hoshmand, 2006); culturally competent practice issues (Lum, 2007); the role of diversity in counseling and psychology (Smith, 2004); theoretical perspectives on multicultural counseling (Sue, Ivey, & Pedersen, 1996); multiple identities in counseling (Robinson, 2005); and cultural life story dialogues within the framework of culture and identity (Thomas & Schwarzbaum, 2006). Each of these writings highlights particular themes relevant to understanding contextual issues with clients, which adds a conceptual infrastructure toward a more full and effective understanding of practice with people of color. My framework as a Latino/Chicano and indigenous male professional has historical support for the development of cultural themes and the role of cultural competency in working with diversity. Consequently, my ethnic and cultural socialization, professional and life experiences, and broad reading in the multicultural area have allowed for several distinct principles to form in working with people of color.

These principles include the following: Initially, it is my world-view belief that all human life is interconnected and serves within a codependent relationship toward the maintenance of stability and eventual growth. The obvious outcome is that as a community of people, we each have a responsibility to recognize this interconnected relationship between person and environment, which allows for its self-preservation and protection. Second, all individuals and their human dilemmas must be understood in context in order to appreciate the fuller arena to one's reality (Anderson & Middleton, 2005). The multicultural literature highlights in significant detail the understanding of context and how that contributes toward a more complete understanding of the individual. Third, both the literature and professional experience have informed me that the dimensions of poverty, social economic status, oppression, racism, and classism frame the lives of many people of color (Robinson, 2005). These areas must have direct consideration, as appropriate, when considering meaningful and effective interventions.

Fourth, all individuals possess varying layers of personal identity that are influenced by ethnicity and culture, sexual orientation, ableness, and religion and spirituality, to name a few (Gaskins, 1999; O'Hearn, 1998). An effective understanding of people needs to allow an informing of this dimension toward the development of the larger picture of who the client is. Fifth, life experiences of the individual permit the appropriate focus relative to how the client is being conceptualized. In brief, families from inner-city environments, regardless of ethnicity or culture, possess a distinct life perspective that needs to be recognized in order to provide meaningful professional consultation (Minuchin, Colapinto, & Minuchin, 2007). Sixth, migration and acculturation are significant life events that have become increasingly part of the human drama with the presence of undocumented families (Falicov, 1998; Cervantis & Mejia, 2009). Effective assessment of these areas may be necessary to evaluate and stabilize the presenting client difficulties. There is an increasing literature base regarding this theme that will help in conceptualizing these issues with immigrant families.

Seventh, language diversity is a salient dimension to the professional care of clients. Ability to speak the socialized language of the client is critical in the ethical provision of service. The role of language in counseling, in particular for Spanish-speaking clients, is an important dimension toward culturally and ethically appropriate professional care (Altarriba & Santiago-Rivera, 1994; Santiago-Rivera & Altarriba, 2002). Eighth, social justice, often framed within the perspective of a liberation psychology, may need to be a required outcome of intervention. In brief, venturing beyond the consultation office may require contact with other social agencies to assist with the emotional behavioral, and psychosocial needs of the clients.

Ninth, knowledge of community resources is a salient information base that supports effective counseling. It is incumbent on the treating therapist to be able to offer other sources of assistance as required. Last, the commitment to a multicultural perspective of the therapist is an essential prerequisite and lifelong learning agenda for the psychotherapist or professional counselor (Ivey et al., 2007; Sue & Sue, 2007). This arena is one that needs to frame the conceptual mind-set and experience of the therapist in order to remain current and aware of the variety of challenges that are part of the experiences of people of color.

Conclusions/Therapeutic Recommendations

The psychological treatment of Donny Ruiz provided significant learning in the understanding of biethnicity. Especially prominent were the role of peer affiliation and association relative to acceptance of individuals who are distinctly different, and the establishment of a therapeutic relationship that was able to evolve into a mentor format. This last aspect proved to be significant for the author as he was able to further learn effective boundaries that could be personal yet professional, and at the same time be helpful therapeutically. A similar outcome was noted in a prior case study described by this author elsewhere (Cervantes, 2006).

A unique feature to the treatment of this case was the role of boundary issues and the evolution of the therapeutic relationship with the therapist. This area has had minimal commentary in the literature, although it was recognized by Parham and Caldwell (2006) that when a therapist is involved in a therapeutic relationship with people of color, there is a conceptual shift in the relationship that evolves over time with a client. This shift may require more appropriate ethical mindset relative to a broader definition of boundary-setting and a redefining of the therapeutic relationship.

My consultation with Donny found him to be personable despite an initial rebellious nature and was complemented by his insightful comments and intellectual understanding of his life circumstances. It felt like a natural process and appropriate sequence to attend his coming-of-age ceremony with his family and subsequently move into a mentor relationship. There was some self-disclosure on the part of the therapist relative to who I was as a man and the life challenges that I undertook toward reaching educational goals and professional stature. It was in the sharing of this information that Donny was found able to integrate this knowledge into his own self-conceptualization, which I believe added to increased security and the deepening of our relationship. However, an interesting question to ask is, What would have happened if I had not allowed this level of disclosure to take place in the relationship? Would there have been the level of progress that occurred with Donny? Would the lack of disclosure have impacted Donny's own movement toward advanced achievement for himself? Would the therapeutic attachment become different without the personal information provided by the therapist? These are interesting questions that help provide additional dialogue relative to what is in the best interest of the client and how this best interest is defined when working with AOC.

Several different principles evolved from the work with this young boy who defined salient aspects of his treatment and offer room for future case conceptualization. These principles in working with biethnic adolescents are noted as follows:

1. It is important to evaluate the level of internal awareness and recognition when adolescents have biethnic identification. This clinical data will provide consistency of goals and meaningfulness of the

counseling process and how this material should be integrated into the counseling process.

2. Recognition of the meaningfulness of biethnic identity further requires the assessment of individual comfort level and role of ethnic conflict or confusion. Internalized assignment of discomfort suggests that ethnic identity may be a significant dimension in the counseling process.

3. Biethnic conflict relevant to the lack of personal integration, personal labeling, prejudice, and peer estrangement results in distinct problem areas that may need further assessment and appropriate intervention. The foundation for these problems has been well documented by Root (1996, 1999). Furthermore, these experiences have been noted by Radina and Cooney (2000), who reviewed national survey data regarding the quality of relationship between multiracial adolescents and their biological parents. It is recommended that these relevant areas of biethnic conflict be carefully addressed so that these dimensions of human experience are not overlooked (Robinson, 2005).

4. The role of oppression and racism are often co-occurring experiences that are impacted by both the larger community and the peer groups where fitting in for adolescents is characteristically difficult. Parents play a critical role in the integration process (Seiffge-Krenke & Shulman, 1990). Engaging parents in the counseling process relative to their parenting styles, messages of ethnic heritage and culture, and level of awareness about their own children's experiences as biethnic or multi-ethnic individuals could be key to the therapeutic process. It is recommended that some assessment of parents and their particular messages of ethnic integration, or lack thereof, be evaluated.

5. Increased cultural and linguistic variation in communities across the country is also supporting the presence of multiethnic partners and subsequent marriages. As a result, mental health professionals will need to attend to a wider scope of knowledge relevant to practice agendas with culturally diverse communities (Hall, 1997; Sue & Sue, 2007). It is recommended that students and young professionals begin the preparation process more systematically toward learning to manage, being exposed to, and integrating a more comprehensive understanding of multicultural individuals and families. This perspective will clearly be the practice arena of the future.

6. The true meaning of biethnic awareness will differ from individual to individual. More consistent and stable integration could depend on numerous factors, including the mental and emotional maturity of the

individual, the level of support from the parent, the assigned role of importance of the peer group, and the level of professional ability for the psychotherapist. It is recommended that, at the appropriate time in the therapeutic process, the following question be asked: "What does it look and feel like to share two or more distinct ethnic identifications?" This qualitative approach will allow for a unique perspective and the recognition of special talents, skills, and interests for the biethnic adolescent.

7. The therapist will need to attend personally and professionally to the role that biethnicity plays in human experience. Whether or not the therapist has dual or multiple ethnicities could play a role in the comfort level for that professional to be able to effectively address those issues. In dealing with biethnic or multiethnic adolescents, the personal review of one's own internal awareness about ethnicity will be salient regarding how the psychotherapist handles this important matter with this clinical population.

8. The role of boundaries with AOC is an important counseling professional theme to consider. This dimension will be a salient dialogue that may require relevant therapeutic navigation between the therapist and client. As Parham and Caldwell (2006) noted regarding the boundaries issue, the role of professional practice will need to accommodate the broad variation of cultural expectations and value systems that are now becoming increasingly evident in service delivery (Goodheart, Kazdin, & Sternberg, 2006; Sue, 2003).

9. Evidence-based psychotherapy and clinical intervention is becoming the theme of the new millennia in practice (Chambless & Ollendick, 2001; Frick, 2007; Goodheart et al., 2006). It will likely be expected that practitioners with people of color pay increased attention to evidence-based methodology and treatment protocols, given that a new level of competency is being suggested by this evolving paradigm.

Discussion Questions

1. How do evidence-based treatments apply to the psychological care of people of color?

2. What is the role of identity when an adolescent is the product of two or more ethnic identities?

3. What other interventions would you propose in dealing with the life problems that described Donny Ruiz?

4. What theoretical framework have you developed to reflect multicultural understanding? How might this framework accommodate the treatment of biethnic clients?
5. What role does family play in your evaluation of client problems, especially when treating people of color?
6. How have you maintained your own professional integrity toward your evolving consciousness as a practitioner of color or as a professional invested in the psychological care of ethnic minority youth?
7. What self-care activities or routines have you developed to remain fresh in your work as a professional?
8. What is your understanding about race, culture, and ethnicity? How comfortable do you feel about addressing these issues in yourself and others?

Additional Resources

There are several other key documents that can be helpful in providing additional understanding relative to cultural diversity and the acknowledgment of ethnic identification as an important factor in the treatment of biethnic or multiethnic individuals. A significant theme noted in this chapter has been the increasing emergence of EBTs that are laying the foundation for more sophisticated care (Goodheart et al., 2006). Some essential references that provide increased awareness to the changing paradigm in the incorporation of an evidence-based practice include Chambless and Ollendick (2001); Frick (2007); Goodheart et al., (2006); Hunsley and Mash (2007); and Kazdin (2004).

There is an increasing literature base that is identifying children and adolescents within the spectrum of evidence-based treatments. Issues related to accountability, appropriate treatment protocols, and consistent findings that can provide results in the effective delivery of mental services for this population are becoming an increasing expectation (Chambers, Ringeisen, & Hickman, 2005). Some of these primary sources include the following: Biglan, Mrazck, Carine, and Flay (2003); Fonagy, Target, Cottrell, Phillips, and Kurtz (2002); Hoagwood (2005); Hoagwood, Burns, Kiser, Ringeisen, and Shoenwald (2001); Kazdin and Weisz (2003); Kratochwill and Shernoff (2004); Marsh and Hunsley (2005); and Wiesz (2004).

The literature base more specific to people of color, particularly adolescents, is still forming. Some of these available sources include Bernal and

Scharron-del-Rio (2001) and Miranda et al. (2005). It is important to recognize the commentaries made by Hall (1997) and Sue (2003), who each echoed the increased need for culturally competent care that recognizes the wide diversity of families and their respective belief systems and practices. As there is increased interpartnering and marriages among culturally different individuals, the role of counseling and psychotherapy will need an additional level of expertise that can competently address issues related to biethnic and multiethnic identity.

References

Achenbach, T. M., & Rescorla, L. A. (2007). *Multicultural understanding of children and adolescent psychopathology: Implications for mental health assessment.* New York: Guilford.

Altarriba, J., & Santiago-Rivera, A. L. (1994). Current perspectives on using linguistic and cultural factors in counseling the Hispanic client. *Professional Psychology: Research and Practice, 25,* 388–397.

American Psychological Association. (2006). Evidence-Based Practice in Psychology. *American Psychologist, 61,* 271–285.

Anderson, N. (1995). Behavioral and sociocultural perspectives on ethnicity and health: Introduction to the special issue. *Health Psychology, 14,* 589–591.

Anderson, S. K., & Middleton, V. A. (2005). *Explorations in privilege, oppression, and diversity.* Belmont, CA: Thomson Brooks/Cole.

Barrera, M., & Castro, F. G. (2006). A heuristic framework for the cultural adaptation of interventions. *Clinical Psychology: Science and Practice, 13,* 311–316.

Baruth, L. G., & Manning, M. L. (2007). *Multicultural counseling and psychotherapy: A lifespan perspective.* Upper Saddle River, NJ: Pearson Prentice Hall.

Bernal, G., & Scharron-del-Rio, M. R. (2001). Are empirically supported treatments valid for ethnic minorities? Toward an alternative approach for treatment research. *Cultural Diversity and Ethnic Minority Psychology, 7,* 328–342.

Biglan, A., Mrazck, P. J., Carine, D., & Flay, B. R. (2003). The integration of research and practice in the prevention of youth problem behaviors. *American Psychologist, 58,* 433–440.

Bowles, D. D. (1993). Biracial identity: Children born to African-American and White couples. *Clinical Social Work Journal, 21,* 417–428.

Castillo, A. (Ed.). (1996). *Goddess of the Americas: Writing on the Virgin de Guadalupe.* New York: Berkeley Publishing Group.

Cervantes, J. M. (2006). A new understanding of the macho male image: Exploration of the Mexican American man. In M. Englar-Carlson & M. A. Stevens (Eds.), *In the room with men* (pp. 197–224). Washington, DC: American Psychological Association.

Cervantes, J. M. (2008a). What is indigenous about indigenous: The mestizo perspective. In B. McNeill & J. M. Cervantes (Eds.). *Latina/o healing practices: Mestizo and Indigenous perspectives* (pp. 3–27). New York: Routledge.

Cervantes, J. M. (2008b). *Mestizo spirituality: A counseling model for Chicano and Native/Indigenous peoples.* Submitted Manuscript.

Cervantes, J. M. & Mejia, O. (2009). Family psychology of immigrant Mexican and Mexican American families. In J. Bray & M. Statton (Eds.). *Handbook of family psychology.* Oxford: Blackwell Publishing, Ltd.

Chambers, D. A., Ringeisen, H., & Hickman, E. E. (2005). Federal, state, and foundation initiatives around evidence-based practices with child and adolescent mental health. *Child and Adolescent Psychiatric Clinics of North America, 14,* 307–327.

Chambless, D. L., & Ollendick, T. H. (2001). Empirically supported psychological interventions: Controversies and evidence. *Annual Review of Psychology, 52,* 685–716.

Chambless, D. L., Sanderson, W. C., Shoham, V., Bennett Johnson, S., Pope, K. S., Crits-Christoph, P., et al. (1996). An update on empirically validated therapies. *Clinical Psychologist, 29,* 5–18.

Choi, Y., Harachi, T. W., Gillmore, M. R., & Catalano, R. F. (2006). Are multiracial adolescents at greater risk? Comparisons of rates, patterns, and correlates of substance use and violence between monoracial and multiracial adolescents. *American Journal of Orthopsychiatry, 76,* 86–97.

Cokley, K. O. (2005). Racialized identity, ethnic identity, and Afrocentric values: Conceptual and methodological challenges and understanding African American identity. *Journal of Counseling Psychology, 52,* 517–526.

Falicov, C. J. (1998). *Latino families in therapy: A guide to multicultural practice.* New York: Guilford.

Fonagy, P., Target, M., Cottrell, D., Phillips, J., & Kurtz, Z. (2002). *What works for whom? A critical review of treatment for children and adolescents.* New York: Guilford.

French, S. E., Seidman, E., Allen, L., & Aber, J. L. (2006). The development of ethnic identity during adolescence. *Developmental Psychology, 42,* 1–10.

Frick, P. J. (2007). Providing the evidence for evidence-based practice. *Journal of Clinical Child and Adolescent Psychology, 36,* 2–7.

Fuligni, A. J., Witkow, M., & Garcia, C. (2005). Ethnic identity and the academic adjustment of adolescents from Mexican, Chinese, and European backgrounds. *Developmental Psychology, 41,* 799–811.

Gaskins, P. V. (1999). *What are you? Voices of mixed-race young people.* New York: Holt.

Gibbs, J. T. (1998). High risk behaviors in African American youth: Conceptual and methodological issues in research. In V. C. McLloyd & L. Steinberg (Eds.), *Studying minority adolescents: Conceptual, methodological, and theoretical issues* (pp. 55–56). Mahwah, NJ: Lawrence Erlbaum.

Goodheart, C. D., Kazdin, A. E., & Sternberg, R. J. (Eds.). (2006). *Evidence-based psychotherapy: Where practice and research meet.* Washington, DC: American Psychological Association.

Hall, C. C. I. (1997). Cultural malpractice: The growing obsolescence of psychology with the changing U.S. population. *American Psychologist, 52,* 642–651.

Hall, G. C. N. (2001). Psychotherapy with ethnic minorities: Empirical, ethical, and conceptual issues. *Journal of Consulting and Clinical Psychology, 69,* 502–510.

Helms, J. E. (1995). An update of Helms' White and people of color racial identity models. In J. G. Ponterotto, J. M. Casas, L. A. Suzuki, & C. M. Alexander (Eds.), *Handbook of multicultural counseling* (pp. 181–198). Thousand Oaks, CA: Sage.

Hoagwood, K. (2005). Family-based services in children's mental health: A research review and synthesis. *Journal of Child Psychology and Psychiatry: Annual Research Review, 46*, 690–713.

Hoagwood, K., Burns, B. J., Kiser, L., Ringeisen, H., & Shoenwald, S. K. (2001). Evidence-based practice in child and adolescent mental health services. *Psychiatric Services, 52*, 1179–1189.

Hoshmand, L. T. (2006). *Culture, psychotherapy and counseling.* Thousand Oaks, CA: Sage.

Hunsley, J., & Mash, E. J. (2007). Evidence-based assessment. *Annual Review of Clinical Psychology, 3*, 57–79.

Ivey, A. E., D'Andrea, M. B., Ivey, M. B., & Simek-Morgan, L. (2007). *Theories of counseling and psychotherapy: Multicultural perspective.* Boston: Pearson/Allyn and Bacon.

Kazdin, A. E. (2004). Evidence-based treatment: Challenges and priorities for practice and research. *Child and Adolescent Clinics of North America, 13*, 923–940.

Kazdin, A. E., & Weisz, J. R. (Eds.). (2003). *Evidence-based psychotherapies for children and adolescents.* New York: Guilford.

Kerwin, C., & Ponterotto, J. G. (1995). Biracial identity development: Theory and research. In J. G. Ponterotto, J. M. Casas, L. A. Suzuki, & C. M. Alexander (Eds.), *Handbook of multicultural counseling* (pp. 199–217). Thousand Oaks, CA: Sage.

Kitahara Kich, G. (1992). The developmental process of asserting a biracial, bicultural identity. In M. P. P. Root (Ed.), *Racially mixed people in America.* Newbury Park, CA: Sage.

Kratochwill, T. R., & Shernoff, E. S. (2004). Evidence-based practice: Promoting evidence-based interventions in school psychology. *School Psychology Review, 33*, 34–48.

Lam, A. G., & Sue, S. (2001). Client diversity. *Psychotherapy: Theory, Research, Practice, Training, 38*, 479–486.

Lame Deer, J., & Erdoes, R. (1972). *Lame Deer, seeker of visions.* New York: Washington Square Press.

Lau, A. S. (2006). Making the case for selective and directed cultural adaptations of evidence-based treatments: Examples from parent training. *Clinical Psychology: Science and Practice, 13*, 295–310.

Lum, D. (2007). *Culturally competent practice: A framework for understanding diverse groups and justice issues.* Belmont, CA: Thomson Brooks/Cole.

Marsh, E. J., & Hunsley, J. (2005). Evidence-based assessment of child and adolescent disorders: Issues and challenges. *Journal of Clinical Child and Adolescent Psychology, 34*, 362–379.

Martin, D. G. (2003). *Clinical practice with adolescents.* Pacific Grove, CA: Thomson Brooks/Cole.

McAdoo, H. (Ed.). (1993). *Family ethnicity: Strength in diversity.* Newbury Park, CA: Sage.

Minuchin, P., Colapinto, J., & Minuchin, S. (2007). *Working with families of the poor.* New York: Guilford.

Miranda, J., Bernal, G., Lau, A., Kohn, L., Hwang, W., & LaFromboise, T. (2005). State of the science on psychosocial interventions for ethnic minorities. *Annual Review of Clinical Psychology, 1*, 113–142.

Neihardt, J. (Ed.). (1961). *Black Elk speaks: Being the life story of a holy man of the Oglala Sioux.* Lincoln: University of Nebraska Press.

O'Hearn, C. C. (1998). *Half and half: Writers on growing up biracial and bicultural.* New York: Pantheon.

Parham, T. A., & Caldwell, C. D. (2006). An African-centered view of dual relationships. In B. Herlihy & G. Corey (Eds.), *Boundary issues in counseling: Multiple roles and responsibilities* (pp. 131–136). Alexandria, VA: American Counseling Association.

Phinney, J. S. (1990). Ethnic identity in adolescents and adults: A review of research. *Psychological Bulletin, 108*, 499–514.

Phinney, J. S. (1991). Ethnic identity and self-esteem: A review and integration. *Hispanic Journal of Behavior Sciences, 13*, 193–208.

Radina, M. E., & Cooney, T. M. (2000). Relationship quality between multiracial adolescents and their biological parents. *American Journal of Orthopsychiatry, 70*, 445–454.

Ramirez, M. (1998). *Multicultural/multiracial psychology: Mestizo perspectives in personality and mental health.* Northvale, NJ: Jason Aronson.

Robinson, T. L. (2005). *The convergence of race, ethnicity, and gender: Multiple identities in counseling.* Upper Saddle River, NJ: Merrill Prentice Hall.

Rodriguez, J. (1994). *Our Lady of Guadalupe: Faith and empowerment among Mexican American women.* Austin: University of Texas Press.

Root, M. P. P. (Ed.). (1992). *Racially mixed people in America.* Newbury Park, CA: Sage.

Root, M. P. P. (1996). (Ed.). *The multiracial experience: Racial borders as the new frontier.* Thousand Oaks, CA: Sage Publications.

Root, M. P. P. (1999). The biracial baby boom: Understanding ecological constructions of racial identity in the twenty-first century. In R. H. Sheets and E. R. Hollins (Eds.). *Aspects of human development: Racial and ethnic identity in school practices* (pp. 90–119). Mahwah, N.J.: Lawrence Erlbaum.

Rowe, W., Behrens, J. T., & Leach, M. M. (1995). Racial/ethnic identity and racial consciousness. In J. G. Ponterotto, J. M. Casas, L. A. Suzuki, & C. M. Alexander (Eds.), *Handbook of multicultural counseling* (pp. 218–235). Thousand Oaks, CA: Sage.

Santiago-Rivera, A. L., & Altarriba, J. (2002). The role of language in therapy with the Spanish–English bilingual client. *Professional Psychology: Research and Practice, 33*, 30–38.

Seiffge-Krenke, I., & Shulman, S. (1990). Copying style in adolescence: A cross-cultural study. *Journal of Cross-Cultural Psychology, 21*, 351–377.

Shih, M., Bonam, C., Sanchez, D., & Peck, C. (2007). The social construction of race: Biracial identity and vulnerability to stereotypes. *Cultural Diversity and Ethnic Minority Psychology, 13*, 125–133.

Smith, T. B. (2004). *Practicing multiculturalism: Affirming diversity in counseling and psychology.* Boston: Allyn and Bacon.

Sue, D. W. (1981). *Counseling the culturally different: Theory and practice.* New York: Wiley.

Sue, D. W., Ivey, A. E., & Pedersen, P. B. (1996). *A theory of multicultural counseling and therapy*. Pacific Grove, CA: Brooks/Cole.

Sue, D. W., & Sue, D. (2007). *Counseling the culturally different: Theory and practice*. New York: John Wiley & Sons.

Sue, S. (2003). In defense of cultural competency in psychotherapy and treatment. *American Psychologist, 58*, 964–970.

Thomas, A. J., & Schwarzbaum, S. (2006). *Culture and identity: Life stories for counselors and therapists*. Thousand Oaks, CA: Sage.

Trimble, J. E., & Fisher, C. B. (Eds.). (2005). *The handbook of ethnic research with ethnocultural populations and communities*. Thousand Oaks, CA: Sage.

Wiesz, J. R. (2004). *Psychotherapy for children and adolescents: Evidence-based treatment and case examples*. Cambridge, UK: Cambridge University Press.

2

Struggling With Research and Practice With a Mexican American Family
The Case of Robert

Olga L. Mejía

Contents

Introduction

In the current climate of psychology, there is increasing consensus that providing culturally responsive clinical treatment is imperative (American Psychological Association [APA], 2000, 2003). Furthermore, the APA (2005) recently approved the "Policy Statement on Evidence-Based Practice in Psychology" (EBPP) that outlines the importance of integrating "the best available research with clinical expertise in the context of patient characteristics, culture, and preferences" (p. 1). However, there seems to be a gap in terms of recognizing the need for culturally responsive treatment and recognizing how to provide those services in a respectful, knowledgeable, and effective manner, particularly when clients present with psychological concerns that intersect a variety of dimensions (Ancis, 2004), such as race, ethnicity, culture, gender, sexual orientation, and disability. Therefore, clinicians often find themselves at a loss in implementing culturally responsive interventions while working with clients from underrepresented groups and/or with clients who present with varying intersections of diversity.

There are a limited number of theoretical models that address psychotherapeutic work with underrepresented groups, including Latino clients. For example, Ancis (2004) emphasized that contemporary counseling theories are used with diverse populations without proper attention given to contextual factors or the intersections of multiple identities; she further stated that clinicians are left with the option of integrating cultural factors into contemporary Western approaches, reconfiguring traditional Western theories, or using and implementing novel strategies. Nonetheless, several authors have made recommendations that can be applied to providing competent mental health services to underrepresented groups. Sue, Arredondo, and McDavis (1992) argued that training culturally competent counselors is imperative and stated that essential components of cultural competence include examining beliefs and attitudes, knowledge, and skills across three dimensions: the counselor examining his or her own assumptions, values, and biases; under-standing the client's world view; and developing appropriate interventions and techniques. In addition, a common factors approach identifies similar underlying aspects across theoretical approaches and has been recommended in work with clients from diverse backgrounds (Fischer, Jome, & Atkinson, 1998). Furthermore, several authors have recommended using an ecological perspective in work with Latina/o youth (Koss-Chioino & Vargas, 1999) and more specifically when working with Chicana/o clients (McNeill et al., 2001; Velásquez, Arellano, & McNeill, 2004).

This chapter will discuss a case study of a 13-year-old Mexican American male named Robert who is enrolled in the seventh grade and struggling with academics; identity, including ethnicity, sexual orienta-tion, and disability; family; and depressive symptoms. A key component in this case study is a discussion of the intersections of diversity that Robert is managing as an adolescent. As a way of contextualizing the therapeutic work, I will introduce a theoretical framework that is cultur-ally sensitive. Next, the discussion will explore the social, cultural, politi-cal, and historical world view of Mexican Americans in the United States. The case study will then be introduced along with session analyses and rationale for interventions. Furthermore, I will reflect on my growth and development as a therapist in working with Robert and his family. The chapter will conclude with general recommendations for working with the Latino community, a sample list of resources, and discussion ques-tions on this chapter.

Theoretical Orientation

My theoretical approach is integrative and draws from psychodynamic, multi-cultural counseling, and feminist theories. Once I began to work with Latino youth and their families at a community mental health agency, which was guided by the medical model and behavioral theory, I quickly realized that I needed to modify my approach. As a recent graduate, I had limited train-ing working with families, and my theoretical approach was at odds with the agency's philosophy. Trained as a scientist practitioner, I searched the litera-ture for appropriate theoretical models that would address work with Mexican American adolescents and their families. The search yielded limited resources. However, the search process did result in one model that has been specifically developed for psychotherapeutic work with Latino families who have adolescents with disruptive behaviors: Structural Ecosystems Therapy (SET).

Jose Szapocznik and colleagues at the University of Miami's Center for Family Studies developed the SET through a span of over 30 years (Robbins, Schwartz, & Szapocznik, 2004). SET evolved out of a previous model developed by this group of researchers, called the Brief Strategic Family Therapy (BSFT) model, which integrates elements of strategic and structural family therapy (Szapocznik & Williams, 2000). The BSFT model was primarily developed as a result of Szapocznik and colleagues being responsive to Latino immigrant families who were experiencing significant conflict with their adolescent children.

A great benefit of SET is that it contains all of the elements of BSFT and further integrates the systemic focus of social ecology (drawn from Bronfenbrenner 1977, 1979, 1986) on the family (Robbins et al., 2004). Therefore, the SET model acknowledges that the adolescents' behavioral problems may be related to factors within the family, but also to a greater ecological context. Szapocznik et al. (1996) argued that integrating family and ecological perspectives is appropriate for Latina/o families given their strong connection and reliance on each other and extended networks.

Core Concepts

The three core concepts highlighted in SET, as described by Robbins et al. (2004), include system, structure, and strategy. The authors defined the family as a system that is made up of interdependent parts that affect each other. However, the authors extended this definition to also include the various systems in the family's social ecology, namely, the peer network, school context, and juvenile justice system, and the parent's or parents' relationship with each of these components or ecosystems.

The structure of SET refers to the patterns that are developed within and between family members. Maladaptive interaction patterns happen when members repeatedly draw out unsatisfactory responses from each other. The premise of the model is that once the family patterns have been modified, the adolescent's disruptive behavior will decrease. Structure, however, also refers to the adolescent and family's interactions with the various ecosystems and any unsatisfactory interactions between them.

Strategy refers to those interventions that are "practical, problem-focused, and deliberate" (Robbins et al., 2004, p. 76). The goal of SET is to intervene in a way that modifies the interactions of the family and the ecosystems, and in the process reduces the adolescent's problem behavior. As a brief treatment model, SET targets only those behaviors and interactions within the family that are directly related to the adolescent's behavior. Therefore, strictly couple or marriage problems would not be addressed within this model.

Interventions and Tasks   In terms of interventions, SET focuses on three main components that are implemented at several levels: joining, diagnosis, and restructuring.

Joining is when the therapist establishes a therapeutic alliance with various entities. For example, the therapist joins with individual family members, family as a system, and the family's ecosystem. The ecosystem components to be potentially engaged include peers, schools, and the juvenile justice system, and which system is engaged depends on the level of influence on the family. Obviously, the therapist must first gain consent from the family to contact those systems. Furthermore, the authors made an important point that the therapist is to function as a form of a facilitator, empowering the parent(s) to become more involved in positive ways with the various ecosystems.

Diagnosis is a process of identifying the interaction patterns within the family that are related to the adolescent's problematic behaviors. The interaction patterns are then examined across five dimensions. The dimensions include (a) organization (examines leadership, hierarchy, and communication patterns); (b) resonance (identifies the level of connectedness from enmeshment, or overinvolved, to disengagement, or underinvolved); (c) developmental stage (addresses the level to which the adolescent is parentified or infantilized, as well as involvement from extended family); (d) identified patienthood (evaluates the level to which the adolescent's problematic behaviors are centralized within the family); and (e) conflict resolution (examines the way the family manages conflict). Last, diagnosis also extends to assess the various interactions between the family and the ecosystems that may be contributing to the adolescent's problematic behavior. Similar to diagnosing family interactions, evaluating interactions between the family and the various ecosystems takes place along the five aforementioned dimensions.

After the diagnosis phase, an intervention plan is developed and implemented; this is called the restructuring process. Key interventions identified in SET include working in the present, reframing, and working with boundaries and alliances. Working in the present focuses on the interactions among family members and between the family and the various ecosystems. As the family members play out their interaction patterns through enactments, the therapist observes their usual way of getting along. Then the therapist is able to begin intervening by avoiding what is known in family therapy as triangulation (Worden, 2003) and redirecting the maladaptive interaction pattern into a more adaptive one by using blocking, reframing, and reorganizing alliances.

When working in the present and within the ecosystems, it is imperative that the therapist both avoids triangulation with the system and creates opportunities for the family to interact directly with the various systems. The authors made an important distinction between SET and case management services. Namely, Robbins et al. (2004) emphasized that SET is not like case management services. In case management, the therapist is likely to intervene directly with the particular ecosystems (e.g., school, social services). On the contrary, the focus of SET is to involve the parent directly with the various ecological systems, and the role of the therapist is to facilitate communication between them.

In reframing, the goal is to turn negative perceptions of the adolescent, family, and ecosystems into positives: reframing also accomplishes the goal of taking the focus off the adolescent, therefore avoiding what is known as "scapegoating" (Worden, 2003) and allowing family members to share responsibility for solving the problem. Furthermore, reframing negative interactions between the family and the various ecosystems allows for a more productive and collaborative atmosphere.

In terms of boundaries and alliances, SET points out that a pattern seen often in youth who are using drugs is the generational crossing of alliances. In other words, rather than the parental unit (if two parental figures are present) allying with each, one parent will ally with the adolescent, whereas the other parent punishes or tries to discipline the adolescent. In treatment, once the parental unit is able to work collaboratively as a team, the generational boundaries are realigned. Ecologically, working with boundaries in families entails the therapist enhancing positive social networks and reducing negative or damaging networks. For example, in facilitating connection between parents and peer systems, the therapist might encourage their parents to meet the adolescent's friends and parents and to develop and track rules for monitoring the adolescent's daily activities. Parents are further encouraged to build support networks through use of extended family, friends, employers, and support groups. The goal of the parental support networks is to allow the parents to better manage their leadership and nurturing role.

One of the unique aspects of the SET model is that it addresses a variety of cultural topics that may be relevant to Latina/o families. SET systematically addresses issues related to immigration, which include extended family separations, the family's lack of knowledge of the new culture, and the varying levels of acculturation between parents and adolescents. Examples of interventions for facilitating the adjustment of immigrant families include inviting third parties into session as a way of building a bridge with children and parents who have been separated because of immigration, encouraging adolescents and parents to expand their perspectives on U.S. and Latino cultures, and addressing underlying fears that family members have for one another.

Evaluating the Theory and Model

It is important to note the reasons why I chose this theory. Given that beginning family therapists tend to get overwhelmed by the amount of information presented by families (Nichols & Schwartz, 2006), SET helped me to organize and conceptualize work with Robert and his family while contextualizing their concerns within the broader ecosystems. Because SET, and its precursor BSFT, were developed specifically for work with Latina/o families, particularly those that have adolescents who have problems with drugs and/or disruptive behavior, this model seemed appropriate. SET not only effectively addresses family interventions, particularly avoiding triangulation and scapegoating, but also offers practical ways to identify and improve family interactions. Additionally, SET offers a comprehensive model that integrates the social ecology of the family.

In closing for this section, the use of the SET theoretical model can be further understood and enhanced by examining tenets of the EBPP and the common factors approach. The process of searching the literature for an appropriate model to work with Latino families is consistent with the guidelines suggested in the EBPP (APA, 2005), whereby I integrated my clinical expertise with the best research practices and the client's characteristics, values, and context. In addition, SET, BSFT, and variations of the two models have been empirically tested in clinical trials and have been shown to significantly improve Latina/o families' functioning (Szapocznik, Kurtines, Foote, Perez-Vidal, & Hervis, 1986; Szapocznik et al., 1989; Szapocznik, Santisteban, Rio, Perez-Vidal, & Kurtines, 1986). The EBPP also recommends sound clinical expertise by conducting a thorough assessment, diagnosis, and treatment plan, all of which are emphasized in the SET model.

The common factors literature proposes that there are underlying common factors across the various types of psychotherapies that facilitate change (Fischer et al., 1998). Frank and Frank (1991) outlined four common factors: (a) "an emotionally charged, confiding relationship with a helping person" (p. 40); (b) a rationale that provides an explanation for the client's symptoms, based on a shared world view between client and therapist, and outlines a procedure for alleviating the symptoms; (c) client expectations for change; and (d) a ritual or intervention for alleviating client distress. The common factors approach has received support from the extensive review of the literature conducted by Wampold (2001), where he found that theories that meet the criteria for the contextual model are about equally effective. It can be argued that the psychotherapeutic work with Robert and his family fits these four common factors, which will be further discussed later.

Culturally Responsive Treatment Implications

This section introduces social, cultural, political, and historical issues to be mindful of when working with the Latina/o community and, more specifically, with Mexican Americans. Interestingly, the Latina/o population in the United States continues to expand, yet psychology offers limited ways for working with this community, particularly Mexican Americans (McNeill et al., 2001; Velásquez et al., 2004). In fact, McNeill et al. (2001) stated that Chicanas/os are "the largest yet least effectively served ethnic population in the United States" (p. 6).

Currently, the minority population in the United States is about 33% of the total population, and Latinas/os are the largest and fastest growing group at 42.7 million (U.S. Census Bureau, 2006). Mexicans constitute the largest subgroup at 59.3%. Generally, Latinas/os can be described as younger, live-in family households that speak Spanish and may be dealing with immigration and acculturation concerns (Ramirez, 2004).

In terms of educational attainment, compared to other Latina/o subgroups, Mexican Americans are less likely to have completed a high school diploma, at 45.8%, or to attain a bachelor's degree, at 7.5%. Finally, 23.5% of all Mexican Americans in the United States live in poverty, compared to 12.4% for the total population (Ramirez, 2004). These data have serious implications for Mexican Americans in the United States in the present and into the future.

Culturally, Mexican Americans can be described as having a collectivistic approach, where the needs of the group are given preference over individual needs (Marin & Marin, 1991), and they are guided by ethnic-oriented constructs such as *familismo*, *respeto*, and *personalismo* (Falicov, 1998b). These constructs have been defined as follows: *familismo* refers to the ways family members depend on each other and extended family for parenting, financial, and problem-solving support; *respeto* refers to showing respect or deference based on age, socioeconomic status, gender, and authority; and *personalismo* refers to an interpersonal communication style with preference for personal, although not informal, contacts (Falicov, 1996; McNeill et al., 2001).

In terms of history, Mexican Americans' presence in the United States dates back to the 1600s. Prior to 1848, most of what is now California, Arizona, western Colorado, New Mexico, Nevada, Texas, and Utah was part of Mexico. Since then, immigration between Mexico and the United States has been characterized by labor demands, economic recessions, and deportations. Currently, the predominant sentiments toward immigrants are unfavorable, as is evident in recent marches in major cities throughout the United States to protest immigration legislation (Associated Press, 2006). The marches were in response to legislation that would make undocumented status in the United States a felony, penalize employers who hire undocumented immigrants, require churches to check legal documentation of parishioners prior to providing assistance, and build fences along part of the U.S.–Mexico border.

In the recent past, several other laws have been passed that specifically restrict the lives of immigrants in the United States. These propositions (187, 209, 227) and decision (Hopwood) deny public services to undocumented immigrants, prohibit state institutions from giving any special consideration to ethnic minorities, abolish bilingual education programs in California public schools, and prohibit consideration of race in admitting students to Texas state universities. Therefore, it can be argued that immigrants' acculturation in the United States is impacted by both the struggles of adjusting to a new culture and the oppressive environment in which they live (Mejía, 2002).

The aforementioned demographics, cultural values, and political and historical background have significant implications for the overall functioning of Mexican Americans in the United States and should be taken into account in psychological treatment.

Case Study

Prior to introducing Robert and his family, I will briefly describe the community mental health program/agency, because it also impacted the psychotherapeutic work.

The Program

The strength-based program was initially developed in California with a federal grant to address the high rates of Latina suicide attempts in the

United States (National Coalition of Hispanic Health and Human Service Organization, 1999). It was free of charge to clients, and had a focus on prevention. Eventually, the program evolved to include families with medical insurance and provided mental health services to minors and their families. Engagement was a key component of the program, and the cultural protective factors of *familismo*, *respeto*, and *personalismo* (defined earlier in this chapter) were integrated from the intake session and throughout treatment.

The program was field based, meaning that therapy took place at a convenient location for clients and their families, such as the clinic, school, or home. The program targeted work with Latino clients, although minors from other ethnic backgrounds received services as well. The focus was family therapy, yet the program also provided individual and group modalities for both the adolescent and the parent(s) as needed. Therapists represented all disciplines (psychology, social work, marriage and family therapy) and were bilingual and bicultural, primarily Mexican American. In addition to comprehensive case management services (including tutoring, transportation, church links, visits to various social services offices, and child care referrals), the program also provided psychiatric services primarily for psychotropic medication.

Intake: Robert and His Family

The intake was conducted at the clinic with the client, Robert, and his mother, Mrs. Martinez. Robert is a 13-year-old Mexican American male born in the United States. His adoptive parents, Mr. and Mrs. Martinez, were born and raised in Mexico. Mr. and Mrs. Martinez adopted Robert when he was 2 years old. Robert was referred for disruptive behavior at home and school (not listening to his parents or teachers, not following rules, arriving late, and leaving early), low grades, and depressive symptoms. Mrs. Martinez spoke primarily Spanish, whereas Robert spoke primarily English. During the intake, Robert also reported struggling with the coming-out process. He had previously disclosed his sexual orientation to his immediate family, and although initially they had some difficulties, they stated they accepted him now. Robert and Mrs. Martinez further described his growing up with a lifelong illness, muscular dystrophy, which caused mobility difficulties. Robert stated that he did not consider his disability a problem, since he had it all his life. Little information was provided about the biological parents, aside from they may have had a history of cancer and problems with drugs. Mrs. Martinez stated that Mr. Martinez used drugs in the past but had been clean for over 10 years.

Mrs. Martinez stated she immigrated to the United States in her early 20s and met her husband several years after. She described having a difficult time as a child growing up in Mexico, primarily because of limited financial resources. She stated she initially struggled in the United States, as she did not have legal documentation at that time, did not speak English, and had difficulty finding employment. As his mother spoke about moving to the United States, Robert showed disinterest and stated he already knew all that information.

As a way to begin understanding the family better, I inquired about other family members and how they got along. The family also included Mr. Martinez, two older brothers who were married and had moved out, and the paternal grandparents, who had recently arrived to live with them. Robert stated that his brothers were not as open about his coming out as his parents were. As a family they generally described getting along well now since Mr. Martinez stopped using drugs, but Mrs. Martinez stated she tended to feel bad for Robert when his father disciplined him. Robert and Mrs. Martinez both reported that Robert was not taking psychotropic medication, and Robert denied suicidality (SI) or homicidality (HI). At the end of the initial session, they agreed to individual sessions for Robert (Mrs. Martinez requested these specifically) and family therapy every other week. Eventually the work focused primarily on family therapy.

It is important to note that according to program guidelines, Robert remained the primary client. Nonetheless, family work and involvement was highly encouraged.

Analysis of Intake Session and Diagnosis

The joining process flowed relatively well from the intake session. Given the premise of the program and Robert's cultural background, the cultural protective factors of *familismo*, *respeto*, and *personalismo* were integrated from the engagement process. Because Mrs. Martinez was more comfortable speaking Spanish and Robert speaking English, I was able to accommodate each of their preferences. In Spanish, I also used the more formal *Usted* format that is traditionally used to show respect to adults and elders. Overall, I communicated a nonjudgmental and open therapeutic environment, allowing space for them to share of themselves as they felt safe to do so. As a way of joining with the various ecosystems, I also inquired about Robert and his family's involvement in the school and peer network.

Being mindful that there may be intergenerational acculturative differences between Robert and his parents, I inquired about their immigration background. The hint that there was some intergenerational acculturative conflict was Robert's disinterest while Mrs. Martinez talked about her immigration experience.

I also noted that as an adolescent, Robert was managing the usual task of figuring out his identity, and additionally was managing the coming-out process and a lifelong disability. Initially, I wrongly assumed that the parents were having a difficult time with his coming out given their Mexican traditional background. However, it seemed that the parents were open and accepting of Robert, although his extended family was not. My assumption was a reminder for me to not jump to conclusions and instead ask for the client's perspective. Furthermore, Robert seemed to not want to talk about his mobility difficulties, as he provided minimal information about it. Mrs. Martinez was more willing to provide information about the muscular dystrophy and how it affected their life. As is evident, Robert is managing several intersections of diversity; the most salient at the time of intake were his ethnicity, sexual orientation, and disability. As an adolescent, it seemed that he was just beginning to be aware of the effects of these intersections and their positive and negative effects on his life.

In terms of diagnosis, I examined the various dimensions outlined by SET throughout the first several sessions within both the family and the ecosystems. In terms of organization, Mrs. Martinez seemed to be much more involved with Robert than the father, and although Mr. Martinez disciplined Robert (for coming home late), for example, Mrs. Martinez would initially support her husband, but then allow Robert to do as he wished. In resonance, it seemed that Mrs. Martinez was highly involved with Robert ever since he was adopted, and he used to have constant doctor's visits because of the muscular dystrophy. At the intake, she seemed to continue to be over-involved with Robert; with the school system, by constantly checking to see if Robert was at school; with doctors, by asking repeatedly what they were doing, and if they could do more; and with peers, by calling often to see where they were and what they were doing. Mr. Martinez, on the other hand, seemed focused on working and became involved only when discipline was required.

It is important to make a point about traditional gender roles within the Mexican culture, which is a collectivistic culture. As a therapist working with Robert and his family, I questioned my hypothesis about Mrs. Martinez's overinvolvement and Mr. Martinez's underinvolvement given that they seemed to be aligned along traditional gender roles, and discussed this in supervision. In the Mexican American culture, it is not unusual for mothers to be much more involved with their children and for offspring to live at home until they marry. The father, on the other hand, traditionally is not as involved with the children and has the provider role (Falicov, 1998b). Through discussion in supervision and accounting for cultural factors, we hypothesized that Mrs. Martinez and Mr. Martinez were overinvolved and underinvolved, respectively.

In terms of developmental stage, Robert's mother seemed to treat him as a young child, which in part may be due to helping him with mobility difficulties, although Robert stated he could do many things for himself. Developmentally, the client was figuring out his identity, was struggling with the coming-out process, was focused on his peers, and wanted to be part of the crowd. In the identified patienthood dimension, Robert's behavior was the focus of family discussions. Furthermore, Mrs. Martinez would often blame the various systems for not helping him do better in school.

When conflict arose in the family, they tended to delve into it, but after much heated arguing, the conflict remained unresolved. In terms of the ecosystems, Robert's mother was often discontent with them for not causing Robert to follow rules better.

Robert and Mrs. Martinez seemed motivated for treatment. The goals for treatment were developed collaboratively with Robert and Mrs. Martinez and included improving communication between family members and decreasing Robert's depressive symptoms. Assessment continued throughout treatment, and as more information was gathered, treatment goals and interventions were modified as necessary.

Last, in analyzing the initial session, one can argue that the four common factors discussed earlier were part of developing a positive therapeutic environment. Through the joining process we started to build a trusting, supportive relationship; we shared a similar world view through Mexican cultural values; the Martinezes seemed motivated to change; and the SET model provided a road map for diagnosis and treatment.

Initial Sessions/Interventions

From the beginning of family sessions, there was often a pull for me to become triangulated with Robert and Mrs. Martinez's interactions and with the various ecosystems. For example, initially Mrs. Martinez would ask me to tell Robert what to do to improve his school functioning. While validating that I could tell that she cared for her son and wanted him to do well, I used redirecting, encouraging her to tell Robert what she wanted and for him to respond to her, therefore encouraging them to enact their discussions.

Then we focused on clarifying communication, verbal and nonverbal, and expressing feelings appropriately. As a way to illustrate verbal and nonverbal communication, I demonstrated a couple of role-plays in session that illustrated a scenario where verbal and nonverbal messages were consistent and another scenario where they were inconsistent. I then asked them to react to the overall messages. As a result, both were encouraged to take responsibility for improving their communication. Through this process, Mrs. Martinez and Robert stated they had not realized the negative impact of nonverbal messages (e.g., facial expression, tone of voice) on their communication. Through this process, it became clearer that they loved each other and that they would make greater efforts to have clearer communication.

As there seemed to be a cross-generational alliance between Robert and Mrs. Martinez, I encouraged them to include Mr. Martinez into family sessions. Because Mr. Martinez's work schedule did not allow for day sessions, I offered to see them as a family on a late evening. After several attempts, the father was able to come in to the clinic. I used reframing, pointing out that as difficult as it was to have a family session, the fact that all three were present showed willingness for the overall situation to improve. As a way of working with boundaries, the parents were encouraged to work as a team and agree on their discipline and consequences, exploring the potential benefits and costs of adhering to consequences. For example, I asked the parents to consider the message to Robert when he continued to receive a fairly high allowance although he was not following rules at home and school. The parents were able to acknowledge the importance of setting boundaries and being firm on the consequences. As a way to help realign the parental unit, the parents were encouraged to spend more time alone, therefore allowing Robert independence with accountability.

As a way to openly incorporate issues of acculturation into family sessions, I encouraged the parents to further discuss their experiences in adjusting to the Mexican and U.S. cultures. The parents discussed how each struggled with being an immigrant. They stated that initially it was difficult finding employment, learning a new language (now they both spoke English, although Mrs. Martinez still felt more comfortable speaking Spanish), finding transportation and housing, and having undocumented status (they both now had legal documentation). Once Robert was able to more clearly listen to his parents, he expressed increased understanding and empathy for their experiences and desire for him to do better. The parents also stated that at times they could not relate to Robert's wanting to go out with his friends, and they wondered why they could not just visit at home. Robert talked with his parents about wanting to fit in with his peers. The parents expressed fear of what could happen when Robert was out with his friends but stated they had greater understanding of why he wanted to go out.

In terms of the ecosystems, Mrs. Martinez had been overinvolved with peers, school, and doctors. As suggested by the theoretical models, and as a way to support her role and refocus more attention on her, Mrs. Martinez was encouraged to attend a parent's group, where she received feedback and support from other parents (the father was not able to attend).

As part of the program and the SET model, I was encouraged to become involved with the various ecosystems. Although I experienced discomfort initially, to be discussed later, I became more involved outside of the therapy room. For example, in addition to making a few home visits, I also attended several school meetings. The home visits gave me an opportunity to be flexible and meet their needs, because the Martinezes did not have transportation on a few occasions, and also to see them interact in their home environment. During school visits, I gained a new perspective from the academic counselor and Robert's teachers. I was mindful of having the parents interact directly with school personnel, and I focused on facilitating clear communication to improve potential negative interactions.

Initial Sessions Analysis

In the initial family sessions, it was challenging to get through any topic, as Robert and his parents would argue and disagree with each other immediately. It seemed important to focus on increasing awareness of how they communicated and the way those interactions affected their relationship. After the role-plays emphasizing verbal and nonverbal messages, they seemed more attentive to how nonverbal cues negatively affected their interactions. They seemed to make an effort to use this information, yet were reminded to use their new skills, as they often reverted to old ways of communicating.

In the initial sessions, it was also important to ask the parents to discuss their immigration experience, which seemed beneficial in several ways. The parents expressed their acculturative process and gained support and validation for their struggles. Robert was able to hear their story and have more empathy for their experiences, and expressed a greater understanding of why they wanted him to do better in school. Likewise, Robert had an opportunity to express how he was trying to fit in with his peers in the U.S. culture and wanting to go out more often. The parents expressed their fears for Robert and stated they would make efforts to understand his point of view.

In terms of being involved outside of the therapy room, I struggled with the decision. Being trained in Western psychology, I initially felt discomfort at leaving my office. I was concerned about the clinical and ethical implications of treating clients therapeutically outside of the therapy room. I discussed my concerns in supervision and gained a greater understanding of how it could be beneficial to be responsive to the greater context, which is emphasized by the SET model. After meeting with Robert and his parents for home visits and attending school conferences, I realized the benefits of leaving my office. I appreciated the broader, more comprehensive picture of Robert, his family, and the impact of the environment on their daily life.

Middle Sessions/Interventions

About 6 months into work with the family, Robert became increasingly depressed. During an individual session (his parents had a work schedule conflict), Robert stated that he was tired of trying to improve and reach the standards being set for him; that he had argued with several of his friends, and that a boy he had met at school was ignoring him. Robert reported that as he talked in therapy, he was feeling confused and did not know why he was feeling so bad about himself. He reported wanting to hurt himself, with a specific plan and intent. He did not agree to a no-harm contract, and after much discussion he volunteered to be hospitalized. The family was contacted and involved in the hospitalization. Robert received psychiatric treatment and prescribed antidepressant medication upon discharge. The parents were encouraged to continue to set firm boundaries with clear and consistent consequences, while balancing with expressions of love and nurturance.

Several sessions after Robert was released from the hospital, he wanted to discuss the coming-out process. Because the theory did not directly address this issue, I drew from my training in graduate school on diversity issues and my personal experiences. Since my undergraduate and graduate studies, I had become more familiar with the lesbian, gay, bisexual, and transsexual community and felt comfortable with LGBT issues. As such, I encouraged Robert to discuss his feelings about coming out to family and friends, as well as attractions to boys at school. Being mindful of the intersections of diversity, I also encouraged him to discuss any concerns he had in terms of being gay and being Mexican American. This discussion was particularly important, because there tends to be strong stigma related to being gay within the Mexican American culture (Rodriguez, 2004). Robert stated that although he felt accepted by his parents, he felt confused about his attraction for boys.

As we processed his thoughts and feelings, it became clearer that he liked boys, but felt confused about how to approach them, and he was unsure about coming out to his other family members and friends. Overall, I provided a supportive and accepting environment.

Furthermore, I noted that at the start of sessions, Robert stated that he did not believe that his disability due to muscular dystrophy was a problem for him. Although I brought it up a few times as a topic of discussion, he did not address the issue for several months. In one family session, he alluded to the frustration of always needing help from others, while at the same time wanting to be independent. Therefore, Robert was experiencing many difficulties, including the appropriate need for independence as an adolescent and the debilitating effects of muscular dystrophy. His ambivalent feelings were validated. Robert was again encouraged to communicate his feelings openly to his parents. Because Robert was able to do many daily activities for himself yet Mrs. Martinez insisted on helping him, we explored ways that Robert could do more tasks and chores on his own to increase his sense of independence.

Robert also touched on the issue of being adopted and how angry he was at his biological parents for having left him. He shared with me that he did not want to be like his biological parents, even though he knew very little about them. Together with his parents, we discussed what it was like when they made the decision to adopt Robert and the family they had built together. He was encouraged to process his feelings of anger and loss. Nonetheless, this was a difficult topic for Robert, and he stated he did not want to discuss it anymore.

Middle Sessions Analysis

In these sessions, it is apparent that Robert is struggling with numerous complex and intersecting concerns. First, developmentally he is struggling with his identity and concerned about how he fits in with his peers. However, Robert has the added dimensions of the coming-out process within the Mexican American culture and managing a lifelong disability. Robert's confusion and depressive symptoms seem an appropriate response to all that is going on around him. Newman and Muzzonigro (1993) stated in a study that in addition to feeling different from other boys, most gay adolescent males of various racial and ethnic backgrounds reported feeling confused during their teen years before reaching the acceptance stage later on in life. As this was the first time that Robert was voicing his feelings about his sexual orientation and disability in a therapeutic setting, I focused on creating a safe environment for him to be able to express the various parts of himself and explore the confusion. I hypothesized that my validation and acceptance, particularly of his sexual orientation, was helpful because we share the same ethnic background. I also focused on facilitating support from his family. His parents seemed accepting of Robert, although the same was not true of their extended family.

An added concern for Robert was the fact that he was coming to grips with being adopted. He wondered about his biological family and why his parents gave him up for adoption. As mentioned earlier, Robert reported having difficulty with this topic and stated he did not want to discuss it anymore. Honoring that he may not be ready to explore this issue further, I let him know we could discuss it again when he was ready to do so.

An important point to make about the therapeutic work is that although Robert has multiple issues affecting him, developmentally he is still an adolescent with adolescent concerns. As such, he is becoming more aware of how these issues affect him, and he is not likely to come to immediate resolutions. He is likely to continue to struggle with these concerns in the years to come.

Termination Sessions

Toward the end of therapy, Robert reported an overall alleviation of depressive symptoms, and he was continuing the antidepressant medication. He stated that he still felt confused about being gay, but that his confusion was about other people's reactions and not about his attraction for other boys. He had decided to come out to his extended family members and other friends, and he had mixed reactions. A few extended family members began to stay away from him. Robert stated that he felt bad about the distance, but that it helped him to have his parents' support. Robert's grades had still not improved significantly, but he had developed a plan that he was trying to follow.

Robert and his parents were communicating more clearly as well. The parents were able to spend more time together, even going away for several weekends alone and doing volunteer work. Robert stayed home and did not get in trouble. The parents had begun to agree more often on having clear and consistent consequences. They still tended to argue with Robert, yet the arguments were not as heated because the parents focused on remaining calm and providing a consistent message. Through the support group, Mrs. Martinez was encouraged to give Robert more independence and to focus more on herself and her husband. The parents were also allowing Robert to go out with his friends more often. Robert did arrive late a few times, but his parents instituted consistent consequences and lately Robert had been following more rules.

As termination approached, the family brought Mexican food and a card signed by all three, stating their thanks. I had not been faced with this situation before in therapy, so I was unsure of what to do. Instinctively, and being familiar with the culture, I accepted their gift and discussed its significance and impact on the therapeutic relationship in session with the family, as well as in supervision.

Termination Sessions Analysis

After Robert was able to talk about his confusion of the coming-out process within the Mexican culture and frustration about having a disability as an adolescent wanting more independence, his depressive symptoms began to decrease. Robert also reported taking his medication consistently. Mr. and Mrs. Martinez seemed to be working together more often to agree on rules and following through with consequences. As Robert and his family were no longer meeting "medical necessity" as described by the program guidelines, we needed to terminate sessions.

In terms of gift giving and receiving, initially I felt uncomfortable with the situation. Given my training, I was again concerned about the therapeutic implications and ethics of receiving a gift from the family. In supervision and through discussion with colleagues, I gained greater understanding on how not accepting the gift may have negative implications for the therapeutic relationship. I learned about the importance of still being mindful of the impact on the therapeutic work, yet also being responsive to the client's cultural background.

Case Conceptualization

I worked with the Martinez family for about a year. It is evident that Robert and his family had numerous complex concerns in their lives, and, more importantly, these concerns are likely to continue to affect them into the future. As a way of organizing the information provided by the Martinez family, this section will examine Robert and his parents from various levels, from broad to more specific.

On a broader level, as a Mexican American immigrant family living in the United States, they were dealing with social, cultural, political, and historical concerns. Both Mr. and Mrs. Martinez had immigrated to the United States from Mexico for financial reasons and to have more educational opportunities. The parents stated they had experienced discrimination when they were searching for employment because of their ethnicity, and because Mrs. Martinez had an accent when she spoke English. Nonetheless, Robert's parents were highly motivated to do well in the United States. They both made efforts to learn English and find employment. They now own their home, and they stated they were thankful to live in a neighborhood where others spoke Spanish as well.

In terms of Robert and the broader level, he was experiencing the effects of homophobia and ableism toward him. In therapy, it became clearer that his confusion about his sexual orientation was more about his environment and others' negative reactions to him. Robert also talked about being teased at school for having mobility difficulties.

The parents had also learned to interact with the various ecosystems. It seemed that Mrs. Martinez had become overinvolved with the ecosystems, including Robert's school, doctor, and peer network, whereas Mr. Martinez remained distanced. Again, here it is important to examine Mrs. and Mr. Martinez's overinvolvement and underinvolvement, respectively, within their cultural background. Being from a collectivistic culture, it is not unusual for the mother to be more involved with her children and to focus on the family as a whole and for the father to be less involved. Nonetheless, through discussions in supervision, we hypothesized that Mrs. Martinez was overinvolved with Robert and the various ecosystems and Mr. Martinez was underinvolved. The interventions then centered on providing a network for Mrs. Martinez to receive support and feedback, focusing more attention on the parental relationship, improving negative interactions with the various ecosystems, and increasing Mr. Martinez's involvement in the family.

In terms of the family level, as noted in the diagnosis section, when the Martinezes came in for treatment, their communication was unproductive and resulted in misunderstandings and hurt feelings. It also seemed that Mr. and Mrs. Martinez were inconsistent in terms of their rules and consequences for Robert. Robert for his part seemed to take advantage of the inconsistent messages to get his way. In sessions, Robert was encouraged to work for what he wanted. Through the therapeutic process, the parents worked together as a team and provided more consistent limits and consequences. Mrs. Martinez stated she benefited from the feedback in the parents' support group. Furthermore, as Mr. and Mrs. Martinez focused on spending more time together, they were allowing Robert to try out his independence.

Another important dimension to the family was intergenerational acculturative conflict. Mr. and Mrs. Martinez were immigrants from Mexico and tended to retain more of the Mexican culture, traditions, and language. Robert, on the other hand, was born in the United States, and as an adolescent, he adhered to U.S. customs. In therapy they stated they gained greater understanding of each others' perspectives.

On an individual level, Robert was managing a variety of complex tasks. In addition to the usual tasks of adolescence in figuring out his identity and wanting to fit into a peer group, Robert was coming out as gay within the Mexican American culture; managing muscular dystrophy, which affected his mobility; and questioning the reasons why his biological parents gave him for adoption. Contextualizing Robert's concerns at the individual and familial levels, and at that of the broader ecosystems, his cognitive, emotional, and behavioral responses seem warranted. As a therapist, I focused on creating a nonjudgmental and accepting environment where Robert could be himself and struggle with the process.

Additional Clinical Considerations

Earlier, I discussed some reasons why SET was helpful in working with Robert and his family. In many ways, because of Robert's age and presenting concern, the model was useful in conceptualizing work with Robert and his family. However, there were also several limitations with the SET model. For example, the SET model focuses on Latina/o families in general, and was primarily developed with families of Cuban descent (Szapocznik & Williams, 2000). Several authors (e.g., McNeill et al., 2001; Velásquez et al., 2004) have emphasized the need to develop theories and models that specifically target the Chicana/o population. Furthermore, Cervantes and Sweatt (2004) noted that overall family models targeting Chicanas/os have not been described well in the psychological literature.

A factor not directly discussed by the SET model is the intersections of diversity that impact clients' lives in significant ways. As mentioned earlier, several authors have advocated accounting for and integrating intersections of diversity into theoretical models (Ancis, 2004; Koss-Chioino & Vargas, 1999; Velásquez et al., 2004). Working with Robert and his family presented a challenge in integrating Robert's ethnicity, culture, sexual orientation, and disability along with intergenerational acculturative stress.

As mentioned earlier, SET is a brief family therapy model, although no session limit is specified. Robert and his family, however, presented with complex issues that were not easily addressed within a brief therapy model. The program/clinic conceptualized clients' functioning using the medical model, which states that as long as medical necessity is met, the client continues to receive services. As such, Robert and his family were seen for a longer period of time than specified by SET.

Another interesting concept to consider is triangulation, which is an essential family therapy concept (Nichols & Schwarts, 2006; Worden, 2003). Falicov (1998a) cautioned against indiscriminately conceptualizing triangulation as pathological and automatically intervening to realign the parental unit. She argued that the conceptualization of triangulation is based on local social constructions, that is, "the American middle-class nuclear family" (Falicov, 1998a, p. 38), and this notion does not necessarily apply to collectivistic cultures. She argued that focusing solely on the parental unit may cut off other central family ties. Falicov's point is well taken and important to account for in family therapy with Mexican American families.

In addition, SET does not directly address the skills or characteristics in the therapist that would allow for the model to flow more effectively. It can be argued that the fact that I am bilingual and bicultural had a significant impact on the therapeutic engagement. For example, Altarriba and Santiago-Rivera (1994) recognized language as a barrier for Chicanas/os seeking mental health services, and Prieto, McNeill, Walls, and Gomez (2001) expressed the great need for bilingual mental health providers. This argument is also consistent with the common factors perspective introduced earlier. Perhaps the cultural similarities between the Martinez family and I helped to develop a strong therapeutic alliance and facilitate the three other common factors cited by Frank and Frank (1991).

Cervantes and Sweatt (2004) recently proposed a model to conceptualize work with Chicano family therapy called TRENSA (Treatment of the Relationship Encounter as Nested Between Self-Disclosure and Professional Awareness) that recommends that the therapist's qualities be accounted for in the therapeutic relationship. In the TRENSA model, the therapist is to account for (a) the therapist's sociocultural experience and history, (b) family therapy theory, and (c) the Chicano family's sociocultural experience and history. The TRENSA model effectively captures the ways that the therapist, theory, and family are interwoven in the therapeutic relationship.

Personal Dimensions of Diversity and World View

Working with Robert and his family was an honor for me. Simultaneously, our work together was a growth experience and presented several challenges. As a recent graduate, I had limited training in family therapy, and my training was primarily in Western psychology, mainly psychodynamic theory. Without a doubt, I found myself feeling overwhelmed and reexamining some of the concepts I learned in graduate school and either unlearning them or modifying them to more accurately account for cultural factors. This process has been examined by Rosenthal Gelman (2004). In her study, she interviewed 15 bilingual and bicultural Latino therapists who were psychodynamically trained. Overall, she found that the therapists extended the psychodynamic approach to include increasing self-disclosure, giving gifts (although being careful to examine possible boundary violations), being more directive and active with Latinos than with other clients, focusing on the therapeutic relationship and increased use of *personalismo*, and using language as a way of building the relationship.

In terms of my personal background, I am a first-generation Mexican female who immigrated to the United States at 9 years old. Therefore, my first language is Spanish, and I believe this skill facilitated the therapeutic work. Nonetheless, I still struggled in translating psychological concepts, which I learned in English, into Spanish.

In addition, the clinic/program required that I get out of my office and meet the family at a convenient location and interact with the various ecosystems. This notion had not been discussed in my graduate training, therefore it presented many discussions in supervision about the ethics of going outside of the office. Eventually, I was able to see and experience the benefits of getting out of my office and the positive effects on the therapeutic work with the Martinez family.

Another issue that presented concern for me was when the family brought food as a gift to therapy sessions. Intuitively, I felt that culturally it would be inappropriate to not accept the gifts. Yet from my previous training, I experienced great discomfort that I brought for discussion to supervision. We discussed the issues and contextualized them within a cultural framework. Although gift giving may be more part of the therapeutic work, I nonetheless engaged in a discussion of the gift's impact on the therapeutic alliance with the client.

Being a Mexican immigrant woman also impacted my work with Robert and his family, both positively and negatively. I believe I made closer contact with the family because we looked and spoke similarly and had Mexican cultural values underlying our interactions. Yet at times I found myself over-identifying with the family members and their struggles, and at times not taking the time to further explore their concerns because there was a perception of mutual understanding. This was salient when the parents discussed their immigration experience, as I was able to relate well to their immigrant struggles. Also, given the more traditional values of the Mexican culture versus the U.S. culture, I wrongly assumed that the parents would not be accepting of Robert's sexual orientation. Therefore, I reminded myself constantly to check in with the family members to ensure I understood them correctly.

Therapeutic Recommendations for Working With Mexican American Families

Drawing from the case study discussion and conceptualization, the following presents some points to be mindful of when conducting psychotherapy with Mexican American families in the United States. Some of these points also apply to Latino families in general.

1. Read and familiarize yourself with the Multicultural Counseling Competencies and Standards, as outlined in both Sue et al. (1992) and Arredondo et al. (1996). Also, Santiago-Rivera, Arredondo, and Gallardo-Cooper (2002) discussed the competencies specifically with the Latino community in their book *Counseling Latinos and la Familia*.
2. When working with Mexican American families, utilize a family systems perspective that integrates cultural dimensions and the broader social ecology.
3. The factors that may be salient in psychotherapeutic work with Latino families are ethnicity and culture, yet remain attentive and open to various intersections of diversity, including sexual orientation, disability, and gender.
4. Learn a second language; if working with the Latino community, learn Spanish. However, it is important to also receive specific training in utilizing Spanish within a psychotherapeutic context.
5. In terms of working with immigrants, these are some points to keep in mind (Mejía, 2002). Learning a new culture and maintaining the home culture is an ongoing process, and the process is not necessarily

pathological; instead, it may be a normal response to a stressful situation (Espin, 1987; Salgado de Snyder, 1987).

6. In the immigration process, immigrants may feel isolated and mourn the loss of family members and familiar surroundings (Ainslie, 1998; Arredondo-Dowd, 1981). Isolation may be further heightened by the unfavorable attitudes toward Latino immigrants in the United States.

7. In working with Latino families and the acculturative process, it is important to focus on positive coping skills. Examples of positive coping include building self-esteem, having flexibility in communication, and improving social support networks.

Conclusions

This chapter is a sample of psychotherapeutic work with a 13-year-old Mexican American male and his family. The case study discussed Robert, his family, and the ways they managed struggles with identity, ethnicity, culture, sexual orientation, disability status, and depressive symptoms. The intersections of diversity that Robert is experiencing were integrated into the therapeutic work, yet his concerns are complex, and he is likely to continue to struggle with them into the future.

I used the SET model in conceptualizing work with Robert and his family. The SET model was especially useful in many ways, including that it was developed particularly for Latino families who have adolescents who present with drug use and/or disruptive behaviors. Through use of the model, I learned that it is imperative to incorporate the family's social ecology into the therapeutic work and conceptualization. Furthermore, I learned valuable interventions on how to integrate the ecological systems perspective into psychotherapeutic work.

However, the SET model presented some challenges as well because it did not directly address how to manage the client's intersections of diversity, the preferred characteristics of the therapist, and Mexican American families specifically. As such, it is recommended that psychotherapeutic models continue to address intersections of diversity, target underrepresented groups, and integrate training specifics for therapists.

The SET theoretical framework in this chapter was further supported and analyzed through the use of the EBPP (APA, 2005) and the common factors approach.

In conclusion, a main recommendation in this chapter for clinicians, researchers, and educators is to develop a means to make successful theoretical models readily available to therapists and to provide the necessary training to effectively implement those models. Many barriers inhibit this connection between science and practice, including financial resources and lack of researcher–clinician networks. Nonetheless, the link between science and practice is integral and necessary to provide competent mental health services to the Latino community.

Discussion Questions

1. The theoretical framework discussed in this chapter was developed for psychotherapeutic work with families who have adolescents who are experiencing disruptive behaviors, which seems to fit well with Robert's presenting concerns. However, the SET model was primarily developed with Cuban American families. How appropriate is it to use the SET model with Mexican American families?
2. How would psychotherapeutic work be different with Robert and his family if the therapist were not bilingual or bicultural?
3. What can be done about the lack of comprehensive theoretical models that account for contextual factors with Mexican Americans?
4. How can researchers and clinicians create more clear lines of communication so that research is readily available to clinicians and vice versa?
5. How can clinicians, particularly in community mental health, have more direct access to relevant research with the population they are working with?
6. While working in community mental health, psychologists are often required to do field visits (e.g., home or school), which are traditionally known in the social work field. In working with the Latino population, how important is it for psychologists to get out of their office and conduct field visits?
7. What interventions would you use as a clinician to be more culturally responsive in working with Latino clients in general?
8. What are the benefits of integrating the client's various intersections of diversity for the client, therapist, and therapeutic relationship?
9. How can more clinicians and researchers become aware of policies such as the "Policy Statement on Evidence-Based Practice in Psychology"?

Cultural Resources

Additional resources for therapists working with Latino (some specifically with Mexican American) families include the following:

1. Santiago-Rivera, A. L., Arredondo, P., & Gallardo-Cooper, M. (2002). *Counseling Latinos and la familia: A practical guide.* Thousand Oaks, CA: Sage.
2. Works authored by Jose Szapocznik and colleagues based out of the University of Miami's Center for Family Studies (http://www.cfs.med. miami.edu/default.htm).
3. Ancis, J. (2004). *Culturally responsive interventions: Innovative approaches to working with diverse populations.* New York: Brunner-Routledge.
4. Works by Celia Jaes Falicov (see References), including *Latino families in therapy: A guide to multicultural practice* (New York: Guilford) and a chapter "Mexican Families" from *Ethnicity and family therapy,* edited by McGoldrick, Giordano, and Pearce (New York: Guilford).
5. Velásquez, R. J., Arellano, L. M., & McNeill, B. W. (2004). *The handbook of Chicana/o psychology and mental health.* Mahwah, NJ: Lawrence Erlbaum.
6. *The Counseling Psychologist* dedicated a complete issue (Volume 29, Number 1) in January 2001 to Chicana/o psychology.

References

Ainslie, R. C. (1998). Cultural mourning, immigration, and engagement: Vignettes from the Mexican experience. In M. Suarez-Orozco (Ed.), *Crossings: Mexican immigration in interdisciplinary perspectives* (pp. 284–300). Cambridge, MA: Harvard University Press.

Altarriba, J., & Santiago-Rivera, A. L. (1994). Current perspectives on using linguistic and cultural factors in counseling the Hispanic client. *Professional Psychology: Research and Practice, 25,* 388–397.

American Psychological Association. (2000). Guidelines for psychotherapy with lesbian, gay, and bisexual clients. *American Psychologist, 55,* 1440–1451.

American Psychological Association. (2003). Guidelines on multicultural education, training, research, practice, and organizational change for psychologists. *American Psychologist, 58,* 377–402.

American Psychological Association. (2005). Policy statement on evidence-based practice in psychology. Retrieved December 20, 2006, from http://www2.apa.org/practice/ebpstatement.pdf

Ancis, J. (2004). Culturally responsive practice. In J. R. Ancis (Ed.), *Culturally responsive interventions: Innovative approaches to working with diverse populations* (pp. 3–21). New York: Brunner-Routledge.

Arredondo-Dowd, P. M. (1981, February). Personal loss and grief as a result of immigration. *Personnel and Guidance Journal*, 376–378.

Arredondo, P., Toporek, R., Brown, S. P., & Jones, J. (1996). Operationalization of the multicultural counseling competencies. *Journal of Multicultural Counseling and Development, 24*, 42–78.

Associated Press. (2006, March 25). 500,000 rally immigration rights in L.A. Retrieved December 20, 2006, from http://www.msnbc.msn.com/id/11442705/

Bronfenbrenner, U. (1977). Toward an experimental ecology of human development. *American Psychologist, 32*, 513–531.

Bronfenbrenner, U. (1979). Contexts of child rearing: Problems and prospects. *American Psychologist, 34*, 844–850.

Bronfenbrenner, U. (1986). Ecology of the family as a context for human development: Research perspectives. *Development Psychology, 22*, 723–742.

Cervantes, J. M., & Sweatt, L. I. (2004). Family therapy with Chicanas/os. In R. J. Velásquez, L. M. Arrellano, & B. W. McNeill (Eds.), *The handbook of Chicana/o psychology and mental health* (pp. 285–322). Mahwah, NJ: Lawrence Erlbaum.

Espin, O. M. (1987). Psychological impact of migration on Latinas: Implications for psychotherapeutic practice. *Psychology of Women Quarterly, 11*, 489–503.

Falicov, C. J. (1996). Mexican families. In M. McGoldrick, J. Giordano, & J. K. Pearce (Eds.), *Ethnicity and family therapy* (pp. 169–182). New York: Guilford.

Falicov, C. J. (1998a). The cultural meaning of family triangles. In M. McGoldrick (Ed.), *Re-visioning family therapy: Race, culture, and gender in clinical practice* (pp. 37–49). New York: Guilford.

Falicov, C. J. (1998b). *Latino families in therapy: A guide to multicultural practice.* New York: Guilford.

Fischer, A. R., Jome, L. M., & Atkinson, D. R. (1998). Reconceptualizing multicultural counseling: Universal healing conditions in a culturally specific context. *The Counseling Psychologist, 26*, 525–588.

Frank, J. D., & Frank, J. B. (1991). *Persuasion and healing: A comparative study of psychotherapy* (3rd ed.). Baltimore: Johns Hopkins University Press.

Koss-Chioino, J. D., & Vargas, L. A. (1999). *Working with Latino youth.* San Francisco: Jossey-Bass.

Marin, G., & Marin, B. V. (1991). *Research with Hispanic populations.* London: Sage.

McNeill, B. W., Prieto, L. R., Niemann, Y. F., Pizarro, M., Vera, E. M., & Gomez, S. P. (2001). Current directions in Chicana/o psychology. *The Counseling Psychologist, 29*, 5–17.

Mejía, O. L. (2002, July/August). Immigration: A dynamic process. *The California Psychologist, 35*, 19.

National Coalition of Hispanic Health and Human Services Organization. (1999). *The state of Hispanic girls.* Washington, DC: COSSMHO Press.

Newman, B. S., & Muzzonigro, P. G. (1993). The effects of traditional family values on the coming out process of gay male adolescents. *Adolescence, 28*, 213–226.

Nichols, M. P., & Schwartz, R. C. (2006). *Family therapy concepts and methods* (7th ed.). Boston: Allyn and Bacon.

Prieto, L. R., McNeill, B. W., Walls, R. G., & Gomez, S. P. (2001). Chicanas/os and mental health services: An overview of utilization, counselor preference, and assessment issues. *The Counseling Psychologist, 29,* 18–54.

Ramirez, R. R. (2004). *We the people: Hispanics in the United States, Census 2000 special reports.* Washington, DC: U.S. Census Bureau.

Robbins, M. S., Schwartz, S., & Szapocznik, J. (2004). Structural ecosystems therapy with Hispanic adolescents exhibiting disruptive behavior disorders. In J. R. Ancis (Ed.), *Culturally responsive interventions: Innovative approaches to working with diverse populations* (pp. 71–99). New York: Brunner-Routledge.

Rodriguez, R. A. (2004). Psychotherapy with gay Chicanos. In R. J. Velásquez, L. M. Arrellano, & B. W. McNeill (Eds.), *The handbook of Chicana/o psychology and mental health* (pp. 193–214). Mahwah, NJ: Lawrence Erlbaum.

Rosenthal Gelman, C. (2004). Toward a better understanding of the use of psychodynamically-informed treatment with Latinos: Findings from clinical experience. *Clinical Social Work Journal, 32,* 61–77.

Salgado de Snyder, V. N. (1987). Factors associated with acculturative stress and depressive symptomatology among married Mexican immigrant women. *Psychology of Women Quarterly, 11,* 475–488.

Santiago-Rivera, A. L., Arredondo, P., & Gallardo-Cooper, M. (2002). *Counseling Latinos and la familia: A practical guide.* Thousand Oaks, CA: Sage.

Sue, D. W., Arredondo, P., & McDavis, R. J. (1992). Multicultural counseling competencies and standards: A call to the profession. *Journal of Counseling and Development, 70,* 477–486.

Szapocznik, J., Kurtines, W. M., Foote, F., Perez-Vidal, A., & Hervis, O. E. (1986). Conjoint versus one person family therapy: Further evidence for the effectiveness of conducting family therapy through one person. *Journal of Consulting and Clinical Psychology, 54,* 395–397.

Szapocznik, J., Kurtines, W., Santisteban, D. A., Pantin, H., Scoppetta, M., Mancilla, Y., et al. (1996). The evolution of structural ecosystems theory for working with Latino families. In J. G. Garcia & M. C. Zea (Eds.), *Psychological interventions and research with Latino populations* (pp. 166–190). Boston: Allyn and Bacon.

Szapocznik, J., Santisteban, D., Rio, A., Perez-Vidal, A., & Kurtines, W. M. (1986). Bicultural effectiveness training (BET): An intervention modality for families experiencing intergeneration/intercultural conflict. *Hispanic Journal of Behavioral Sciences, 6,* 303–330.

Szapocznik, J., Santisteban, D., Rio, A., Perez-Vidal, A., Santisteban, D. A., & Kurtines, W. M. (1989). Family effectiveness training: An intervention to prevent drug abuse and problem behavior in *Hispanic adolescents. Hispanic Journal of Behavioral Sciences, 11,* 3–7.

Szapocznik, J., & Williams, R. A. (2000). Brief strategic family therapy: Twenty-five years of interplay among theory, research and practice in adolescent behavior problems and drug abuse. *Clinical Child and Family Psychology Review, 3,* 117–134.

U.S. Census Bureau. (2006). Nation's population one-third minority. Retrieved October 15, 2006, from http://www.census.gov/Press-Release/www/releases/archives/population/006808.html

Velásquez, R. J., Arellano, L. M., & McNeill, B. W. (2004). *The handbook of Chicana/o psychology and mental health*. Mahwah, NJ: Lawrence Erlbaum.
Wampold, B. E. (2001). *The great psychotherapy debate: Models, methods, and findings*. Mahwah, NJ: Lawrence Erlbaum.
Worden, M. (2003). *Family therapy basics* (3rd ed.). Pacific Grove, CA: Brooks/Cole.

3

Conversations in Marriage ©
An African–Centered Marital Intervention

Daryl M. Rowe and Sandra Lyons Rowe

Contents

Conversations in Marriage © (CIM) is a community empowerment program that promotes marriage education through a series of semistructured seminars or conversations. CIM was developed to address the disturbing decline of marriage within the African American community. CIM grew out of more than 30 years combined experience providing counseling and psychotherapy with African American couples, families, and individuals, and is grounded in African-centered metatheory. Consistent with African-centeredness, key ethical features of various African proverbs have been used in this family intervention to provide insight into how to facilitate engagement and change. A 12-week curriculum overview is provided along with suggestions for facilitating the program.

Introduction

There is clear evidence that culture and ethnicity play significant roles in shaping the relational experiences of African Americans (Allen & Olson, 2001; McAdoo, 1998). The fragility and vulnerability of African American marriage has been well documented during the past 40 years (Allen & Olson, 2001; Lawson & Thompson, 1994; Patterson, 1998; Staples, 1981; Tucker & Mitchell-Kernan, 1995). Various positions have been put forth underscoring the salience of competing factors: (a) economic issues, related to both the declining employment status of African American men and the increasing economic independence of African American women (Cherlin, 1998); (b) unequal sex ratio, related to multiple factors—higher death rates from disease, poorer health care, violent crime, higher rates of drug and alcohol abuse, gang activity, incarceration, and sexual orientation—that further reduce the number of desirable males available for marriage (Darity & Myers, 1995; Pinderhughes, 2002); (c) sociocultural issues, related to both the retention of African cultural values and the delicate adaptations to hostile societal oppression, restrictions, and shifts (Patterson, 1998); and (d) relational struggles, tied to gender role flexibility, couple communication, fidelity, power, and intimacy (Boyd-Franklin & Franklin, 1999; Patterson, 1998).

Nationwide estimates of the U.S. Census Bureau suggest that of the African American women who had given birth in the past 12 months, 60% of those births were to unmarried women; that 30% of African American children live with single mothers; that and almost 40% of African American adults were married (U.S. Census Bureau, 2007). These data reflect a disturbing trend that has been growing over the past 40-plus years. For example, in 1960, a married couple was found in approximately 78% of African American households; decreasing to 64% in 1970; by the late 1980s, only 48% of African American households included both a husband and a wife

(Pinderhughes, 2002). According to Billingsley and Morrison-Rodriguez (1998), this downward trend continued, reaching a low of 39% by 1993.

Given these data, it becomes important to examine more innovative strategies that can be developed to redirect the downward trends. Although some have argued that declining African American marriage rates are related to a lower desire to marry (South, 1993), others have stressed that desirability is not waning, but that unrealistic expectations, economic stressors, and conflict between the genders have contributed to the deteriorating bonds of marriage (Bulcroft & Bulcroft, 1993). Last, clinicians have sought African antecedents to current African American values in their efforts to develop more effective clinical interventions (Boyd-Franklin, 1989). Thus, the purpose of the proposed chapter is to describe and discuss the usefulness of CIM as a community intervention program to address the particular marital stressors with which African American couples with multiple social identities (religiosity, class, ethnicity, age) struggle.

Theoretical Orientation: African-Centered Metatheory

The theoretical framework of the CIM program is consistent with African-centered metatheory. African-centered metatheory is a promising theoretical advancement in the social sciences that is responsive to the specific sociocultural contexts, strengths, preferences, and issues attendant to the unique features of persons of African descent (Nobles, 1998). The framework reflects the more than 40-year examination by African American psychologists and therapists, using available evidence and clinical expertise, to devise more culturally responsive treatment paradigms for understanding the mental and psychological health of African Americans (Boyd-Franklin, 2003). African-centered metatheory is consistent with the mission of the Association of Black Psychologists (2003) and the American Psychological Association (APA) 2005 Presidential Task Force on Evidence-Based Practice (APA, 2005). The APA task force set forth a number of domains to consider in determining whether psychological practices are evidence-based, as follows: best available research, clinical expertise, and patients' values, characteristics, and context. However, as Wampold (2001) argued, based on his notable meta-analytic review of treatment efficacy studies, "the commonalities among treatment are responsible for the benefits" (p. 77) of psychotherapy, notwithstanding theoretical and therapeutic processes. He further argues that grounding treatment approaches in the cultural contexts of the persons to be served seemed potentially more relevant to the efficacy of those approaches than the specific components of particular therapies. Finally, he suggested that the more congruent the rationale is for a therapeutic approach with the client's world view, the more likely that the client would continue with treatment. Thus, the implication is that if clients seek relief through psychotherapeutic healing practices, the available evidence suggests that psychotherapy is effective, with different psychotherapies not demonstrating substantively different effects. Moreover, appealing to clients' world views appears to influence the degree to which they will engage psychotherapeutic healing practices and thus benefit from the approaches.

African-centered metatheory, therefore, can provide an explanation for how changes can occur within African-descent communities, consistent with their world views. It emerges out of Asante's work (1987, 1990) in rhetoric, in which he advanced that African values and ideals must be placed at the center of discussion involving persons of African descent, culture, and behavior, and that Africans are subjects—not objects—in the examination of human ethos (Rowe, 1991). Asante's work ushered in a paradigmatic shift in how the behavior of persons of African descent has been conceptualized. Asante's construct has been applied across a number of domains including Black studies (Karenga, 1993), education (Murrell, 2002), history (Diop, 1989), social work (Schiele, 1996), and psychology (Akbar, 1984; Akinyela, 2005; Azibo, 1989; Nobles, 2006). However, because the delineation of those very African ideals has been the result of ongoing research and deliberation, it is and has been quite difficult to put forth fixed, authoritative parameters of what composes African-centeredness. As an African proverb states, "One always learns from someone else." Thus, the very process of theorizing about the constitutive positions of African-centeredness leads to continuous refinement and reconsideration of key conceptual frameworks and terminology that influence its conceptualization. Nonetheless, African-centered metatheory considers sociocultural and familial factors, environmental context and stressors, readiness to change, and level of social support to develop more effective alternative interventions for persons of African descent (APA, 2005).

Nobles (1986) argued that there has been continuity in the reemergence of African-centeredness, that independent of shifting theories, sociopolitical pressures, and deepening insights into African cultural structures, scholars of African descent have long questioned Western social science's ability to explain the Black experience (Nobles & Goddard, 1993, p. 132).

Historically, there has been considerable variation in the terms utilized to center one's understanding of the psychology of persons of African descent. The terminology has ranged from "Black Psychology" (Thomas, 1971; White, 1991), to African American psychology (Burlew, Banks, McAdoo, & Azibo, 1992), to Afrocentric psychology (Myers, 1993), to Africentric psychology (Azibo, 1989; Baldwin, 1981), to African (Black) psychology (Kambon, 1998), to African psychology (Grills, 2004; Nobles, 1986), to African-centered psychology (Nobles & Goddard, 1993). The use of terminology seems to reflect both shifting theoretical notions about how to best capture this emerging (or reemerging—see Nobles, 1986) paradigm and mere pragmatism, where terminology is used because of its idiomatic currency, seemingly without sufficient theoretical deliberation.

The result of terminology variance has had both positive and negative impacts on the development of African-centered metatheory. From a positive perspective, the ongoing attempts to attribute an African-derived designation to theoretical, research, and applied initiatives concerning health and healing approaches to persons of African descent has created significantly more discursive space for continued investigation and refinement of a centered African psychological paradigm: "Someone destined to be lost does not meet a relative." The implication is that more and more psychologists of African descent are at least considering, as a necessary heuristic, a grounding of their ideas for understanding and examining the behavior and mental processes of persons of African descent in African cultural principles.

However, a less favorable outcome of terminology variance is the conceptual murkiness that results both from the employment of African-centered designations to theoretical, methodological, and applied frameworks that owe their conceptual heritage to non-African conceptions and from the failure of scholars to define their use of terminology in setting forth either theoretical, methodological, or applied initiatives. The African proverb, "No matter how well an idol is made, it must have something to stand on," provides insight into why setting forth definitional foundations is essential to the continued refinement of African-centered metatheory.

According to Nobles (1998),

> African centeredness represents a concept which categorizes a "quality of thought and practice" which is rooted in the cultural image and interest of people of African ancestry and which represents and reflects the life experiences, history and traditions of people of African ancestry as the center of analyses. ... In essence, African centeredness represents the fact, that as human beings, people of African ancestry

> have the right and responsibility to "center" themselves in their own
> subjective possibilities and potentialities and through the recentering
> process reproduce and refine the best of the human essence. (p. 190)

Nobles's definition is critical because it shifts the debate from merely conceptual issues to the meanings and methods of African-centered psychology,
because it places emphasis on the quality of thought and practice (Rowe
& Webb-Msemaji, 2004). As such, psychology centered in African thought
and practice reflects African people's intimate knowledge of their subjective
human experiences as they interact with the world—nature, the cosmos,
geographical location, others, and one's self.

As Nobles (1986) argued, the efforts to articulate African psychology are
still in flux, thus:

> The work we do is constantly changing and we continue to inform our
> efforts by the need to transform psychology. ... [Current efforts] ...
> should not be taken as an example of "the African (Black) psychology,"
> at least not in the sense of the complete or developed African (Black)
> psychology. Most of the work of Black psychologists should be seen as
> "African (Black) psychology becoming." (pp. 109–110)

Thus, Rowe and Webb-Msemaji (2004) suggested that the term African-
centered best reflects how to encapsulate the various efforts for discussing
the psychology of persons of African descent at this point in history. By
"centered," they suggested that the current level of understanding is not sufficiently informed to have formal distinctive boundaries for what explicitly
constitutes African cultural thought and practices, and that scholars examining these issues should intentionally locate their theories, methods, and
practices within the ever-deepening investigation into and reclamation of
African cultural ways. They suggested four criteria for assessing parameters
of African-centered psychology, as follows: (a) it utilizes African cultural
patterns and styles for understanding human behavior; (b) it reflects the various ways African peoples have sought to understand, articulate, and project
themselves to themselves, others, and the world; (c) it emphasizes values that
are more dynamic, circular, communal, and situational; assumptions that are
more integrative or diunital; and methods that are more symbolic, affective,
and metaphorical; and (d) it relies on African sources, that is, oral literature
(proverbs, myths, tales, and stories), praise songs and moral teachings, spiritual system scripts, prayers, and the dynamic interdependence of community,
nature, and spirit. Thus, each of us seeking to contribute to the elaboration of

African-centered psychology must not merely identify our efforts as African centered, but specify how and why our work sits within the paradigm.

Similarly, Nobles (2004) suggested that African-centered psychology must address the oral tradition—how beliefs and traditions are handed down from one generation to the next. As a result, we contend that an additional domain of African psychology can be discerned through a descriptive analysis of moral language, the sanctions used to enforce morality, and a review of proverbs, tales, and myths that refer to the moral beliefs of the peoples. As Chinua Achebe (1964) indicated, conversation, particularly as handled by elder members of traditional African society, is one of the greatest repositories of African wisdom that portrays authentic African life and experience.

Treatment Implications: An Overview of CIM

CIM, an African-centered marital intervention, is a community empowerment program designed to strengthen relationship skills and sustain healthy marriages among African American couples by promoting marriage education through a series of semistructured seminars. CIM was developed in 2002 and has been conducted with over 70 couples to date to address the disturbing decline of marriage within the African American community (Allen & Olson, 2001). CIM grew out of more than 30 years combined experience providing counseling and psychotherapy with African American couples, families, and individuals. From those experiences, several insights were gleaned that facilitated the development of this culturally specific community intervention program.

First, it became clear that in working with African American couples, especially African American men, initially highlighting the legacy of healthy African American families within the context of community needs and community survival was more helpful in facilitating their readiness for change than merely stressing the individual couple's marital health. According to Murrell (2002),

> Basing ... explorations of such topics as "community" or "family" in the narratives of oral history creates a real and authentic reason for [participants] to listen to, analyze, and work with stories. Stories become the vehicle for purposeful investigation of significant ideas and information. (p. 114)

African American men are often reluctant to engage in dialogue about their personal family and relationship issues; consequently, African American men have to be included in marriage education in such a way that respects their gender role identification and motivates them to leave a legacy of hope for African American families (Whitfield, Markman, Stanley, & Blumberg, 2001). Thus, as opposed to first exploring one's personal marital relationship, marriage education needs to occur within the context of African American community development and empowerment.

Second, we recognized that participatory discussions facilitated more disclosure and openness from participants than did didactic instruction and exercises because these discussions reflect a communal framework that can reconnect participants to a sense of homeplace (Burton, Winn, Stevenson, & Lawson-Clark, 2004). African American couples tended to participate more freely when material was presented in a more narrative than didactic style. Both African American men and women were more likely to share insights and opinions when the discussion mirrored the storytelling style more consistent with African American culture (Murrell, 2002).

Third, we discovered that introducing and incorporating African proverbs stimulated more discussion and prompted more insights into strategies for sustaining healthy marriages among African American couples. There is preliminary data that suggest that the intentional use of metaphors can enhance conceptual and emotional understanding and alliance (Devlieger, 1999; Martin, Cummings, & Hallberg, 1992).

Finally, we observed that structuring repetitive group recitations centered in African American cultural principles helped foster a sense of shared purpose among participants (Watts & Abdul-Adil, 1997). Each session was initiated by and concluded with a poem that encapsulated the culturally grounded, community-oriented, participatory intervention program.

The seminars or conversations emphasize a sharing process wherein couples discuss strategies to help individuals and couples improve their marital relationship skills, institute different standards for determining marital relationships, and develop long-term commitment to sustaining healthy marriages for the betterment of African American communities. Conversations are different ways of learning—allowing for active involvement, multidirectionality, and egalitarianism versus passivity, unidirectionality, or inequality (Zuniga, 1992).

Good conversations invite participants to join in, wind along, dip in and out—sometimes superficially, sometimes deeply—and then circle back and enter the discussion again. Each time, participants can uncover more about themselves, others, and processes of sustaining healthy marriages. The conversations can be tightly structured or organized, or more spontaneous, moving quickly sometimes and more slowly at other times. Conversations allow participants to grasp meaning out of expression—to hold it and give it back to others—providing a glimpse into their understanding of marriage among African Americans. The goal of these conversations is to lift up, support, and encourage African American couples in their quest to be better men and women—together. An African proverb that captures this focus: "He who begins a conversation does not foresee the end."

CIM emphasizes community because community is the outgrowth of family, and marriage is the basis of family. We use community in ways similar to Burton et al.'s (2004) idea of homeplace. They described homeplace as

> multilayered, nuanced individual and family processes that are anchored in a physical place that elicits feelings of empowerment, belonging, commitment, rootedness, ownership, safety, and renewal. Critical elements of the homeplace include social attachments and relationships characterized by distinct cultural symbols, meanings and rituals ... [that] ... shape individuals' and families' sense of social and cultural identity. (pp. 397–398)

We place emphasis on community because traditionally, marriage has occurred within the context of community; it has been the marker of adulthood and the focus of existence and the point where all members of a given community meet—the departed, the living, and those yet to be born (Mbiti, 1970). Marriage establishes and maintains family, creates and sustains the ties of kinship, and is the basis of community. Thus, from a historical perspective among persons of African descent, marriage was seen as a duty, a requirement for society, essential for community—the basis of civilization (Gyekye, 1996). This sense of community or homeplace can be seen as a sanctuary from the often cruel realities of living in a stratified society where ethnicity, poverty, education, and political disenfranchisement can lead to difficult lives (Burton et al., 2004). Our position is that the homeplace originates from the union of persons, initially through marriage, and the resultant knitting together of families into vibrant communities. From such a perspective, marriage is and has to be seen as bigger than mere personal happiness—marriage is about building community and preserving a viable homeplace (see Burton et al. for a fuller discussion of the theoretical and pragmatic implications of homeplace among African American families).

Through this program, we suggest that marital relationships are not private, but they belong to the community (Some, 1999). This is a powerful idea for transforming marriage within the African American community. These notions of community place emphasis on the responsibility of community to safeguard the voices of its members, such that community members hear each person—valued and affirmed—and cultivate each person's gifts that then are freely given back to the larger world (Some, 1999). Thus, community serves to anchor persons to something larger than merely their partners or spouses, providing a sense of belonging and purpose.

Rationale for Interventions: African Proverbs

West African proverbs serve to stimulate discussion about key marital struggles and strategies for ameliorating those challenges. There is a clear link between the articulation of African-centered psychology and the reliance on African sources of which proverbs are a critical aspect.

> Proverbs are deeply rooted in this [African] culture and almost everyone who grows up in a village, becomes a living carrier of proverbs. They are interwoven in local languages. At the same time, they constitute a sub-language of their own. This language of proverbs, this way of speaking by employing proverbs, is known by many people who use it with various skills more or less throughout their lives ... the language of proverbs is a whole way of seeing the world, a way of speaking with other people, a way of feeling the atmosphere in society in which they live. (Opoku & Mbiti, 1997, p. ix)

African proverbs are collections of metaphorical statements, usually short and to the point, that convey general truths about life, people, and community (Ackah, 1988). These statements are offered in particular situations, and if they are received by others as being wise and reflective of the shared beliefs or "social conscience" (p. 49) of members of the social system, they can become popular idioms in the group's language system and purveyors of the social conscience. "Proverbs are the distilled genius of oral cultures, perhaps even an encapsulation of the whole. ... They identify and dignify a culture, bringing life into wisdom and wisdom into life," according to Nussbaum (1998). However, proverbs gain their power from their situational context, they originate from experience and convey insights metaphorically (Dalfovo, 1998). Thus, the true meanings of an African psychological system can be found only when examined in the context of its practical meanings.

> Proverbs are rooted in the same reality that prompts human beings to forge their cultures. They are expressions of culture, and thus they reflect reality because they both stem from it and lead back to it. They

are the very features that help to identify a specific culture. These expe-
riential and cultural dimensions guarantee that an interest in proverbs
is an interest in an authentic expression of culture. (Dalfovo, 1998,
pp. 42–43)

Nwoga (1975) emphasized that proverbs always must be examined both for
what they say and for how they say it. The what and how situate the proverb
such that it can always be relevant and meaningful across situations, contexts,
and persons. Similarly, Opoku and Mbiti (1997) argued that proverbs serve
as catalysts of morals, ethics, knowledge, wisdom, and philosophy—they
stimulate further reflection and necessitate deeper thinking. For example,
"The water boils but never forgets its home," and "The head is best known
by the owner."

Traditionally, proverbs have been used to instruct members about the
customs and traditions of particular communities. Dzobo (1992) described
proverbs as "normally short and pithy sayings … very popular devices used to
state metaphorically certain general truths about life" (pp. 94–95). A Yoruba
proverb states, "a proverb is a horse which can carry one swiftly to the discovery of ideas." This proverb demonstrates the overall function of proverbs:
to describe the essence of human relationships, situations, happenings, and
behavioral patterns of people.

According to Dzobo (1992), proverbs can be used for four primary purposes: (a) to express truths that are difficult to comprehend; (b) as guides for
conduct—as bases for determining the unacceptability of certain forms of
behavior; (c) as commentary on human behavior—proverbs help to delineate
the styles humans reflect in negotiating life; and (d) to express values—to
reflect the centered values characteristic of Africans, from the psychological,
moral, spiritual, humanistic, economic, and intellectual to the material.

Thus, African proverbs are particularly useful for sharing the key elements of each conversation's focal point. Proverbs are brief, serving as simple
ways to convey elegant truths; are flexible, such that they can be used across
a variety of situations and points in time (Parker & Wampler, 2006); are
profound, by stimulating further reflection and calling for deeper thinking
about commonplace occurrences (Zuniga, 1992); and are communicative,
by promoting conversation (Monye, 1996). Proverbs in such settings are like
the seasonings, used to strengthen points made by different participants in
the conversation. An African proverb states, "knowledge is like a garden:
If it is not cultivated, it cannot be harvested." CIM stresses that marriage is
the garden, and the challenge is to recreate cultivation skills that allow the

gardens of African American marriages to harvest healthy children and to reestablish the foundation of healthy communities.

Our Curriculum

The project uses a curriculum, piloted over the past 3 years, that, although not formally evaluated, has provided excellent feedback in preliminary applications. The CIM curriculum is 12 weeks long, emphasizing the following themes:

1. Marriage: Meaning and Purpose—examining the importance of marriage within historical African community development; a key proverb used to center that dialogue is "When a tree builds on its own roots, it will be healthy."
2. The Historical Role of Marriage—examining the idea that marriage is the focus of existence and the basis of civilization; a key proverb used is "You may be a giant of a man, you may begin to grow gray hair, you may be bald and toothless with age, but if you are unmarried—you are nothing."
3. Marriage: A Labor of Love—examining realistic struggles and expectations of marriage for African Americans given the historical legacy of oppression and discrimination in the broader society; a key proverb used is "Once you have made up your mind to cross the river, by walking through it, you do not mind getting your stomach wet."
4. Marriage Myths—examining salient myths that interfere with the fulfillment of one's duty and obligations toward marriage and community building; a key proverb used is "Happiness is temporary, and commitment is eternal."
5. Marriage Rituals—examining strategies or repetitive processes for sustaining healthy marriages including connecting, conversational, continuity, commitment, forgiveness, and rejuvenation rituals; a key proverb used is "The person who goes to draw water does not drink mud."
6. Gender Relations—examining gender role issues that have undermined the viability of African American marriage, for example, respect, fidelity, commitment, violence and intimidation, and trust; a key proverb used is "If you are planning for 1 year, grow rice; if you are planning for 20 years, grow trees; but if you are planning for centuries, grow Women."

7. Making Marriage Meaningful—examining the idea that meaningful marriage happens when we fulfill our purpose in life through providing our gifts; a key proverb used is "What one cultivates is what one harvests."

8. Preserving Friendship in Marriage—examining the importance of establishing and sustaining deep, open, and intimate friendships with one's spouse; a key proverb used is "Friendship is like a field you can harvest every season."

9. Marriage Choice and Commitment—examining the necessity of making good choices to facilitate long-standing commitment; a key proverb used is "The pot will smell of what is put into it."

10. Marriage Celebrations and Ceremony—examining the importance and necessity of celebrating and creating ceremonies to mark the progress of one's continued journey in marriage; a key proverb used is "Don't let the emotions of the moment interfere with the celebrations of a lifetime."

11. Marriage: Faith and Forgiveness—examining the need to understand that problems are commonplace and to learn how to acknowledge and move forward together; a key proverb used is "To one who does not know, a small garden is a forest."

12. Marriage Rebirthing and Rejuvenation—examining the necessity of renewing long-term commitment to marriage regularly; a key proverb used is "He who does not mend his clothes will soon have none."

Throughout each conversation, Dzobo's framework is used to situate new learning for the participants. Thus, to express truths, the following proverbs have been shared:

1. That which is good is never finished.
2. The freedom that comes from ignorance enslaves the one who entertains it.
3. If you know the beginning well, the end will not trouble you.
4. There is nothing so good, it can not be improved.

As guides for conduct, the following proverbs have been shared:

1. Before shooting, one must aim.
2. You must act as if it is impossible to fail.
3. We should put out the fire while it is still small.
4. Goodness must be repaid with goodness.

As commentary on human behavior, the following proverbs have been shared:

1. I pointed out to you the stars, and all you saw was the tip of my finger.
2. It is the heart that gives; the hands only let go.
3. Talking with one another is loving one another.

To express values, the following proverbs have been shared:

1. A people with power look for the source of problems within themselves.
2. To grow and be good is better than to be born with goodness.
3. All wisdom is from God.
4. Only one who goes into the forest comes back with firewood.
5. Rain does not fall on one roof alone.
6. If relatives help each other, what evil can hurt them?

Conceptualization: Sample CIM Conversation

Each conversation begins with an introduction and overview of CIM and is structured to last between 2 and 3 hours, depending on the number of participants. First, we begin with the recitation of a poem that stresses a community imperative for strengthening relationships among African American men and women. All participants are invited to recite the poem, and we begin by discussing its meaning and relevance to marriage. Following the initial recitation, the facilitators present themselves, sharing their expertise, marriage history, goals, purposes, and format of the conversation. Participants are invited to ask questions and/or share comments on any of the above. The aim of these activities is to highlight the unique contextual factors within which African American relationships and marriages must function and negotiate.

In discussing the format, we place special emphasis on the conversational nature of the gathering, where we seek to honor each participant's story, questions, and concerns, and emphasize the idea that our goal is to invite public discussion of relationships and marriages. We also let the participants know that we will use African proverbs to illuminate different aspects of marriage and provide brief examples and a rationale for their use. Last, we briefly share our assumptions about what marriage is and why promoting it is critical to sustaining the African/Black community. Again we invite participants to ask questions and/or share comments on any of the above. These activities situate our efforts within existing interlocking stories that center participants in a broad sociohistorical context, unique to persons of African descent.

For first meetings, we then move to share inspirational ideas gleaned from African/Black thinkers—poets, philosophers, psychologists, historians, sociologists, religious representatives, educators, elders, and so on—regarding relational and marital issues congruent with the focus of that conversation. If the conversation is continuing from a previous gathering, a brief recap of the previous conversation occurs. The inspirational ideas serve as the introductory comments to frame the discussion for the day, to which we liberally sprinkle African proverbs to foster insight and promote deepening exploration. These proverbs may have varied aims, consistent with Dzobo's framework. Throughout this portion of the conversation, participants are encouraged to share both general and specific comments from their own and others' marital experiences. As much as possible, we attempt to facilitate participants speaking directly with one another to support, counter, or extend comments and commentary.

Following discussion, we proceed to summarize key issues raised and suggest specific strategies for addressing the concerns raised, congruent with each conversation's focus. We continue to offer African proverbs to underscore the specific suggestions offered and suggest that the participants seek to continue these conversations among their naturally occurring social networks (friends, colleagues, family members, etc.). Finally, we close with another group recitation that is a pledge of commitment to marriage and community development.

Additional Clinical Considerations

Five primary benefits have been discerned through couple and individual participation in CIM, as discussed next.

First, participants tend to develop a sociohistorical and community perspective toward marriage sustainability within the African American community. Participants report a deeper appreciation of the broader social and contextual issues that impinge upon African American marriages, including but not limited to underlying gender roles, isolation, fragmented neighborhoods, economic disparities, racial segmentation, and indifferent public policies (Patterson, 1998). For example, according to 1890 census data, following emancipation, 88% of men and 92% of women aged 35 to 44 were married or widowed (Pinderhughes, 2002). Second, participants report an expansion of their understanding of gender relational issues that influence marriageability, such as values of commitment, respect, fidelity, and communication, in addition to economic domains (education, income, job status, etc.). Participants explore the impact of male dominance and female independence on the prevalence of distrust and conflict that has been documented within African American gender relationships (Tucker & Mitchell-Kernan, 1995).

Third, participants report developing ongoing skills and strategies for sustaining their marriages. Specifically, participants report exploring ways of building and maintaining friendship, affection, and emotional intimacy; managing choices and commitment; improving communication and companion skills; identifying marriage myths and other indicators of marital difficulties; managing the impact of parenthood on marriage; building and sustaining trust and cooperation; managing and deescalating conflicts; and developing strategies for periodically renewing and rejuvenating marriage (Whitfield et al., 2001).

Fourth, participants report that they can identify and access community structures that support sustaining marriage, including services to assist with parenting issues, financial and job search issues, substance and alcohol issues, domestic violence issues, and faith-based issues.

A final component of the program is our use of "Marriage Mentors," African American couples married for at least 20 years, who provide ongoing support, encouragement, and problem solving for participants during the period of the program and for 3 months following the conclusion of the program. Marriage Mentors serve as a community resource and have access to additional community resources that support sustaining marriage.

There are a number of facilitation tips that aid in managing these conversations and that are consistent with African-centered metatheory. For example, in attempting to help couples understand particular marital and relational challenges, we try to help couples see their problems as a combination of personal, family and significant others, community, social system, and world view and beliefs aspects. Similarly, the conversations seek to reconstruct marital and relational stories from participants' fragments of memory, gossip, news, history, and reports to help them rediscover by going back through evidence. Telling stories reflects deep thought through words, movements, rhythm, and harmony (Akinyela, 2005). Thus, through the telling of stories, deep connections—touching the heart—can occur.

The idea of touching the heart—Kugusa Mtima—was introduced by Nobles, Goddard, and Cavil (1998) and embodies the "experience of being touched, moved, affected by a self-conscious created form and force … through transcendence and transformation" (p. 15). This idea reflects the capacity to move from one phenomenological reality to another (transcend) and from one material condition to another (transform); for marital and relational challenges, it means that couples can experience and develop new perspectives about marriage within African/Black communities. In this way, touching the heart is seen as a process of reconnecting a misaligned relationship or marriage with African cultural power—to make a path to healthier relating.

The following attributes are particularly important in handling these conversations: (a) facilitator skill should be determined by the ability to touch the heart—to transcend and transform human consciousness; (b) facilitators must be capable of responding to emotion—to anticipate and articulate affect that may be unstated or understated; (c) facilitators must be willing to use metaphorical speech and overlaid speech—to communicate using the symbolic and rhythmic flow of conversation; (d) facilitators must be more direct and clear about insights instead of tentative and ambiguous; and (e) facilitators must be willing to utilize a higher degree of activity versus a lower degree of activity (Rowe & Msemaji-Webb, 2004).

Authors' Personal Dimensions of Diversity

The first author is an African/Black male, in his 50s, born and raised in the Midwest of the United States. He is the third child and second son of a family of four siblings, from working-class roots. He is a product of segregated elementary schooling, integrated secondary schooling, undergraduate training from a historically Black college/university (HBCU), and graduate training from a large midwestern research university for both master's and doctoral studies. He is son, brother, nephew, cousin, uncle, husband, father, friend, colleague, and teacher: "He who learns, teaches," according to an African proverb.

The second author is an African/Black American female, in her 50s, born and raised on the East Coast of the United States. She is the first born, with one younger sibling, from working-class roots. She is a product of integrated schooling from elementary through high school. Her undergraduate and graduate education was completed on the West Coast. She is a daughter, sister, cousin, aunt, granddaughter, wife, mother, friend, and colleague: "Anticipate the good so you may enjoy it," according to an African proverb.

With more than 30 years' combined experience as practicing psychologists working with African/Black individuals, couples, and families, we have spent considerable time clarifying our world views and negotiating differences in world view (a) with persons in distress, (b) across theoretical perspectives (strategies and interventions), and (c) within systems (agencies of care). Our work has occurred at the nexus of person, power, privilege, perspectives, and problems. These features are reflected indelibly in both our therapeutic approaches (theories and techniques) and our styles (the nuanced attempts to form collaborative relationships with clients often disinclined to value our work, a priori).

The following themes regarding good clinicians reflect our combined points of view. First, we believe good clinicians must possess an articulated conception of optimal human functioning—they must have clear ideas about their goals and the outcomes of their connections. They must also be able to communicate those goals to clients in understandable, nontechnical terms so clients can decide whether the goals are consistent with their own values. From our perspective, working with African/Black persons has to be grounded within our own subjective possibilities and potential, thus creating a process for reproducing and refining the best of ourselves. Thus, we believe African-centeredness is the basis of optimal functioning.

Second, we believe good clinicians must possess a clinical presence—a blend of acumen, insight, judgment, style, and sensitivity, tempered by experience, that conveys a fundamental respect for the value and worth of humans within the context of their collective group memberships. We believe that clients are simultaneously members of various interlocking social networks that provide meaning to their behavior. Good clinicians respect and value those various networks, through which clients realize their meaningfulness. In our work with African/Black persons, we believe it is critical to have a solid working foundation across multiple dimensions of identity, encompassing age and generation, gender, class, and religiosity and spirituality, among other dimensions.

Third, we believe good clinicians must possess an extensive repertoire of ideas, strategies, and styles to attend to and connect with people experiencing a range of distressing human dilemmas. Because clients are people reflecting a broad range of interlocking social networks, clinicians must have a variety of strategies accessible to increase the chances for effective treatment.

Fourth, good clinicians must possess the ethical integrity to refrain from taking advantage of clients' trust and vulnerability. Clarity regarding one's role and functions is essential. Last, good clinicians are not bounded by established theory and technique, but maintain a level of creativity and rigor to continuously seek to expand the number of available treatment options for a particular client or set of clients with distinctive issues in various contexts. The nature of human distress is limitless, so good clinicians must continually seek to bring forth different methods to intervene.

Our experiences with appropriating existing clinical and counseling theories and techniques to render them more useful for African/Black populations, both practically and theoretically, have had the most critical impact on our insights into and understandings of clinical intervention. It is our belief that unless we, as clinicians and scholars, systematically examine the processes for working with all humans, our understanding of any human behavior and the delineation of effective approaches will remain hampered.

Therapeutic Recommendations

There are a number of recommendations that can aid in working with African Americans in general, and with African American couples, more specifically, as follows:

1. The major problem when discussing therapeutic work with African Americans is that none of the tools with which mental health professionals have been equipped in their training in applied clinical and counseling psychotherapy have been designed or developed with African Americans in mind. Although some things might work, we simply haven't been asking enough questions regarding what to do, under what particular circumstances, with what sets of presenting problems, for which kinds of people, taking into account what types of contextual variables are most helpful for addressing the unique and particular concerns of African Americans.

2. Although we argue that there are broad unifying assumptions that can be utilized in developing conceptual approaches for working clinically with persons of African descent, it is important for clinicians to recognize that African Americans will present as heterogeneous individual adults, children, families, and couples. African Americans vary by age, religiosity, social-economic status, regions, education, and gender (to name but a few). Clinicians need to attend to the following principles with this heterogeneity in mind.

3. Given the long-standing and pervasive impact of racism, African Americans tend to be wary of mental health and psychological treatment and thus may present in a somewhat more cautious or guarded

fashion, being very attentive to a broad array of metacommunication issues; for example, congruence between what a therapist says and how he or she says it, the therapist's comfort with stylistic nuances (vocalisms, volume, speed, gesturing, etc.), and the therapist's comfort with thematic material (discussions about real and perceived experiences of racism and discrimination, privilege, and power).

4. Therapists must develop familiarity with the linguistic nuances of African Americans. Dialectical differences, patterns, and styles of communication have roots in the language patterns of continental Africans. Although not all African Americans speak Ebonics, especially with its current infusion with street slang, the ability to code-switch—to move from Standard English to Ebonics—tends to be available to large numbers regardless of socioeconomic status, education, or profession. As is the case in other primary or original language systems, Ebonics is the language of primary emotions. Many African Americans will rely on Ebonics as a primary communication style during points of strong emotional experience.

5. In terms of communication patterns, African Americans more often are more demonstrative; have higher energy, faster responses, and less emotional restraint; tend to use more physical attributes to highlight communication—more touching, movement, hand gestures; and are more likely to use more spiritual references and intensity when communicating. Often, there is an overlap of conversation between one speaker and the next such that both often speak at the same time, and there is often an expectation of verbal acknowledgment of understanding. This communication style is also discussed as call and response where the listeners voice their acknowledgment of the speaker, and the speaker's ideas are constructed and affirmed through this feedback process. The style supports a theory of collective construction of reality.

6. Therapeutic style is crucial for creating an environment where change can occur. Given the lack of proven legitimacy of accepted therapeutic approaches and practices, the person of the therapist becomes the single most important tool or technique for establishing effective therapeutic and healing relationships. Thus, therapists must convey a certain humility that conveys knowledge, comfort, and familiarity while simultaneously relating as colleague and guide. Implied is therapist appreciation of the various sociocultural elements of the client's experiences which contextualize them more fully.

7. Therapists must convey an open invitation to question, encouraging questions about the therapist, therapeutic process, theoretical leanings, length of time of treatment, possibility for the involvement of others, rules of engagement, expectations about client and therapist role, and responsibilities for the client and therapist. Therapist credibility is enhanced by allowing the client to scrutinize the process. It is important to assume that questions exist, and the therapeutic task is to make the asking of them normal and commonplace.

8. Therapists must be willing to use metaphorical speech which is overlaid as well. Metaphorical speech is speech that relies on descriptions of feelings and dilemmas using commonplace and everyday expressions (hence, the use of proverbs). The idea is to share meaning systems with the commonplace versus abstract terminology. The more abstract the message, the less feeling there is, and as a result, less meaningfulness occurs. African American speech tends to be more contextually determined; thus, the spaces between the words are often more powerful than the words themselves. Overlaid speech reflects the rhythmic flow or cadence of talking, such that the spaces or lack thereof are indicative of the sense of extension into the other person. The more overlaid speech, the more connective the relationship.

9. Last, therapists must be willing to engage in a degree of self-disclosure about the congruence of role, person, context, and intent. Often, therapist credibility is less influenced by training and expertise as by authenticity, grasp of cultural issues, and willingness to engage and admit shortcomings.

Conclusions

Marriage has the capacity to provide us with ongoing insight into who we are, have been, and will become. As such, marriage is as much about building community as being in love. Our goal is to initiate a series of conversations that center persons of African descent in the joys and challenges of holding hands over time and throughout life. Given the particular challenges with which African/Black folks must grapple in the multifaceted realities of the United States, we grow more and more convinced that we must look backward to move forward; that is, we must develop strategies that emerge out of our shared cultural wellsprings to craft solutions to seemingly intractable problems. Strengthening marriages and improving relationships within our community provides a unified approach for addressing multiple complex issues. The prolific African American poet Haki R. Madhubuti, who has written extensively on the necessity of strengthening marriage, is eloquent on this imperative, as follows:

> What matters is the renewing and long running kinship seeking common mission, willing work, memory, melody, song. Marriage is an art, created by the serious, enjoyed by the mature, watered with morning and evening promises. ... So that your nation will live and tell your stories accurately, you must be endless in your loving touch of each other, your unification is the message, continuance the answer. (1987, p. 8)

An African proverb states, "Happiness is temporary, commitment is eternal." Our work is aimed at helping to make commitment to marriage commonplace and contagious within the African American community.

Discussion Questions

1. Discuss your ideas about the obstacles to maintaining relationships and marriages in general.
2. Discuss your ideas about the obstacles to maintaining relationships and marriages within the African American community. How do these obstacles contribute to the declining numbers of marriages within the African American community?
3. What do you see as the major contributions of African-centered metatheory for understanding the psychological and mental health of African Americans?
4. What are the strengths and limitations of using culturally specific theoretical orientations for thinking about the behavior of different ethnic and cultural groups?
5. How does CIM differ from traditional marriage education programs? What limitations do you see in its approach?
6. How are African proverbs useful for promoting discussion among African American couples?
7. What are the primary purposes for using African proverbs? Could other sets of proverbs be as effective?
8. Discuss the benefits of the CIM program for African American couples. Do you think it might be useful for a wider range of couples?

9. What ethical concerns, if any, emerge for you as you consider the recommendations for working with African Americans? How would you reconcile those ethical dilemmas to ensure that you provide the best available treatment for African Americans?

Cultural Resources: Suggestions for Further Reading/Sources

Ani, M. (1994). *Yurugu: An African-centered critique of European cultural thought and behavior.* Trenton, NJ: Africa World Press.

Belgrave, F. Z., & Allison, K. W. (2006). *African American psychology: From Africa to America.* Thousand Oaks, CA: Sage.

Boyd-Franklin, N. (2003). *Black families in therapy: Understanding the African American experience* (2nd ed.). New York: Guilford.

Gyekye, K. (1996). *African cultural values: An introduction.* Philadelphia: Sankofa.

Jones, R. (1998). *African American mental health.* Hampton, VA: Cobb & Henry.

Jones, R. (1999). *Advances in African American psychology.* Hampton, VA: Cobb & Henry.

Jones, R. (2004). *Black psychology* (4th ed.). Hampton, VA: Cobb & Henry.

Kambon, K. K. (1998). *African/Black psychology in the American context: An African-centered approach.* Tallahassee, FL: Nubian Nation.

McCubbin, H. I., Thompson, E. A., Thompson, A. I., & Futrell, J. A. (Eds.). (1998). *Resiliency in African-American families.* Thousand Oaks, CA: Sage.

Nobles, W. W. (2006). *Seeking the Sakhu: Foundational writings for an African psychology.* Chicago: Third World Press.

Nussbaum, S. (1998). *The wisdom of African proverbs: Collections, studies, bibliographies.* Colorado Springs, CO: Global Mapping International.

Some, S. E. (1999). *The spirit of intimacy: Ancient teachings in the ways of relationships.* Berkeley, CA: Berkeley Hills Books.

Whitfield, K. E., Markman, H. J., Stanley, S. M., & Blumberg, S. L. (2001). *Fighting for your African American marriage.* San Francisco: Jossey-Bass.

References

Achebe, C. (1964). *Arrow of God.* New York: Anchor Books.

Ackah, C. A. (1988). *Akan ethics: A study of the moral ideas and the moral behavior of the Akan tribes of Ghana.* Accra, Ghana: Ghana Universities Press.

Akbar, N. (1984). *Chains and images of psychological slavery.* Chicago: Third World Press.

Akbar, N. (1991). *Visions for Black men.* Nashville, TN: Winston-Derek.

Akinyela, M. M. (2005). Testimony of hope: African-centered praxis for therapeutic ends. *Journal of Systemic Therapies, 24*(1), 5–18.

Allen, W. D., & Olson, D. H. (2001). Five types of African-American marriages. *Journal of Marital and Family Therapy, 27*(3), 301–315.

American Psychological Association. (2005). Report of the 2005 presidential task force on evidence-based practice. Retrieved January 5, 2007, from http://www.apa.org/practice/ebpreport.pdf

Asante, M. K. (1987). *The Afrocentric idea.* Philadelphia: Temple University Press.

Asante, M. K. (1990). *Kemet, Afrocentricity and knowledge.* Trenton, NJ: Africa World Press.

Association of Black Psychologists. (2003). Mission, purpose and goals. Retrieved January 12, 2007, from http://www.abpsi.org/mission_vision.htm

Azibo, D. A. (1989). African-centered theses on mental health and a nosology of Black/African personality disorder. *Journal of Black Psychology, 15*(2), 173–214.

Baldwin, J. A. (1981). Notes on an Africentric theory of Black personality. *Western Journal of Black Studies, 5*(3), 172–179.

Baldwin, J. A. (1986). African (Black) psychology: Issues and synthesis. *Journal of Black Studies, 16*(4), 67–76.

Billingsley, A., & Morrison-Rodriguez, B. (1998). The Black family in the 21st century and the church as an action system: A macro-perspective. *Journal of Human Behavior in the Social Environment, 1*(2/3), 31–47. New York: Haworth Press.

Boyd-Franklin, N. (1989). *Black families in therapy: A multisystemic approach.* New York: Guilford.

Boyd-Franklin, N. (2003). *Black families in therapy: Understanding the African American experience* (2nd ed.). New York: Guilford.

Boyd-Franklin, N., & Franklin, A. J. (1999). African American couples in therapy. In M. McGoldrick (Ed.), *Re-visioning family therapy: Race, culture and gender in clinical practice* (pp. 268–281). New York: Guilford.

Bulcroft, R., & Bulcroft, K. (1993). Race differences in attitudinal and motivational factors in the decision to marry. *Journal of Marriage and the Family, 55,* 338–355.

Burlew, A. K., Banks, W. C., McAdoo, H. P., & Azibo, D. A. (1992). *African American psychology: Theory, research, and practice.* Newbury Park, CA: Sage.

Burton, L. M., Winn, D.- M., Stevenson, H., & Lawson Clark, S. (2004). Working with African American clients: Considering the "homeplace" in marriage and family therapy practices. *Journal of Marital and Family Therapy, 30*(4), 397–410.

Cherlin, A. J. (1998). Marriage and marital dissolution among Black Americans. *Journal of Comparative Family Studies, 29*(1), 147–159.

Dalfovo, A. T. (1997). African proverbs and African philosophy. In W. Saayman (Ed.), *Embracing the Baobab tree: The African proverb in the 21st century* (pp. 37–48). Pretoria, South Africa: Unisa Press.

Darity, W., & Myers, S. (1995). Family structure and the marginalization of Black men: Policy implications. In M. Tucker & C. Mitchell-Kernan (Eds.), *The decline of marriage among African-Americans* (pp. 263–308). New York: Russell Sage.

Devlieger, P. J. (1999). Frames of reference in African proverbs on disability. *International Journal of Disability, Development and Education, 46*(4), 441–451.

Diop, C. A. (1989). *The cultural unity of Black Africa: The domains of matriarchy and of patriarchy in classical antiquity*. London: Karnak House.

Dzobo, N. K. (1992). *African symbols and proverbs as source of knowledge and truth*. Washington, DC: Council for Research in Values and Philosophy.

Grills, C. N. (2004). African psychology. In R. Jones (Ed.), *Black psychology* (4th ed., pp. 171–208). Hampton, VA: Cobb & Henry.

Gyekye, K. (1996). *African cultural values: An introduction*. Philadelphia: Sankofa.

Kambon, K. K. (1998). *African/Black psychology in the American context: An African-centered approach*. Tallahassee, FL: Nubian Nation.

Karenga, M. (1993). *Introduction to Black studies* (2nd ed.). Los Angeles: University of Sankore Press.

Lawson, E., & Thompson, A. (1994). Historical and social correlates of African-American divorce: Review of the literature and implications for research. *Western Journal of Black Studies, 18*(2), 91–103.

Madhubuti, H. R. (1987). *Killing memory, seeking ancestors*. Chicago: Third World Press.

Martin, J., Cummings, A. L., & Hallberg, E. T. (1992). Therapists' intentional use of metaphor: Memorability, clinical impact, and possible epistemic/motivational functions. *Journal of Consulting and Clinical Psychology, 60*(1), 143–145.

Mbiti, J. S. (1970). *African religions and philosophies*. Garden City, NY: Anchor Books, Doubleday.

McAdoo, H. P. (1998). African-American families: Strengths and realities. In H. I. McCubbin, E. A. Thompson, A. I. Thompson, & J. A. Futrell (Eds.), *Resiliency in African-American families* (pp. 17–30). Thousand Oaks, CA: Sage.

Monye, A. A. (1996). *Proverbs in African orature: The Aniocha-Igbo experience*. Lanham, MD: University Press of America.

Murrell, P. C., Jr. (2002). *African-centered pedagogy: Developing schools of achievement for African American children*. Albany: State University of New York Press.

Myers, L. J. (1993). *Understanding an Afrocentric worldview: Introduction to an optimal psychology* (2nd ed.). Dubuque, IA: Kendall/Hunt.

Nobles, W. W. (1986). *African psychology: Toward its reclamation, reascension and revitalization*. Oakland, CA: Institute for the Advanced Study of Black Family Life and Culture.

Nobles, W. W. (1998). To be African or not to be: The question of identity or authenticity—some preliminary thoughts. In R. L. Jones (Ed.), *African American identity development* (pp. 183–206). Hampton, VA: Cobb & Henry.

Nobles, W. W. (2004). African philosophy: Foundation for Black psychology. In R. Jones (Ed.), *Black psychology* (4th ed., pp. 57–72). Hampton, VA: Cobb & Henry.

Nobles, W. W. (2006). *Seeking the Sakhu: Foundational writings for an African psychology*. Chicago: Third World Press.

Nobles, W., & Goddard, L. (1993). An African-centered model of prevention for African American youth at high risk. In L. Goddard (Ed.), *An African-centered model of prevention for African-American youth at high risk* (DHHS Publication No. SMA 93-2015, pp. 115–129). Rockville, MD: U.S. Government Printing Office.

Nobles, W. W., Goddard, L., & Cavil, W. (1998). *An introduction to the African centered behavioral change model for the prevention of HIV/STDs*. Washington, DC: Association of Black Psychologists.

Nussbaum, S. (1998). *The wisdom of African proverbs: Collections, studies, bibliographies.* Colorado Springs, CO: Global Mapping International. [*CD*].

Nwoga, D. (1975). *Igbo traditional verse.* Burlington, MA: Heinemann.

Nwoga, D. I. (1975). Appraisal of Igbo proverbs and idioms. In F. C. Ogbalu and E. N. Emenanjo (Eds.) *Igbo Language and Culture* (pp. 186–204). Ibadan, Nigeria: Oxford University Press.

Opoku, K. A., & Mbiti, J. S. (1997). Hearing and keeping Akan proverbs. *African Proverbs Series,* Vol. 2. Accra, Ghana: Asempa Publishers.

Parker, T. S., & Wampler, K. S. (2006). Changing emotion: The use of therapeutic storytelling. *Journal of Marital and Family Therapy, 32*(2), 155–166.

Patterson, O. (1998). *Rituals of blood: Consequences of slavery in two American centuries.* New York: Basic Civitas Books.

Pinderhughes, E. B. (2002). African American marriage in the 20th century. *Family Process, 41*(2), 269–283.

Rowe, D. M. (1991). Africentricity: A multidimensional paradigm. *Psych Discourse, 23*(2), 11–12.

Rowe, T. D., & Webb-Msmejai, F. (2004). African-centered psychology in the community. In R. Jones (Ed.), *Black psychology* (4th ed., pp. 701–721). Hampton, VA: Cobb & Henry.

Schiele, J. H. (1996). Afrocentricity: An emerging paradigm in social work practice. *Social Work, 41*(3), 284–294.

Some, S. E. (1999). *The spirit of intimacy: Ancient teachings in the ways of relationships.* Berkeley, CA: Berkeley Hills Books.

South, S. (1993). Racial and ethnic differences in the desire to marry. *Journal of Marriage and the Family, 55,* 357–370.

Staples, R. (1981). Race and marital status: An overview. In H. P. McAdoo (Ed.), *Black families* (pp. 173–176). Newbury Park, CA: Sage.

Thomas, C. W. (1971). *Boys no more.* Beverly Hills, CA: Glencoe.

Tucker, M., & Mitchell-Kernan, C. (1995). Trends in African American family formation: A theoretical overview. In M. Tucker & C. Mitchell-Kernan (Eds.), *The decline of marriage among African-Americans* (pp. 8–26). New York: Russell Sage.

U.S. Census Bureau. (2007). The American Community—Blacks: 2004: American Community survey reports. U.S. Department of Commerce, Economics and Statistics Administration. Retrieved April 15, 2007, from www.census-gov/prod/2007pubs/acs-04.pdf

Wampold, B. (2001). Contextualizing psychotherapy as a healing practice: Culture, history, and methods. *Applied and Preventive Psychology, 10,* 69–86.

Watts, R. J., & Abdul-Adil, J. (1997). Promoting critical consciousness in young African American men. *Journal of Prevention and Intervention in the Community, 16,* 63–86.

White, J. L. (1991). Toward a Black psychology. In R. Jones (Ed.), *Black psychology* (3rd ed., pp. 5–14). Berkeley, CA: Cobb and Henry.

Whitfield, K. E., Markman, H. J., Stanley, S. M., & Blumberg, S. L. (2001). *Fighting for your African American marriage.* San Francisco: Jossey-Bass.

Zuniga, M. E. (1992). Using metaphors in therapy: Dichos and Latino clients. *Social Work, 37*(1), 55–60.

4

Intersecting Multiple Identities
The Case of Lehua

Laurie "Lali" McCubbin

Contents

Introduction

The case study of Lehua is about the intersection of multiple identities that individuals may have within themselves, among their family members, and in their community. The intersection of ethnicity, sexual orientation, and religious affiliation across different contexts can create situations where identity salience and congruence among these identities can become challenging. As people develop and grow across different contexts, their identities also develop and change. The stressors associated within each context such as oppression, discrimination, heterosexism, historical trauma, and racism can make navigating each context a challenge for even the most resilient person. Therefore various coping strategies must be drawn on, and consistent self-care and internal self-acceptance of all of one's identities can be essential in navigating the contexts within one's life.

A common factors approach can be vital to creating a safe and supportive environment for self-acceptance and harmony among identities within oneself to occur. Although each context has its unique stressors, the counseling sessions can be one context where an individual can find a safe place to work through conflicting emotions and freely express the challenges and difficulties of living in a complex world. In the treatment and conceptualization of these intersecting identities, the author will draw from the contextual model (Wampold, 2001), common factors (Hubble, Duncan, & Miller, 1999), Native Hawaiian indigenous psychology (McCubbin, Ishikawa, & McCubbin, 2007), and developmental models and research on gay, lesbian, and bisexual (GLB) clients (McCarn & Fassinger, 1996; Rust, 1992).

Theoretical Orientation: The Contextual Model and Common Factors

The contextual model is a metatheory, rather than a psychological or therapeutic theory, indicating that the treatment procedures used in therapy are beneficial to the client because of the meaning attributed to those procedures, rather than to their specific psychological effects (Wampold, 2001). These procedures within the contextual model are as follows: (a) there is an emotionally charged, confiding relationship with a helping person; (b) the context of the relationship is a healing setting; (c) there is a rationale or conceptual schema in understanding symptoms and providing treatment for a client; and (d) there is a ritual that requires both the client and the therapist to participate to help the client alleviate symptoms.

A common factors approach (Hubble et al., 1999) proposes there are essential factors that are common to most counseling theories and treatment, rather than specific ingredients of a particular theory, that are responsible for change to occur. The four major common factors are as follows: (a) factors in the client's life that cause or facilitate change; (b) the counseling relationship, also referred to as the "therapeutic alliance" between the client and the counselor, and a warm, caring, and empathic relationship based on acceptance and affirmation; (c) the client's belief that he or she will get better (expectations by the client of the outcome of therapy); and (d) the model or technique used in therapy. Wampold (2001) in his extensive review of the treatment efficacy literature provided empirical support for the common factors approach, finding that theories meeting the criteria of the contextual model have been found to be more or less equally effective.

Culturally Responsive Treatment Considerations: Native Hawaiian Psychology

In working with Pacific Islanders and, specifically, Native Hawaiians, counselors should utilize indigenous psychology and the world view of Native Hawaiians (McCubbin et al., 2007). The Hawaiian concept of self, which is grounded in social relationships (Pukui, Haertig, & Lee, 1972a), is based on the belief that the individual, society, and nature are inseparable and are essential to psychological and physical health (McCubbin & Marsella, in review). Therefore, identity and self-concept are embedded in the social relationships and the contexts that a person lives in. Some parallels can be seen in feminist theory and its emphasis on development in the context of connectedness and relationships with others.

The well-being of Native Hawaiians is viewed holistically, encompassing body, mind, and spirit, as well as a mutual embeddedness in the family, land, and spiritual world (Judd, 1998; Marsella, Oliveira, Plummer, & Crabbe, 1995). Key values in the Native Hawaiian culture demonstrate this holistic perspective and can give insight into understanding how Native Hawaiians view mental health and the etiology of mental illness, and how to resolve issues and determine treatment.

Three components of the Hawaiian culture are essential to mental health: *'aina* (land), *'ohana* (family), and *mana* (spirit) (McCubbin et al., 2007). *'Aina* can be translated to refer to the earth, land, or nature (Kanahele, 1986; Pukui & Elbert, 1986; Rezentes, 1996). According to Kanahele and Rezentes, *'aina* has three dimensions: physical, psychological, and spiritual. The environment embodies physical *'aina*, marking both ancestral homelands and the substance required to nourish the body. Psychological *'aina* is related to mental health, particularly in regard to positive and negative thinking. Spiritual *'aina* speaks to daily relationships between Native Hawaiians and the spiritual world. Traditionally, the spiritual world is a source of strength for Native Hawaiian people.

'Ohana, meaning family or kin group (Kanahele, 1986; Pukui & Elbert, 1986; Rezentes, 1996), is a strong source of support and identity in Hawaiian culture. *'Ohana* can consist of extended family and informal relationships with friends and family members of friends. Thus, the *'ohana* can be considered an extended and complex arrangement of roles and relationships and plays a key role in defining one's self in relation to others.

Mana means divine or spiritual power (Kanahele, 1986; Rezentes, 1996) and evokes respect for one's gods. In terms of Native Hawaiian health, *mana* can refer to how the individual experiences the relationship between health and sense of place (Oneha, 2001). *Mana* emanating from ecological elements or nature has the power to calm, energize, heal, and relax (Oneha, 2001). *Mana* is the life energy that binds and connects person, family, land, and the spirit world. The concept of *mana* can coexist with a belief in Christianity. Indigenous spiritual beliefs are not necessarily incompatible with the Christian faith. In fact, the Native Hawaiians overthrew their own preexisting religious structure and *kapu* system in the 19th century. Native Hawaiians, although colonized by the missionaries, were able to translate the Bible and its lessons from Greek text into the Native Hawaiian language, assisting Hawaiians in claiming their religious identity with their own language.

The conceptual schema in understanding mental health and well-being can be viewed in the Native Hawaiian culture as *lokahi*, meaning harmony and unity (Pukui & Elbert, 1986). According to Rezentes (1996), *lokahi* can be understood as a triangle formed by *'aina* (nature), *kanaka* (humankind), and *ke akua* (god[s]). Native Hawaiian health requires *lokahi* or a sense of harmony between mind, body, spirit, and land. Psychological and spiritual well-being can be seen as having relational and emotional bonds free from conflict.

The Native Hawaiian schema for conceptualizing mental illness develops when there is a disequilibrium or disharmony in relationships including the family (*'ohana*), land (*'aina*), and God (*ke akua*). According to Pukui, Haertig, and Lee (1972a, 1972b), mental illness has two different etiologies: *ma'i mai waho* and *ma'i ma loko* (Pukui, Handy, & Livermore, 1934). *Ma'i mai waho* refers to sickness caused by outside (*waho*) forces such as spirits or gods. A ritual for alleviating mental illness would be traditional faith healing practice, be *la'au kahea*, which would involve prayer and restoration of *lokahi* of the body, mind, and spirit (Judd, 1998). In addition, resolving these conflicts with family members, the god(s), and the land would be acts to "set right" the transgression or to seek forgiveness or resolution of the conflict(s).

Although faith healing may be available for some Native Hawaiians, because of the oppression and cultural genocide of the Hawaiian culture, some Hawaiians do not have access to traditional healers. Therefore, Native Hawaiians may seek out help from their church, religious leaders, extended family, and/or friends. A proportion may seek out mental health services. Western models of therapy such as person-centered theory and feminist therapy may be helpful in alleviating symptoms; however, an understanding of Native Hawaiians' conceptualization of health and mental illness can be instrumental in creating an environment that is culturally congruent and accepting for the client. Native Hawaiians may not fully articulate Native Hawaiian mental health conceptualization as written in this chapter; however, a counselor having this knowledge may be helpful in understanding varying Native Hawaiian world views.

Cultural Considerations

The history of the loss of the nation, the population decimation, and the loss of culture has had significant effects on the Native Hawaiians and has been referred to as cultural trauma (Salzman, 2001) and cultural genocide. Native Hawaiians have high rates of substance abuse, depression, and anxiety disorders compared to non-Hawaiians (Guerrero, Hishinuma, Andrade, & Bell, 2003; Marsella et al., 1995; Prescott et al., 1998). The cultural trauma has contributed to a condition of long-term psychosocial cultural trauma similar to that experienced by other colonized indigenous peoples (Salzman, 2001). The native people were subjected to persistent ridicule and discrimination. Hawaiians were viewed as stupid and lazy people. Cook, Withy, and Tarallo-Jensen (2003) characterized this adverse situation as "cultural wounding," and this wounding, it is argued, is related to the present-day negative health status of Native Hawaiians.

Prior to reading this case study, readers should have some knowledge about Native Hawaiian culture. In most multicultural counseling textbooks, Pacific Islanders, if addressed, are usually combined with Asian Americans. Despite the use of Asian Americans as the umbrella term with Pacific Islanders subsumed under the title, the history of Pacific Islanders may seem more similar to American Indians and Native Alaskans. This is in part due to the influences of American colonialism and the presence of missionaries from the Christian and Mormon faith in the Pacific Rim.

State policies, such as movement toward legalizing same-gender marriages in Hawai'i, may lead people to make generalizations about Pacific Islanders and their attitudes toward GLB citizens. However, as within most societies and communities of color, attitudes, perspective, and stereotypes of GLB people may vary within the multiple ethnic groups found on the Hawaiian Islands. Because of the strong presence of Christianity and Mormonism among Pacific Islanders, homophobic attitudes can be prevalent within certain sections of the Pacific Islander community. The intersection between colonization processes instilled by missionaries and one's identity as a Christian and Native Hawaiian can lead to internal and external conflicts for GLB individuals and families. Because a client has had to deal with Christianity and colonization throughout the generations, there is a process where these seemingly incongruent identities can come together in a peaceful resolution.

The majority of Native Hawaiians are multiracial; estimates vary from 66% to 99%. The rapid decline of the Native Hawaiians, referred to as the cultural genocide or "holocaust" by some writers (Stannard, 1989), contributed to the increase in interracial marriages in the islands. This led to the development of a complex multiethnic and multiracial population in subsequent generations in which Native Hawaiian ancestry is now charted in $1/16$ or even $1/32$ blood quantum levels. People may define themselves solely as Native Hawaiian, multiracial, multiethnic, or *hapa* (part Caucasian part Hawaiian, or it can also mean "mixed" race), independent of their biological racial heritage. A common misperception about Native Hawaiians is that anyone who lives on the Hawaiian Islands is considered Hawaiian. This assumption is erroneous; rather than being "Hawaiian," they are considered "local." Native Hawaiians are indigenous to the land and resided on the islands prior to Western contact in 1778. Native Hawaiians had their own government, monarchy, and parliamentary system and were recognized as having their own nation prior to the overthrow of the monarchy by U.S. businessmen (for more information about Hawaiian history, see McCubbin et al., 2007).

Traditional Theoretical Orientation

My theoretical orientation is based primarily on person–client-centered theory and feminist theory. The goals of therapy are to promote self-acceptance, empowerment, and self-care. The purpose of therapy with Lehua is to bring together her multiple identities and allow her the room to explore their development and meanings and how they intersect. In addition, the goals in therapy for Lehua are (a) to provide ways for her to cope with challenges in the external world and within herself that may be creating distress because of conflicting expectations of her multiple identities (e.g., as a woman, Pacific Islander, Christian, lesbian, daughter, and partner) and (b) to move from a sense of incongruence with conflicting identities to congruence with all of her identities and to trust her own inner sense of self. The process of change in therapy would focus on providing the foundation of person-centered theory (genuineness, unconditional positive regard and empathy) consistently throughout the sessions while also incorporating interventions from the feminist approach (gaining empowerment, recognizing types of oppression, and reframing experiences and coping mechanisms).

Treatment Implications

Although person-centered and feminist theories can help in conceptualizing clients' issues and developing treatment plans, additional resources are needed to fully understand the unique aspects of Lehua's case. Developmental theories on identity such as ethnic and racial identity (Helms, 1990; Phinney, 1992), gay and lesbian identity (McCarn & Fassinger, 1996; Rust, 1992), and spiritual identity (Fowler, 1981) can assist a counselor in understanding Lehua's developmental processes and her multiple identities. With each identity Lehua has, conflicting issues with other identities can occur (being a Christian and being lesbian). Native Hawaiian concepts can also be incorporated into treatment to provide a culturally responsive intervention. Research on GLB clients (Parks, Hughes, & Matthews, 2004) can also inform the counselor in understanding Lehua.

Case Study

Lehua has come to the university counseling center based on a recommendation of a classmate in her master's program. Lehua is a first-year graduate student and recently moved from Hawai'i to the U.S. mainland (Midwest). She is feeling sad, lonely, and depressed as she is missing home and finding the transition to be challenging. This is her first experience in counseling. Her skin tone has a slight olive complexion, giving her an ambiguous ethnic look. One could perceive her ethnicity as Latina, Italian, Native Hawaiian, Samoan, or European American. She is the eldest in the family, with two younger brothers, ages 12 and 17. Her parents have been married for 30 years.

Sessions Analyses and Rationale for Interventions

Sessions 1 and 2: Building Rapport and Talking Story The first session focused on what brought Lehua into counseling. Lehua was tearful and appeared embarrassed by her emotions and coming into counseling. Lehua was hesitant to talk at first and was not clear how therapy worked. She seemed shy yet accommodating to my questions and efforts to get to know her. To be transparent and equalitarian, I explained my theoretical orientation and philosophy in counseling and offered some information about who I am (I am Native Hawaiian, Japanese, and Caucasian, and have lived on the islands as well as on the mainland). The self-disclosure was to provide information about me as Lehua was sharing her story and to build the relationship with some commonalities. Using the island concept of "talk story," I asked Lehua to tell me about herself.

Lehua had recently moved to the mainland from Honolulu and was very homesick and having difficulties adjusting to the new area and graduate school. When asked "What do you miss back home?" she talked at great length about the lifestyle of the islands, the food, and her extended family. She missed the slower pace and family style of the islands, such as people calling each other auntie and uncle. She missed small things like Zippy's, Foodland, and Longs Drugs Store, where she could get local food such as kalua pig, sushi, fresh fruit, and Japanese snacks. She missed talking pidgin and the way people greeted her with a kiss on the cheek and a hug. The purpose of encouraging Lehua to talk about home, foods, and the cultural factors she missed was to help alleviate her anxiety about coming to counseling and to help build our relationship.

The second session focused on the differences between the islands and the Midwest and what challenges she saw in adjusting to this new area. Prioritizing these differences, we were able to come up with the stressors that were causing distress for Lehua. Her main concerns were as follows: (a) not having family nearby, (b) missing the Hawaiian and local culture, (c) being the only Pacific Islander in her program, and (d) interacting with her classmates. Despite assertions from her classmates that they were not racist and had no stereotypical thoughts about Hawaiians, they continually talked about Hawai'i in terms of sun and relaxation. They also held assumptions about the islands that "racism did not exist" and did not understand how Lehua could describe herself as "Native Hawaiian" as Hawai'i was a state and therefore she was like "one of us." In addition, because Lehua could "pass" as being White given her biracial heritage, classmates did not understand her need to assert her Native Hawaiian identity. This was compounded by Lehua's need to maintain harmony in her relationships and to avoid conflict even if it meant personal sacrifice for the benefit of the group.

Her classmates' comments bothered Lehua, which led to her feelings of being incongruent with her culture and how she presented herself to her classmates. She tried to fit in and did not want to challenge peoples' stereotypes about the islands and Native Hawaiians as she did not want to create interpersonal conflict. However, the price of creating a sense of false harmony in her relationships was feelings of despair, isolation, loneliness, and feeling misunderstood.

When asked how she handled these stereotypes and assumptions from people in the past, she reported talking with her family, cousins, and friends and praying. Her family and friends validated her identity and the ignorance people had about their shared common culture. Every Sunday, her extended family (parents, grandparents, aunts, uncles, and cousins) and friends back home would gather at her cousin's house located in the Hawaiian homelands and talk story, eat, and play games. Family friends who were "*hanai'ed*," or informally adopted as part of the family, were also included. The family consisted of multiple races and ethnicities, including European American, Asian, Pacific Islander, and Latino. Most of her blood-related relatives were part Hawaiian; however, her *hanai'ed* family members were European American, Filipino, and Japanese. Sometimes the talk would be serious, but mostly it was about being together. Lehua described how in the neighborhood in which she lives in the Midwest, she rarely saw anyone outside their homes, and no one interacted beyond brief polite interactions. This is in stark contrast to her family's and cousin's neighborhood, where kids were playing together and most neighbors were outside and talking to one another. Also the lack of touch in the Midwest (e.g., no hugs or brief kisses on the cheek as a greeting) was strange, and she missed these expressions of affection and kinship. When dealing with these differences, Lehua talked about the power of prayer and how she sought consolation and compassion in her relationship with God and Jesus Christ. Lehua indicated that she did not belong to a church in the Midwest. I gave Lehua a pamphlet produced by the multicultural student center about various religious institutions, including churches in the area, ethnic food restaurants and grocery stories, and the Hawaiian student club for her to review and for us to discuss next time.

Analysis of Sessions 1 and 2   The purpose of these sessions was to build a rapport with Lehua. Talking story is a local term on the islands for telling each other about themselves and their families. I began the session talking story to help relax Lehua in an informal way, as she seemed hesitant about counseling. Discussing food can be a way to recognize one's culture, as it brings part of your home and culture with you in a new place. Food can also be a bonding experience and a way to get to know one another in a less threatening way.

Self-disclosing about my own ethnic and racial heritage, and indicating that I lived on the islands, can be complicated. Within group differences, what it means to be Hawaiian, or *hapa*, can be found. In addition, indicating where I lived on the islands can also tell the client my socioeconomic status, which may affect how the client sees me.

Sometimes among Hawaiians, legitimacy or authenticity testing can occur, focusing on "How Hawaiian are you?" or "How local are you?" Questions about one's family are common so that one can see possible connections in the Hawaiian community. One may ask about another's knowledge or experience with Hawaiian culture, cultural practices, and Hawaiian language. Therefore, my disclosure of my identity was a risk that could have helped or hindered the counseling relationship; luckily, in this case it was the former. Counseling theories and multicultural textbooks do not address this authenticity and the legitimacy testing that may occur in therapy or how to deal with this dynamic. Prior to disclosing their identity (ethnic [if necessary], spiritual, or sexual orientation), counselors need to be aware where they are developmentally in their respective identities, and how this may affect interactions with clients. Racial identity models (Helms, 1990) can also be helpful in understanding the dynamics between Lehua and her classmates.

The purpose of the second session was to assess the level of the acculturative stress Lehua was experiencing and how these stressors were impacting her and her current coping mechanisms. As a counselor, being aware of different resources in the community (e.g., churches, restaurants, groceries, and campus groups) can help a client adjust to a new culture or environment.

Session 3: Coming Out   Lehua reported that she wanted to talk to me about the pamphlet with descriptions of the churches in the area. She reported feeling uncomfortable and guilty about not being "completely honest" with me. She talked about her fear of my disapproval and that I may have made certain assumptions about her. Recognizing that as a counselor I may have misinterpreted or jumped ahead with my assumptions of the client, I encouraged her to tell me what was bothering her and asked how I could help.

Taking a deep breath, Lehua talked about her partner, Emily, who moved with her to the Midwest. Lehua was working in a hospital after college graduation where Emily was a nurse. They began a romantic relationship about 3 years ago, and Emily was the one who encouraged her to get a master's degree. Emily is European American and has lived in several places, including the mainland, abroad, and Hawai'i. Emily spent the majority of her life in Hawai'i, as her father was in the military and now currently runs a security firm on the islands. Her mother is a homemaker. Emily is out to her parents and has been since her late teens. Emily is open about her lesbian identity in her family, her social circles, and her workplace. Emily is 4 years older than Lehua and has been in two previous serious relationships with women.

We spent some time talking about Lehua's concerns about my reactions to this disclosure and her feelings about me giving her the brochure without knowing this important part of her life. She was deeply concerned about my own religious beliefs and my attitudes about sexual orientation. I explained my openness and acceptance of her sexual orientation and her faith, and added that my intention for giving Lehua the brochure was to acknowledge her religious affiliation and identity, and to consider possible support systems. We discussed possible assumptions that I could have made about this gesture, about her spirituality, faith, need for a religious community, and sexual orientation. We talked about everyone needing to unpack their "privileged" backpacks, including me as her therapist. I talked briefly about multiple identities and how, depending on a client's comfort level, the disclosing of these identities would follow their own course in therapy. I acknowledged her courage and honesty in telling me what was bothering her.

Lehua appeared relieved by my reaction, and I asked more about possible challenges in identifying as a lesbian and a Christian. This was the first time Lehua had used the "L word" to describe herself. She talked about how the categories and the "L word" troubled her because she felt it did not capture her feelings for Emily. The second half of the session focused on her feelings and relationship history, including the respect, gratitude, and love she felt for having Emily in her life. Prior to Emily, Lehua had never had a same-sex relationship. She dated a male classmate during high school whom she met in a local Christian youth group. Though they dated throughout high school, she reported very little sexual activity and felt they both stayed in the relationship to avoid sexual desires and a need to model a healthy nonsexual Christian relationship. She remembered this relationship fondly, but also saw it retrospectively as more of a friendship than a romantic relationship. Throughout college, Lehua was actively involved in her church and a Native Hawaiian activist group. She felt her college days really focused on her identity as a Native Hawaiian and connecting herself to her heritage. However, Lehua reported feeling "different" since middle school and was embarrassed or ashamed when she had sexual feelings for other females. She was in denial during high school, focusing solely on her religion, and found companionship among her fellow Native Hawaiian peers in college. She had a crush on a very close friend during college, but kept her feelings private.

Lehua was working at a hospital when she met a group of friends (three women including Emily). During this time, she began to examine her feelings toward women and struggled a great deal with her faith. Despite ongoing prayers, Lehua felt an attraction toward Emily. She was close friends with Emily for 2 years and knew about Emily's sexual orientation. Lehua continued to have conflicting emotions about possibly wanting to have a relationship with a woman, but she was also scared because she had been raised to believe that this was a sin. She finally disclosed to her cousin that she thought she was gay and that she had a crush on her coworker. Her cousin was very supportive and did not act surprised by her secret. Her cousin asked Lehua, "Why would God put someone like her in your life and give you these feelings of love if He meant it to be a sin?" Lehua spent a great deal of time pondering this, searching in her heart to find how deeply she cared for Emily and if she desired for a romantic relationship. After a long talk, Emily and Lehua had their first date, and they have been together for 3 years. They have been cohabiting for 6 months, 3 in Hawai'i and 3 on the mainland.

At the end of the session, when asked how she felt about it, she reported feeling good and glad that she had told me her concerns. I asked her how she was different in the past (in high school, in college, and 3 years ago) compared to who she is today. In response, she talked about how far she has come from those days when she struggled so much about possibly dating Emily.

She recognized that she had made the right decision to be with Emily and that she truly changed her life in a positive way. I commented on how Lehua had shared her life story: first her religious identity (in high school), then her Native Hawaiian identity (in college), and her lesbian, or "L," identity in the past 3 years. I asked her to think about how she would like to define her identity now and in the future.

Analysis of Session 3 According to Pedersen (1978), recovery skills are needed to help a counselor in those situations in which he or she is not culturally empathic or misses an opportunity to explore cultural factors. Pedersen stated, "If a counselor is not making mistakes while counseling a client from a culture that is totally unfamiliar to the counselor, then the counselor may very well not be taking enough personal risk" (p. 483). Most multicultural case studies demonstrate multicultural competence skills; however, very few textbooks or cases discuss what to do if you make a "cultural" mistake.

My gesture in offering information about churches without asking or knowing Lehua's sexual orientation could indicate my heterosexual privilege and possible assumptions made when a client reveals she is a Christian. When working with GLB clients, and in my own development as a psychologist, I am continually increasing my awareness and challenging myself about my heterosexual privilege communicated in my attitudes and behaviors that I demonstrate every day. Although I did not disclose my heterosexual orientation verbally to Lehua, she may know through my language and nonverbal behaviors. Therefore, supervision for me is critical in order to discuss possible blind spots in therapy and to increase my awareness and development.

This session demonstrates two levels of interactions going on: (a) Lehua's concern about my approval or disapproval about her sexual orientation and/or religious affiliation, and (b) her own internal and external conflicts about these identities. The focus on subsequent sessions would be on exploring possible challenges and finding ways to cope with these stressors. Lehua has indicated two coping strategies in therapy: praying and relying on Emily. As we explore in more depth in therapy about her identities and internal struggles, it is important for us to continue using empathy, positive regard, and genuineness. In addition, using a feminist approach, consequent sessions might also focus on incorporating additional coping strategies to help her deal with the multiple oppressions she is encountering.

Session 4: To Pule or Not to Pule *Pule* in Hawaiian means prayer. Typically, at the beginning of meetings or a project, and before sitting down to eat,

Native Hawaiians will ask an elder to say the *pule* to guide the project or purpose of the meeting. The *pule* can be used to focus a group's energy and allow everyone time to put their personal agendas aside for the sake of the family, organization, or group. The *pule* is practiced in Native Hawaiian culture prior to *ho'opono pono* practices, which are family gatherings to set right any issues of conflict occurring in the family.

Lehua, based on our conversations during our previous session, as well as her struggle with Christianity and being with Emily, asked if we could *pule* before we began the session. Typically, the elder says the *pule*, but because this was Lehua's time, I asked Lehua to say the prayer, and I would pray with her. Lehua prayed aloud, "Lord, I ask you that this session be fruitful and helpful. Lord, I am grateful and blessed to have this time with Lali to talk, connect and heal. Please guide me in your path. In Jesus' name we pray. Amen."

I thanked Lehua for this prayer and asked what she thought about doing *pule* in our sessions. She reported that she thought a lot about who she wanted to be now and in the future. She had decided that she was tired of compartmentalizing her life and feeling like she had to sacrifice one part of herself for the other. She was tired of pretending and not being fully honest with people, including herself. She was tearful and exclaimed, "I just feel all over the place with all these pieces of me that don't fit together, and I don't know if they ever will." When asked to elaborate on these feelings, she talked about how she suspected her parents knew about her relationship with Emily. Emily is considered part of the family and attends the Sunday dinners. Her mother refers to Emily as their "*hanai'ed* daughter" and always includes her in family events such as baptisms, weddings, and showers. She feels her mother and father are affirming of their relationship without saying anything directly. Her father is quiet and reserved, but she describes their relationship as "very close." They have a special bond, and she worries about what he thinks of her knowing that she and Emily live together. Prior to her leaving for the mainland, her father pulled her aside and said, "All I want for you is to be happy," which felt to her like a blessing. Lehua's paternal aunt is very vocal about her beliefs that homosexuality is a sin and prays for other families with a gay son or daughter.

Lehua is also very close to her paternal grandmother and describes her as a constant comfort and teacher of the old Hawaiian ways. It was her grandmother and her stories that inspired Lehua to become active in the Native Hawaiian rights movement in college. Her grandmother is a strict Catholic, and, when Lehua was a child, they attended Sunday mass together every week. She is the matriarch of the family, and everyone goes to her for advice and defers to her judgment. People may not agree with Grandma, but "you will respect and honor her by following her requests." However, since moving away and living with Emily, Lehua has not gone to church.

Some of Emily's new friends are very much involved in the gay rights movement and believe that anyone who is not out by their criteria have serious issues and will continue to be under the oppression of the heterosexist society. Lehua, because of her culture, and out of respect for her elders and her religion, does not feel she can be fully out. Although Emily really is enjoying her new friends, Lehua feels very uncomfortable around them. They put down organized religion and stereotype those who are Christian. Emily is supportive of Lehua's faith and has attended church with her in the past, but does not strongly identify with Christianity.

Lehua has made some friends in the Christian group on campus, but is out only to one female, who says that she accepts Lehua for who she is, but she cannot condone the sin that she is living. Lehua wants to find a religious community that can accept and honor her partnership with Emily and her spiritual development. Lehua described feeling conflicted about how the way she was raised as a Catholic may not fit with who she is today. She felt a connection and a loss at the same time when she attended church back home last year, finding comfort in the rituals, but realizing she could never be fully a part of it; thus, she has stopped attending services. As her relationship with Emily deepened, she realized the losses she will have (e.g., not getting married in her family's church, or not having her children baptized by her family's priest). Her hesitancy to go to a new church in this community stems from her continued feelings of loss and fear that making this commitment would mean breaking away from part of her heritage, her family, and her childhood.

Lehua's homework for the next 2 weeks was to read an excerpt from *The Good Book: Reading the Bible With Mind and Heart* by Peter J. Gomes (1997) and to meet with an openly gay minister at a local Episcopal church. We talked about what the expectations and goals were for these two assignments.

Analysis of Session 4   Several multicultural interventions were conducted within this session. First, for some people of color, the power of prayer is important and can help focus the session's energies. It can also help in understanding the client's goals and perhaps what he or she may be struggling with spiritually. To be ethical and empower the client, I will ask the client to say the prayer aloud and that I will bear witness to the prayer or pray with him or her. If one feels uncomfortable with prayer in session, clients can sing a hymn (for Hawaiians it is the doxology in the Hawaiian language). This serves two purposes: (a) to center the client and (b) to help with diaphragmatic breathing if a client is anxious or experiencing pain.

Lehua opened up more about her extended family, the various views about same-sex relationships, and the varying degrees of coming out. Sometimes, in communities of color, coming out is a process that can be nonverbal and behavioral, such as bringing Emily to all major family events and family members accepting her as one of the family. Laird (1998) discussed the variability in reactions of families of origin to same-sex partnerships and provided some excellent examples to help describe the complexity of this process.

For many people of color, because of the importance of Christianity and the church within the culture and family, there may be varying degrees of being out. In Lehua's case, some of the elders are not explicitly aware of her sexual orientation. Lehua does not directly state her orientation, partly out of respect for her elders and because at this stage of her coming-out process, she made conscious choices about what is comfortable for her and culturally appropriate for the family. Sometimes allies, like Lehua's cousin or the minister, can help Lehua to have her identity as a lesbian within the familial, cultural, and religious contexts of her life.

The homework assignments are consistent with feminist theory's interventions for change in raising social consciousness about oppression, and also help to build a community to discuss with others who have encountered and lived through multiple oppressions. As a counselor, it is critical for me to establish relationships in the community (in this case the openly gay minister) that can help as resources for clients. This particular person is in a committed relationship and has struggled with similar issues that Lehua is facing. In addition, this minister has events at his home for members of his church where same-sex couples are welcome. This may help Lehua in meeting other lesbian couples who are also Christian. Navigating safe zones for GLB clients can be stressful and time-consuming, but helping clients to find these places can be instrumental to their adjustment.

Lehua's intersecting identities can be conceptualized using developmental models of spiritual identity (Fowler, 1981) and sexual orientation. Lehua is in transition between spiritual stages. The loss she feels is her movement away from the synthetic-convention faith seen in childhood (characterized by the importance of faith in bringing together family, congregation, and the community). Lehua questioned her spirituality and faith in relation to her personal issues (attraction for Emily) and critically examined her beliefs in relation to her values and lifestyle 3 years ago, which is the individuating–reflective stage. She is now moving into the conjunctive stage where she is dealing with the paradoxes in her faith journey, and learning her own path-way to faith rather than following another's path (e.g., her aunt's beliefs). In terms of Lehua's sexual orientation and coming-out process, McCarn and Fassinger's (1996) distinction between individual and group identity pro-cesses can be applied to Lehua in that she is out to herself personally and engaging in a same-sex relationship, but because of her ethnic and religious identities, her group identity process is different.

In this session, lateral oppression was presented, which can occur within oppressed groups. Emily's friend who was active in the gay rights movement needed to come out as part of her healing path. However, each person's devel-opmental process of coming out may be different, and people may be at various stages. This does not mean that one person is more healthy or better than the other; rather, one needs to accept that this is a developmental pro-cess and to respect one another in their respective places. In addition, some communities that support one identity (e.g., Christian group) may condemn another identity (sexual orientation), creating conflicts in the external world that can also be found internally.

Session 8: Finding a Church and Going Home   Lehua had been attending the Episcopal church and went to weekly events at the minister's and his partner's home. She has found this community, although different from her church back home, very welcoming and comfortable. Emily recently joined her for Sunday services and a movie night with members from the church. Lehua still feels conflicted about her sexual orientation and her religious identity, but at least now she has Christian friends with whom she can truly talk about these issues. She and the minister have had two long talks, and she reports feeling like "he gets it," but she would also like to find a female who has gone through similar experiences. She was really excited and happy about having Emily there and having their relationship be so warmly accepted by fellow Christians, which was a "blessing."

Lehua had recently gone home for a break and gave me a gift of some local food that she remembered talking about early on in our sessions. I offered for us to share the food together in session. Both she and Emily went home for the holidays, and she described it as relaxing and really focused on family time. She reported that although she cried leaving Hawai'i, she found that she was looking forward to going back to their apartment and just having alone time with Emily again. She felt sad and homesick for the first few days, but it was nice reconnecting with Emily. Both of them recognized that they were also creating an *'ohana* in the Midwest.

I asked her, "What was it like going back after being gone for 4 months?" She reported that the trip home helped her to see that although some things remained the same, she also saw things differently since being away. When asked to elaborate on this, she reported that she recognizes how hard it must have been at first for Emily to fit in with her family, and listen to homophobic comments and be silent. Lehua felt these things as well, cringing inside, but this time it was different, like she could stand up for herself and for Emily, whereas before she was afraid to rock the boat. Lehua found ways through her sense of humor to challenge her younger brothers' homophobic comments. Even when her aunt went on another homophobic tirade, she felt more distant from it and less reactive toward her aunt. Before, Lehua would have had all these emotional reactions, which led to feelings of helplessness or despair. Now, she felt she could pull away and categorize the behaviors in a way that was more manageable. The emotions were still there, but the feelings of insecurity, helplessness, and frustration were more tempered than before.

We talked about the need to be compassionate and connected to our families, but also able to recognize when certain interactions or comments were toxic, and therefore we needed to pull away. Being true to her cultural values and heritage (such as 'ohana and lokahi) is essential to her relationships and her cultural identity. It is also necessary to recognize that even our families can have oppressive prejudicial views that may be unhealthy, but we can withdraw from these comments and still be congruent with our culture and family. Lehua felt she had more information about the Bible (referring to "The Good Book"), and although she is not ready to confront her aunt, she felt inside she could combat some of the stereotypes (which her aunt was voicing) for her own well-being.

Lehua and I talked about resilience among Native Hawaiians and how research (Werner & Smith, 2001) has found that the ability to cope by distancing oneself from a family member and also having compassion for that family member was a way to be congruent with one's family values ('ohana and lokahi) regarding one's sexual orientation and well-being (having compassion, but also having the self-care to pull away from oppressive or prejudicial attitudes). Navigating the complex and difficult terrain of one's sexual orientation, religious identity, and ethnic identity means needing the tools and skills to make that journey manageable.

Using the 'aina (land) as a metaphor, we talked about the big island where the miracle of the birth of land is occurring at Kilauea. Lehua and Emily had both been down to the big island and hiked toward Kilauea. One can see from a distance or by boat the red glow of the lava flowing into the ocean and the steam rising as new land is being made. Walking on the path toward Kilauea can be difficult, as the rock is hard with jagged edges like glass. Therefore, a hiker needs to be skillful in navigating this terrain, including having equipment, skills, and the knowledge about what is safe and unsafe. Part of Lehua's journey is navigating this terrain with the various pitfalls of oppression, prejudicial attitudes, discrimination, and challenges in the intersection of her multiple identities. However, this interplay of her identities is similar to the birth of land. One needs the water and the hot lava for the birth of the land. Her identities, like the ocean and the lava, are powerful and may seem opposite or incompatible at times, but they have the capacity to make something, like 'aina or mana, that is everlasting.

Analysis of Session 8   This session focused on the coping mechanisms and reframing of different situations for Lehua in dealing with her family, and her conflicting issues about being lesbian and Christian. Lehua has added additional coping mechanisms, such as relying on her minister and new friends at the church, being able to be compassionate toward family members while also distancing herself from toxic comments, and reframing her experience in moving to the Midwest to building a new 'ohana rather than losing her 'ohana on the island. Using the concept of 'aina and events going on in the islands, we drew a metaphor to relate this to Lehua's journey and coming to peace with her multiple identities.

Case Conceptualization

Lehua was struggling to find *lokahi* (harmony) between her relationship with God, her relationship with Emily, and her relationship with her family and culture (using a Native Hawaiian conceptualization). The conflictual nature of having these multiple relationships and complex identities created conflict and discord, resulting in a sickness within Lehua. The stressors associated with these identities and their lack of congruence with one another manifested into symptoms found in adjustment disorder with mixed anxiety and depressed mood. Because of the incongruency between her real self and her public self, feelings of loneliness, sadness, and isolation emerged (using person-centered theory). Using person-centered and feminist approaches with Lehua helped to explore various issues and concerns and assisted in developing new coping mechanisms to deal with the distress in her life. Interventions such as unconditional positive regard, genuineness, and empathy helped to create a safe place for Lehua to explore her issues and to build rapport between her and I as the counselor. Increasing social consciousness and awareness, addressing different forms of oppression, developing new coping mechanisms, and reframing circumstances also helped Lehua achieve her goal of being at peace with herself, her identities, and her relationships with others (using feminist theory). Combining a Native Hawaiian conceptualization of health and mental illness with the interventions and concepts from person-centered and feminist theories helped to develop a coherent treatment plan for Lehua.

Evidence-Based Practice in Psychology

Within the American Psychological Association, there has been a need for evidence-based practices within psychology to promote effectiveness of treatment, including "psychological assessment, case formulation, therapeutic relationship, and intervention" (American Psychological Association, 2005, p. 1). One of the concerns regarding evidence-based practices is the lack of samples that include racial and ethnic minorities. Because of cultural characteristics, world views, development processes, and stressors unique to people of color, culturally appropriate treatment interventions are warranted. However, there remains a paucity of research on the effectiveness of these treatments ("mainstream" treatments such as cognitive behavior therapy and culturally based treatment protocols) among Pacific Islanders. The literature on counseling with Native Hawaiians and Pacific Islanders focuses more on individual case studies or examples of application of techniques, such as dream interpretation (e.g., Rezentes, 1996). Clinicians have also made recommendations on theoretical orientations that may be useful with Native Hawaiians; however, there remains a lack of empirical investigation of the efficacy of these types of therapy (indigenous or Western-based models) with Native Hawaiians.

Empirical evidence has been found with regard to assessment tools that can be used in therapy for the evaluation of self-esteem (Miyamoto et al., 2001), depression (Prescott et al., 1998), anxiety (Hishinuma et al., 2000), life stressors (Miyamoto et al., 2001), and substance abuse (Nishimura et al., 2001) among Native Hawaiian adolescents. The following measures have been found to be valid and reliable with this population: (a) the Rosenberg Self-Esteem Scale (Rosenberg, 1965), (b) the Major Life Events Checklist (Andrews, Levisohn, & Hops, 1993), (c) the State-Trait Anxiety Inventory (STAI; Spielberger, Gorsuch, & Lushene, 1970), (d) the Center for Epidemiologic Studies Depression Inventory (CES-D; Radloff, 1977), and (e) selected items from the

Substance Abuse Subtle Screening Inventory–Adolescent (SASSI-A; Miller, 1990) in the prediction of substance abuse and dependence. In addition to these empirically supported assessment tools used with Native Hawaiian adolescents, patient cultural characteristics, such as family ethnic schema (e.g., cultivation of the family's or *'ohana's* identity, values, beliefs, rules, and boundaries within an ethnic context), have been found to predict higher levels of individual physical, emotional, and social well-being (McCubbin, 2006). However, more research is needed to determine the efficacy and utility of these assessment instruments and cultural characteristics in promoting effective psychological practices and interventions among Native Hawaiians.

Additional Clinical Considerations

Future directions with Lehua may include exploring her biracial identity, her continued spiritual path in her faith, and the stages of her relationship with Emily (committed partnership, children). Being in a cross-cultural relationship with Emily can bring up certain issues that may need to be addressed in a culturally responsive manner. Questions about Lehua's biracial identity and Emily's White identity as well as their interactions in the different contexts of their lives may come into play if they consider having children together. Lehua will also need to work on acquiring social skills to handle situations dealing with stereotypes, oppression, and discrimination. Having social skills and coping mechanisms to deal with these situations can be preventive for Lehua and protect her from feelings of frustration, guilt, anger, and hurt.

Identification of Author's Personal Dimensions of Diversity and World View

As discussed in the analyses of the sessions, my identity as a heterosexual female and a Native Hawaiian also impacted my world view and how I saw this client's issues and concerns. I may have overidentified with Lehua about being Native Hawaiian. Defining one's identity as Native Hawaiian can vary from client to client, therefore it is important for me to continually be aware of my own identity development, world view, and biases. Also, my heterosexual privilege may have affected my interactions with Lehua and my interventions (such as referring her to churches without prior knowledge about her sexual orientation). I think with many beginning counselors (and seasoned therapists), there is a pressure to be multiculturally right or perfect in our sessions; however, mistakes or misunderstandings can occur, and may in fact be the norm. How one recovers from these moments can also be essential and great learning opportunities to continue to develop multicultural counseling competency skills and provide culturally responsive treatments.

Therapeutic Recommendations

In the case study, the author made an effort to discuss some possible challenges in working with people of the same ethnicity. Assumptions about pairing a therapist and a client on the basis of ethnicity or race can also bring about some additional challenges, such as salience of one's ethnic or racial identity, authenticity or legitimacy testing, socioeconomic status differences, and possible connections outside of the therapeutic setting (e.g., belonging to the same organizations or having mutual friends). Working with people outside of one's ethnicity, race, sexual orientation, or religion can also have unique challenges. Several guiding principles can be helpful in assisting clinicians in working with Pacific Islanders.

First, it is important to understand that Pacific Islanders have their own cultural values, beliefs, and practices that are unique to their respective island and heritage. Although Pacific Islanders have been aggregated with Asian Americans, there are several differences between these groups, such as values, world views, cultural practices, issues related to discrimination and oppression, and psychological and physical risk factors. The consolidation of Pacific Islanders with Asian Americans in the counseling literature can lead to erroneous conclusions about diagnoses, treatment interventions, and therapeutic goals. Another suggestion is to consider some theories, models, and practices related to American Indians, such as postcolonial psychology and historical trauma, which may be more relevant for Native Hawaiians given the history of colonization and genocide.

In addition, when working with Native Hawaiians, counselors need to make a distinction between "local" identity and "Native Hawaiian." "Local" identity refers to the common island culture; however, this does not supersede one's ethnicity. For example, a Caucasian person can be local, born and raised on the Hawaiian Islands, but this does not mean he or she is Native Hawaiian. Native Hawaiians were indigenous to the land prior to Western contact. One refers to a geographic identity (regional), whereas the other is related to one's ethnicity, culture, and/or heritage.

Another recommendation when working with Pacific Islanders is to gain some knowledge and awareness about the historical context and current political issues of their respective island and culture, and their relationship with the United States in terms of war, policies, and rights and privileges (e.g., house representative, senator) within the U.S. government. This would help in reducing overgeneralizations, stereotypes, or erroneous assumptions about the island's history, the current issues facing them, and the survival of their culture. Reading current literature and research on Pacific Islanders is also warranted to understand Pacific Islanders and their cultural values, beliefs, and practices. For example, several books have been published regarding the stereotypes and erroneous depictions of Samoan and Polynesian culture in Margaret Mead's work that have led to stereotypes and discrimination of Pacific Islanders. Therefore, clinicians need to be up-to-date on knowledge about Pacific Islanders, as well as understand the stereotypes they may encounter.

These last guidelines are based on the intersection of multiple identities. First, identities (ethnicity, sexual orientation, and religious affiliation) can grow and change over time. Sometimes measures are based on the premise that values, beliefs, and practices are consistent over time; however, because of unique stressors of people of color, such as cultural genocide and discrimination, these identities and their respective practices may need to adapt and change over time to survive. As people adapt their identities to various challenges in their lives, these changes should be viewed through the lens of adaptation, resilience, and recovery, rather than on a continuum of "strong" or "weak." Also, having a strong identity in one area does not equate a weakened identity in another area. They can grow and adapt simultaneously. In addition, most Hawaiians are multiethnic; therefore, a person may have multiple cultural values, beliefs, and practices, and these can vary from person to person based on the family's background. Finally, as with all groups, heterogeneity within groups exists, therefore generalizations about Pacific Islanders, religious affiliation, and sexual orientation must be used with caution, as context and time can shape and change each person and how his or her identities come together.

Conclusions

The purpose of the case of Lehua is to demonstrate the complexity of multiple identities, including sexual orientation, spiritual development, and ethnic and racial identity development and how this complexity can impact one's mental health. Utilizing a culture's conceptualization of mental illness and the respective ritual(s) in healing can be instrumental to providing culturally responsive and responsible care. Finding ways to integrate traditional counseling theories with indigenous perspectives can also greatly enhance one's awareness, knowledge, and skills in working with diverse clients. The study of the intersection between multicultural counseling competence, indigenous world views, and evidence-based practices is still in its infancy, and therefore it is critical that practitioners, scholars, and researchers come together to address these issues so that every client is able to receive culturally responsive and appropriate counseling services.

Discussion Questions

1. What types of acculturative stress do you see in the case of Lehua? Why is the term "acculturation" difficult to apply to indigenous peoples?
2. What impact does cultural trauma have on Lehua and her relationship with Emily?
3. How would you as a counselor help Lehua deal with people's assumptions, oppression, and discrimination, given her identity as a Christian, a lesbian, and a biracial Native Hawaiian?
4. How do you recover in therapy when you have made a cultural mistake with a diverse client such as Lehua?
5. How may a heterosexual counselor exhibit heterosexual privilege, and how might this impact a client?
6. What do you see as the developmental stages for GLB clients incorporating their spirituality, religiosity, and coming-out process? How do you see multiple identities (ethnic and racial identity, religious identity, and sexual orientation) interact and develop over time?

Cultural Resources

Gomes, P. J. (1997). *The good book: Reading the Bible with mind and heart*. Boston: Compass.

Lease, S. H., Horne, S. G., & Noffsinger-Frazier, N. (2005). Affirming faith experiences and psychological health for Caucasian lesbian, gay and bisexual individuals. *Journal of Counseling Psychology, 52*(3), 378–388.

McCubbin, L. D., Ishikawa, M., & McCubbin, H. I. (2007). Kanaka Maoli: Native Hawaiians and their testimony and resilience. In A. Marsella, J. Johnson, P. Watson, & J. Gryczynski (Eds.). *Ethnocultural perspectives on disaster and trauma: Foundations, issues and applications* (pp. 271-298). New York, NY: Springer.

O'Neill, C., & Ritter, K. (1992). *Coming out within: Stages of spiritual awakening for lesbians and gay men.* San Francisco: Harper and Row.

Parks, C. A., Hughes, T. L., & Matthews, A. K. (2004). Race/ethnicity and sexual orientation: Intersecting identities. *Cultural Diversity and Ethnic Minority Psychology, 10*(3), 241–254.

Phinney, J. S. (1992). The Multigroup Ethnic Identity Measure: A new scale for use with diverse groups. *Journal of Adolescent Research, 7*(2), 156–176.

References

American Psychological Association. (2005). Policy statement on evidence-based practice in psychology. Retrieved March 28, 2007, from http://www2.apa.org/practice/ebpstatement.pdf

Andrews, J. A., Levisohn, P. M., & Hops, H. (1993). Psychometric properties of scales for the measurement of psychosocial variables associated with depression in adolescence. *Psychological Reports, 73*, 1019–1046.

Cook, B. P., Withy, K., & Tarallo-Jensen, L. (2003). Cultural trauma, Hawaiian spirituality and contemporary health status. *California Journal of Health Promotion, 1*, 10–24.

Fowler, J. (1981). *Stages of faith.* New York: Harper and Row.

Gomes, P. J. (1997). *The good book: Reading the Bible with mind and heart.* Boston: Compass.

Guerreo, A. P. S., Hishinuma, E. S., Andrade, N. N., & Bell, C. K. (2003). Demographic and clinical characteristics of adolescents in Hawaii with obsessive-compulsive disorder. *Archives of Pediatrics and Adolescent Medicine, 157*(7), 665.

Helms, J. E. (Ed.). (1990). *Black and White racial identity: Theory, research, and practice.* Westport, CT: Greenwood.

Hishinuma, E. S., Miyamoto, R. H., Nishimura, S. T., Nahulu, L. B., Andrade, N. N., Makini, G. K., Yuen, N. Y. C., Johnson, R. C., Kim, S. P., Goebert, D. A., & Guerrero, A. P. S. (2000). Psychometric properties of the State-Trait Anxiety Inventory for Asian/Pacific Islander adolescents. *Assessment, 7*, 17–36.

Hubble, M. A., Duncan, B. L., & Miller, S. D. (1999). *The heart and soul of change: What works in therapy.* Washington, DC: American Psychological Association.

Judd, N. L. K. (1998). La'au Lapaau: Herbal healing among contemporary Hawaiian healers. *Pacific Health Dialog, 5*, 239–245.

Kanahele, G. H. S. (1986). *Ku kanaka: Stand tall.* Honolulu: University of Hawaii Press.

Laird, J. (1998). Invisible ties: Lesbians and their families of origin. In C. J. Patterson & A. R. D'Augeli (Eds.), *Lesbian, gay, and bisexual identities in families: Psychological perspectives* (pp. 197–228). New York: Oxford University Press.

Marsella, A. J., Oliveira, J. M., Plummer, C. M., & Crabbe, K. M. (1995). Native Hawaiian (Kanaka Maoli) culture, mind, and well-being. In H. I. McCubbin, E. A. Thompson, A. I. Thompson, & J. E. Fromer (Eds.), *Resiliency in ethnic minority families: Native and immigrant American families* (pp. 93–113). Madison: University of Wisconsin.

McCarn, S. R., & Fassinger, R. E. (1996). Revisioning sexual minority identity formation: A new model of lesbian identity and its implications for counseling and research. *The Counseling Psychologist, 24*, 508–534.

McCubbin, H. I., & McCubbin, L. D. (1997). Hawaiian American families. In M. K. DeGenova (Ed.), *Families in cultural context: Strengths and challenges in diversity* (pp. 239–266). Mountain View, CA: Mayfield.

McCubbin, L. D. (2006). The role of Indigenous family ethnic schema on well-being among Native Hawaiian families. *Contemporary Nurse, 23*(2), 170–180.

McCubbin, L. D., Ishikawa, M., & McCubbin, H. I. (2007). Kanaka Maoli: Native Hawaiians and their testimony of trauma and resilience. In A. Marsella, J. Johnson, P. Watson, & J. Gryczynski (Eds.). *Ethnocultural perspectives on disaster and trauma: Foundations, issues and applications* (pp. 271–298). Springer. New York, NY.

McCubbin, L. D., & McCubbin, H. (2005). Culture and ethnic identity in family resilience: Dynamic processes in trauma and transformation of indigenous people. In M. Unger (Ed.), *Handbook for working with children and youth: Pathways to resilience across cultures and contexts* (pp. 27–44). Thousand Oaks, CA: Sage.

Miller, G. (1990). *The SASSI adolescent manual.* Spencer, IN: Spencer Evening World.

Miyamoto, R. H., Hishinuma, E. S., Nishimura, S. T., Nahulu, L. B., Andrade, N. N., Johnson, R. C., et al. (2001). Equivalencies regarding the measurement and constructs of self-esteem and major life events in an Asian/Pacific Islander sample. *Cultural Diversity and Ethnic Minority Psychology, 7*, 152–163.

Nishimura, S. T., Shihinuma, E. S., Miyamoto, R. H., Goebert, D. A., Johnson, R. C., Yuen, N. Y. C., et al. (2001). Prediction of DISC substance abuse and dependency for ethnically diverse adolescents. *Journal of Substance Abuse, 13*, 597–607.

Oneha, M. F. M. (2001). Ka mauli o ka oina a he mauli kanaka: An ethnographic study from a Hawaiian sense of place. *Pacific Health Dialog, 8*, 299–311.

Parks, C. A., Hughes, T. L., & Matthews, A. K. (2004). Race/ethnicity and sexual orientation: Intersecting identities. *Cultural Diversity and Ethnic Minority Psychology, 10*(3), 241–254.

Pedersen, P. (1978). Four dimensions of cross-cultural skill in counselor training. *Personnel and Guidance Journal, 57*, 480–484.

Phinney, J. S. (1992). The Multigroup Ethnic Identity Measure: A new scale for use with diverse groups. *Journal of Adolescent Research, 7*(2), 156–176.

Prescott, C. A., McArdle, J. J., Hishinuma, E. S., Johnson, R. C., Miyamoto, R. H., Andrade, N. N., et al. (1998). Prediction of major depression and dysthymia from CES-D scores among ethnic minority adolescents. *Journal of American Academy of Child and Adolescent Psychiatry, 37*(5), 495–503.

Pukui, M. K., & Elbert, S. H. (1986). *Hawaiian dictionary.* Honolulu: University of Hawaii Press.

Pukui, M. K., Haertig, E. W., & Lee, C. A. (1972a). *Nānā I Ke Kumu (Look to the source) (Vol. 1)*. Honolulu, HI: Hui Hanai.

Pukui, M. K., Haertig, E. W., & Lee, C. A. (1972b). *Nānā I Ke Kumu* (*Look to the source*) (*Vol. 2*). Honolulu, HI: Hui Hanai.

Pukui, M. K., Handy, E. S. C., & Livermore, K. (1934). *Outline of Hawaiian physical therapeutics: Bulletin 126.* Honolulu, HI: Bishop Museum.

Radloff, L. S. (1977). The CES-D scale: A self-report depression scale for research in the general population. *Applied Psychological Measurement, 1,* 385–401.

Rezentes, W. C. (1996). *Ka Lama Kukui Hawaiian psychology: An introduction.* Honolulu, HI: A'Ali'i Books.

Rosenberg, M. (1965). *Society and the adolescent self-image.* Princeton, NJ: Princeton University Press.

Rust, P. C. (1992). The politics of sexual identity: Sexual attraction and behavior among lesbian and bisexual women. *Social Problems, 39,* 366–386.

Salzman, M. B. (2001). Cultural trauma and recovery: Perspectives from terror. *Trauma, Violence and Abuse, 2,* 172–191.

Spielberger, C. D., Gorsuch, R. L., & Lushene, R. E. (1970). *Manual for the state trait anxiety inventory.* Palo Alto, CA: Consulting Psychologist Press.

Stannard, D. E. (1989). *Before the horror: The population of Hawaii on the eve of Western contact.* Honolulu: University of Hawaii Press.

Wampold, B. E. (2001). *The great psychotherapy debate: Models, methods, and findings.* Mahwah, NJ: Lawrence Erlbaum.

Werner, E. E., & Smith, R. S. (2001). *Journeys from childhood to midlife: Risk, resilience and recovery.* Ithaca, NY: Cornell University.

5

Psychotherapy Within an American Indian Perspective

Jeff King

Contents

Introduction

> I see and admire your manner of living, your good warm houses, your extensive fields of corn, your gardens, your cows, oxen, workhouses, wagons, and a thousand machines, that I know not the use of. I see that you are able to clothe yourselves, even from the weeds and grass. In short you can do almost what you choose. You whites possess the power of subduing almost every animal to your use. You are surrounded by slaves. Every thing about you is in chains and you are slaves yourselves. I fear if I should exchange my pursuits for yours, I too should become a slave.
>
> **—Big Soldier, Osage Chief, describing his perception of White Man's ways to an Indian agent (Deloria, 1999, p. 4)**

These words spoken by Big Soldier in 1820 set the tone for this chapter. Psychotherapy with American Indians in many ways runs contrary to mainstream psychological theories because of significant differences in world view, values, traditions, history, and life-ways.

When writing about counseling in Indian Country, as many American Indians call Native American culture, it is important to first determine whether there is an American Indian psychology that is different from mainstream psychology. My answer is a resounding "Yes!" The rationale for this distinction results from converging themes of American Indian existence and history. Although there are many different beliefs among the over 500 federally recognized tribes in the United States, there are many common themes as well.

The first and most basic common theme is that most, if not all, tribes hold to a world view in which humans are seen as equal to the rest of creation. This is to be contrasted with mainstream society (and psychology) in which humans are thought to be superior to the rest of creation. Views of self, family, society, nature, time, and communication emerge from this basic world view. It is at this point where the two societies diverge and develop ways of life very different from each other.

World Views and Their Effects

If one holds the perspective of mainstream society in which the individual is superior to the rest of creation, then it follows that the primary purpose in life for humans is to gain greater mastery and control over creation. The scientific enterprise is a primary example of this. In mainstream society, science is for the purpose of gaining greater knowledge about the world and how it works for many reasons. Yet the primary underlying reason is for greater control of nature. Psychology assumes these same goals because it is inextricably linked to the scientific enterprise. Nature is seen as something to conquer, and the non-human elements of life are seen as subservient to the goals of human beings.

Contrast this perspective with an American Indian world view in which humans are believed to be equal to the rest of nature. In this view, the purpose is not to have mastery and control, but to live in effective coexistence with creation. Therefore, nature is respected as a fellow living creature and a "co-collaborator" in living life well. Again, the late Vine Deloria Jr. (Jensen, 2000, p. 6) explained this dynamic when asked about the fundamental difference between the Western and indigenous ways of life. He replied, "I think the primary difference is that Indians experience and relate to a living universe, whereas Western people, especially scientists, reduce all things, living or not, to objects."

It is clear that the way people go about living their life is very different within each of these world views. People in the "superior to creation" world view will see nature more as a curiosity and challenge to tame or conquer, and thus approach the world with an attitude of superiority and view all of life as pointing to them. In contrast, American Indians will approach life with a respectful and honoring attitude and view each aspect as containing meaning and lessons for living together, each aspect of life having meaning in itself.

Robert Coles, in his book *The Spiritual Life of Children* (Coles, 1990, p. 25–26), explained this gap caused by differing world views in his telling of meeting a young American Indian (Hopi) girl who explained why he wasn't getting much response from the tribe to his research work: "My grandmother says that [you] live to conquer the sky, and we live to pray to it, and you can't explain yourself to people who conquer, just pray for them, too."

The Concept of Self Varies From Mainstream Psychology

The perception of what constitutes a healthy individual also differs across cultures. In the mainstream culture, it is the person who can do it himself or herself and who is his or her "own person," autonomous, and self-confident. Among Native people, the healthy individual is one who is an integral part of the tribe or community. This person is interdependent, seeks to understand his or her role within the tribe, and works to maintain the harmony within the community. In my tribe (Muscogee), for example, the words for a healthy individual are *geemonzeet heenleen ahdli doeezh*, meaning "this person is there, a person of good repute, around and available to help." Lakota terminology for healthiness is *tiwahe eyecinka egloiyapi nahan oyate op unpi kte*, meaning "the family moving forward interdependently while embracing the values of generosity and interdependence." In Tewa, the term is *ta e go mah ana thla mah*, which translates to "this person is of good demeanor, kind and empathetic to the people and generous to those in need, including the animals." Among the Dine', the term *Hozho* refers to the person living in balance with all of nature, thus being in a state of well-being.

These are but a few examples of how mainstream and Native cultures differ. One can surmise that the values of psychology are embedded in mainstream culture and thus do not reflect those of Native tribes.

Historical Effects and Their Dynamics

American Indian history leads to another of the many converging streams affecting the differences between mainstream and American Indian culture. Because Western European societies have seen themselves as superior to creation, they have also assumed that their way of viewing the world is superior to other cultures as well. Western European society has attempted to change the cultures of the world to its own set of values and ways of life for hundreds of years. American Indians were not excluded from this process, and were subject to the oppression of non-Indian invaders to this country who attempted to subjugate, assimilate, and/or eradicate in the name of what is best for America. This dynamic continues to this day. In fact, most tribes deal daily with scientists, researchers, politicians, policy makers, administrators, educators, and the media insisting they conduct themselves according to the values of mainstream America. For mainstream psychology in particular, the Native client is required to accept a system of psychotherapy that has its origins in mainstream culture.

Evidence-Based Practice as Applied to Counseling American Indians

Evidence-Based Practice in Psychology (EBPP) is the integration of the best available research with clinical expertise in the context of patient characteristics, culture, and preferences (American Psychological Association, 2005). Sadly, there is very little research to demonstrate which techniques are most effective in Indian Country (Whaley & Davis, 2007). In fact, there is evidence indicating that counseling services designed around conventional (researched) methods are inappropriate for Native communities (LaFromboise, Trimble, & Mohatt, 1990). As stated previously, differences in tribal culture, geographical location, and the individual add to the complexity of providing quality services to this population.

There is a considerable amount of research documenting the prevalence of mental illness, behavioral difficulties, substance abuse, domestic violence, poverty, and child welfare issues in Indian Country, but there is very little information providing specific strategies for genuine healing in the therapeutic context (Nebelkopf & Phillips, 2004; Trimble & Gonzales, 2008; Witko, 2006). The general findings indicate that the use of culturally based healing modes within a particular therapeutic context is more effective than not. However, many of these "traditional" treatments, such as the use of the medicine wheel, the sweat lodge, smudging, and the talking circle, are pan-Indian and not necessarily tribal specific. In fact, most of these techniques are generally drawn from Plains tribal groups and are not applicable to or practiced by many other tribes in the United States.

This leaves us to consider how one employs "best practices" based on the best research when there is no research upon which to base these practices. In keeping with the goals of EBPP, when there is a lack of empirically validated treatment effectiveness, there is the call for research on effective clinicians or clinics in their respective communities as a means to study efficacy (Westen, Novotny, & Thompson-Brenner, 2005).

Whaley and Davis (2007) noted that "cultural adaptations" to current EBPP evidence has been shown to be more effective in various communities. Currently, in Indian Country there is a movement underway to contact tribes and mental health workers to determine what has worked well in their respective communities (Isaacs, Huang, Hernandez, & Echo-Hawk, 2005). Similar to the recommendations presented by Westen et al. (2005), Isaacs et al. (2005) gathered information from both practitioners and community members as to what works best in Indian Country. They termed this methodology practice-based evidence and defined it as a range of treatment approaches and supports that are derived from, and supportive of, the positive cultural attributes of the local society and traditions.

Theoretical Orientation

The theoretical orientation in this case study is anchored in American Indian psychology. The type of work that is effective with traditional American

Indian people is not represented among the notable mainstream theorists or theories. Rather, it is anchored within an American Indian world view that focuses more on process than on outcome, relationship over professionalism, indigenous healing methods rather than research-based outcomes, a willingness to journey with clients within their world view and their perceptions of healing, and an equal power dynamic in the therapeutic relationship (Trimble & Gonzales, 2008). When therapy is successful in this context, clients will feel more fully themselves as human beings and as members of their tribal culture. This conception is considered healing, and is viewed as restoration to wholeness. This wholeness includes one as a cultural being. The outcome of therapy should be not that clients have embraced an "outside set of techniques or therapy style" as part of their healing but rather that they have found the healing processes within themselves and the therapy congruent with their own culture. This process of healing reverses a historical dynamic of racism and oppression in which Native people were forced to embrace the ideas and ways of the dominant culture to be successful or get well.

There are over 550 federally recognized tribes and over 150 distinct languages, and tribal beliefs are oftentimes very distinct (even within tribes). These differences include concepts of disease and mental illness, variability in degree of acculturation between and within tribes, and tribal relationships to the land (e.g., tribes on original land versus those relocated). Thus, a set of standard guidelines within an American Indian therapeutic orientation is hard to define because therapy necessarily manifests itself in multiple ways across different tribes in distinct settings.

However, there are underlying processes that are common. American Indian psychology moves away from techniques or formulas for treatment effectiveness and focuses more on the process of healing itself. American Indian psychology is primarily rooted in the world view of Native peoples, and thus acknowledges and respects the history, beliefs, traditions, and spirituality of each tribe or nation it serves. As mentioned previously, American Indian psychology applies itself in such a manner that the persons served become more fully who they are meant to be as both tribal members and cultural beings.

American Indian psychology, although utilizing theories and techniques developed within Western European science, recognizes the limitations of these approaches in applicability to Native cultures. It broadens the psychological approach to healing by acknowledging the spiritual realm, the importance of traditional healing practices, ceremony, and the sacredness of place, person, and life. It may incorporate these aspects into counseling, study, or intervention, depending on permission or invitation by the person, family, or tribe.

There is a broader perspective toward the presenting problem. For example, in many tribal settings, there is a greater degree of hardships or problems experienced by individuals in the months preceding a major ceremony or pilgrimage. Although these might be viewed in isolation or even within a family by mainstream psychological theories, a Native view would consider the fact that prayers have been offered in the previous year (and generations for that matter), and these current difficulties are part of a design to prepare (strengthen) the individual (or family and community) for the ceremony or journey.

American Indian psychology assumes a background of oppression, racism, genocide, and mistreatment by the dominant culture for each individual, family, and community. Furthermore, it is assumed that there is a deep pain experienced that is "the pain of the people." This pain is related to the history of the tribe and the many tragic events that occurred at the hands of White people. It is a collective pain (Brave Heart & DeBruyn, 1988). Today, there are ceremonies to bring healing for this pain, such as the "Wiping of the Tears." American Indian psychology embraces traditional activities as strength for the individual, family, and community. It builds on the existing efforts toward healing. Oftentimes, there are referrals made for a client to seek the help of a medicine man or woman because his or her knowledge extends into realms of life and spirituality that psychologists and counselors typically do not understand. Insight and deep knowledge many times emerge from participation in pilgrimages, ceremonies, peyote meetings, or dances held by the tribe. The degree to which these elements are discussed in therapy depends on the tribal beliefs about disclosing sacred activities to nontribal members. Nevertheless, they are respected and honored by the therapist for the healing they bring.

The dynamic in the therapy room is also very different. Power differentials are reduced significantly. In many traditional circles, academic and professional credentials do not indicate credibility or competence. It is the character of the therapist that matters. I once provided an article to a client about post-traumatic stress disorder. He later stated that he began to read it, but became dissatisfied. He said, "I don't want to know what these other people are saying about this. I want to know what you have to say from your own learning. I can't trust these people in the paper because I don't know them. If you tell me what you know yourself, then I can begin to trust you."

American Indian psychology is still in development and perhaps always will be. Native cultures have always taken in new information and integrated it into tribal ways. As we "put our minds together," there will emerge greater clarity as to what makes up American Indian psychology. What I have described as American Indian psychology does not mean that techniques such as cognitive therapy, behavioral approaches, and so on are not used within Indian Country. Rather, they are employed within a much broader context than is typical within mainstream psychology. There are cultural issues still to consider, such as the 50-minute session (a necessity of billing requirements, but how can one determine the needed time on a particular day?), the therapy office (there are thoughts and feelings associated with offices and "going there" that are in opposition to community values), diagnosis and treatment (although the *Diagnostic and Statistical Manual of Mental Disorders* [American Psychiatric Association, 2000] acknowledges cultural diagnoses, insurance companies do not, and they typically do not reimburse for nontraditional treatment strategies), and collaborative intervention (if a medicine person is called in as part of the overall treatment, there is not a billing designation for reimbursement or a procedure code that acknowledges this form of intervention).

The client's unique interpretations of his or her experiences are considered paramount to any psychotherapeutic model or heuristic. The tribal life-ways and contexts are utilized as vital information to the client's story. In keeping with this particular style of interpreting information, I will use the story of the client to inform the reader more about the malleability of the theoretical orientation. Clearly, there are significant differences between mainstream psychology and psychology among American Indians. The case presented here contains many of these factors and serves to illustrate the points made earlier in this chapter.

Treatment Implications

Treatment implications for this type of therapy are vast. American Indian psychology is the study and practice of what composes the well-being of Native peoples. In this context, both well-being and ill-being are understood as they relate to each person, family, and tribe or nation according to their world view, values, beliefs, and life-ways. Treatment differs from mainstream psychology on many levels. First, the therapist–client dynamic may be very different. The therapist may be known by the client in other societal roles.

In fact, the therapist's credibility may be in question if he or she is not known in other community roles. Furthermore, the power differential is more equalized in the client–therapist relationship. In the case of this particular case study, I knew the client in many other community roles. This "knowing of the other" almost necessitates a more equal power balance in the therapy session. However, this balance is also more congruent with traditional ways of relating. Because of this dynamic, there needs to be greater assurance that confidentiality is paramount. It has been my experience that the discomfort associated with coming into contact with one's therapist in other social settings is minimal to nonexistent in Indian Country, whereas in mainstream psychology there is considerable effort placed on maintaining boundaries and proper protocol when these situations occur and avoiding "dual relationships." The boundary lines are drawn very differently in Native communities.

As illustrated in the case that follows, therapy embraces as important information what the client experiences in traditional spiritual activities and what was being told to her by a medicine man. Life experiences, dreams, and visions are viewed as critical messages indicating the direction life should take. Our therapy incorporated and built on these messages. In fact, these messages served to guide our sessions. Again, the focus was not on a particular technique, but rather on the process that was occurring both outside and inside the therapy room.

Techniques, such as visualization (trance state), are applied given that the client was experienced and comfortable with these states, having related a number of significant dreams, visions, and other experiences with the spirit world. These visualizations were based on the images that had come to her via dreams or visions. It was important that I, as the therapist, stayed very connected to her journey and let that lead the way for our work together. Once again, the importance of the relationship and the sense of shared space were of absolute necessity for therapy to be effective.

Sara's Story

Sara was a 30-year-old Native woman of Blackfeet and Lakota heritage and an acquaintance in the community where I lived at that time. She was married to a Lakota man and had two children through the marriage. Both she and her husband lived in the Lakota way, attending sweat lodges regularly, participating in Sun Dance and Vision Quest, and using traditional healers when necessary. The Sun Dance is considered very central to

Lakota spirituality. It is a new year's ceremony celebrated in the summer, usually on a full moon and lasting for 28 days. However, the last 4 days are the ones on which the dancing and most of the ceremony take place. The person who participates in Sun Dance must be invited, and he or she spends a year in preparation. Typically, there is a 4-year commitment, and one's spiritual journey and well-being are evaluated in these 4-year increments. Each year is spent in sweat lodge ceremonies, as the sweat lodge is a place of spiritual refuge and mental and physical healing, a place to obtain answers and guidance by asking Spirit for needed strength, wisdom and power, meditation, and perhaps vision quests. Vision quests (*Hanblecheyapi*) are times of solitude in a remote sacred place designated by a Holy Man. Literally, the term means "crying out for a vision." It is a time of focused prayer to receive knowledge and understanding from the spirit world.

Initial Sessions

Sara sought out counseling from me because she knew I understood and respected tribal ways and views. She reported to me that she had already been to several non-Indian therapists who were nice, but it became painful to her when they were not able to understand the cultural aspects of her story. Because she already knew me, she was reluctant to ask for therapy, knowing there might be an ethical breach. However, she had made many efforts to get into therapy and had, at one time, traveled to another city to see a therapist. However, none of these efforts were to her satisfaction, as it became clear she needed someone to understand her culture if she were to benefit from therapy.

I was concerned as well and sought supervision from another psychologist in our city. The supervisor thought, given my client's efforts to get therapy elsewhere without success, we should give it a try while making sure we stayed clear in our minds on both our personal and our therapeutic relationships. Interestingly, back in history, this issue would not have been a concern in a tribal community, where the counselors or other healers would be friends, relatives, coworkers, or definitely someone known by the help-seeker. In my experience, Native people do not draw these lines between relationships in the community and in the office, and they do not show up as concerns in the relationship between counselor and client. In fact, one's credibility is diminished as a therapist in the tribal community if he or she is not involved in the community in other roles.

We began our therapy with Sara's talking about how difficult and painful it had been trying to talk to therapists who could not understand her cultural outlook on what was happening to her. She was extremely relieved to have someone who would not blink an eye at her perceptions.

She explained that she had been extremely anxious and afraid for quite some time. She was afraid to sleep with the lights turned off. She had this sense that there were spirit-monsters under her bed, and she was extremely afraid to be by herself. She related her history in which her father had been in the Marines and was an alcoholic. Her father had passed away many years ago, yet there were still disturbing feelings when she remembered him.

When she was a child, her father would bring his military buddies over to the house to drink. She didn't remember much of her childhood or of these experiences when her father was drinking, but she wondered if at some point she had been sexually abused by either her father or one of his friends. She noted that when she became anxious she felt tingling sensations around her wrists and ankles (as if they were tied by a rope). Even in the course of our therapy together, at certain points in our conversations she would experience these sensations.

Early Sessions, Beginning Interventions

In the discussion of her personal history, Sara related that she did not remember much about her childhood. To help facilitate memories, I suggested she draw a floor plan of the house. She had trouble remembering all the rooms, but did the best she could as memory served. I then asked her if she had any feelings associated with the various rooms in the house. Sara replied that there were definite feelings about the various rooms, and when it came to talking about the basement, she became very upset and the tingling sensations became noticeable. I suggested a visualization exercise in which we, together, stood at the top of the stairs. My reason for placing myself with her in the visualization was that if trauma had occurred to her when she was a child, she had experienced it alone. My presence with her in this memory recall could reverse the effect of being alone in that situation.

Sara was able to visualize herself with me at the top of the stairs, and I asked if it was OK to go down the stairs. Hesitatingly, she agreed, and we went down as far as the platform at which the stairs turned at an angle to more stairs leading to the basement floor. It was at this point where her feelings of distress became very intense, and she explained that she could not go any further. I was concerned about her emotional rawness of this experience and wanted to bring closure of some kind before we ended our session. Interestingly, and consistent with an American Indian approach to therapy, earlier in the month I had another Native counselor tell me of a strategy for bringing some control and closure to reviewing traumatic events. I employed this strategy into our session and asked Sara to take a Polaroid snapshot picture of the stairs and basement, then take the picture and place it there on the stairs. She related (while still in the visualization) that there was a place above the door to put the picture. This brought relief and closure to the terror Sara felt, and she was able to go with me back up the stairs and then come back into the present in the therapy room. We discussed the notion that these images and feelings were part of the healing process beginning to open up and take her to the areas necessary for resolve of past trauma. I encouraged her to take these images into the sweat lodge as well and pray for protection and healing as she makes this journey.

Sara was willing to continue this process in our next session. We went into the visualization and went down the stairs to the platform where we had stopped last time. As we started down the next part of the stairs to the basement floor, Sara reported that she became a child of about age 4. We again discussed the notion that this journey was one of healing, and it was necessary for her to become that child. We received these images as from Tunkashila (Grandfather/Creator/God) and therefore considered that we had the protection and guidance from Tunkashila. We had to stop at the bottom of the stairs because the basement seemed very threatening, ominous, and evil. The floor, Sara said, was very cold, and she was unwilling to step down onto it. Once again, we put closure to this experience with gratitude to the Creator and were able to end the session with a pleasant sense that important things were being accomplished through this exercise.

The next session, we again went to the basement, and this time I asked Sara to ask Spirit (Tunkashila) for what she needed to take the next steps. She said that she was given warm slippers, a shawl, and a doll to hold. Drawing strength from these images, she stepped down onto the basement floor. She was very frightened and said she saw the monster-spirits further back in the basement. These were the same monster-spirits she had experienced in her bedroom. I asked her to look for signs of protection from Spirit to let her know that she will be OK as she figures out why they are there. She stated she saw a huge figure of an eagle up on the ceiling. Sara visibly showed relief and settled down after receiving this image. Please note that I was not giving her these images, but rather trusting the process that she would be given what she needed as we went along.

It is important to note that in the process of therapy, we were working on current relationships and struggles in her everyday life. We worked at setting healthier boundaries with family members and determining trust levels among acquaintances, colleagues, and friends. One interesting aspect of this work was dealing with abandonment issues. Sara was open to the messages by her healing and felt two circumstances were important messages for her. The first was when she was camping in a tent at the bottom of a hill upon which her husband was undergoing a vision quest on top of the hill. The medicine man had told her someone would come and keep her company. Sara was extremely afraid of being alone. For example, when her husband was gone from the house on overnight business, she would always either ask a relative or friend to stay with her, or she would go stay at someone else's home. While in the tent, she never heard anyone arrive and felt she was alone, that there must have been some miscommunication and believed no one had come to stay at camp with her. She tossed and turned all night with fear and anxiety over being left alone. At daylight, she emerged from her tent only to find the medicine man's nephew sleeping in a sleeping bag nearby. Sara had not been alone!

The second instance of learning came (and not too distant in time from the other) when Sara felt she was alone at home, and a similar sleepless night occurred. In the morning she came out of her bedroom only to find that her son had been home all along. She felt the message was clear in a spiritual way: that when she thinks she is alone, she is not. Sara translated this spiritually, in the sense that Tunkashila sees her and is with her at all times. Even when she feels alone, she is not. These lessons were not "cognitive thoughts she used to replace irrational thoughts," but rather actual events in her life that synchronistically lined up with what she was currently dealing with in therapy. I believe this kind of learning embeds the lessons deep within one's psyche and emotions because it is not something the client made up, but a lesson out of real-life experience.

I also wondered if this was part of a preparation for someone in her life leaving. Interestingly, soon after these life lessons, a best friend announced that she was moving overseas as a result of a last-minute opportunity to teach disadvantaged youth in Brazil. Ordinarily, Sara's abandonment issues would have manifested in a significant manner. However, having learned these lessons, her friend's leaving was difficult but manageable. Sara saw this incident as both a test and proof of the healing that occurred and, in turn, served to deepen the healing.

The visualization work was seen as complementary to the life-situation work. We viewed her progress with setting boundaries with family and others as a means to move further into the basement in the visualizations. This progress seemed to correspond very well with the timing of what she saw and did in the basement and with her everyday circumstances. One prepared her for the other. Analysis of this dynamic suggests that as Sara set boundaries in her relationships with family and others, she felt more secure in herself and emboldened to step further into the basement and confront the monsters. The success with confronting the monsters in the basement gave her inner strength to set even healthier boundaries in daily relationships.

Along the way, she would remark about changes that had occurred in her daily life: "I can sleep with the light out in the bedroom now! … The monsters are no longer under my bed. They are gone!"

We continued the visualization work in additional sessions and came to the point where Sara was able to step out into the basement and begin to communicate with the monsters. They had at first appeared threatening and dangerous, but they became weaker in facial expression and mannerisms as she came closer. They actually hid from her behind the basement pillars and piping. One of the monsters turned out to be her father, who had been abusive, but now appeared to be sad. At a process–analysis level, as one confronts one's demons, they tend to lose their power. They will also reveal their secrets as to why they were there in the first place.

As the monsters lost their power, they indicated there was a door to another room in the basement. Sara had forgotten about this door, and when she became aware of the room, she became extremely upset. She was terrified of what might be behind it. We drew on the strengths of what had been given to her already, recognizing that she had been prepared for this time. It took a couple of sessions before we were able to open the door.

When the door was opened, Sara went in the room and saw a bed. She felt that if she was sexually abused, this place was probably where it happened, and she was extremely upset. Equally upsetting was that she saw a younger version of herself (approximately age 9) in the room. She cried and told me how this girl looked vacant, empty, and devoid of hope. The girl had been in the room for such a long time and appeared to have lost hope of anything ever changing. Sara was so distraught over this girl that she was sobbing and feeling her hopelessness. Although it was near the end of our session time, I could not see how we could end with things as they were. So I asked Sara what she could communicate to this girl to give her some sense of hope. Sara told the girl she would be back and gave her the doll she had been given months earlier in one of our visualizations. Interestingly, the doll was given to Sara several weeks back for this very moment, and the healing process knew this. However, neither Sara nor I knew this!

Last Sessions

By the time we were completing our work in therapy together, Sara still had the monster-spirits in the basement, but they were no threat to her. They were no longer in her bedroom, as she could sleep with the lights off and was able to sleep well even when alone. Sara reported toward the end of therapy that she even looked forward to having evenings alone! She also stated that she had begun to wear bracelets. This, too, was significant given the history of sensations of feeling like her wrists had been tied when she was young and the fact that she had never worn bracelets beyond childhood.

Sara's healing continues even though she no longer attends therapy sessions with me. During our time together, she was able to connect in deeper ways to her own healing path and spirituality. She continues to strengthen herself in this way and trust her healing to lead her where she needs to go. She knows my door is always open.

Case Conceptualization and Evidence-Based Common Factors

Recognizing that there are no research studies upon which EBPP can be built in working with Native clients, there are general principles used in the context of culturally competent counseling in Indian Country that are part of EBPP's guiding principles.

Therapy consisted of a number of venues: relationship building, cultural identification with values and cultural practices, storytelling, history gathering, boundary setting, visualization, dream interpretation, and spirituality in perspective taking. All of these are consistent with within-tribal values and beliefs and the emphasis of EBPP on cultural-contextual considerations. The visualization was not an unfamiliar venue because trance-like states occur during many ceremonies or during prayer (Krippner, 1993), and visions in American Indian culture are not uncommon. Thus, the visualization was not seen as an imaginary journey. Rather, it was akin to a journey (if not an actual journey) into a parallel spirit world where healing could take place. Sara had similar experiences in the past and therefore was able to invite the memories and images fairly easily. From a mainstream psychological approach, these notions may not make sense or be understandable. Within a Native world view, however, these disparate notions are accepted (e.g., what I do in the physical world affects what I am able to do in the spirit world). There is more room for mystery, and logical understanding of events and perceptions are not necessary. Furthermore, logic may get in your way. In other words, within a Native approach, healing may often come in ways not understood by the conscious mind; however, Native people accept this and feel comfortable with not knowing and simply accepting. Thus, there is a need that the way Native people participate in their healing is a reflection of the differences in culture. This process would not need explanation in traditional American Indian circles.

Overall, I recognized that the client was a woman who was very traditional in her approach to the world, and thus therapy, would need to respect, honor, and build on her traditional outlook. If Sara were more assimilated to mainstream culture in its outlook, therapy would have been very different. Furthermore, her traditional spirituality would need to be an integral part of our therapy, because it formed the core principles by which she lived her life. Thus, it was necessary to align myself with her journey and be a helper along the way. My conceptualization acknowledged that Sara was a woman who had been significantly abused in her past, with very little recognition or memory of what the specific abuse was. She was experiencing a high degree of anxiety and fear of abandonment that interfered with her ability to trust others and to feel good about herself. She had a significant amount of resources in her traditional spirituality and sense of community, family, and friends. Furthermore, she had unique gifts of exquisite sensitivity and openness to the spirit world. These strengths would be built on and trusted to guide the course of therapy. There would be no predetermined plan for therapy but rather a trusting of Sara's spiritual process to bring to the sessions the necessary life situations, dreams, images, and insights to show what the next steps would be.

Additional Clinical Considerations

There have always been healers in Indian Country. Psychotherapy has manifested itself in many forms in many tribes. Modern psychotherapy, as used in tribes, must be seen as an art and not as a technique. If one utilizes a theory and the techniques contained therein, one is acting as a technician, not an artist. Healing in Indian Country is an art. The focus must be on the healing process as it manifests itself within the particular individual and as part of the tribal culture. Healing wears the costume of culture, and as clinicians we must learn to recognize it in its culturally congruent form. Our therapy must be adapted to the culture to the extent that when the therapeutic process is completed, clients feel even more fully the cultural being they are. In this context, they believe the healing is theirs, not the therapist's. The effective practice in Indian Country is one in which the history of the tribe is known, felt, and honored as the world view of the tribe is understood and taken into account in the counseling process. Consequently, the background factors of historical trauma, the dynamics of racism, White supremacy, and oppression are, in effect, reversed in the therapy room and in the healing process.

This conceptualization is a very different way of approaching psychotherapy. However, if we are serious in our efforts to provide best practice in Indian Country, the hard work of changing our own views about psychology and healing must be undertaken. It is not that these efforts have been made and have failed. It is that the task at hand has been found difficult and therefore untried.

Author's Personal Dimensions of Diversity and World View

I am a tribally enrolled member of the Muscogee (Creek) Nation of Oklahoma. My father's ethnicity was White. Growing up, our family was more connected to my mother's side of the family and our Native heritage. We would attend stomp dances, gatherings, funerals, and other tribal activities when we were living in Oklahoma. My aunt served on the tribal council for 13 years. My mother's own journey was similar to many American Indians of her generation. She did not speak English until she was school aged, as her mother never spoke English. She also attended an American Indian boarding school for part of her education, which she stated was inferior to public school education and racist. My mother experienced harsher forms of racism than I. She remembered when the signs on the stores said, "No dogs or Indians allowed!" Given this harsh treatment, she vowed that her children would not experience the pain she had undergone. Therefore, she deliberately did not pass on the language or the culture to her children. However, unbeknownst to her, she did pass on a lot of the culture. Values, mannerisms, and other background nonspecific behaviors were passed on to us children. I grew up knowing I was Creek, but did not make much about it. Rarely did I experience discrimination, and it was not until I was in college studying psychology that I began to look at the issues confronting American Indian people. I was extremely alarmed at the ethnocentric bias in the research and the lack of cultural sensitivity in the textbooks and theories of psychotherapy. This reaction only fueled my determination to discover and make evident these important aspects.

My studies focused on cross-cultural psychology in general and American Indians in particular. My thinking was that you could not understand Native people without an understanding of other ethnic minorities in the United States, and you could not understand the ethnic minority experience in the United States without knowledge of what minorities around the world were experiencing.

My learning has been threefold: the academic pursuit of information, the participation in Native communities, and the clinical knowledge derived as a practitioner. These converging dimensions have led to an approach to psychotherapy that has been illustrated in this chapter. I do not believe that expertise comes from academic studies or necessarily being a clinician. Rather, I strongly believe (and my clients have taught me) that there is a healing process woven into the fabric of the universe and of which we can learn its processes. My journeying with clients in their healing has allowed me to discover some of the patterns and principles of this healing process. There is much to communicate about what all this means, but suffice it to say that the healing process manifests itself through culture, through the individual's own experience, and through the clinician's own life processes. It uses whatever means are available. It is up to the person to pay attention to his or her healing and learn to hear it, to see it, and to trust it. Once this healing begins, wonderful things occur.

Therapeutic Recommendations

The following are general guidelines for characteristics necessary for effective counseling with American Indian clients.

1. Be flexibile. Overall conclusions by both practitioners and researchers suggest this is the most important characteristic for counseling effectiveness with Native Americans and other ethnic minorities. Flexibility

refers to a willingness to let go or set aside one's previous assumptions about how therapy is supposed to work and hear from the client and community to determine one's approach. Second, it refers to how one views the role of counselor (i.e., Do you stay only in your office, or do you visit clients in their homes? Do you seek additional help by consulting with local medicine persons? Are you willing to self-disclose?).

2. Be genuine. It is the authentic person who will gain the respect and confidence of a Native client. Native people are quite sensitive to "wannabees," those who "want to be" Indian, but aren't. Counselors should be comfortable in their own skin and not want to co-opt Native ways for themselves. I had one client state this about non-Indians: "They have taken our land, our children, our men, our life-ways, and now they even want to take our beliefs!" Be willing to admit you don't know. Be willing to admit your ignorance. Be willing to admit your lack of knowledge about the tribe. You must also be willing to "come out from behind the desk." That is, you must not identify yourself so much with the counselor role that you cannot be authentic in the session.

3. Be knowledgeable. Seek to become knowledgeable about the history, world view, and other specific tribal information about the population you are serving. This goes deeper than simply reading or hearing people talk; it requires listening with one's heart and feeling the information. My own conviction is that if you cannot feel "the pain of the people," you will be limited in your ability to connect with your clients.

4. Be willing. Be willing to learn, listen, read, and seek out information regarding the population you serve. This is a bit sensitive, as you do not want to be assertive in your information gathering. This is typically seen as rude and self-inviting. Rather, by being willing, you can eventually sense when you get the invitation to acquire information related to the tribe. It is then when your clients (or community members) will tell you their stories.

5. Be aware of acculturation issues. Much of this chapter has focused on Native people who identify as traditional or bicultural. However, Native people range from being very traditional to thoroughly assimilated to White culture. It is important to determine where in this sphere your client is moving. Discussion of traditional healing may not be important to someone who is assimilated, and he or she may prefer counseling that is rooted more in Western European models of therapy. Usually, by listening to the client, you can determine where he or she is in this process. It is typically rude to ask.

6. Be aware of traditional healing. Carolyn Attneave, one of the first American Indian psychologists, talked about how traditional healers could be right under practitioners' noses and they not know it. They could be assistants or maintenance persons at the clinic. It is extremely important to know that most, if not all, tribes have traditional healers. Even in urban areas, there is a strong preference to seek out traditional healers. This is a difficult area to negotiate, because there are also many people who proclaim to be traditional healers but are phony. It is important to learn what makes someone authentic as a traditional healer and what to look for to identify imposters. Typically, traditional healers will not self-identify, and you will have to find out about them by word of mouth. Another aspect of knowing about traditional healing is that oftentimes your counseling can be more effective if it is in alignment with what your client is getting from the traditional healer and corresponds to the timing of the ceremonies and other spiritual activities. There are typically "curious hardships" experienced by tribal people just before important ceremonies or activities. It is believed that these are preparations for entering into these important times. Finally, if your client is traditional, it may be helpful to make a referral to a traditional healer who can address the client's problem from an entirely different perspective.

7. Be aware of medication issues. Sometimes clients will be taking herbs or other remedies prescribed by a medicine man or woman or folk healer. There is the possibility that these can counteract with any medications prescribed by the psychiatrist or physician.

8. Understand world view differences. As part of one's study of the tribe or community, it should become readily apparent that Native people see the world differently. It is extremely important to understand one's own world view and its implications for viewing life and developing values, conceptions of self, relationships, and so on. One Native person stated, "I'll tell you what an identity crisis is. It is when you do not know the land, and the land doesn't know you." Clearly, this illustrates an outcome of a certain world view that is different from mainstream society. Thus, it is important not only to first understand your own world view but to also understand the world view of your client and to work within that world view as much as possible.

9. Be comfortable with silence. This is related to world view and life-ways, but many Native people tend to be quieter than non-Indians. It is not unusual in Indian Country to have a guest who sits in your house and does not talk that much. It is not the talk that makes the get-together

meaningful, but rather one's presence. Silence in counseling may create a comfort level for a Native client. One Native commented on a White therapist "filling the air with noise," referring to how talkative the counselor was. Silence is not necessarily a defense!

10. Maintain eye contact. I have had clients who looked at me perhaps two or three times during our session. It is part of the culture. Unfortunately, I have read reports that have used amount of eye contact as a measure of progress. Lack of eye contact is not a sign of low self-esteem or avoidance—it is cultural!

11. Have humor. As opposed to the stereotype of the American Indian as stoic, Native people have a great sense of humor and enjoy good laughs—even at their own expense. It has also been a deep coping strategy for tribal people for dealing with the very difficult times and situations many face on a daily basis. Using humor to laugh at yourself may be a means for building the therapeutic relationship.

12. Dress casually. Typically, dressing professionally is a barrier in communication to Native people. It represents the values of White society and suggests that you identify with that part of White society. It further suggests that you are not willing to identify with your client and his or her community.

13. Make room for mystery. Traditional Native thinking is not the same as the logical, linear communication style found in mainstream society. Thus, seemingly disparate notions such as "shape-shifting"—people or spirits appearing in another form, such as an animal—are not disputed by traditional Indians. Seeing spirits or having visions or other experiences rarely seen in the White world are common for Native people. It is not necessary for the counselor to believe these things to be true for himself or herself; however, it is necessary for the counselor to believe these things to be true for the client. If one tries to explain all the phenomena that Native people may present in session, one will cause discomfort and create a barrier in the counseling relationship. Rather, make room for mystery. Truly, we don't know everything, and everything cannot be explained.

14. See spirituality as an integral part of life. It is sad that within science, and more particularly psychology, spirituality is largely ignored. It is sad because it forms the core of most people in the world, and definitely among American Indians. Spirituality is not seen as separate from everyday life. Rather, it is interwoven into all aspects of life and conveys meaning throughout the various daily experiences.

Discussion Questions

1. What are the different ways that the cultural backgrounds of many American Indians influence the psychotherapeutic relationship?
2. How might a counselor prepare himself or herself for this type of culturally congruent counseling?
3. Given this chapter's information, should the underlying world views of psychotherapy and counseling be reevaluated? If so, in what way? If not, why?
4. How does one begin to understand the healing process as it manifests itself in Native culture?
5. If psychotherapy is the acquiring of effective techniques for addressing psychological distress, what are the important skills, attitudes, and so on that a counselor needs to acquire?
6. If psychotherapy is more of an art than use of proven strategies, then what are the important skills, attitudes, and so on that a counselor needs to acquire?

Resources

Deloria, V., Deloria, B., Foehner, K., & Scinta, S. (Eds.). (1999). *Spirit and reason: The Vine Deloria reader*. Golden, CO: Fulcrum.

Duran, E., & Duran, B. (1995). *American Indian post-colonial psychology*. Albany: University of New York Press.

Katz, J. (1985). The sociopolitical nature of counseling. *The Counseling Psychologist, 13*(4), 615–624.

McIntosh, P. (1988). *White privilege and male privilege: A personal account of coming to see correspondences through work in women's studies*. Wellesley, MA: Wellesley College, Center for Research on Women.

Mohatt, G., & Eagle Elk, J. (2002). *The price of a gift: A Lakota healer's story*. Lincoln: University of Nebraska Press.

Pinderhughes, E. (1989). *Understanding race, ethnicity, and power: The key to efficacy in clinical practice*. New York: Free Press.

Sage, G. (1997). Counseling American Indian adults. In C. C. Lee (Ed.), *Multicultural issues in counseling: New approaches to diversity* (2nd ed., pp. 35–52). Alexandria, VA: American Counseling Association.

Smedley, A. (1999a). Antecedents of the racial worldview. In *Race in North America: Origin and evolution of a worldview* (pp. 41–71). Boulder, CO: Westview Press.

Smedley, A. (1999b). The rise of science: Sixteenth-to-eighteenth century classifications of human diversity. In *Race in North America: Origin and evolution of a worldview* (pp. 150–168). Boulder, CO: Westview Press.

Voss, R. W., Douville, V., Little Soldier, A., & Twiss, G. (1999). Tribal and shamanic-based social work practice: A Lakota perspective. *Social Work, 44*(3), 228–241.

Whaley, A. L., & Davis, K. E. (2007). Cultural competence and evidence-based practice in mental health services: A complementary perspective. *American Psychologist, 62*(6), 563–574.

Yamato, J. (1992). Something about the subject makes it hard to name. In P. S. Rothenberg (Ed.), *Race, class, and gender in the United States: An integrated study.* New York: St. Martin's.

References

American Psychiatric Association. (2000). *Diagnostic and statistical manual of mental disorders* (text rev.). Washington, DC: Author.

American Psychological Association. (2005). Policy statement on Evidence-Based Practice in Psychology. Retrieved from http://www2.apa.org/practice/ebpstatement.pdf

Brave Heart, M. Y. H., & DeBruyn, L. (1988). The American Indian Holocaust: Healing unresolved grief. *American Indian and Alaska Native Mental Health Research*, 8(2), 56–78.

Coles, R. (1990). *The spiritual life of children.* Boston: Houghton Mifflin.

Deloria, V. (2000). How science ignores the living world. Retrieved from http://www.thesunmagazine.org/buffalo.html

Isaacs, M. R., Huang, L. N., Hernandez, M., & Echo-Hawk, H. (2005). The road to evidence: The intersection of evidence-based practices and cultural competence in children's mental health. Policy paper, National Alliance of Multi-Ethnic Behavioral Health Association. Retrieved from http://www.nambha.org/Documents/RoadtoEvidence_93006.pdf

Jensen, D. (2000, July). Where the buffalo go: How science ignores the living world. An interview with Vine Deloria. *The Sun, 6*(295). Chapel Hill, NC: Sun Publishing Company.

Krippner, S. (1993). Cross-cultural perspectives on hypnotic-like procedures used by Native healing practitioners. In S. Rhue, S. J. Lynn, & I. Kirsch (Eds.), *Handbook of clinical hypnosis.* Washington, DC: American Psychological Association.

LaFromboise, T. D., Trimble, J. E., & Mohatt, J. R. (1990). Counseling intervention and American Indian tradition: An integrative approach. *The Counseling Psychologist, 18*, 628–654.

Nebelkopf, E., & Phillips, M. (2004). *Healing and mental health for American Indians: Speaking in red.* Walnut Creek, CA: AltaMira Press.

Trimble, J. E., & Gonzales, J. (2008). Cultural considerations and perspectives for providing psychological counseling for American Indian Indians. In P. B. Pedersen, J. G. Draguns, W. J. Lonner, & J. E. Trimble (Eds.), *Counseling across cultures* (6th ed., pp. 93–111). Thousand Oaks, CA: Sage.

Westen, D., Novotny, C., & Thompson-Brenner, H. (2005). EBP EST: Reply to Crits-Cristoph et al. (2005) and Weisz et al. (2005). *Psychological Bulletin, 131*, 427–433.

Whaley, A. L., & Davis, K. E. (2007). Cultural competence and evidence-based practice in mental health services: A complementary perspective. *American Psychologist, 62*(6), 563–574.

Witko, T. M. (2006). *Mental health care for urban Indians: Clinical insights from Native practitioners.* Washington, DC: American Psychological Association.

6

Spirituality and Psychotherapy
A Gay Latino Client

Fernando Ortiz

Contents

Introduction

Spirituality and religion are particularly important in the Mestizo world view (Ramirez, 2004). The religious diversity of Latinos/as may include affiliations to Christian (e.g., Catholic, Protestant, Evangelical, and nondenominational institutions) and non-Christian groups (e.g., Jewish and Muslim). The popular religiosity of Latinos/as may also include spiritual practices and beliefs in *curanderismo* (folk healing), Spiritualism, *Santería*, *brujería* (witchcraft), Buddhism, and transcendental meditation (Baez, 1996; Baez & Hernandez, 2001). For centuries, Latinos/as and other ethnic minorities have integrated these beliefs into their life, and they have attributed special meaning, including therapeutic and healing power, to their religious practices (Dudley-Grant, 2003; Mio & Iwamasa, 2003). Cultural competence entails knowing this prominence given to religion and spirituality and, more specifically, how to integrate research findings with clinical practice (Sue & Sue, 2003).

Research on Religion and Spirituality

Literature exploring the significance of religious and spiritual meaning in psychotherapy is abundant (Bergin, 1991; Bergin, Masters, & Richards,

1987; Clay, 1996; Helminiak, 2001; Pargament, 1997; Schulte, Skinner, & Claibom, 2002; Shafranske, 1996). In an extensive review of the literature published during the past century, Powers (2005) found that the number of publications on religiousness and spirituality in psychotherapy dramatically increased in the 1970s. Walker, Gorsuch, and Tan (2004) conducted a meta-analysis and concluded, among other things, that many therapists are already incorporating religion and spirituality in therapy.

In general, meta-analyses and reviews of the empirical literature on the relationship between religion and spirituality and mental and physical health have found many positive associations. Some of these include personal adjustment, recovery from physical and mental illness, control of compulsive behaviors, absence of psychological symptoms, lower mortality, and mental well-being (Bergin, 1983; George, Larson, Koenig, & McCullough, 2000; McCullough, Hoyt, Larson, Koenig, & Thoresen, 2000). Studies have also found a negative correlation with depression, anxiety, and substance abuse (Knox, Catlin, Casper, & Schlosser, 2005). Recently, an issue of *American Psychologist* specifically addressed this linkage between spirituality and mental and physical health and its importance for psychological research and practice (Hill & Pargament, 2003; Miller & Thoresen, 2003; Powell, Shahabi, & Thoresen, 2003; Seeman, Fagan-Dubin, & Seeman, 2003).

In spite of the significant role played by spirituality and religiosity for certain ethnic groups and the extensive extant research, two issues remain problematic for researchers and practitioners: how to clearly define religious and spiritual experience, and how to effectively incorporate it into psychotherapeutic practice (Steinfel, 2000; Zinnbauer, Pargament, & Scott, 1999). Without a clear scientific operational definition, most authors have conceptually differentiated the two concepts and suggested that religion or religiousness implies behavioral adherence to institutional practices and rituals and doctrinal assent to beliefs, dogmas, and precepts (Miller & Thoresen, 2003; Worthington & Sandage, 2001). Spirituality, on the other hand, is often seen as personal, subjective, emotional, inward, and unsystematic (Hill & Pargament, 2003). However, some have warned about the dangers of this conceptual polarization, claiming that it leads to simplistic categorizations (e.g., "spirituality is good," "religion is bad") and unnecessary bifurcations because many people experience spirituality within the context of organized and institutional religion (Hill et al., 2000; Hill & Pargament, 2003; Knox et al., 2005; Pargament, 1999).

Integration of religiousness and spirituality into psychotherapy can be a challenging task, especially in our era of empirically supported treatments or evidence-based interventions (Chambless & Hollon, 1998; Pargament, Murray-Swank, & Tarakeshwar, 2005). Many practitioners have reported that they are not adequately trained to work sensitively and effectively with clients whose world views and lifestyles are deeply spiritual or religious. Some may also be ambivalent about bringing religion and spirituality into the psycho-therapeutic setting because of fears of imposing their own values (Mack, 1994). Their uncertainty may be related as well to the minimal coursework, supervision, and training regarding the place of religion and spirituality in therapy (Brawer, Handal, Fabricatore, Roberts, & Wajda-Johnston, 2002; Richards & Bergin, 2000; Schulte, Skinner, & Claiborn, 2002; Shafranske & Gorsuch, 1984; Shafranske & Malony, 1990). More important, religious and spiritual experiences are very complex and multidimensional, and they usually occur in interaction with other important aspects of one's culture and identity (Walker et al., 2004).

This chapter offers some considerations on the integration of religious-ness and spirituality and psychotherapy in the context of a culturally diverse client. Religiousness and spirituality are basic dimensions of the human condition (Sue, Bingham, Porché-Burke, & Vasquez, 1999) and particularly salient for the optimal human functioning of people of color (Constantine & Sue, 2006). A case is presented, followed by a detailed discussion of the main issues revolving around three main themes: culture, seropositive status, and religion and spirituality. The case exemplifies the complexity of psychosocial, cultural, and spiritual dimensions often embedded in clients' experiences. A theoretical conceptualization of the issues is described, along with specific interventions used. Discussion of interventions is informed by empirically based perspectives (Pargament et al., 2005) and evaluated from the perspec-tive of the Principles of Empirically Supported Interventions (Wampold, Lichtenberg, & Waehler, 2002), with special emphasis on multicultural perspectives (Quintana & Atkinson, 2002).

Case

Gabriel, a 25-year-old Mexican American male, came to therapy and, dur-ing the first session, after some initial rapport building, hesitantly revealed to the counselor that he was gay. However, Gabriel reported that he was not out to most of his family and friends for fear of being shunned from family reunions, social gatherings, and church activities. He considered himself fairly acculturated (bicultural) and speaks Spanish, especially with his mother, who is an immigrant from Mexico. He described his family as relatively traditional in gender issues, sexuality, and religious values (i.e., Catholic). He reported feeling self-conscious in family interactions, especially when interacting with the other males in the family, whom he described as *muy hombres* (very manly) and often telling homophobic jokes. He mentioned that he is dreading the reaction they might have when they find out his true identity. He feared being stigmatized by the family and ostracized from his close family and friends.

The client was prompted by his physician to see this counselor after becoming infected with HIV. He indicated that he most likely contracted it while having sex with other Latino men who consider themselves to be heterosexual. He reported feeling emotionally and spiritually conflicted. He indicated that recently he had been attending a Buddhist temple where he was learning about mindfulness and acceptance. He highlighted the fact that he considers himself spiritual, but not necessarily religious. He described his spiritual journey as conflicted and isolated. He noted that he felt like he had to live a double life, hiding his sexuality from a judgmental community and vengeful God. He also learned that homosexual acts were sinful, and thus he had struggled to reconcile his spirituality and sexuality. He characterized his life as one of sexual silence, internalized homophobia, and anger at God. He also possessed a strong sense of shame, fear of rejection, fear of judgment by God, and low self-esteem.

The client expressed a need for self-acceptance, a sense of belonging, and meaningful relationships. He yearned for intimacy with others, in which he could be his true self and reveal his gay identity without the fear of rejection. Given his recent diagnosis, he expressed existential concerns about his future, the meaning of life, and the prospect of effectively coping with the possibility of failing health and possible death. He found it challenging to rid himself of deeply entrenched negative self-views and damaging self-talk.

Multilayered presenting problems require multilevel interventions. Gabriel's presentation includes at least these important world view components: ethnicity, acculturation, family cultural dynamics, religion, spirituality, sexual orientation, gender roles, homophobia, seropositivity, perceived stigma, and psychological distress. The therapeutic approach consisted of (a) spiritually oriented and multiculturally sensitive psychotherapeutic interventions, (b) mindfulness-based suggestions, and (c) cognitive-behavioral strategies.

Theoretical Orientation: Multiculturally Informed and Spiritually Integrated

In the context of Gabriel's ethnic identity, it is important to keep in mind the following principles of Mestizo psychology (Ramirez, 2004) when addressing Gabriel's complex clinical presentation: (a) the person is an open system (i.e., inseparable from the physical and social environments in which he or she lives); (b) the spiritual world holds the key to destiny, personal identity, and life mission; (c) community identity and responsibility to the group are of central importance in development; (d) the foundations of a good adjustment to life (mental health) are liberation, justice, freedom, and empowerment; (e) total development of abilities and skills is achieved through self-challenge (i.e., endurance of pain and hardship); (f) the search for self-knowledge, individual identity, and life meaning is a primary goal; and (g) duality of origin, life in the universe, and education within the family play a central role in personality development (i.e., polar opposites—male and female, good and evil, God and human, sin and virtue, illness and health—were often fused in Latino/a indigenous cosmologies).

From the perspective of the Principles of Empirically Supported Interventions, several principles can aid in selecting empirically supported interventions. Interventions can be identified at various levels depending on their level of efficacy (Wampold et al., 2002). Both qualitative and meta-analytic reviews provide substantial evidence supporting general efficacy of cognitive-behavioral approaches and mindfulness-based interventions. However, there is less empirical evidence supporting the use of these interventions with Mexican Americans. Further research needs to demonstrate clinical success with clients from ethnic and sexual minority backgrounds struggling with specific problems, as with the case of Gabriel (Bernal & Scharrón-Del-Rio, 2001; Quintana & Atkinson, 2002). Ethical guidelines suggest that existing psychotherapies be modified to become culturally appropriate for ethnic minority persons. Nagayama Hall (2001), for example, identified interdependence, spirituality, and discrimination as constructs that are particularly salient for ethnic minorities and can be incorporated in culturally sensitive theoretical models of psychotherapy for multiple ethnic minority groups.

There has been some psychological literature that has favorably presented the use of cognitive-behavioral interventions with Latinos/as (Organista & Muñoz, 1996). However, outcome research on the efficacy of cognitive-behavioral therapy (CBT) with Latinos/as has been extremely limited. It could be especially helpful with Latino/a clients whose expectations include immediate symptom relief, guidance and advice, and a short-term, problem-centered approach (Miranda, 1976; Torres-Matrullo, 1982). Comas-Díaz (1981) found CBT to be significantly efficacious in treating depression with Puerto Rican mothers. In addition, Organista, Muñoz, and Gonzalez (1994) found significant pre-to-posttreatment reductions in depression in a sample of Latinos/as. Elligan (1997) reported the successful integration of CBT to treat a bicultural male client (Mexican Palestinian) with dysthymia. Hendricks and Thompson (2005) successfully treated a Latina woman suffering from bulimia nervosa by integrating both CBT and interpersonal psychotherapy. Gelman, Lopez, and Pérez-Foster (2005) found significant before–after treatment improvement in a 12-session CBT protocol for depression with Latinas. In their analyses of evidence-based interventions for diverse populations, Muñoz and Mendelson (2005, p. 791) concluded, "Despite the fact that CBT was originally developed and tested with predominantly European American populations, we predicated that its core principles would be applicable to diverse groups provided that they are presented in a culturally sensitive manner."

Research on the clinical efficacy of mindfulness practices with Latinos/as has been more limited. Gillispie (2006) found positive mental health outcomes among Latinos using mindfulness procedures. More specifically, the use of mindfulness-based interventions was related to decreased trait anxiety levels and significantly related to biculturalism, that is, a more flexible acculturation transition. At the broadest level of extant empirical evidence, the combination of mindfulness-based cognitive therapy has considerable empirical support in treating personality disorders (Huss & Baer, 2007). Several studies have found mindfulness to be associated with psychological well-being (Brown & Ryan, 2003). Mindfulness, in combination with CBT interventions, significantly reduced relapse in recovered depressed patients (Teasdale et al., 2002). A special issue of *Clinical Psychology: Science and Practice* critically reviewed clinical interventions based on mindfulness (Baer, 2003; Hayes & Wilson, 2003; Kabat-Zinn, 2003; Roemer & Orsillo, 2003; Teasdale, Segal, & Williams, 2003). After an extensive and empirical review of the literature using meta-analytic techniques, Baer (2003) concluded that some mindfulness-based interventions may be helpful in the treatment of several disorders. Kabat-Zinn (2003) highlighted the importance of mindfulness-based interventions and how they can be sensitively used in cross-cultural settings. Mindfulness has been heavily influenced by spirituality, primarily Eastern meditative and Christian contemplative traditions, and thus can be suitably integrated into psychotherapy in the form of meditation practices (e.g., sitting and walking meditation) and other forms of mindfulness practice (e.g., mindfulness of eating, breathing, etc.) (Dimidjian & Linehan, 2003).

Treatment Implications

For clarity, this section describes treatment considerations along three major dimensions that are considered to be the main areas of therapeutic emphasis. Critical issues are highlighted in the form of questions at the end of each dimension.

Cultural Dimension

As a second-generation gay Mexican American male, Gabriel has learned to navigate between two different ethnic and cultural world views: the Euro-American culture and the Mexican culture. Mexican culture differs from Euro-American culture in many ways. For example, Hofstede (1980, 2001) ranked 53 cultures along four value-based dimensions. On the Individualism dimension, Mexico ranked 32nd and the United States ranked 1st. As noted by others (e.g., Díaz-Loving & Draguns, 1999), Mexican culture is relatively collectivistic, with a strong emphasis on close family and social relations. Loyalty in a collectivistic culture is paramount, especially to the family. For Mexican and Mexican American gay and lesbian people, this is an especially important factor as they may feel conflict because of values of respect (*respeto*) and family honor and loyalty (*familismo*). It can make the identification and integration of one's sexual orientation (coming-out process) even more difficult. In addition, possible family rejection deeply affects these Mexicans and Mexican Americans, who are rooted in these family values. Thus, the loss of the family as the primary support group is paramount to Mexican American clients.

Among other value differences, Mexico ranked much higher on the Power Distance dimension (tied for 5th) than the United States (38th), suggesting a greater acceptance of unequal power and status in Mexican culture. Cultural institutions (e.g., church, traditions) enjoy a certain status and influence as well. Mexico also ranked higher (6th) than the United States (15th) on the Masculinity dimension, perhaps reflecting the greater differentiation of gender roles in Mexican society. Masculinity (*machismo*) enjoys a certain status in the culture (Díaz-Guerrero, 2001). On the Uncertainty Avoidance dimension, Mexico ranked 82nd and the United States ranked 43rd, indicating the Mexican society's low level of tolerance for uncertainty. In an effort to minimize or reduce this level of uncertainty, strict rules, laws, policies, and regulations are adopted. The ultimate goal of this culture is to control everything to eliminate or avoid the unexpected. The combination of Catholicism and the cultural dimensions may reinforce a world view predicated in the belief that there is an absolute Truth (Hofstede, 2001).

Moreover, according to Díaz-Guerrero (1967), every culture develops a system of interrelated historic-socio-cultural premises (HSCPs) which give shape to most psychological processes of the individual. An HSCP is an affirmation underlying the specific logic of the group (Díaz-Guerrero, 2001). These premises are typically endorsed by the majority of the culture's members because they embody the culture's values, norms, beliefs, traditions, and prescriptions for behavior (Díaz-Guerrero, 1992). Díaz-Guerrero (1993) categorized the HSCPs as prescriptive or as related to coping style. Nine HSCPs were derived in a factor analysis of 123 belief and value statements: machismo (male supremacy over women), affiliative obedience (obedience toward parents and figures of authority), value of virginity, abnegation (sacrifice of personal needs for the sake of others), fear of authority, family status quo (women's faithfulness to husbands, and children's emulation of parental traits), respect over love (attitudes toward parents based on respectful obedience), family honor, and cultural rigidity (parental strictness and restrictions on women's work and courting) (Díaz-Guerrero, 1982).

Based on these cultural dimensions, the following critical questions warrant exploration in therapy: What is Gabriel's level of acculturation and relative endorsement of traditional Mexican values? Which HSCPs can be used as a framework to understand his intrapersonal conflict with religion and spirituality? To what extent are his values and sexual orientation conflicting? How can Gabriel be assisted to integrate his cultural values and sexual orientation?

Seropositive Status

As a self-identified gay Mexican American male with seropositive status, Gabriel has encountered stereotypical and homophobic views that have brought up considerable shame, guilt, and psychological distress (Carballo, 1989). This set of psychosocial experiences (i.e., oppression, stigma, homophobia, and discrimination) has been identified as extremely devastating for sexual minorities, particularly for ethnic minority groups (Díaz, Ayala, Bein, Henne, & Marin, 2001; Díaz, Ayala, & Bein, 2004; Hoffman, 1993). Some have suggested that the relatively high prevalence of HIV infection among Latinos/as may be due to social context and internalized sociocultural experiences, which likely affect sexual behavior and sexual risk management (Zea, Reisen, & Díaz, 2003). Traditionally, sexual behavior has been conceptualized as highly personal and individualistic. The emphasis has been placed on the person's sense of identity, knowledge, attitudes, beliefs, and perceptions. This results in assessment, treatment, and prevention models for HIV that lack cultural sensitivity and validity.

On the other hand, Díaz (1998, 2000) proposed a theoretical model that explains the sexual behavior of Latino gay men as a personal dialectic between cultural values and the internalization of these into sexual scripts. Not only are sexual orientation and identity about the individual, but in a highly collectivistic culture, sexual identity also reflects the family and the social group. Sexual categorization is also dependent on cultural notions of masculinity and femininity. In European American culture, individuals self-identify themselves in sexual categories (e.g., gay, bisexual, and straight), whereas Latinos' sexual categorization, especially in the case of gay male relationships, is primarily based on the relational category within the dyad (e.g., active or passive, top or bottom). Therefore, some gay Latino males may not necessarily refer to themselves as gay, especially in more traditional cultural settings, and yet prefer sex with other men (Díaz, 2000).

Thus, from a clinical perspective, several critical issues need to be considered: What messages or scripts regarding gender identity and sexual orientation has Gabriel internalized, and how much do they influence his sexual behavior? What role, if any, have these external sociocultural forces and internalized psychosocial scripts played in putting him at risk for contracting HIV? What cultural images of sexual minorities was he exposed to in his ethnic sociocultural context, and what characteristics (positive, negative, neutral, contradictory) did these images evoke for him? How does Gabriel relate to and cope with the broader gay community, which may not necessarily hold similar sociocultural constructions of gender and identity?

Spiritual and Religious Struggles

Gabriel indicated that religion and spirituality have played an important role in his life. Historically speaking, most Latinos/as have ancestry in Latin

America, a continent known for its devout religiosity. Catholicism has been an influential institution shaping the world view of a large number of Latinos/as. It has defined theological notions such as God and sin and instituted certain moral codes. Of particular relevance to our case are moral precepts regarding sexuality. Official Catholic teaching has consistently judged all homosexual activity as "gravely sinful" (McBrien, 1994). Gay Catholics who may experience a difficult time accepting the institutional moral teachings may report a greater sense of alienation, higher degree of anxiety about their sexuality, cognitive dissonance, or the inability to integrate seemingly contradictory identities (Loseke & Cavendish, 2001; O'Brien, 1991).

When struggling with seemingly contradictory identities, some Catholics opt to leave the institutional practice of Catholicism and may join religious groups or institutions with a more accepting and tolerant view of homosexuality (McNeill, 1993). Such is the case of Dignity, a Catholic community for lesbian, gay, bisexual, and transgendered (LGBT) people. Wagner, Serafini, Rabkin, Remien, and Williams (1994) found that involvement in Dignity fosters positive attitudes in integrating one's homosexuality and religious identity.

It would be a distorted view to claim that all religious institutions promote teachings or views that are characteristically homophobic or in some way oppressive and marginalizing of LGBT people (Bouldrey, 1995). Although some positive pastoral developments have been made toward the inclusion and acceptance of LGBT people into religious communities, some of the largest religious bodies (e.g., Catholicism, Islam) continue to struggle theologically regarding the acceptance of more progressive views on gay and lesbian issues (e.g., same-sex partnerships, ordination of openly gay and lesbian individuals, etc.). Some religious writers have advanced positive theological views that have the human dignity of LGBT people as a basic premise, saying they deserve respect and human rights (Alexander & Preston, 1996; Balka & Rose, 1989).

From the analysis of the literature and from clinical experience working with gay and lesbian clients struggling with religious and spiritual issues, one may find three broad levels of affiliation: religiously committed, religiously compliant, and religiously conflicted. The religiously committed would include most LGBT people who are associated with a religious group, active in the respective religious practices of the institution, and, for the most part, are receptive to the religious views on sexuality and specifically the institutional teaching on homosexuality (Greene & Herek, 1994; Tigert, 1996). The religiously compliant may include the LGBT people who self-identify as members of the religious institution and adhere to the general religious rules and practices (Comstock, 1996; Glaser, 1996). This level especially occurs in the case of family tradition (e.g., nominal gay Catholic versus observant or truly practicing gay Catholic) where it is mere compliance and generally lacking deep, personal commitment. The religiously conflicted refers to LGBT people who are members of a religious institution or who have left the religious institution for a variety of reasons. This may include dissenting views on sexuality, homophobic practices or beliefs, religious discrimination and bigotry, and other forms of marginalization (Buchanan, Dzelme, Harris, & Hecker, 2004; Shallenberger, 1998).

These three categories are not mutually exclusive, but they help us to understand some of the intrapersonal and contextual dynamics of clients. Some religiously committed clients, for example, may have recently been exposed to a bigoted statement in their church community, and despite their dedication to their faith, they may feel internally conflicted. One may also encounter closeted religious individuals who profess a certain religious affiliation publicly and comply with some religious practices, but deep in their conscience are on the verge of abandoning or relinquishing their religious affiliation. These levels of affiliation and commitment might also be associated with different emotional reactions and ways of coping, which range from spiritual self-surrender and conscious acceptance to negativism, rage, resentment, and other forms of distress (Barret & Barzan, 1996).

Therefore, these therapeutic considerations deserve clinical attention. In Gabriel's experience, how can he reconcile his two seemingly contradictory identities, and would he ultimately want to be devoutly religious and proudly gay? How can he heal from his perceived sense of moral condemnation? How can he continue to strengthen his spirituality vis-à-vis his religiosity and experience self-acceptance, a sense of belonging, intimacy, and meaning in his life?

Analysis of Sessions and Rationale for Interventions

Structurally, psychotherapy consisted of seven sessions, with two sessions mainly dedicated to assessment and exploration of issues, approximately four sessions incorporating specific spiritual and cognitive-behavioral interventions, and one session for the conclusion of therapy. Because the psychotherapeutic process is a fluid and dynamic process, it is difficult to have a clear delineation of clinical issues and session goals and interventions. Yet, for illustration and training purposes, I have briefly outlined the main foci and goals of every session, followed by some of the exchanges with the client. I also discuss the main interventions utilized and the rationale for their implementation.

First Session

The focus of this session was (a) to establish rapport and to develop a therapeutic relationship, (b) to evaluate coping skills and current resources, (c) to assess suicidal potential and other crisis issues, and (d) to be culturally sensitive and to offer support. I initially engaged in a small casual conversation (*plática*) with Gabriel about the hassle of parking around our facility. After I introduced myself, I proceeded to explain how I approach counseling and to find out what expectations he had, especially because he had been referred by a physician and did not have prior experience with psychotherapy. Confidentiality and its exceptions were explained.

Gabriel introduced himself, and at one point he interrupted the conversation to inquire about my ability to speak Spanish, to which I responded in Spanish and briefly disclosed about my Mexican background. He was visibly engaged and described his family as originally from Mexico. He then explained the reason of his referral. Upon further inquiry on my part, he elaborated about his recent medical diagnosis and hesitatingly disclosed his sexual orientation, identifying himself as gay. During this sensitive time of self-disclosure and rapport building, I consciously made use of appropriate attending skills while maintaining moderate levels of eye contact, being aware of cultural experiences, and listening with a third ear (listening attentively to verbal and nonverbal messages).

In terms of actual content, he reported feeling isolated from his family, community, and God. He described the diagnosis of seropositivity as catastrophic and feared being stigmatized, though he was still in the early stages of the disease and therefore relatively asymptomatic. He presented with negative attributions and perseveration. He feared employment and housing discrimination. He saw this as a major transition in his life and appeared confused as to how he was going to cope. He noted that some of his peers believe that becoming HIV infected is the individual's "own fault," and it is frequently stigmatized as highly contagious and repulsive. He talked about some of the unknowns that lay ahead regarding the progression of the disease and the likelihood of premature death.

Specific interventions used during the session included an assessment of interpersonal and institutional support systems. Gabriel reported feeling confused as to where to turn to for help. He expressed fears of rejection, abandonment, and the loss of existing relationships. He indicated that, paradoxically, he was emotionally and physically distancing himself from friends, family, and colleagues as a way of keeping his status a secret and yet having a stronger desire for support.

Given my client's seropositive status, I consulted with my supervisor regarding ethical dilemmas, specifically about the limits of confidentiality and duty to warn (*Tarasoff v. Regents of the University of California*, 1976). Apparently, dishonesty regarding one's infectious state is common and may represent a threat to uninformed partners. Suggestions from my supervisor included an assessment of potential harm (e.g., the extent to which my client engages in behaviors that carry a high risk of transmission) and inquiring about potential identifiable victims.

Rationale

Rapport building with Latino/a clients is essential. Initiating the session with a small *plática* can be seen as part of the Latino/a cultural value referred to in counseling as *personalismo*, which involves listening to others, having a genuine interest in getting to know others, and demonstrating good social skills. My intentional decision to selectively self-disclose about my background is also part of being personally caring and respectful (showing *respeto*).

Regarding appropriate assessment and interventions for seropositive clients, Hoffman (1991) proposed a psychosocial model that is sensitive to cultural minorities. Some of my interventions in this first session—for example, assessing the client's prediagnosis or presymptom social support system versus his or her postdiagnosis support system—are derived from Hoffman's model.

Second Session

This session focused on (a) further assessing his emotional reactions to HIV infection and diagnosis, (b) exploring strategies to increase and maintain sources of support, (c) building support through effective coping, and (d) further examining spiritual and existential issues. When asked about how his week had been, he quipped, "As my abuelita used to say, '*Ayúdate que Dios te ayudará*' " (Help yourself and God will help you). To which I responded,

"*Dios mediante*" (God willing!). I asked him to tell me the story of his grand-mother and his upbringing. He briefly chronicled his life story growing up in a predominantly Latino neighborhood with a large immigrant presence. He also recounted growing up in a close-knit family that instilled values such as loyalty to the family, love for God, and respect for elders.

Gabriel attributed blame to himself, others, and God for his current situation, which had generated feelings of self-loathing and guilt. He also experienced a drop in self-esteem as a result of multiple psychosocial stressors. He attributed his self-condemnation to an overly rigid church that, in his opinion, unjustly labeled him a sinner. In addition, he felt marginalized in a Latino *machista* community and in an overly pious Catholic Church.

Specific interventions utilized during this session included discussion of community services for seropositive clients for example, referral to a support group at the local gay and lesbian support center. I continued to assess for attributions (cognitive appraisal), psychosocial competence, and his ability to function in the various social and cultural contexts in which he was living and working. An assessment of general coping revealed that he was not abusing substances or resorting to self-destructive or reckless behaviors, and he did not display suicidal ideation.

Rationale

My initial question suitably prompted Gabriel to respond with a *dicho*, or Spanish proverb. Comas-Díaz (2006) recommended the use of sayings in psychotherapy because they embody the wisdom of the culture and reveal life outlook, beliefs, attitudes, and feelings. One cannot fail to notice the sense of spirituality that is linguistically encoded in these Latino sayings about God and the internal locus of control. By purposely responding with a saying that metaphorically captures the equivalent meaning of God being in control, Gabriel proceeds to talk about religious and spiritual struggles. A theme emerges; Gabriel's religious upbringing instilled in him an image of himself that conflicts with his sexual orientation, and he would like to reconcile these two aspects of his identity.

Asking Gabriel to tell me the story of his family is an intervention supported by Arredondo et al.'s (2006, p. 18) *Psychohistorical Approach to Psychotherapy*. Arredondo et al. generally invited clients to tell the family story, while the counselor listens for "themes of identity conflict, acculturation stress, loss and grief, homesickness, guilt, and other emotions." It continues the rapport-building process, as I continue to learn about him as an individual, while at the same time assessing for the influence of family history and values on the presenting issues.

Third Session

This session focused on (a) further exploring Gabriel's sense of identity and supporting him in the development of his gay identity development, (b) discussing his coming-out process, and (c) assessing potential sources of prejudice and discrimination and coping. Gabriel described his experience with homophobia, stereotypes, and other negative influences. I encouraged Gabriel to speak about his feelings and reactions to stigma and homophobic attitudes and behaviors, specifically coming from his family, his religion, and society in general. I was especially interested in the internalization of these negative social influences and how they have impacted his self-concept and self-esteem and contributed to his emotional distress.

He indicated that he has been very selective about his coming-out process, disclosing his true sexual identity to those individuals he considers safe and non-judgmental. We discussed the pros and cons of coming out to other people in his life; for example, his family and close friends. Regarding his church, I offered information about the various groups and pastoral outreach programs available. I also offered resources not directly associated with the church (e.g., GLSEN: Gay, Lesbian, and Straight Education Network). I also provided him with some education brochures, including bilingual resources for LGBT people.

Rationale

Research consistently confirms that LGBT people are vulnerable to stereotypes, bigotry, abuse, and violence. Research has suggested that higher rates of mood disorders, anxiety disorders, and substance abuse among LGBT are mainly attributed to such psychosocial stressors and pressures. Thus, I considered it very important to listen to Gabriel and to assess to what extent he had been exposed to these negative influences and determine the negative emotional impact on him.

Fourth Session

Our goals were (a) to continue evaluating emotional coping (access to resources and support, and suicidal potential), (b) to discuss specific spiritual practices, and (c) to cognitively appraise self-explanations. Gabriel had just returned from a local Buddhist temple, where he had briefly met with a Zen master, and had been participating in meditative practices. I listened attentively as he shared his interest in Buddhism and asked him to share with me how he initially got involved with it. He enthusiastically described how meaningful he found the teachings and practices of Buddhism at this point in his life. Displaying a respectful, receptive, and inquisitive engagement, I asked him to share with me what he had found particularly striking. "Compassion, community, and care ... the three Cs I've been longing for," he emphatically stated. He explained that he saw Buddhism as different from most religious institutions because it teaches tolerance and sees all human beings as belonging to a universal, loving community. Moreover, this universal human family is afflicted by suffering stemming from attachment to transient things in life. With a jovial demeanor, he shared that his meditative practices are giving him a sense of belonging and a deeper understanding and awareness of his own suffering.

Specific interventions included positive reinforcement and validation of current meditative practices. I also introduced a psychoeducational approach and explained the concept of mindfulness, which involves intentionally bringing one's attention to the internal and external experiences occurring in the present moment. We identified some specific issues (existential concerns, despair, isolation, images of God, and negative self-attributions) and discussed them in light of the new insights and experiences he derived from Buddhism. He was able to gradually reframe some of these issues using the concept of enlightenment, which he understood as the path toward ultimate peace and human happiness, obtained through detachment from transient realities and the exercise of meditation and study. He was going through a transformation from relating to what he had experienced as the institutional, vengeful God to his current experience of the loving presence within him and a feeling of being connected with all of creation.

Rationale

Integration of spirituality into psychotherapy requires a respectful attitude, and I have consistently exhibited this for the client. This is evidenced in my receptive demeanor, genuine inquisitiveness, and validating affirmations. These interventions are an integral part of the therapeutic alliance and pave the way for integration of spirituality. From a cognitive perspective, we used mindfulness to explore the client's thinking and underlying cognitions that may be very adaptive for Gabriel.

A cognitive therapist is especially alert to cognitive distortions, which often develop as a result of life experience and form the basis for personality and the way one construes the world. These schemas are usually formed during the early and influential years of childhood and adolescence and are later reinforced by experiences. One of Gabriel's interpretative tendencies seems to be "I am a worthless and sinful person in God's eyes." Some of the intervention strategies used included collaborative empiricism and Socratic dialogue.

Collaborative empiricism refers to a collaborative relationship in which dysfunctional or distorted cognitions are identified, evaluated, and gradually modified (reframed). In this process, one should not tell the client that these beliefs are wrong, especially if these beliefs are religiously derived; rather, it is the client's decision regarding what beliefs will be maintained and what beliefs will be discarded. Empathy, genuineness, and warmth are used to foster the progression of the collaborative relationship (Beck, Rush, Shaw, & Emery, 1979; Beck & Weishaar, 1989).

In Socratic dialogue, the therapist asks questions with the purpose of helping the client examine his or her thinking and formulate additional interpretative alternatives. When done correctly, Socratic questioning will not trap the client into a specific answer or put the client on the defensive. In this process of guided discovery, the therapist helps the client to discover experiences in the past that are affecting his or her current thinking (e.g., early religious experiences or concepts). All of these techniques help clients learn to interpret information in a more neutral or adaptive manner (Beck & Weishaar, 1989).

Fifth Session

To a certain degree, this session was a consolidation of the previous session and so the focus was (a) to continue some of the cognitive focused work we initiated, specifically examining some of the images he had internalized and their emotional associations; (b) to review some of the insights he had acquired from participating in a support group; and (c) to continue integrating spiritual practices into his life.

He expressed gratitude for the referral to the support group for seropositive gay males. He shared some of the topics the group had been discussing, which included coping skills, mastery, grief work, cognitive reframing, and reordering of priorities. We spent some time connecting some of the skills and insights he had learned to our therapy, and he noted that he had found cognitive reframing particularly helpful.

I creatively included the intervention of "progressive image modification," which is the process by which damaging perceptions of clients might be gradually transformed into more rational perceptions. I asked Gabriel to concentrate on the key pattern connected with his images of God and self-concept and asked him to describe them fully. I asked him to form the emerging themes into visualizations to the extent that it was possible. After employing some relaxation to help him concentrate, I asked him to imagine the themes again, but to change some component of the pattern (e.g., by incorporating some of the new images he has learned in Buddhism). I suggested that he could change some visual or emotional component or some other aspect of the pattern. Gabriel engaged in this progressive image modification, and we discussed the experience and emotions associated with it.

Rationale

Progressive image modification has been successfully used by cognitive-behavioral theorists (Lazarus, 1977; Singer & Pope, 1978). The purpose of progressive shaping is to get clients to disrupt their thinking patterns just enough to remove the source of negative emotion. The client is gradually led through a process of changing various components in his or her general belief structures until the person is able to isolate the source of distressing emotions.

Sixth Session

The focus of this session was to (a) evaluate progress made in therapy and anticipate setbacks, (b) continue assessing self-efficacy (e.g., personal belief that he can control certain events) in several areas of his life, (c) monitor affect regulation, and (d) integrate spiritual practices in his life. Gabriel and I revisited some of the mutually agreed-on goals and discussed other areas that needed to be explored. He expressed concern about two specific issues: potential setbacks in the future and medication compliance. He expressed feeling a deeper sense of meaning in his life and a more accepting attitude of his seropositive status. He also reported a more positive relationship with the transcendent and sacred dimensions of his life and a forgiving and embracing attitude toward others. He noted that recently he had been meeting with the Zen master at the temple and having spiritual direction. It is surprising that he had also participated in an ecumenical prayer meeting for world peace that brought together people of various faiths, and he felt a sense of community support, even when praying to, what he called, the "God of Christianity."

I asked Gabriel to identify specific strengths and skills he had learned and setbacks he may potentially encounter. We created a hierarchy of situations in which he felt the least and most efficacious. With his help, we prepared a self-talk dialogue to be used during the vulnerable situations. We realistically anticipated negative emotions and reviewed steps to follow to overcome these situations. We rehearsed the dialogue for each item on the hierarchy. Regarding his prescribed medication, for example, he expressed mixed feelings about adherence to the recommended regime. We reviewed some of the mindfulness strategies to be more aware of fear-based responses and reactions and to identify stressful situations.

Rationale

Many clients expect to fail miserably. Bandura (1977) and others have described this expectation as "low self-efficacy," the belief that one cannot execute the behaviors required to produce positive outcomes. Clients exhibiting this expectation consistently underestimate their ability to cope with various situations. After a while, these expectations tend to become self-fulfilling prophecies. However, coping statements can avert this pattern, helping improve clients' self-efficacy. Rehearsing the dialogue with the coping statements is a modeling procedure (Meichenbaum, 1977) that can be very effective for clients to use when the need arises.

Seventh Session

The sixth session suitably set the tone for the exploration of existential issues. By this time, Gabriel had confronted negative feelings related to his faith and sexual orientation. With more insight into the underlying issues affecting him, the primary focus of this session was (a) to discuss his fears of progressive physical illness and possible death, (b) to further clarify some value conflicts, and (c) to introduce conclusion of therapy and discuss posttherapy plans. Gabriel reported dreading to confront the prospect of dying and death. He kept asking one existential question: Why me? His existential concerns appear to be aggravated by the fear of early death associated with HIV. I asked Gabriel to think about the meaning of his life in the context of his family and the Buddhist concept of a universal community. He described the meaning of soul and afterlife. His sharing seemed to gradually put his existential concerns into perspective and attach meaning and purpose to his life. We then read a passage from Viktor Frankl's *Man's Search for Ultimate Meaning* (1975/1997) and reflected on it. The passage dealt with meaning in suffering, based on Frankl's own testimonial of survival from Auschwitz.

Rationale

It is common for clients dealing with terminal and serious illness to confront existential themes related to death, freedom, meaning, and isolation (Shepherd-Johnson, 2003; Yalom, 1980). Feeling connected to a transcendent reality was especially helpful for Gabriel (Simoni, Martone, & Kerwin, 2002). This relationship with a spiritual and infinite reality, through meditation and reflection on his spiritual gifts, helped him put his personal struggles into perspective. He reported feeling a sense of peace by surrendering his attachments to health and accepting and embracing each moment as it came. My approach in dealing with Gabriel's existential and spiritual questions regarding mortality is consistent with Rousseau's (2000) palliative approach, which includes seven steps: (a) controlling physical symptoms; (b) providing a supportive presence; (c) encouraging life review to assist in recognizing purpose, value, and meaning; (d) exploring guilt, remorse, forgiveness, and reconciliation; (e) facilitating religious expression; (f) reframing goals; and (g) encouraging meditative practices, focusing on healing rather than cure.

Eighth Session

This session was devoted to (a) reviewing the course of therapy and the insights and skills learned, (b) providing additional resources for support, and (c) discussing contingency plans and future potential challenges. I encouraged Gabriel to continue attending the support group and to continue accessing community resources. I reframed this last session from being a "termination" to being a "passage" into a different phase in his "life journey" or "pilgrimage." We used these metaphors to process the session and to put it in context. I was especially cognizant of his previous struggles with isolation and separateness from others. After reviewing his goals for therapy and what he had addressed,

I provided him with some resources in the community and mentioned to him that he could return at any time. I mentioned this is just a passage into a different phase, to which he jokingly replied with a very popular Mexican saying: *Borrón y cuenta nueva* (Erase and start a new account).

Rationale

For a religiously oriented client such as Gabriel, who also struggles with existential concerns related to finality, I purposely used widely used metaphors in the spiritual traditions. Life is usually seen as a journey or pilgrimage. Journey connotes a final and purposeful destination. The human person is not an aimless wanderer, but rather a spiritual pilgrim with a purpose. Therapy can be seen as a stopover or passage along this meaningful path.

Case Conceptualization

Values are cognitive representations of desirable goals. Similar to needs, motives, and goals, values motivate actions. They vary in their importance as guiding principles in people's lives (Schwartz, 1992). From a cultural perspective, cultural schemas (values, beliefs) are dependent on cultural learning. In Gabriel's case, the following cultural values and HSCPs, characteristic of the Mexican culture, appear to be very salient: familism (family loyalty), Catholicism, affiliative obedience, family honor, and abnegation. As a self-identified Mexican American individual with a fairly high level of acculturation, he also reported a relatively strong level of endorsement of some traditional Mexican values, especially the cultural mandates referring to family relationships (obedience, honor, and *respeto*), due in part to his close relationship with his mother, who was Mexican born and Spanish speaking.

Whereas most of these values are socially and culturally desirable and usually serve an adaptive role, a cognitive assessment of Gabriel yielded the hypothesis that some of them may have been contributing to his intrapersonal conflict. As a religiously compliant individual, Gabriel grew up Catholic, following a long family tradition of strict adherence to religious practices and teachings. However, a value conflict was apparent between his religious affiliation and his sexual orientation. Being sexually active with other men and being exposed to family and church views forbidding homosexuality was extremely conflicting for him. He once stated, "I pride myself on being *bien educado* [well raised]", and he didn't want to bring shame to his family, yet he couldn't deny his sexual orientation. Thus, feelings of guilt and loneliness resulted from living a double life. On the one hand, he was trying to adhere to family values and cultural expectations, and on the other, he was involved in gay relationships and wanted to be able to live an authentic lifestyle.

We were also able to identify some cognitive distortions. Gabriel's dichotomous thinking was apparent when he tended to classify himself as either good or bad, sinful or virtuous, or adequate or inadequate (i.e., self-efficacious), depending on whether he had managed to observe or follow certain religious or cultural prescriptions. The diagnosis of HIV had a tremendous negative impact on his self-concept. This resulted in self-blame and personalization (i.e., making a connection between some other event and himself, without supporting evidence), unfairly assuming that he was solely responsible for his actions and seropositive status. Gabriel was encouraged to see, without relinquishing total responsibility, other sociocultural factors contributing to his circumstances. Special relevance was given to stigma, oppression, and negative stereotypes, particularly in the Latino community, as affecting his sexual identity and self-concept.

Additional Clinical Considerations

The *Diagnostic and Statistical Manual of Mental Disorders* (DSM-IV; American Psychiatric Association, 2000) has included a new diagnostic category titled religious or spiritual problem under Other Conditions That May Be a Focus of Clinical Attention. For the first time, there is acknowledgment of distressing religious and spiritual experiences as nonpathological problems (Turner, Lukoff, Barnhouse, & Lu, 1995). This category (V62.89) is usually used "when the focus of clinical attention is a religious or spiritual problem." Some examples include "distressing experiences that involve loss or questioning of faith" and "questioning of spiritual values." In Gabriel's case, the use of this label would be an accurate diagnostic assessment because part of the distress he is experiencing seems to be directly associated to his religious beliefs. In addition to this, Gabriel's presenting problems met DSM-IV criteria for major depressive disorder, and I initially obtained authorization (release of information) to consult with his treating physician.

Identification of Personal Dimensions of Diversity and World View

Being aware of oneself as a cultural being has been considered a competency and a prerequisite for competent multicultural counseling (Sue, Arredondo, & McDavis, 1992). More specifically, Sue et al. (1992) indicated that it is crucial that one is aware of one's own cultural heritage, values, and biases and is comfortable with differences that might exist between therapist and client in terms of race, gender, sexual orientation, and other sociodemographic variables. Differences should not be seen as being deviant. The term cultural countertransference has been coined to describe the therapist's reactions (affective, cognitive, and behavioral) to cultural experiences in therapy that might potentially impede the therapeutic endeavor (Stampley & Slaght, 2004).

From my first encounter with Gabriel, I gradually became aware of our identity similarities and differences. Similarities in background and values can be helpful in relating to and understanding the client. It can also present some challenges. Supervision was very important in examining some of my reactions, assumptions, and ethnocultural biases. For instance, I identified the potential risk of ethnic overidentification, which I experienced as the affective and cognitive tendency to misperceive Gabriel as overly similar to me. I was mindful that every client is unique and may share some similarities in values, beliefs, and attitudes. However, objectivity and competence may be compromised by one's selective perceptual and attitudinal focus on what is common, similar, and familiar.

Values and belief systems are core elements of one's identity. Most people take pride in these defining characteristics because they describe one's total outlook on life, including society and its institutions. They also serve as guiding principles for one's behavior. In many ways, our values are the interpretative lens one uses to understand reality and one's existence within it. Some of Gabriel's problems stemmed from conflicts with his cultural and religious value orientations. It was a delicate balance between clarifying the conflict and not imposing my own biases or assumptions. My approach was to initially explore where the source of the conflict was and then gently and gradually guide Gabriel in his own discernment and sorting out of underlying conflicts. It was a matter not of altering his values or beliefs, but of primarily working with the feelings ("I feel like a worthless sinner") stemming from the value conflict and the self-punitive and self-loathing assumptions

("God hates all gays like me"), interpretations ("This means the church condemns all gays"), and extrapolations ("I wonder if I will be saved") made from some of these values.

Integrating spirituality and religiosity presented its own challenges. These are some of the most sacred and profound experiences that human beings are capable of having. They may become a rich repertoire of meanings and fulfillments, aspirations and longings, and, paradoxically, conflict and distress. As a person of faith, and someone who strives for therapeutic mindfulness, I have been able to learn to observe my experience, to become more aware of my process, and, in gaining a sense of separateness and reflexivity, to be accepting of others. I bring this mindful and meditative stance to my therapeutic work, thus opening a holding space for my client that is, to the extent that it might be possible, devoid of my own agenda.

Therapeutic Recommendations

1. Use multidimensional assessment and conceptualization of issues (ethnicity, acculturation, sexual orientation) and think holistically in structuring treatment goals.
2. Develop an integrative approach that incorporates both culturally appropriate and evidence-based intervention strategies that you can effectively use when working with LGBT Latino/a clients.
3. Know that Latino/a families handle LGBT topics, especially when a family member discloses a gay or lesbian sexual orientation, in different ways. Psychologists have to be well prepared to work with different family experiences.
4. Attend to your own personal definitions and experiences of religiosity and spirituality, and know how they differ or overlap with your client's.
5. Focus on differences between you and your client regarding sexual orientation and ethnicity and how you would address these differences.
6. Recognize that clients with different religious experiences (e.g., religiously committed, religiously compliant, and religiously conflicted) present different issues in psychotherapy and require different psychotherapeutic approaches.
7. Become aware of your response to homophobia and religious systems that promote intolerance and religious beliefs found to be detrimental to LGBT clients.

8. Establish consultative relationships with spiritual and religious leaders and consultants in the LGBT community.
9. Learn about sexual identity development and models of spiritual and religious development and clinical implications.
10. Explore the source of internalized homophobia (e.g., societal, religious, cultural, family), and facilitate the description and expression of these negative messages in a supportive therapeutic environment.

Conclusions

I would like to offer two caveats regarding the content of this chapter. First, although the primary objective is to offer considerations for the integration of religiosity and spirituality, my clinical experience has been primarily with gay and lesbian people affiliated with religious groups within the Christian tradition. Therefore, the spiritual struggles of the client presented in this chapter, and corresponding clinical conceptualization and interventions, may or may not generalize to clients with similar conflicts and concerns from non-Christian traditions. It is the ethical responsibility of the culturally sensitive therapist to judiciously discern what considerations may be applicable to a specific case.

Any kind of therapeutic integration requires a keen perspective into what compatible and discrepant components might fit into a workable theoretical whole. With this mind, the ethically responsible and culturally helpful practitioner will use sound clinical judgment to incorporate spiritual practices and interventions that are consistent with the client's desired therapeutic goals and conceptually compatible with the therapist's theoretical orientation. In this case, Gabriel sought out Buddhist practices and integrated them into his life through meditation and spiritual support. This may not be the case for all religiously oriented people. Some LGBT people may find a pastoral support program within their own faith traditions.

Second, not every intervention and therapeutic approach herein presented met a rigorous scientific test of empirical validation according to the strict criteria of empirically supported criteria. I carefully reviewed the existing literature on empirically supported therapies for Latinos and LGBT clients. One has to be mindful that most psychotherapies have been developed with Euro-American and heterosexual participant samples or with samples where ethnic minority identity or sexual orientation was unknown. Transferring the use of these therapy approaches to LGBT and ethnic minority clients should be done closely following the best practice guidelines developed by the American Psychological Association. Theoretically, most of the interventions included in this chapter can be conceptualized from a cognitive-behavioral approach, multicultural perspective, and use of mindfulness-based strategies. The efficacy of the interventions, instead of being solely evidence-based practices, is mostly supported by practitioner-based evidence. My client reported a generalized sense of improvement in various areas of functioning.

Discussion Questions

1. Why is it meaningful to distinguish between religion and spirituality? Consider some of the descriptors from popular usage and experiences associated with each. What would be some of the clinical issues associated with someone who experiences a conflict between religion and spirituality?

2. Discuss how aspects of identity (ethnicity, acculturation, gender, sexual orientation) interact with religion and spirituality. To what extent are they related, and how complementary or incompatible are they?

3. Discuss some issues of oppression, homophobia, and discrimination in relation to HIV. What psychosocial factors make ethnic minorities especially vulnerable and at risk for HIV infection? What biases would make current models of diagnosis, prevention, and treatment not suitable for ethnic minorities?

4. What criteria should psychotherapists adopt for implementing effective interventions for specific clinical issues in complex cases? To what extent are manualized treatments appropriate for ethnic minorities?

5. For the culture or ethnic group that you know best, discuss any specific beliefs, stereotypes, stigmas, or prejudices they may have about sexual minorities. How do they differ from the case presented in this chapter in regard to (a) family dynamics, (b) religion and spirituality, and (c) attitudes toward HIV?

6. Why are some therapists reluctant to integrate religion and spirituality into psychotherapy? If the therapist has previously felt ambivalent or hesitant about spirituality in psychotherapy, how could he or she deal with a client who unexpectedly introduces spiritual or religious material into the session? Consider ethical implications.

7. What are some of the potential risks, abuses, or detrimental experiences for clients in regard to (a) involvement in spiritual or religious practices and (b) pseudoscientific claims attached to "spiritually based psychotherapies"?

8. What is your ethnic, cultural, and/or religious heritage? Is there anything about your value or belief system that you find conflicting, distressing, salutogenic (promoting or enhancing health and well-being), or pathogenic (causing impairment or disease)? What parts do you embrace? What parts do you reject?

9. Discuss how a self-identified nonreligious therapist might treat a client who (a) prays every day and lives a devotional and pious life (e.g., frequent church attendance, observance of religious holidays, adherence to spiritual guidance of religious leaders or pastors), (b) makes moral decisions guided by a religious code (e.g., commandments, virtue, grace), and (c) makes sense of events in life in general by referring to spiritual entities (God and heaven, devil and hell, saints and demons, soul and spirit). What helpful approaches might this therapist follow to be sensitive and respectful of this world view?

10. Read the following scenarios about cultural countertransference to religious clients: (a) a therapist is thinking that a female client sounds "narrow minded," "overly traditional," and/or "cognitively inflexible" when she decides not to have an abortion because for her this is a sinful crime; (b) a therapist is feeling uncertain or ambivalent or has mixed feelings regarding a client who believes homosexuality is a sin; and (c) a therapist personally thinks celibacy is a "repression" of sexuality, and she is currently working with a seminarian who struggles with masturbation and would like to stop because for him this is a breach of his vow to a celibate and chaste lifestyle. Discuss how these issues could be addressed or resolved in the context of therapy.

Cultural Resources

Suggested Film

Philadelphia (1993) is a historically important film in raising consciousness about AIDS. Tom Hanks plays a lawyer dismissed from his firm, apparently for incompetence, but really he has AIDS. Denzel Washington, a personal injury attorney, is initially homophobic. He agrees to take on the case and learns about his misconceptions about the disease, about those who contract it, and about gay people in general. He ends up overcoming his intolerance and fighting for justice.

The Wedding Banquet (1993) is about Wai-Tung (Winston Chao), an undocumented Chinese immigrant, who meets Simon (Mitchell Lichtenstein), and they begin dating. However, Wai-Tung's parents have not the slightest inkling of Wai-Tung's sexual orientation. The movie creatively portrays the interaction of ethnicity, sexual orientation, and the coming-out process.

Suggested Readings

Comas-Díaz, L., & Griffith, E. E. H. (Eds.). (1998). *Clinical guidelines in cross-cultural mental health.* New York: John Wiley & Sons.

> This excellent resource offers very practical guidelines for working with clients from diverse ethnocultural backgrounds. It addresses specific cultural dimensions (ethnicity, language, religion, family values) and their relation to mental health.

Garnets, L. D., & Kimmel, D. C. (Eds.). (2003). *Psychological perspectives on lesbian, gay, and bisexual experiences.* New York: Columbia University Press.

> The book has readable chapters on the meaning of sexual orientation, psychological dimensions of sexual prejudice, discrimination and violence, identity development and stigma management, and diversity among lesbians, bisexuals, and gay men. Some chapters also have a focus on sexual orientation throughout the life span.

Greene, B. (Ed.). (1997). *Ethnic and cultural diversity among lesbians and gay men.* Thousand Oaks, CA: Sage.

> This is part of the series *Psychological Perspectives on Lesbian and Gay Issues,* sponsored by the Society for the Psychological Study of Lesbian, Gay, and Bisexual Issues, Division 44 of the American Psychological Association. This edited book brings together some fine papers by multicultural authors on various ethnic populations (e.g., Native American, Jewish, Black South African, older African American males, Greek American lesbians) and their struggles with ethnic identity, racism, acculturation, and the coming-out process.

Pargament, K. I. (1997). *The psychology of religion and coping.* New York: Guilford.

> The author provides a comprehensive analysis of religion and coping. Examples of chapters include the sacred and the search for

significance, when people turn to religion, when they turn away, when religion fails, and problems of integration in the process of coping. The author is a well-published scholar, and he integrates scientific theory with clinical practice.

Stern, M. E. (1985). *Psychotherapy and the religiously committed person.* New York: Haworth.

This practical and readable book includes chapters from several authors who provide a balanced explanation of important spiritual issues and how they can be integrated into psychotherapy.

Velásquez, R. J., Arellano, L. M., & McNeill, B. W. (Eds.). (2004). *The handbook of Chicana/o psychology and mental health.* Mahwah, NJ: Lawrence Erlbaum.

This is a great reference on mental health issues affecting Chicanas/os. Topics include Mestiza and Chicano/a psychology, acculturation, ethnic identity development, stereotypes, folk healing, psychological assessment, domestic violence, substance abuse, and folk healing. It covers these topics with scholarly discussions and yet is very readable and applicable.

Suggested Web Sites

http://www.apa.org/about/division/div44.html
This Web site of Division 44, the Society for the Psychological Study of Lesbian, Gay, and Bisexual Issues of the American Psychological Association focuses on the diversity of human sexual orientations by supporting research, promoting relevant education, and affecting professional and public policy.

http://www.ac.wwu.edu/~culture/readings.htm
This site offers online readings in psychology and culture from the Center for Cross-Cultural Research at Western Washington University. This is an outstanding compilation of readings from multicultural and cross-cultural experts dealing with topics of culture and psychology. Every reading includes discussion questions and resources.

http://www.fetzer.org/
This is the official Web site of the Fetzer Institute, which conducts rigorous scientific research on religion and spirituality. It brings together renowned scholars and leaders to scientifically study religion

and spirituality. Their research projects have specific applications; for example, current investigations include altruism in America, racial healing, and end-of-life research.

References

Alexander, M. B., & Preston, J. (1996). *We were baptized too: Claiming God's grace for lesbians and gays.* Louisville, KY: Westminster John Knox Press.

American Psychiatric Association. (2000). *Diagnostic and statistical manual of mental disorders* (text rev.). Washington, DC: Author.

Arredondo, P., Davison Avilés, R. M., Zalaquett, C. P., Gracioso, M. P., Bordes, V., Hita, L., & Lopez, B. J. (2006). The psychohistorical approach in family counseling with Mestizo/Latino immigrants: A continuum and synergy of worldviews. *The Family Journal: Counseling and Therapy for Couples and Families, 14,* 13–27.

Baer, R. A. (2003). Mindfulness training as a clinical intervention: A conceptual and empirical review. *Clinical Psychology: Science and Practice, 10,* 125–143.

Baez, A., & Hernandez, D. (2001). Complementary spiritual beliefs in the Latino community: The interface with psychotherapy. *American Journal of Orthopsychiatry, 71,* 408–415.

Baez, E. J. (1996). Spirituality and the gay Latino client. *Journal of Gay and Lesbian Social Services, 4,* 69–81.

Balka, C., & Rose, A. (1989). *Twice blessed: On being lesbian or gay and Jewish.* Boston: Beacon Press.

Bandura, A. (1977). Self-efficacy: Toward a unifying theory of behavior change. *Psychological Review, 84,* 191–215.

Barret, R., & Barzan, R. (1996). Spiritual experiences of gay men and lesbians. *Counseling and Values, 41,* 4–15.

Beck, A. T., Rush, A. J., Shaw, B. F., & Emery, G. (1979). *Cognitive therapy of depression.* New York: Guilford.

Beck, A. T., & Weishaar, M. E. (1989). Cognitive therapy. In R. Corsini & D. Wedding (Eds.), *Current psychotherapies* (pp. 285–320). Itasca, IL: F. E. Peacock.

Bergin, A. E. (1983). Religiosity and mental health: A critical reevaluation and meta-analysis. *Professional Psychology: Research and Practice, 14,* 170–184.

Bergin, A. E. (1991). Values and religious issues in psychotherapy and mental health. *American Psychologist, 46,* 394–403.

Bergin, A. E., Masters, K. S., & Richards, P. S. (1987). Religiousness and mental health reconsidered: A study of an intrinsically religious sample. *Journal of Counseling Psychology, 34,* 197–204.

Bernal, G., & Scharrón-Del-Río, M. R. (2001). Are empirically supported treatments valid for ethnic minorities? Toward an alternative approach for treatment research. *Cultural Diversity and Ethnic Minority Psychology, 7,* 328–342.

Bivens, A. J., Neimeyer, R. A., Kirchberger, T. M., & Moore, M. K. (1995). Death concern and religious belief among gays and bisexuals of variable proximity to AIDS. *Omega, 30,* 105–120.

Bouldrey, B. (1995). *Wresting with the angel: Faith and religion in the lives of gay men.* New York: Riverhead Books.

Brawer, P. A., Handal, P. J., Fabricatore, R. R., Roberts, R., & Wajda-Johnston, V. A. (2002). Training and education in religion-spirituality within APA-accredited clinical psychology programs. *Professional Psychology: Research and Practice, 33,* 203–206.

Brown, K. W., & Ryan, R. M. (2003). The benefits of being present: Mindfulness and its role in psychological well-being. *Journal of Personality and Social Psychology, 84,* 822–848.

Buchanan, M., Dzelme, K., Harris, D., & Hecker, L. (2004). Challenges of being simultaneously gay and lesbian and spiritual and/or religious: A narrative perspective. *American Journal of Family Therapy, 29,* 435–449.

Carballo, D. A. (1989). Hispanic culture, gay male culture, and AIDS: Counseling implications. *Journal of Counseling and Development, 68,* 26–30.

Chambless, D. L., & Hollon, S. D. (1998). Defining empirically supported therapies. *Journal of Consulting and Clinical Psychology, 66,* 7–18.

Clay, R. A. (1996). Psychologists' faith in religion begins to grow. *The APA Monitor, 27*(1), 46–48.

Comas-Díaz, L. (1981). Effects of cognitive and behavioral group treatment on the depressive symptomatology of Puerto Rican women. *Journal of Consulting and Clinical Psychology, 49,* 627–632.

Comas-Diaz, L. (2006). Latino healing: The integration of ethnic psychology into psychotherapy. *Psychotherapy: Theory, Research, Practice, Training, 43,* 436–453.

Comstock, G. (1996). *Unrepentant, self-affirming, practicing: Lesbian, gay, and bisexual people within organized religion.* New York: Continuum.

Constantine, M. G., & Sue, D. W. (2006). Factors contributing to optimal human functioning in people of color in the United States. *The Counseling Psychologist, 34,* 228–244.

Díaz, R. M. (1998). *Latino gay men and HIV: Culture, sexuality, and risk behavior.* New York: Routledge.

Díaz, R. M. (2000). Cultural regulation, self regulation, and sexuality: A psycho-cultural model of HIV risk in Latino gay men. In R. G. Parker, R. M. Barbosa, & P. Aggleton (Eds.), *Framing the sexual subject: The politics of gender, sexuality, and power* (pp. 191–215). Berkeley: University of California Press.

Díaz, R. M., Ayala, G., & Bein, E. (2004). Sexual risk as an outcome of social oppression: Data from a probability simple of Latino gay men in the U.S. cities. *Cultural Diversity and Ethnic Minority Psychology, 10,* 255–267.

Díaz, R. M., Ayala, G., Bein, E., Henne, J., & Marin, B. V. (2001). The impact of homophobia, poverty, and racism on the mental health of gay and bisexual Latino men: Findings from 3 U.S. cities. *American Journal of Public Health, 91,* 927–932.

Díaz-Guerrero, R. (1967). Sociocultural premises, attitudes and cross-cultural research. *International Journal of Psychology, 2,* 79–87.

Díaz-Guerrero, R. (1982). The psychology of the historic-sociocultural premises. *Spanish-Language Psychology, 2,* 383–410.

Díaz-Guerrero, R. (1992). The need for an ethnopsychology of cognition and personality. *Journal of Human Behavior, 29,* 19–26.

Díaz-Guerrero, R. (1993). Mexican ethnopsychology. In U. Kim & J. W. Berry (Eds.), *Indigenous psychologies: Research and experience in cultural context* (pp. 44–55). Thousand Oaks, CA: Sage.

Díaz-Guerrero, R. (2001). *Psicología del Mexicano: Descubrimiento de la etnopsicología* [Psychology of the Mexican: Discovery of ethnopsychology] (5th ed.). Mexico City: Trillas.

Díaz-Loving, R., & Draguns, J. G. (1999). Culture, meaning, and personality in Mexico and in the United States. In Y. T. Lee, C. R. McCauley, & J. G. Draguns (Eds.), *Personality and person perception across cultures* (pp. 103–126). Mahwah, NJ: Lawrence Erlbaum.

Dimidjian, S., & Linehan, M. (2003). Defining an agenda for future research on the clinical applications of mindfulness practice. *Clinical Psychology: Science and Practice, 10*, 166–171.

Dudley-Grant, G. R. (2003). Perspectives on spirituality and psychology in ethnic populations. In J. S. Mio & G. Y. Iwamasa (Eds.), *Culturally diverse mental health: The challenge of research and resistance* (pp. 341–360). New York: Brunner-Routledge.

Elligan, D. (1997). Culturally sensitive integration of supportive and cognitive behavioral therapy in the treatment of a bicultural dysthymic patient. *Cultural Diversity and Mental Health, 3*, 207–213.

Frankl, V. F. (1997). *Man's search for ultimate meaning.* New York: Plenum Press. (Original work published 1975)

Gelman, C. R., Lopez, M., & Pérez-Foster, R. M. (2005). Evaluating the impact of cognitive-behavioral intervention with depressed Latinas: A preliminary report. *Social Work in Mental Health, 4*, 1–16.

George, L. K., Larson, D. B., Koenig, H. G., & McCullough, M. E. (2000). Spirituality and health: What we know, what we need to know. *Journal of Social and Clinical Psychology, 19*, 102–116.

Gillispie, Z. (2006). Mindfulness theory and cultural identity: Predicting positive mental health outcomes among Latino students (Doctoral dissertation, Pacific Graduate School of Psychology, 2006). *Dissertation Abstracts International, 67*, 3449.

Glaser, C. (1996). *Uncommon calling: A gay Christian's struggle to serve the church.* Louisville, KY: Westminster John Know Press.

Greene, B., & Herek, G. (1994). *Lesbian and gay psychology.* Thousand Oaks, CA: Sage.

Hayes, S. C., & Wilson, K. G. (2003). Mindfulness: Method and process. *Clinical Psychology: Science and Practice, 10*, 161–165.

Helminiak, D. A. (2001). Treating spiritual issues in secular psychotherapy. *Counseling and Values, 45*, 163–189.

Hendricks, P. S., & Thompson, J. K. (2005). An integration of cognitive-behavioral therapy and interpersonal psychotherapy for bulimia nervosa: A case study using the case formulation method. *International Journal of Eating Disorders, 37*, 171–174.

Hill, P. C., & Pargament, K. I. (2003). Advances in the conceptualization and measurement of religion and spirituality. *American Psychologist, 58*, 64–74.

Hill, P. C., Pargament, K. I., Hood, R. W., Jr., McCullogh, M. E., Swyers, J. P., Larson, D. B., & Zinnbauer, B. J. (2000). Conceptualizing religion and spirituality: Points of commonality, points of departure. *Journal for the Theory of Social Behaviour, 30*, 51–77.

Hoffman, M. A. (1991). Counseling the HIV-infected client: A psychosocial model for assessment and intervention. *The Counseling Psychologist, 19*, 467–542.

Hoffman, M. A. (1993). Multiculturalism as a force in counseling clients with HIV-related concerns. *The Counseling Psychologist, 21*, 712–731.

Hofstede, G. (1980). *Culture's consequences: International differences in work-related values.* Newbury Park, CA: Sage.

Hofstede, G. (2001). *Culture's consequences, comparing values, behaviors, institutions, and organizations across nations* (2nd ed.). Thousand Oaks, CA: Sage.

Huss, D. B., & Baer, R. A. (2007). Acceptance and change: The integration of mindfulness-based cognitive therapy into ongoing dialectical behavior therapy in a case of borderline personality disorder with depression. *Clinical Case Studies, 6*, 17–33.

Kabat-Zinn, J. (2003). Mindfulness-based interventions in context: Past, present, and future. *Clinical Psychology: Science and Practice, 10*, 144–156.

Knox, S., Catlin, L., Casper, M., & Schlosser, L. Z. (2005). Addressing religion and spirituality in psychotherapy: Client's perspectives. *Psychotherapy Research, 15*, 287–303.

Lazarus, A. (1977). *In the mind's eye: The power of imagery for personal enrichment.* New York: Rawson.

Loseke, D. R., & Cavendish, J. C. (2001). Producing institutional selves: Rhetorically constructing the dignity of sexually marginalized Catholics. *Social Psychology Quarterly, 64*, 347–362.

Mack, M. (1994). Understanding spirituality in counseling psychology: Considerations for research, training, and practice. *Counseling and Values, 39*, 15–32.

McBrien, R. P. (1994). *Catholicism.* San Francisco: Harper.

McCullough, M. E., Hoyt, W. T., Larson, D. B., Koenig, H. G., & Thoresen, C. (2000). Religious involvement and mortality: A meta-analytic review. *Health Psychology, 19*, 211–222.

McNeill, J. J. (1993). *The church and the homosexual.* Boston: Beacon Press.

Meichenbaum, D. (1977). *Cognitive-behavior modification: An integrative approach.* New York: Plenum.

Miller, W. R., & Thoresen, C. E. (2003). Spirituality, religion, and health. *American Psychologist, 58*, 24–35.

Mio, J. S., & Iwamasa, G. Y. (Eds.). (2003). *Culturally diverse mental health: The challenges of research and resistance* (pp. 341–360). New York: Brunner-Routledge.

Miranda, M. R. (Ed.). (1976). *Psychotherapy with the Spanish-speaking: Issues in research and service delivery* (Monograph No. 3). Los Angeles: Spanish-Speaking Mental Health Research Center, University of California.

Muñoz, R. F., & Mendelson, T. (2005). Toward evidence-based interventions for diverse populations: The San Francisco General Hospital prevention and treatment manuals. *Journal of Consulting and Clinical Psychology, 73*, 790–799.

Nagayama Hall, G. C. (2001). Psychotherapy research with ethnic minorities: Empirical, ethical, and conceptual issues. *Journal of Consulting and Clinical Psychology, 69*, 502–510.

O'Brien, T. (1991). A survey of gay/lesbian Catholics concerning attitudes toward sexual orientation and religious beliefs. *Journal of Homosexuality, 21*, 29–44.

Organista, K. C., & Muñoz, R. F. (1996). Cognitive behavioral therapy with Latinos. *Cognitive and Behavioral Practice, 3*, 255–270.

Organista, K. C., Muñoz, R. F., & Gonzalez, G. (1994). Cognitive behavioral therapy for depression in low-income and minority medical outpatients: Description of a program and exploratory analyses. *Cognitive Therapy and Research, 18*, 241–259.

Pargament, K. I. (1997). *The psychology of religion and doping: Theory, research, practice.* New York: Guilford.

Pargament, K. I. (1999). The psychology of religion and spirituality? Yes and no. *International Journal for the Psychology of Religion, 9*, 3–16.

Pargament, K. I., Murray-Swank, N. A., & Tarakeshwar, N. (2005). An empirically-based rationale for a spiritually-integrated psychotherapy. *Mental Health, Religion and Culture, 8*, 155–165.

Powell, L. H., Shahabi, L., & Thoresen, C. E. (2003). Religion and spirituality: Linkages to physical health. *American Psychologist, 58*, 36–52.

Powers, R. (2005). Counseling and spirituality: A historical review. *Counseling and Values, 49*, 217–225.

Quintana, S. M., & Atkinson, D. R. (2002). A multicultural perspective on Principles of Empirically Supported Interventions. *The Counseling Psychologist, 30*, 281–291.

Ramirez, M. III. (2004). Mestiza/o and Chicana/o psychology: Theory, research, and application. In R. J. Velásquez, L. M. Arellano, & B. A. McNeill (Eds.), *The handbook of Chicana/o psychology and mental health* (pp. 3–19). New Jersey: Lawrence Erlbaum Associates.

Richards, P. S., & Bergin, A. E. (2000). Towards religious and spiritual competence for mental health professionals. In P. S. Richards & A. E. Bergin (Eds.), *Handbook of psychotherapy and religious diversity* (pp. 3–26). Washington, DC: American Psychological Association.

Roemer, L., & Orsillo, S. M. (2003). Mindfulness: A promising intervention strategy in need of further study. Clinical Psychology: *Science and Practice, 10*, 172–178.

Rousseau, P. (2000). Spirituality and the dying patient. *Journal of Clinical Oncology, 18*, 2000–2002.

Schulte, D. L., Skinner, T. A., & Claibom, C. D. (2002). Religious and spiritual issues in counseling psychology training. *The Counseling Psychologist, 30*, 118.

Schwartz, S. H. (1992). Universals in the content and structure of values: Theoretical advances and empirical tests in 20 countries. In M. P. Zanna (Ed.), *Advances in experimental social psychology* (Vol. 25, pp. 1–65). New York: Academic Press.

Seeman, T. E., Fagan-Dubin, L., & Seeman, M. (2003). Religiosity/spirituality and health: A critical review of the evidence for biological pathways. *American Psychologist, 58*, 53–63.

Shafranske, E. P. (1996). *Religion and the clinical practice of psychology.* Washington, DC: American Psychological Association.

Shafranske, E. P., & Gorsuch, R. L. (1984). Factors associated with the perception of spirituality in psychotherapy. *Journal of Transpersonal Psychology, 16*, 231–241.

Shafranske, E. P., & Malony, H. N. (1990). Clinical psychologists' religious and spiritual orientations and their practice of psychotherapy. *Psychotherapy, 27,* 72–78.

Shallenberger, D. (1998). *Reclaiming the spirit: Gay men and lesbians come to terms with religion.* New Brunswick, NJ: Rutgers University Press.

Shepherd-Johnson, L. (2003). Facilitating spiritual meaning-making for the individual with a diagnosis of a terminal illness. *Counseling and Values, 43,* 230–240.

Simoni, J. M., Martone, M. G., & Kerwin, J. F. (2002). Spirituality and psychological adaptation among women with HIV/AIDS: Implications for counseling. *Journal of Counseling Psychology, 49,* 139–147.

Singer, J., & Pope, K. (Eds.). (1978). *The power of human imagination.* New York: Plenum.

Stampley, C., & Slaght, E. (2004). Cultural countertransference as a clinical obstacle. *Smith College Studies in Social Work, 74,* 333–347.

Steinfel, G. J. (2000). Spiritual psychology and psychotherapy: Is there theoretical and empirical support? *Journal of Contemporary Psychotherapy, 30,* 353–380.

Sue, D. W., Arredondo, P., & McDavis, R. J. (1992). Multicultural counseling competencies and standards: A call to the profession. *Journal of Counseling and Development, 70,* 477–486.

Sue, D. W., Bingham, R. P., Porché-Burke, L., & Vasquez, M. (1999). The diversification of psychology: A multicultural revolution. *American Psychologist, 54,* 1061–1069.

Sue, D. W., & Sue, D. (2003). *Counseling the culturally diverse: Theory and practice* (4th ed.). New York: Wiley & Sons.

Tarasoff v. Regents of the University of California, 17 Cal. 3d 425, 551 P. 2d 334, 131 Cal. Rptr. 14 (cal.1976).

Teasdale, J. D., Moore, R. G., Hayhurst, H., Pope, M., Williams, S., & Segal, Z. V. (2002). Metacognitive awareness and prevention of relapse in depression: Empirical evidence. *Journal of Consulting and Clinical Psychology, 70,* 275–287.

Teasdale, J. D., Segal, Z. V., & Williams, J. M. G. (2003). Mindfulness training and problem formulation. *Clinical Psychology: Science and Practice, 10,* 157–160.

Tigert, L. C. (1996). *Coming out while staying in: Struggles and celebrations; Lesbians, gays, and bisexuals in the church.* Cleveland, OH: United Church Press.

Toman, J. A. (1997). Dual identity: Being Catholic and being gay (Doctoral dissertation, Cleveland State University, 1997). *Dissertation Abstracts International, 58,* 1942.

Torres-Matrullo, C. (1982). Cognitive therapy of depressive disorders in the Puerto Rican female. In R. M. Becerra, M. Karno, & J. I. Escobar (Eds.), *Mental health and Hispanic Americans* (pp. 101–113). New York: Grune & Stratton.

Turner, R. P., Lukoff, D., Barnhouse, R. T., & Lu, F. G. (1995). Religious or spiritual problem: A culturally sensitive diagnostic category in the DSM-IV. *Journal of Nervous and Mental Disorders, 185,* 435–444.

Wagner, G., Serafini, J., Rabkin, J., Remien, R., & Williams, J. (1994). Integrating one's religion and homosexuality: A weapon against internalized homophobia? *Journal of Homosexuality, 26,* 91–109.

Walker, D. F., Gorsuch, R. L., & Tan, S.-Y. (2004). Therapists' integration of religion and spirituality in counseling: A meta-analysis. *Counseling and Values, 49,* 69–80.

Wampold, B. E., Lichtenberg, J. W., & Waehler, C. A. (2002). Principles of empirically supported interventions in counseling psychology. *The Counseling Psychologist*, *30*, 197–217.

Worthington, E. L., & Sandage, S. J. (2001). Religion and spirituality. *Psychotherapy*, *38*, 473–478.

Yalom, I. (1980). *Existential psychotherapy*. New York: Basic Books.

Zea, M. C., Reisen, C. A., & Díaz, R. M. (2003). Methodological issues in research on sexual behavior with Latino gay and bisexual men. *American Journal of Community Psychology*, *31*, 281–291.

Zinnbauer, B. J., Pargament, K. I., & Scott, A. B. (1999). The emerging meanings of religiousness and spirituality: Problems and prospects. *Journal of Personality*, *67*, 889–919.

7

Incorporating Affirming, Feminist, and Relational Perspectives
The Case of Juan

Marie L. Miville,
LeLaina Romero, and
Melissa J. Corpus

Contents

Juan is a 25-year-old multiracial (Filipino and African American) man coming to therapy at a community mental health center in a large city in the northeastern United States because he feels "anxious" and "wants to stop procrastinating." He is attending a local community college part-time, earning his associate's degree, and working full-time as a retail assistant at a local electronics store. He lives with and cares for his mother, who is chronically ill. His parents divorced when he was very young, and he is estranged from his father and extended paternal family. Juan also lives with two younger brothers, ages 18 and 19, from his mother's second marriage. During the course of treatment, Juan expresses frustration with his mother and his aunts, who expect him to be constantly available to them and who often chastise him for the amount of time he spends at work and school. He also begins describing a feeling of not "fitting in" with his mother's family at times and a desire to know his father's family. The client discloses that his mother is Filipina, and although Juan has always played an important role in his family as the oldest son, he often feels as if his extended family treats him differently than his male cousins, who are "pure Pinoy." Juan feels that his mother's family is "too traditional—it's suffocating!" and wonders if his father's family is different because they are "from the States."

Juan describes close friendships with a few people from work and school. He is dating a Puerto Rican American man whom he met at an event sponsored by a multicultural lesbian, gay, and bisexual (LGB) club on campus. He states that he is "grateful" for his friends and partner, but often feels pulled between family obligations and other relationships. Although Juan is out to his family as a gay man, he does not feel his family members entirely accept his male partner, and they sometimes make homophobic comments in front of him. At the same time, Juan's mother has been confined to the house because of her illness for the past month, which means that Juan has been a caretaker for his brothers and mother more frequently. Juan states that he is having trouble sleeping at night, and when he gets home from work or school, all he wants to do is "pass out." When he does have the time and energy to do his schoolwork, he sometimes has "trouble breathing" because all he can think about is what he is going to do when he graduates with his associate's degree. Juan would like to eventually earn a bachelor's degree in engineering, but is worried that he will not be able to handle the stress because of his family obligations and his need to work to support himself.

(Adapted from Miville & Romero, 2007)

Introduction

Juan sits at the intersection of multiple worlds. He is a gay man and a person of color with working-class roots living in the United States, and his race and sexual orientation certainly have been devalued or denigrated at various points throughout his life. Moreover, as a biracial person, particularly as a child of parents from two different racial minority groups, Juan most likely has been marginalized even within his own racial-ethnic communities, perhaps rendered invisible because he does not "fit" clearly into a specific group, including his own family. These challenges to his identities further may be contextualized within his current developmental, family, and career struggles. Moreover, although gay men, people of color, and biracial and multiracial people are marginalized in the larger society, it is important to view the sources of strength that Juan may derive from these identities. In this chapter, we will discuss counseling issues specific to working with LGB people and biracial and multiracial people, integrating Juan's presenting concerns to provide examples. Because it will be optimal to employ a myriad of culturally responsive theoretical orientations when working with Juan, we have chosen to work from a feminist relational perspective, embedded in LGB affirmative and multicultural competence frameworks.

Although all clients can benefit from a feminist relational perspective, we believe this approach to be particularly relevant to Juan, who is facing multiple challenges in part because of his identity as a biracial (Filipino and Black) gay man, perhaps from working-class or working-poor roots. In addition, from what he describes, he is facing challenges in his relationships with family members and perhaps with friends and his partner. In the next sections, we will define our theoretical frameworks applied to the case of Juan. Throughout the chapter, we will integrate relevant information from the evidence-based practice literature in addressing the anxiety symptoms that Juan presents, bearing in mind that there is a dearth of research on how these techniques apply to individuals from nondominant groups.

LGB Clients and LGB Affirmative Counseling

An LGB affirmative framework is crucial when working with clients such as Juan who are lesbian, gay, or bisexual. Because LGB clients face societal oppression and subsequent internalized homophobia or biphobia, sexual orientation should be a central focus of therapy with LGB clients. To foster a therapeutic alliance within an LGB affirmative framework, counselors should not assume their clients' willingness or desire to directly address the issue of sexual identity in the context of counseling (Murphy, Rawlings, & Howe, 2002). Although sexual identity may or may not be related to clients' presenting problems, practitioners need to be aware that clients may not choose to disclose their sexual identification because of their concern of therapists' attitudes toward LGB individuals. Furthermore, Palma and Stanley (2002) posited that practitioners can create therapeutic environments that suggest they have the capacity to affirm LGB communities. For example, therapists may familiarize themselves with LGB-affiliated books, political and social organizations, and social venues to help demonstrate awareness of LGB culture. At the same time, practitioners should not mislead their clients, but instead be genuine about aspects of LGB culture of which they are unsure or unaware. Subsequently, to be an effective LGB-affirmative counselor, practitioners must be equipped to address any number of salient issues surrounding the LGB population. These include a comprehensive understanding of sexual orientation and sexual identity development, coming-out processes, same-sex relationships, parenting and familial concerns, and the unique experiences of LGB individuals who are ethnic minorities, religious, and/or aging (Pachankis & Goldfried, 2004).

It is important for counselors to be aware of heterosexism as well as of homophobia. Like racism and sexism, heterosexism is a form of oppression that privileges heterosexual activities, beliefs, values, attitudes, and behaviors as the norm while rejecting or looking down on homosexuality and bisexuality (Miville & Ferguson, 2006). Heterosexism is linked with sexism in that both heterosexual norms and gender-appropriate roles are expected in the larger society. LGB people often are viewed as "deviant" in terms of both gender and sexual orientation. To increase effectiveness with LGB clients, counselors can become aware of their own heterosexist attitudes, whether or not they are heterosexual. In addition, it is important to pay attention to the ways in which LGB clients internalize negative attitudes about themselves and how these attitudes may be related to their presenting concerns.

When working with Juan, we suggest that it also might be beneficial to conceptualize Juan's sexuality through an LGB identity development model (e.g., Cass, 1979; McCarn & Fassinger, 1996). Many gay and lesbian identity development models provide helpful frames of reference to explore the conflicts and resolutions that LGB individuals such as Juan may experience while formulating their sexual identities. These models primarily address the various milestones and common struggles that occur for many individuals in their search for a positive sexual identity. In addition to intrapsychic changes, LGB identity development is influenced by various environmental factors.

On the basis of the available information concerning Juan, we thought he likely endorsed a relatively positive perspective of his gay identity. For example, his steady relationship with a male partner suggests that Juan is comfortable being in a same-sex relationship. In addition to having a certain level of self-acceptance, Juan demonstrates an ability to be out to his family. That is, he appears to be open to his mother, siblings, and other relatives about his sexuality and his relationship with his partner. Unfortunately, despite his openness around his family members, Juan's family experiences ambivalence regarding Juan's sexual orientation and, at times, alienate him. The lack of unconditional acceptance by his family members may lead Juan to experience both internal and external struggles surrounding his continued sexual identity development. We further suggest that although LGB identity models provide excellent sources for understanding potential conflicts, it is important to help Juan articulate what an LGB identity means for him.

In addition to conceptualizing Juan's case through an identity development model, we urge mental health practitioners to consider self-exploration and receive appropriate training to effectively treat LGB clients. According to a recent study, 99% of practitioners reported seeing at least one gay or lesbian client during their professional career (Murphy et al., 2002). Research also suggests that gay and lesbian clients utilize individual therapy more frequently than heterosexual individuals. Although there is ample evidence to demonstrate that LGB and heterosexual individuals share the same rate of psychological functioning, Murphy et al. posited that LGB clients possess unique additional concerns (i.e., the coming-out process, antigay harassment, eating disorders, and substance abuse). These related factors may be attributed to the additive effects of oppression related to both gender and sexual orientation. The prevalence of LGB clients necessitates the need for practitioners and trainees to evaluate their own attitudes and beliefs regarding LGB individuals (Hancock, 2000). Hancock (2000) suggested that practitioners and trainees who hold negative feelings toward LGB persons may engender harm toward their clients. Practitioners who harbor this attitude are at the risk of perpetuating and exacerbating internalized homophobia that clients may possess.

Biracial and Multiracial People and Counseling

As described earlier, Juan is a biracial individual. The terms biracial and multiracial generally describe individuals with parents of different racial categories, irrespective of their personal racial self-identity (Rockquemore & Brunsma, 2002; Miville & Romero, 2007). These terms also can refer to individuals who have parents of the same socially designated race, if one or both of the parents are multiracial or if there is an acknowledgment of cross-racial mixing in the family history (Root, 1996). Multiracial is a broader term that includes people who claim two or more racial backgrounds (e.g., Black, White, Asian), such as individuals who have at least one parent who self-identifies as biracial and another parent of a different racial background (Root, 1996).

The 2000 U.S. Census marked a critical moment in which multiracial individuals finally began to gain governmental legitimacy with respect to their rich and complex racial heritage (Miville, 2005). Indeed, according to the 2000 census, nearly 7 million people checked more than one racial category, representing 2.4% of the total U.S. population. Prior to this time, biracial and multiracial people were often in legal and social limbo, given laws against interracial marriage and strict rules regarding hypodescent (i.e., percentage of so-called Black blood) (Fernandez, 1996). Thus, it is only within the past two decades that most theory and research describing the unique experiences of multiracial people has been proposed and conducted. With the publication of several book-length works (e.g., Brown, 2001; Rockquemore, 2002; Root, 1992, 1996), pioneering scholars have recently been able to present a variety of theories, methodologies, findings, and suggestions for interventions regarding multiracial people in a single forum (Miville, 2005). Moreover, a number of conceptual models have been proposed describing the racial identity development of biracial and multiracial people (e.g., see Kerwin & Ponterotto, 1995; Poston, 1990; Root, 1998).

To date, most of the available research focuses on multiracial people with one White parent, and far less information is available regarding individuals whose parents are from differing racial-ethnic minority groups (Miville, 2005). Thus, in a case like Juan's, it will be important for counselors to develop an understanding of the cultural dynamics of first-generation Filipino young adults and of African American people, keeping in mind that Juan grew up around more Filipinos than African Americans. In addition, counseling psychologists have developed specific recommendations and guidelines for working with multiracial people. Root (in Wehrly, 1996, cited in Miville & Romero, 2007) identified six key themes that may affect multiracial clients in counseling:

1. Uniqueness. Uniqueness is a predominant theme that likely interacts with other clinical issues. A sense of uniqueness may lead to behaviors misdiagnosed as pathological or maladjusted. Moreover, as Wehrly (1996) noted, "Living as a unique individual all of one's life sometimes leads to strong feelings of isolation and depression" (p. 128).

2. Acceptance and belonging. As a multiracial participant in a study by Miville, Constantine, Baysden, and So-Lloyd (2005) noted, "I think a lot of us are chameleons," meaning that many multiracial people can fit into a number of social groups, but perhaps never fully participate or feel connected to any one group, except perhaps with other multiracial people. Social barriers to full group membership may give rise to feelings of loneliness, anxiety, and depression.

3. Physical appearance. A unique physical appearance can lead to multiple experiences of being openly stared at or questioned; for example, the matching of their name with their physical presence. Constant questioning of who or even what someone is may be associated with feelings of being judged or negatively evaluated by others.

4. Sexuality. The exotic nature with which multiracial individuals, particularly women, are viewed in the larger society, as well as a presumption of promiscuity, may lead to outright discrimination as well as feelings of evaluation and objectification by others. Relationship issues may occur for both multiracial individuals and their partners in dealing with internalized stereotypes or fantasies based on prevailing sexual myths about multiracial individuals.

5. Self-esteem. Being or feeling different or unique may lead some (though not all) multiracial individuals to struggle with their self-esteem and to strive to excel to feel better about themselves. At the same time, it is important for counselors to not presume that low self-esteem is automatically a concern for their multiracial clients and to explore positive feelings their clients might have about being who they are (different and unique as well as parallels with others).

6. Identity. As noted earlier, identity issues may be of concern for multiracial clients. However, it is important to support clients in their efforts to identify and emphasize strengths of their multiracial heritage. Some strengths may involve an ability to negotiate with a variety of social groups and settings and to cross rigid social boundaries, along with an awareness of the importance of doing so. Moreover, multiracial individuals may privately identify as such but publicly identify as a member of a particular racial or ethnic group (e.g., Black or Asian). Part of facilitating identity development may be to support the simultaneous adoption of multiple labels, as well as to help find a supportive social network.

Feminist Therapy and Relational Approaches

Because of the uniqueness of Juan's background, we suggest the use of relational and feminist approaches for therapy. Relational or interpersonal approaches endorse the perspectives that humans are social by nature and that intrapsychic conflicts are always to some extent rooted in interpersonal dynamics (Teyber, 2000). Working from a feminist perspective, the therapist is aware of power dynamics both inside and outside of the therapy room (Brown, 1994), allowing for attention to oppressed social identities based on gender, race, sexual orientation, and social class. Though early feminist frameworks of therapy emphasized gender as the most important variable of analysis, other feminists who call themselves "radical," "multicultural," and "third wave" believe in the interconnectedness of oppression and power. In short, feminist therapy is inadequate without a focus on all facets of human diversity (Brown, 1994).

Feminist and relational approaches to counseling complement one another quite well because a central feature of feminist therapy is an egalitarian relationship between client and therapist. Combining relational perspectives with a feminist theoretical orientation also acknowledges that individuals have relationships with social systems. Checking in with clients about how the counseling relationship is proceeding with attention to power dynamics can help both therapists and clients to understand other relationships in clients' lives, particularly those in which there may be an abuse of power. Some feminist therapists have combined principles of relational and feminist therapy together in a framework called relational-cultural theory (RCT), which emphasizes the need for healthy connections. Jordan and Walker (2004) summarized this approach:

> The complexity of connection and of relationships arises from unequal power, from working with difference, or from trying to manage conflict creatively. RCT recognizes that all relationships are punctuated by disconnections, misunderstandings, and conflict. Connecting in a real, growthful way with others is not always harmonious or comfortable; we all experience fear, anger, and shame. We move away to protect ourselves, particularly if we are not met with empathic responsiveness or if we feel we do not matter to the other person. But when we can renegotiate these inevitable disconnections, the relationship is enhanced and personal feelings of well-being, creativity, and clarity increase. (p. 6)

RCT not only emphasizes relationships as important for healing, but also places connection with others and the self at the center of what it means to be healthy and to thrive. Unequal power can disrupt or complicate connections. Juan may be experiencing a "crisis of disconnection" with his family because of his gay identity. Perhaps his mother had expectations for him to marry a woman and have a family, and his "failure" to meet those expectations is affecting their relationship. This disconnection may be very difficult for Juan because he continues to play a central role in his family.

Though typically conceived of as an appropriate framework with women (Devoe, 1990), the principles of feminist therapy may be applied to all clients, particularly those from marginalized groups. A framework that empowers clients within a relationship that strives to be egalitarian would certainly be a helpful foundation for working with Juan. Feminist therapy also provides an understanding of the harm done to men by rigid models of masculinity arising from patriarchy, which penalize men for deviating from masculine norms (Brown, 1994). This may be particularly important to highlight with Juan. As a gay man raised with traditional Filipino values, Juan may be struggling to develop his gender and sexual identity with few positive masculine role models that mirror him. In addition, Juan may choose to act hypermasculine to avoid discrimination based on his gay identity.

Multicultural Counseling: Addressing Intersections and Interconnections

Research and training on multicultural competence in counseling has focused on three important areas for counselors: awareness, knowledge, and skills (American Psychological Association, 2003). Awareness refers first and foremost to the counselors' understanding of their own cultural identities, world view, and biases. Counselors also need to have specific knowledge of the cultural groups they are likely to encounter in their work and the skills that go beyond traditional training in psychotherapy (e.g., advocacy skills). In addition to the three dimensions of multicultural competence, multicultural psychologists have proposed three characteristics of multiculturally competent practitioners: a commitment to actively engaging in a process of understanding their own attitudes, including values and biases; a commitment to understanding the world view of clients who are culturally different; and a commitment to developing intervention strategies that are appropriate and relevant for each client based on their cultural experiences (Sue, Arredondo, & McDavis, 1992).

When working with LGB people of color, mental health practitioners must consider how sexism, heterosexism, and racism may collectively affect clients. Each form of social oppression may be overt or covert, conscious or unconscious, and intentional or unintentional (Miville & Ferguson, 2006). Mental health practitioners need to recognize that these intersections may be of varying significance at different times in their client's lives. Miville and Ferguson (2004) proposed that LGB people of color often are forced to choose one community over another, such as family, their religious community, the LGB community, or their racial or cultural community. Thus, practitioners need to be cautious in utilizing prescriptive treatments and instead jointly work with clients to cultivate their personal identities, at the discretion of the clients.

Juan is grappling with his identities of being gay, biracial (Filipino and Black), and male, and the integration of these multiple identities can be difficult to achieve. Juan, who has been raised by his biological Filipina mother, may be greatly influenced by Filipino cultural norms. For example, Filipino culture defines the family as the most important social institution (Lee, 2002). In addition, profamily and promasculine standards are abundant and highly treasured among Filipinos (Lee, 2002). Moreover, the values of raising a family through a heterosexual union impart a message that homosexual relations are not valued. As Bridges, Selvidge, and Matthews (2003) noted, LGB "relationships are not just seen as wrong; there is simply no frame of reference for even articulating or understanding them" (p. 119). Therefore, Juan's belief that he is not accepted by his Filipino family members may stem from not only his biracial heritage, but their disdain toward his sexual identity as well. The fact that he is not fulfilling the cultural prescription of getting married and raising children may be construed as a breach in loyalty to his family and culture. Although Juan partly fulfills his masculine expectations through his ability to work full-time and provide for his needs and perhaps those of his family, fulfilling such expectations may present an internal conflict for Juan. In short, his familial responsibilities may compete with his desire to concentrate on his academic and professional aspirations, as well as adopt a nonconforming gender role.

In addition, being a gay man of color may pose a social status conflict for Juan. For example, gay men of color may find that the social status connected with being male may make it difficult to fully identify and integrate an LGB identity because of the presumed lower social status attributed to gender nonconformity (Miville & Ferguson, 2006). When considering these potential conflicts, mental health practitioners may find it beneficial to help clients develop a sense of how these identities present both internal and external conflicts.

In light of these concerns regarding multiple identities, practitioners can be cognizant of imposing oppressive values, thoughts, or beliefs onto their client. The foundation of theoretical orientations within mental health is couched in Eurocentric, patriarchal, heterocentric, and individualistic beliefs. Therefore, practitioners need to be aware of how these frameworks may eclipse the impact of societal oppression. In addition, mental health practitioners who work with LGB people of color cannot assume that this population is a homogenous entity. Moreover, a treatment that is found effective with one LGB client of color may not be beneficial for other LGB clients of color.

Session Analysis

Juan was seen for 10 sessions at the counseling center at his community college, which provides personal counseling, career counseling, and academic advising. On his application, he stated that he wanted to participate in counseling because of "family stress, having a hard time sleeping, and anxiety that makes it hard to breathe sometimes." He also indicated that he preferred to see a therapist who was gay or lesbian, or at least one who was very knowledgeable about LGB people. The counseling center director assigned him to a graduate student intern, Ana, who is an openly lesbian woman, and who identifies as multiracial (Latina/White; ethnically, Puerto Rican and European American).

The waiting room and counseling rooms all contain literature and symbols welcoming diverse groups of people, including LGB and transgendered people, people of different racial and ethnic groups, and people with disabilities. The counseling center offers support groups for people from minority groups, such as a group for LGB students of color.

During the first two sessions, Juan was mainly concerned about being understood. Issues of trust were at the forefront, and he seemed very cautious and hesitant to speak. The counselor's focus was on creating a safe space and explaining the nature of the counseling relationship, as this was Juan's first time in counseling. Here is a vignette from the first session:

> *Juan:* It's just…I haven't talked about this to anyone before. Just my boyfriend, really.

Counselor: And I'm really a stranger to you.

Juan: Yeah. And I'm talking about my family. I don't want you to get the wrong idea, to think that I'm like putting them down. It's like I'm betraying my mom.

Counselor: This is difficult, then…coming here to try to get help for how anxious you're feeling, and then feeling protective of your family because they love and support you, but you have other feelings too…

Juan: (*silence*). I'm just not sure you're going to get where I'm coming from. I mean, I'm glad that I got a lesbian counselor, but my family is Filipino and we're very tight. I don't know if you'll get that.

Counselor: Well, there are definitely differences between us, and there might be times when I don't understand, but I hope we can work through that and talk about those differences…

Juan's disclosure of his fear that his counselor will not understand him because of his culture opened up a door for him and Ana to talk about race, ethnicity, and culture in the first session. Ana shared that she identifies as multiracial, but acknowledged the privilege that she has because of her lighter skin. Juan began to talk a bit about being Black, but having no one to identify with in his family. At the end of the session, Ana checked in with Juan about how he felt, validating that it really is difficult to begin this process, but that she had hope that a counseling relationship has something to offer him.

As sessions progressed, Juan talked more about the pressure that he feels as he negotiates his roles in school, his family, and his relationship with his boyfriend. This vignette shows what could be a clash of cultural values and how it was worked through from a relational perspective.

Juan: I'm just so tired all the time…I feel like my family puts so much pressure on me to do everything! It's like everything would fall apart if I wasn't taking care of things.

Counselor: It must be really hard to focus on you, to take care of yourself.

Juan: (*with anger*) Well, I have no choice! And anyway, I wouldn't have it any other way…my mom needs me. What do you mean "take care of myself?" You think I'm not taking care of myself?

Counselor: You seem angry…

> *Juan:* Well, yeah! I mean, you make it sound so easy, just to "take care of myself."
>
> *Counselor:* …well, maybe what I said sounded kind of judgmental…and a bit disconnected from who you are. The idea that taking care of yourself is separate from taking care of your family is pretty American…I'm wondering if you've felt like this before.
>
> *Juan:* Well, a lot of my American friends, especially my White friends, give me the same advice. I'm kind of sick of it. And in here I've felt like I could trust you, so it really pissed me off…

In this session, Ana attempted to acknowledge how hard it was for Juan to focus on himself, to "take care of himself." Juan responded with frustration at Ana, who then was able to own that her statement might have been judgmental and not in tune with Juan, as well as where else this has occurred for Juan. They next talked a little about how this interaction reminded him of others in his life and how confusing it was to have so many messages about taking care of others, especially family (Filipino), and taking care of self (White American). Juan also wondered aloud how his father's family dealt with these kinds of problems.

Juan missed the next session, stating he was out "sick" with the flu, but then came back the following week.

> *Counselor:* How have the past couple of weeks been?
>
> *Juan:* You know, same old stuff. I still am not sleeping well, and last night I had an argument with my boyfriend.
>
> *Counselor:* What about?
>
> *Juan:* He was feeling lonely since I'd not been able to see him for a few days. I just told him sometimes family comes first.
>
> *Counselor:* Sounds like you might have been feeling a little pulled to take care of him too…
>
> *Juan:* Yeah, maybe…
>
> *Counselor:* So what's it like to come back to talk with me…
>
> *Juan:* To tell you the truth, I was a little nervous about coming back. You know, we had a good talk last time, but I was still doubting a little what you're here for.
>
> *Counselor:* Well, thanks for saying that—I was wondering how it felt for you. I also think that telling me that is important to our work here…Helps us stay connected… You know, last time we met, we talked about mixed messages you got from different family

members and friends, and feeling expectations to take care of loved ones, you know, to "be a good son," yet feeling so burned out...Can you tell me who you mean when you use the word "family"?

Juan: Well, I guess that would be my mother and brothers, aunts and cousins...

Counselor: Anyone else?

Juan: My boyfriend I guess...

Counselor: That makes a lot of sense...but I might guess you don't feel like you have the "right" to devote time to him, like you do with your other family members, let alone have him devote time to you...

Juan: Mmm, I never thought about it that way...I just try to do what I need to do, and I know I'm not ashamed of who I am...

In this session, Ana checked into what it was like for Juan to come back to counseling after their last session, acknowledging that being able to express his feelings of apprehension about coming back for therapy was important. She also asked Juan to articulate what "family" meant to him, affirming his recognition of his boyfriend as part of his "family" and how this may become a more supportive aspect of his life (i.e., normalizing that he had a right to devote attention to his partner). Remaining sessions focused on areas of confusion and mixed messages in Juan's life, whether it was from family and friends, parent and partner, mother and father (who was absent). Juan also began to take a yoga class which he really liked, and began to feel more accepting of finding ways to rest and relax, especially since this helped him to better help his family.

Evidence-Based Practice Implications

In the past two decades, evidence-based treatments have emerged in the field of professional psychology. Managed health care's agenda to reduce costs has played a pivotal role in the movement toward briefer, more prescriptive treatment. Moreover, mental health practitioners are expected to utilize empirically supported interventions to ensure more efficient and effective outcomes. Perhaps for the first time since the conception of the scientist–practitioner model, science is of immediate relevance to practitioners (e.g., Acierno, Hersen, & Van Hasselt, 1996, in Chwalisz, 2003). As a consequence of the demand for brevity and empirically based treatment, there has been a preponderance of workshops, curricula, and symposia that addresses this need for mental health professionals. In addition, in 1996, in response to the need for clarity of scientific bases for various intervention practices in counseling psychology, as well as a professional practice environment that increasingly insists on accountability, truth in advertising, and cost effectiveness, Gerald Stone (then president of Division 17) and James Lichtenberg (then the division's vice president for science) proposed the formation of a Special Task Group on empirically supported interventions in counseling psychology (Wampold, Lichtenberg, & Waehler, 2002).

Despite the trend in employing evidence-based practice, a number of psychologists have expressed their opposition to specific, manualized treatments. Sturdee (2001) noted, "Scientific evidence cannot provide proof, it can only affirm our commitment to the conceptual structures and the theoretical constructs provided by the paradigm within which what counts as evidence has already been defined" (p. 499, in Chwalisz, 2003). Furthermore, Antony and Rowa (2005) elucidated a multitude of reasons that erode the potency of evidence-based practice. First, empirically based interventions necessitate a concrete diagnosis from the *Diagnostic and Statistical Manual of Mental Disorders* (American Psychiatric Association, 2000). The need for a solidified diagnosis eclipses the treatment of other presenting mental health concerns that a client may grapple with (i.e., depression). In addition, individuals who fail to satiate the requisite diagnostic features cannot benefit from evidence-based treatment. Moreover, when utilizing empirically supported interventions, individuals need to meet all the requirements for a specific diagnosis because treatment is solely tailored for a specific, individual diagnostic taxonomy.

In addition to the previously mentioned concerns regarding empirically supported treatment, it is important to consider the utility of empirically based interventions when working with specific populations. The empirical evidence surrounding treatment is based on the general population of adults (Baez, 2005). Consequently, the narrowly defined sample base limits the generalizability of treatment toward other crucial populations, namely, college populations, populations of color, and LGB populations.

Clinical symptoms presented by Juan point to a possible anxiety disorder. These disorders represent the most common mental health concern in the United States and are among the most frequently reported in college mental health (Baez, 2005). Statistics demonstrate that anxiety disorders often have a detrimental impact on students' academic performance, attendance, retention, career selection, and relationship development, as well as on their physical health and general well-being (Baez, 2005). In addition, symptoms of anxiety can emerge in a variety of ways. For example, anxiety can manifest in response to a traumatic situation (i.e., physical or sexual assault), academic-related concerns (i.e., tests), and during unexpected times of the day (i.e., waking up with panic-like symptoms). Moreover, it is important to consider that other presenting symptoms can mask the presence of anxiety. Depression and alcohol and illicit drug use are prevalent mental health concerns that often emerge to manage anxiety. When treating Juan, it is important to consider his multiple identities, and to conceptualize his case holistically.

Despite the prevalence of anxiety disorders among college students, university counseling centers markedly lack empirically supported interventions hinged upon a college-aged constituency (Baez, 2005). The dearth of empirical evidence germane to college students is based solely on nonclinical samples (i.e., psychology undergraduate students who volunteer for research studies). Although college counseling centers seem to be an ideal place to adopt evidence-based treatment because they afford short-term therapy, college counseling centers average only approximately 3.3 sessions per client (Draper, Jennings, Baron, Erdur, & Shankar, 2002). In contrast, at least 20 sessions per client are rendered short term in evidence-based practice. This marked difference threatens the applicability of evidence-based treatment within college settings. Unfortunately, empirically supported interventions fail to accommodate for other mental health issues that a client may also present with. Baez asserted that practitioners who work in college settings must employ a holistic assessment, meaning clinicians should be cognizant of other components such as normative developmental concerns relating to college and other mental health disorders.

Although there is a conspicuous dearth of empirically supported interventions concerning anxiety disorders among college students, significant results for this population are found in a few studies. Borkovec et al. (1987) found significant results for the treatment of generalized anxiety disorder with a combination of relaxation training and cognitive therapy. Furthermore, Valdez (2003) conducted a study illustrating that cognitive restructuring among White American and Mexican American college students is an effective treatment module to reduce the level of anxiety surrounding school-related issues. For panic disorders, studies have shown that therapist efficacy and clinical experience (average 8.9 years) are instrumental factors in the effective practice of cognitive-behavioral therapy.

As noted earlier, Juan presents with anxiety-related symptoms that manifest physiologically (i.e., Juan has trouble breathing and sleeping). As we discussed earlier, it is critical to conceptualize Juan's case holistically and account for environmental or oppression factors that may contribute to his anxiety level. For example, Juan juggles work and school responsibilities, while taking care of his chronically ill mother. Juan also worries that his role as a caretaker and his responsibility to work may serve as an impediment to pursuing his goals of obtaining a bachelor's degree. Utilizing a feminist and multicultural framework, we see there is an apparent conflict between U.S. values (i.e., individualism and goal attainment) and his mother's traditional Filipino values (i.e., collectivism and family is priority). It is imperative to honor the client's narrative and world view rather than to impose Western-oriented views of therapy that convey autonomy as the most adaptive and healthy therapeutic goals. A clinician who works with Juan may want to empower him with strategies on identifying anxiety-provoking contexts and managing these symptoms.

A major challenge in considering evidence-based practice for this case is the scant research that exists on biracial men, particularly gay biracial men. We urge that additional research be conducted on working with biracial and multiracial individuals of "multiple minority" status because the issues they face, in addition to the distinct challenges and unique resiliencies, may be similar to those of other biracial people (e.g., ambiguous appearance, exoticizing). For the time being, it is clear that therapists must practice caution in applying manualized treatments for anxiety for clients such as Juan. In addition to cognitive-behavioral strategies for managing anxiety, and given the preponderance of external or environmental stressors beyond Juan's control, along with ensuing internal struggles, helping Juan articulate these conflicts while emphasizing his strengths in the face of these challenges may be effective.

Identification of Authors' Personal Dimensions of Diversity and World View

As lesbian and bisexual women of color, we bring a unique perspective to this case. Our experiences negotiating multiple identities in our families and in our professional lives impact the ways in which we choose to work with Juan. Certainly our choice of a feminist relational framework is impacted by our gendered experiences. Two of the authors identify as biracial Latinas, and one author identifies as Filipina. Our multiple identities reflect experiences of oppression, and we discussed the similarities and differences between our cultural experiences as we worked on this chapter.

A perspective that we share based on our experiences negotiating multiple identities is that one identity is not inherently more important than another. Though sometimes asked to choose among our allegiance to race(s), gender, and the LGB community, we know this is an "impossible choice" (Miville & Ferguson, 2004). We are all of these identities at the same time and thus cannot deny or minimize any one group membership. We understand that our identities and social group memberships are fluid and dynamic, rather than static, over time and situation. On the basis of our experiences, we know that identity is not a simple linear development process, and we assume the same for Juan. Perhaps there are aspects of Juan's experience that we as women may have overlooked. However, because we come from a world view that encourages counselors to keep their eyes open to power dynamics and the influence of socially constructed categories on personal and relational experiences, we hope our work with Juan will be as dynamic as his (and our) identities.

Conclusions and Recommendations for Practitioners

We presented the case of Juan, utilizing several approaches we believe are important to integrate for competent practice, including LGB affirming, feminist, and relational perspectives. We also highlighted unique challenges of incorporating EBPP with clients like Juan for whom there is likely little research evidence supporting the validity of manualized treatments. Although we believe that empirically based interventions may be helpful for Juan, we urge practitioners to proceed with caution in applying such interventions and heed their clinical observations when doing so. Indeed, we believe that to ignore the environmental and oppressive structures that currently affect Juan may lead to a further exacerbation of his presenting issues rather than their effective treatment.

In thinking about Juan's case, we suggest that professionals who may not share significant aspects of his identities (e.g., race, ethnicity, gender, and sexual orientation) consider the following when working with him:

- Explore in depth how/why Juan does not feel like he "fits in" with his mother's Filipino family. It will be important to explore how Juan identifies racially and ethnically. What are his ties to Filipino culture? How have Black/African American people and other people of color treated him? Has he been treated differently by his family because of his racial heritage and identity? It is possible that Juan has internalized negative beliefs about himself because of messages that he has heard about Black people, Filipino people, or people of color in general. Because of his biracial identity, he may have experienced invalidation with family members and with peers. It will be important to create a therapeutic environment that is supportive of Juan's chosen racial identity. This may be the first environment in which he experiences that support, providing a "corrective emotional experience" in the context of the therapeutic relationship (Teyber, 2000).

- In addition, explore in depth how/why Juan may feel that he does not fit in with his family because he is gay. For example, his behavior and appearance may deviate from traditional heterosexual male norms within his family. Religion also may play a role. Filipino families typically practice Catholicism, and he may have heard negative messages about homosexuality growing up. Assessing the support that Juan has for his gay identity will be crucial. For example, are there extended family members (e.g., cousins of his generation) that embrace or might embrace his identity? Does his peer network embrace both his racial identity and gay identity? Has he found a network of LGB people of color, in addition to his boyfriend? Juan mentioned attending an event sponsored by a multicultural LGB club. How involved is he with these types of organizations on his campus or elsewhere? Practitioners may create a supportive environment in which Juan authentically explores his gay identity. Internalized homophobia may be confronted and explored in a gentle and supportive manner. Exploring Juan's feelings about being "out" to his family will be helpful.

- Further, exploring sources of support for his relationship with his partner beyond his family also is critical. Is his partner's family accepting of him and of their relationship? Are friends supportive of their relationship? In order to strengthen Juan's social support around issues of racial identity and sexual orientation, therapists will need to have knowledge about support groups and other community resources. Part of this may be helping to affirm a more expansive understanding of "family" for Juan.

- Explore how/why Juan perceives his family as "too traditional" and seeks a connection with his father's side of the family. This concern may stem from a clash in cultural values between Juan and his maternal family. Thus, Juan's interest in connecting with his paternal family may reflect both genuine curiosity and frustration about his current family situation. Juan also may yearn for a relationship with his father. Again, this yearning may be shaped, in part, by his disconnection from his maternal family by not being "pure Pinoy." He further may feel disconnected by his father's family because his father was not as involved in his life.

- Explore Juan's anxiety from a holistic, strengths-based perspective. Objectively, Juan may not have the time to take care of himself with his current schedule. However, in working with Juan, it will be important to locate problems that are external to him: the pressures he is facing from his family, along with daily encounters of racism and homophobia. It also is important to assess the severity of his anxiety symptoms. Therapists may ask any number of the following questions: Are the symptoms preventing him from engaging in his daily work/school routine, and from taking care of himself? How does Juan generally feel, and what is he thinking about when he experiences problems with sleeping and breathing? How does he feel about his responsibilities to his mother and his families? Are these in alliance with his values? Is Juan experiencing conflict with traditional Filipino values about family? How does he reconcile his personal values and beliefs with those of his family? How are these beliefs shaped by being "from the States," like his father? It is possible that worry about Juan's mother's health is contributing to his anxiety. How does he feel about his mother being chronically ill? Is Juan taking on too much at school or work because of unrealistic expectations that he has for himself? How are these expectations shaped by social class, race, ethnicity, and gender? For example, Juan may feel that as the oldest child, especially as the oldest son, he is obligated to take care of his family. Perhaps other siblings are able to work, but he feels guilty asking for help.

In sum, the therapeutic relationship may be the first place for Juan where a "many/and," rather than an "either/or," approach honors and validates his various identities, regardless of the background of the therapist. From a relational perspective, this may be crucial to envisioning new types of supportive relationships for Juan, and for helping him to cope with the invalidation he has experienced in multiple contexts, including the intimate context of family. Therapists need to explore potential barriers to creating an empathic environment for Juan in which he can process painful feelings about race and other identities. As Miville and Ferguson (2006) note,

> Oppression affects individuals uniquely, such that their impact may affect people differentially.... As such, we recommend that mental health professionals help their clients to deconstruct their oppressive experiences [and environments] to define positive identities that incorporate their unique wishes, values, and contexts/communities. In this way, clients can develop a more holistic sense of self. (pp. 100–101)

Incorporating theoretical frameworks that allow for open dialogue, and recognition and support of the sources and psychological impact of oppression will be fruitful means of helping Juan, not only in alleviating anxiety symptoms, but also in finding health and hope in his identity and relationships with others.

Discussion Questions

1. What is meant by "LGB affirmative" counseling? How does such an approach help clients? How responsible should therapists be for knowing this approach?
2. What are relational and feminist perspectives? How might these approaches work with clients who are not female or who do not endorse feminist beliefs?
3. How do evidence-based interventions incorporate racial-ethnic, gender, and sexual orientation variables? What evidence currently exists to support the use of manualized treatments for people of color, women and men, and LGB populations? How might you incorporate your clinical skills and clients' backgrounds to develop effective EPPs for clients with multiple identities?
4. How might you integrate process-oriented therapy approaches (e.g., feminist) attuned to oppression issues with evidence-based interventions?
5. How important are experiences of oppression and privilege to developing a counseling relationship? How might your experiences with

oppression and privilege affect how you conceptualize a client with multiple oppressed identities?

6. How might you work with a client who has a different set of salient identities than yours (e.g., he strongly identifies as White gay man, and you identify as a Latino heterosexual man)?

7. How does your definition of healthy sexuality affect your professional relationship-building with an openly LGB client? With a client who is not "out" to himself/herself?

8. How important is "outness" as an LGB individual to psychological well-being? What are important factors in helping to facilitate this process with a client?

9. What attitudes do you have about multiracial people? Are some mixed race individuals more easily acceptable by you, for example, a client who mirrors part of your racial/ethnic background?

10. How does culture affect gender roles? How do you incorporate cultural beliefs and norms in working with a client who is nonconforming in their gender roles or sexual orientation?

11. How important is it to involve family and/or partners into your professional relationships? What impact might each individual (e.g., parent, same-sex partner) have on your therapeutic relationship?

Resources

Biracial/Multiracial Resources

Books

Delmin, C. (2002). *Burnt bread and chutney: Growing up between cultures- A memoir of an Indian Jewish girl.* New York: The Ballantine Publishing Group.

Gaskins, P. F. (Ed.). (1999). *What are you? Voiced of mixed-race young people.* Markam, Ontario: Fitzhenry & Whiteside Ltd.

Habibi, N. (2003). *Atul's quest.* San Diego, CA: Aventine Press.

Johnson, K. R. (1999). *How did you get to be a Mexican? A White/Brown Man's search for identity.* Philadelphia, PA: Temple University Press.

Massey, S. (1997). *The salaryman's wife.* New York: HarperTorch.

McBride, J. (1996). *The color of water: A Black man's tribute to his White mother.* New York: The Berkley Publishing Group.

Miville, M. L., & Romero, L. (2007). Counseling multiracial people: Attending to multiple selves in multiple contexts. In W. M. Parker, & M. A. Fukuyama (Eds.), *Consciousness raising: A primer for multicultural counseling* (3rd ed., pp. 161–180). Springfield, IL: Charles Thomas.

Senna, D. (1998). *Caucasia*. New York: The Berkely Publishing Group.

Walker, R. (2001). *Black, White, & Jewish: Autobiography of a shifting self.* New York: The Berkley Publishing Group.

Web Sites

Fulbeck, K. (2009). The Hapa Project. Retrieved January 26, 2009 from http://www.seaweedproductions.com/hapa

The FUSION Program for Mixed Heritage Youth (2009). fusionprogram.org. Retrieved January 26, 2009 from http://www.fusionprogram.org/index.php

MAVIN Foundation (2009). mavinfoundation.org. Retrieved January 26, 2009 from http://mavinfoundation.org/

Mixedasians (2009). mixedasians.com. Retrieved January 26, 2009 from http://www.mixedasians.com

The Multiracial Activist (2009). multiracial.com. Retrieved January 26, 2009 from http://www.multiracial.com/site/

Swirl (2009). swirlinc.org. Retrieved January 26, 2009 from http://www.swirlinc.org/

Films

Brosnan, P. (Producer) and Brady, E. (Director). (1998). *The Nephew* [*Motion Picture*]. Ireland: Irish Dream Time.

Chono-Helsley, M. (Producer) and Chono-Helsley, M. (Director). (1993). *Do 2 Halves Really Make a Whole?* [Documentary]. United States: Visual Communications.

Fulbeck, K. (Producer) and Fulbedk, K. (Director). (1991). *Banana Split* [*Documentary*]. United States: Seaweed Productions.

Kelley, M. (Producer) and Leroy, J. (Director). (2005). *Chasing Daybreak: A Film about Mixed Race in America* [*Documentary*]. United States: The MAVIN Foundation.

Lo, C. M. (Producer) and Lo, C. M. (Director). (2000). *Catfish in Black Bean Sauce* [*Motion Picture*]. United States: Black Hawk Entertainment.

Rossignon, C. (Producer) and Kassovitz, M. (Director). *Café au lait* (*aka Métisse*) [*Motion Picture*]. France: Canal+.

LGB Resources

Books

Garnets, L. D., & Kimmel, D.C. (Eds.). (1993). *Psychological Perspectives on Lesbian and Gay Male experiences.* New York: Columbia University Press.

Greene, Beverly (Ed.). (1997). *Ethnic and cultural diversity among lesbians and gay men.* Thousand Oaks: Sage Publications, Inc.

Hemphill, E. & Beam, J. (Eds.). (2007). *Brother to Brother, New Writings by Black Gay Men.* Washington, DC: Redbone Press.

Kumashiro, Kevin K (Ed.). (2004). *Restoried selves: Autobiographies of Queer Asian/Pacific American activists.* Binghamton: Harrington Park Press/The Haworth Press.

Longres, John F. (Ed.). (1996). *Men of color: A context for service to homo-sexually active men.* New York: Haworth Press.

Reid-Pharr, R. F. & Delany, S.R. (Ed.). (2001). *Black Gay Man: Essays. New York, NY: NYUPress.*

Savin-Williams, R.C & Cohen, K. M. (Eds.). (1996). *The lives of lesbians, gays, and bisexuals: Children to adults.* Orlando: Harcourt Brace College Publishers.

Sullivan, G. & Jackson, P.A. (Eds.). (2001). *Gay and Lesbian Asia: Culture, Identity, Community.* New York: Haworth Press.

Web Sites

APA Lesbian, Gay, and Bisexual Concerns Program. (2009). apa.org. Retrieved January 24, 2009, from http://www.apa.org/pi/lgbc/

Gay Asian & Pacific Islander Men of New York. (2009). Gapimny.org. Retrieved January 24, 2009, from http://www.gapimny.org/

Gay Men's Health Crisis. (2009). gmhc.org. Retrieved January 24, 2009, from http://www.gmhc.org/

National Gay and Lesbian Task. (2009). thetaskforce.org. Retrieved January 24, 2009, from http://www.thetaskforce.org/

Parents, Families & Friends of Lesbians and Gays. (2009). pflag.org. Retrieved January 24, 2009, from http://www.pflag.org/

Pride in the City. (2008). Prideinthecity.com. Retrieved January 24, 2009, from http://www.pridenthecity.com/

Films

Lee, A. (Producer), & Lee, A. (Director). (1993). *The Wedding Banquet* [*Motion Picture*]. China: Central Motion Pictures.

Lim, D. & Tulchinsky, K. X. (Producer), & Lim, D. (Director). (2005). *Floored by Love* [*Motion Picture*]. Canada: Reel Fang Productions.

Riggs, M. & Freeman, B. (Producer), & Riggs, M. (Director) (1990). *Tongues United: Black Men Loving Black Men* [*Documentary*]. United States: Frameline Productions.

Spadola, M. (Producer), & Spadola, M. (Director). (1992). *Orientations, Our House: Lesbians and Gays in the Hood* [*Motion Picture*], United States: Sugar Pictures Productions.

Wu, A. (Producer), & Wu, A. (Director). (2005). *Saving Face* [*Motion Picture*]. United States: Sony Pictures.

Wise, S. J. (Producer), & Wise, S. J. (Director). (2001). *A Different Kind of Black Man* [*Documentary*]. United States: Frameline Productions.

References

American Psychiatric Association. (2000). *Diagnostic and statistical manual of mental disorders* (text rev.). Washington, DC: Author.

American Psychological Association. (2003). Guidelines on multicultural education, training, research, practice, and organizational change for psychologists. *American Psychologist, 58*, 377–402.

Antony, M. M., & Rowa, K. (2005). Evidence-based assessment of anxiety disorders in adults. *Psychological Assessment, 17*, 256–266.

Baez, T. (2005). Evidence-based practice for anxiety disorders in college mental health. *Journal of College Student Psychotherapy, 20*, 33–48.

Borkovec, T. D., Mathews, A. M., Chambers, A., Ebrahimi, S., Lytle, R., & Nelson, R. (1987). The effects of relaxation training with cognitive or nondirective therapy and the role of relaxation-induced anxiety in the treatment of general anxiety. *Journal of Consulting and Clinical Psychology, 55*(6), 883–888.

Bridges, S. K., Selvidge, M. M. D., & Matthews, C. R. (2003). Lesbian women of color: Therapeutic issues and challenges. *Journal of Multicultural Counseling and Development, 31*, 113–130.

Brown, L. S. (1994). *Subversive dialogues: Theory in feminist therapy.* New York: Basic Books.

Brown, U. M. (2001). *The interracial experience: Growing up Black/White racially mixed in the United States.* Westport, CT: Praeger.

Cass, V. C. (1979). Homosexual identity formation: A theoretical model. *Journal of Homosexuality, 4,* 219–235.

Chwalisz, K. (2003). Evidence-based practice: A framework for twenty-first century scientist practitioner training. *The Counseling Psychologist, 31*(5), 497–528.

Cooper, S. (2005). Evidence-based psychotherapy practice in college mental health. *Journal of College Student Mental Health, 20,* 1–6.

Devoe, D. (1990). Feminist and nonsexist counseling: Implications for the male counselor. *Journal of Multicultural Counseling and Development, 69,* 33–36.

Draper, M. R., Jennings, J., Baron, A., Erdur, O., & Shankar, L. (2002). Time-limited counseling outcome in a nationwide college counseling center sample. *Journal of College Counseling, 3,* 26–38.

Fernandez, C. A. (1996). Government classification of multiracial/multiethnic people. In M. P. P. Root (Ed.), *The multiracial experience: Racial borders as the new frontier* (pp. 15–36). Thousand Oaks, CA: Sage.

Hancock, K. A. (2000). Lesbian, gay, and bisexual lives: Basic issues in psychotherapy training and practice. In B. Greene & G. Croom (Eds.), *Education, research, and practice in lesbian, gay, bisexual, and transgendered psychology* (pp. 91–131). Thousand Oaks, CA: Sage.

Jordan, J. V., & Walker, M. (2004). Introduction. In J. V. Jordan, M. Walker, & L. M. Hartling (Eds.), *The complexity of connection: Writings from the Stone Center's Jean Baker Miller Training Institute* (pp. 1–8). New York: Guilford.

Kerwin, C., & Ponterotto, J. G. (1995). Biracial identity development: Theory and research. In J. G. Ponterotto, J. M. Casas, L. A. Suzuki, & C. M. Alexander (Eds.), *Handbook of multicultural counseling* (1st ed., pp. 199–217). Thousand Oaks, CA: Sage.

Lee, R. B. (2002). Psychosocial contexts of the homosexuality of Filipino men in heterosexual unions. *Journal of Homosexuality, 42,* 35–63.

McCarn, S. R., & Fassinger, R. E. (1996). Revisioning sexual minority identity formation: A new model of lesbian identity and its implications. *Counseling Psychologist, 24,* 508–534.

Miville, M. L. (2005). Psychological functioning and identity development of biracial people: A review of current theory and research. In R. T. Carter (Ed.), *Handbook of racial-cultural psychology and counseling, Volume I: Theory and research* (pp. 295–319). New York: Wiley.

Miville, M. L., Constantine, M. G., Baysden, M. F., & So-Lloyd, G. (2005). Chameleon changes: An exploration of racial identity themes of multiracial people. *Journal of Counseling Psychology, 52,* 507–516.

Miville, M. L., & Ferguson, A. D. (2004). Impossible "choices": Identity and values at a crossroad. *The Counseling Psychologist, 32,* 760–770.

Miville, M. L., & Ferguson, A. D. (2006). Intersections of sexism and heterosexism with racism: Therapeutic implications. In M. G. Constantine & D. W. Sue (Eds.), *Racism as a barrier to cultural competence in mental health and educational settings* (pp. 87–106). New York: Wiley.

Miville, M. L., & Romero, L. (2007). Counseling multiracial people: Attending to multiple selves in multiple contexts. In W. M. Parker, & M. A. Fukuyama (Eds.), *Consciousness raising: A primer for multicultural counseling* (3rd ed., pp. 161–180). Springfield, IL: Charles Thomas.

Murphy, J. A., Rawlings, E. I., & Howe, S. R. (2002). A survey of clinical psychologists on treating lesbian, gay, and bisexual clients. *Professional Psychology: Research and Practice, 33*, 183–189.

Palma, T. V., & Stanley, J. (2002). Effective counseling with lesbian, gay, and bisexual clients. *Journal of College Counseling, 5*, 74–89.

Poston, W. S. C. (1990). The biracial identity development model: A needed addition. *Journal of Counseling and Development, 69*, 152–155.

Rockquemore, K. A. (2002). *Beyond Black: Biracial identity in America.* Thousand Oaks, CA: Sage.

Rockquemore, K. A., & Brunsma, D. L. (2002). Socially embedded identities: Theories, typologies, and processes of racial identity among Black/White biracials. *Sociological Quarterly, 43*, 335–356.

Root, M. P. P. (1992). *Racially mixed people in America.* Newbury Park, CA: Sage.

Root, M. P. P. (1996). *The multiracial experience: Racial borders as the new frontier.* Thousand Oaks, CA: Sage.

Root, M. P. P. (1998). Experiences and processes affecting racial identity development: Preliminary results from the Biracial Sibling Project. *Cultural Diversity and Mental Health, 4*(3), 237–247.

Root, M. P. P. (2002). Methodological issues in multiracial research. In G. C. N. Hall & S. Okazaki (Eds.), *Asian American psychology: The science of lives in context* (pp. 171–193). Washington, DC: American Psychological Association.

Sue, D. W., Arredondo, P., & McDavis, R. (1992). Multicultural counseling competencies and standards: A call to the profession. *Journal of Counseling and Development, 70*, 477–486.

Teyber, E. (2000). *Interpersonal process in psychotherapy* (4th ed.). Belmont, CA: Wadsworth/Thomson Learning.

Valdez, G. (2003). *Comparing the relative efficacy of cognitive restructuring between Anglo American and Mexican American college students.* Unpublished master's thesis, University of Texas, Austin, Texas.

Wampold, B. E., Lichtenberg, J. W., & Waehler, C. A. (2002). Principles of Empirically Supported Interventions in counseling psychology. *The Counseling Psychologist, 30*, 197–217.

Wehrly, B. (1996). *Counseling interracial individuals and families.* Alexandra, VA: American Counseling Association.

8

The Conflict of Navigating Cultural Expectations
The Case of Sam

Matt Englar-Carlson and Sophia Rath

Contents

Introduction

This chapter explores the case of Sam, a young adult male college student of Cambodian descent. Sam's life clearly shows how the recent sociopolitical history of Cambodia influences the mental health and acculturation of many Cambodians. This case example reviews the difficulties Sam experiences in living up to the cultural and familial expectations of being the eldest male child within his Cambodian culture, highlighting the intersection of ethnic and gender identities. Furthermore, this case will examine Sam's conflict in navigating family and traditional Cambodian notions of behavior compared with his own experiences in the Western world. Sam's struggle of acculturation and his means of trying to meet the expectations of his multiple identities are explored in psychotherapy. The case analysis explores Cambodian cultural themes and integrates a gender-sensitive therapeutic approach.

The current emphasis on evidence-based practice in psychology has been critiqued by many (Atkinson, Bui, & Mori, 2001; Bernal & Scharron-del-Rio, 2001; Whaley & Davis, 2007) who questioned whether the contemporary push for evidence-based practice has appropriately integrated a cultural perspective. Whaley and Davis (2007) offered the complementary notion of blending practice guidelines of culturally competent services (American Psychological Association [APA], 2003) with the need for evidence-based practice. They noted that one point of convergence between these two models is the development and use of culturally adapted interventions. Cultural adaptation is focused on modifying exiting evidence-based treatments to accommodate the cultural beliefs, expectations, attitudes, and beliefs of the client. Levant and Silverstein (2005) and Cochran (2005) highlighted that gender is an aspect of diversity that is often not addressed in evidence-based practice or in psychotherapy as commonly practiced in the community. However, numerous authors (see Brooks & Good, 2001; Englar-Carlson & Stevens, 2006; Rabinowitz & Cochran, 2002) have outlined gender-based cultural adaptations that can be made within the psychotherapy relationship to accommodate male clients of diverse backgrounds. Clinical expertise, as defined by the ability to identify and integrate the best research data with clinical data (APA, 2006), can guide psychotherapists to develop effective treatments with gender-based adaptations for male clients. Other research (Norcross, 2001; Wampold, 2001) on common components of effective psychotherapy has continually highlighted the contribution of the psychotherapy relationship or working alliance to successful outcome. Gender-based adaptations in service of creating effective psychotherapy relationships practice are grounded in a combination of existing theory and research about the new psychology of men with an integration of a clinician's own interpersonal expertise, assessment and judgment, decision making, and understanding of the contextual differences. In the treatment and conceptualization of the case of Sam, we look at the intersection of ethnicity and gender and the development of a strong therapeutic alliance as a way to practice culturally competent, evidence-based psychotherapy.

Theoretical Orientation

As a psychotherapist, I (MEC) have been theoretically influenced by Adlerian (Carlson, Watts, & Maniacci, 2006) and humanistic-existential (Bugental, 1978; Yalom, 1980) schools of psychology and by the emerging scholarship from the new psychology of men and masculinity (Englar-Carlson & Stevens, 2006; Levant & Pollack, 1995; Pollack & Levant, 1998). From Adlerian theory, I am specifically drawn to encouragement and social interest. Encouragement is a process of focusing on a person's resources and giving positive recognition to build a person's self-esteem, self-concept, and self-worth (Dinkmeyer, McKay, & Dinkmeyer, 1997). Encouragement begins with acknowledging that life can be difficult and instilling faith in clients that they have the potential to change. Building hope and expectation is viewed as a core component to successful therapy outcomes and has been viewed as a common component of successful therapies (Hubble, Duncan, & Miller, 1999; Wampold, 2001). Social interest is the kind of empathic bonding people feel for each other and the responsible actions and attitudes they take toward one another, a sense of belonging and participating with others for the common good. Developing greater compassion for others helps clients resolve their individual problems.

A considerable influence has been the wealth of multicultural and gender-aware guidelines and theories of practice. As a clinician, I have focused my practice on working with boys and men, and my approach tends to explore how multiple identities influence psychological well-being. Among other identity factors, gender is now recognized as a salient organizing variable of clients' lives and experiences. Understanding the gendered nature of masculinity is an important cultural competency (Levant & Silverstein, 2005; Liu, 2005; Mellinger & Liu, 2006). Guidelines developed for multicultural counseling competency (APA, 2003) and for practice with girls and women (APA, 2007) offer some direction and considerations in regard to helping psychologists work with men. These guidelines highlight the importance of the sociocultural context in tailoring psychotherapy to embrace the diverse identities of clients. Cochran (2005) noted the adoption of evidence-based practice as a dominant paradigm in psychology. In an age of theoretical integration, evidence-based practice is guided more by the use of research-based evidence for diagnosis and treatment, the use of clinical expertise to guide judgment, and the consideration of client values and preferences. Cochran observed that though the psychology of men is recognized as a distinct area of clinical practice, there has yet to be controlled studies that demonstrate the effectiveness of specific treatments with men. Thus, the field is guided more by integrating clinical expertise with masculinity ideologies and values.

The wealth of scholarly research and writing in the psychology of men has demonstrated an interesting paradox. Even though most of the theoretical work on psychotherapy was historically predicated on the lived experiences of men's lives, men themselves may not fully benefit from existing and accepted models of clinical treatment (Liu, 2005). Many men face unique psychosocial, cultural, and interpersonal challenges associated with masculine socialization experiences and changing cultural expectations of both male behavior and the roles of men (Brooks & Good, 2001). In terms of Asian American men, Liu (2002) found that Asian men endorsed traditional masculine ideology and that some traditional Asian values (such as controlled emotional expression and success for familial recognition) were related to dominant masculine values (Liu & Iwamoto, 2006). Furthermore, Asian American men often cope with racist and external pressure against their masculinity (Abreau, Ramirez, Kim, & Haddy, 2003), hegemonic gendered expectations (Chen, 1999; Liu, 2002, 2005), and traditional male Asian cultural expectations (e.g., avoidance of shame, collectivism, conformity to norms, deference to authority, emotional self-control, family recognition through achievement, filial piety, humility, and hierarchical relationships) (Kim, Atkinson, & Umemoto, 2001; Kim, Atkinson, & Yang, 1999).

When it comes to observing my clinical work in action, one could easily see a relational approach grounded on what I believe is the true foundation of effective therapy: a healthy and respectful client–therapist relationship. The APA Division of Psychotherapy Task Force (Norcross, 2001) clearly noted that the therapeutic relationship has consistently been an important contributor to outcome in the now extensive research on psychotherapy. Specific features of evidence-based practices emphasize the use of such relationship factors as the therapeutic alliance, empathy, and goal consensus (Hubble et al., 1999). Within the therapy relationship, I specifically address the working alliance (Bordin, 1994) with an emphasis on developing an agreement on the goals and tasks of therapy and experiencing an emotional bond with each other. Related to the working alliance, I am particularly aware of the real relationship. In this regard, I have been influenced by Gelso and Hayes (1998) by conceptualizing the real relationship in terms of genuineness (e.g., being honest, open, authentic, and congruent with one's inner being) between clients and myself and having realistic perceptions of each other that are not colored by transference distortions. For male clients, that often translates into more self-disclosure as a means to building a relational bridge and creating a sense of psychotherapy as a shared endeavor.

Cultural Considerations

The term Asian American is often used to refer to individuals residing in the United States who are indigenous to the Asian continent. Despite the heterogeneity that exists among Asian cultures, Asian Americans are often viewed as a single homogenous group (Chae, 2001; Okazaki & Hall, 2002). Although sharing Asian ancestry and aspects of Asian cultural heritage, Asian American is a broad term at best, as it encompasses a great diversity of nationalities and cultures that defy simple characterizations. Knowledge about one of these cultures may not necessarily apply to other Asian cultures. Although a growing body of literature addresses the counseling of Asian Americans, resources that attend to the counseling of Cambodian-descended clients is limited. This section will review some cultural considerations that can be useful to integrate into culturally adapted interventions for Cambodian-descended clients.

Many Cambodians in the United States are recent immigrants who fled the Cambodian Civil War. In 1975, the Khmer Rouge communist regime took over the nation's capital, Phnom Penh, and during the next 4 years, an estimated 1.5 to 3 million men, women, and children died in what has been touted as "the killing fields" (Kurlantzick, 2000; Lay, 2001; Peang-Meth, 1991). The client presented in this chapter, Sam, was born shortly after his mother and father escaped from a labor camp and traveled to a refugee camp in Thailand in the late 1970s. Like many other Cambodian families, Sam's family immigrated to Southern California in 1979. Cambodians compose one of the largest refugee groups in the United States, with approximately 150,000 refugees admitted since 1975 (U.S. Committee for Refugees, 1992; Wong et al., 2006). Despite having lived in the United States for several years, many Cambodian Americans continue to struggle with the repercussions of the traumas experienced in Cambodia, the immigration process, and acculturation. According to the Surgeon General's Report on Mental Health, "This national trauma, as well as the stressors associated with relocation, including English language difficulties and cultural conflicts, continues to affect the emotional health of many Cambodian refugees and other immigrants" (U.S. Department of Health and Human Services [USDHHS], 2001).

In a sociological-cultural overview of Cambodian, or Khmer, history and culture, Peang-Meth (1991) asserted that Cambodian values and beliefs are largely influenced by the religious and spiritual tenets of Theravada Buddhism and Hindu Brahmanism. Brahmanism specifically played a role in framing the castelike hierarchical structure that marks Cambodian societal and family structure to the present day. It is also from Brahmanism that Cambodians derive their belief in a spirit world. It is often during religious ceremonies that rituals are performed to encourage the blessings of benevolent spirits and ancestors while warding off more malevolent spirits (Boehnlein, Leung, & Kinzie, 1997).

Theravada Buddhism, meanwhile, plays a significant role in establishing a cultural tradition that encourages the virtues of harmony, tolerance, and acceptance. Excessive displays of emotion are frowned upon. Not only do emotional displays disrupt the harmony of the peaceful environment prized by traditional Cambodian culture, but an individual who reacts to an upsetting situation contradicts the ideal that although one is in sole control of one's destiny, one cannot avoid suffering. One must simply deal with the hand one has been dealt and focus on life as it is rather than on what it could be (Peang-Meth, 1991).

The Khmer Buddhist is taught to be peaceful, compassionate, agreeable, and understanding (Peang-Meth, 1991). What may be interpreted as disinterest or passivity may actually be a reflection of dual beliefs. Because of beliefs in karma and reincarnation, seeking peace and tranquility in this life will help to ensure a better station in the next. Conversely, the value of conservatism compels the Khmer to avoid risky situations and confrontation unless directly threatened. Though the individual may not always follow through, most requests will be responded to with "yes, it can be done." Refusal of a request by saying "no" is considered to be disrespectful. Honor and dignity are also highly valued within the Khmer culture, and a Khmer individual's key goal in life is to bring honor and goodness to one's family.

Although Cambodian American immigrants and their families may have resided in the United States for many years, cultural differences between traditional Eastern values and mainstream Western values can be a source of significant individual and interpersonal conflict. These difficulties are often influenced by parents' traditions and adherence to traditional norms, and by adolescents' acculturation to Western and American values (Xiong, Eliason, Detzner, & Cleveland, 2005).

In a discussion of the Cambodian American family, Boehnlein et al. (1997) described its dynamics in the context of the influence of recent history, the organization of the traditional Cambodian family, and acculturation. Because traditional Cambodian values are often imbedded in a strong sense of family identity, interdependence rather than independence is fostered from a young age. Even through adulthood, children are expected to defer to the advice and opinions of older family members and to orient personal interests to reflect the interests of the group. This is especially salient in the Cambodian culture in which children, including adult children, are expected to defer to filial piety. Because of their age and life experience, family elders are accorded the utmost respect and authority. Decisions made by parents and grandparents are not to be challenged; even adult children are expected to abide by the wishes of their families. The child is a member of the family and therefore is morally obligated to behave in a manner that upholds the family's traditions or "face" (Smith-Hefner, 1999). If a child misbehaves, then it reflects poorly on the entire family's reputation. For many Cambodian parents, the high expectation of retaining traditional values within the family is associated with their own experiences with the Khmer Rouge's attempts to eradicate these values (Rousseau, Drapeau, & Rahimi, 2003).

Research specific to the acculturative experiences of Cambodian immigrants to life in the United States is limited. Despite drastic mental health needs, there is limited guidance as to providing psychological services for this population. Many of the current references regarding acculturative adjustment and mental health for Cambodian refugees are confined within primary studies of psychopathology, such as post-traumatic stress disorder (PTSD), depression, and anxiety (Chung, 2001; Chung & Bemak, 2002; Hinton, Hsia, Um, & Otto, 2003), with little guidance as to culturally appropriate clinical work.

Culturally Responsive Treatment Considerations

There has been some research on the specific mental health needs and treatment of Cambodian-descended clients that can form the basis of effective evidence-based practice. Many Cambodians who came to the United States experienced the traumatic repercussions of Cambodia's seizure by the Khmer Rouge. Many Cambodian refugees are beset by high levels of current poverty, substantial exposure to pre- and postmigration trauma, and high rates of psychopathology (Marshall, Schell, Elliot, Berthold, & Chun, 2005). The Surgeon General's Report identified Cambodian refugees as a population with particularly high needs given their substantial rates of trauma exposure, poverty, and distress (USDHHS, 2001). These experiences have undoubtedly impacted the manner in which Cambodian refugees practice culture and child rearing (Boehnlein et al., 1997; McKenzie-Pollock, 2005). In reference to the effects of the war and social upheaval that took place in Cambodia, Peang-Meth (1991) asserted that the "rending of the social fabric will surely alter the force of traditionalism in Khmer society" (p. 451). Subsequently, it can also be presumed that these factors have affected how second-generation Cambodian Americans negotiate their roles as Americans in the context of their heritage and the environment in which they have been raised.

In the Cambodian culture, it is not uncommon for mental illness to be attributed to the presence of ancestral spirits (Nishio & Bilmes, 1987). Furthermore, because of the negative stigma associated with mental illness, some Asian American clients express emotional distress psychosomatically (Root, 1998). For many Cambodian people, emotional distress is presented as physical pain (McKenzie-Pollock, 2005). Chung (2001) noted that traumatized Cambodian women may express psychological distress through neurasthenia, a condition in which psychological distress is manifested in somatic symptomatology. Neurasthenia complements the traditional Asian belief that the mind and body are intermingled. Akutsu and Chu (2006) recommended a culturally sensitive yet concerted effort to probe for underreported issues of a sensitive or private nature. Whereas Southeast Asians tend to report more somatic complaints, it is possible that somatic complaints are a culturally sanctioned script on speaking about mental illness. Psychologists can be aware of this and look to probe deeper, beyond somatic symptoms. This is particularly significant because the reporting of somatic complaints may not be viewed as acute distress and may lead to later intake appointment assignments (Akutsu, Tsuru, & Chu, 2006). Yet, it is possible that somatic complaints mask more acute and severe mental health conditions that warrant swift clinical attention.

Despite the growing availability of mental health programs geared toward diverse populations, much of the available research on Asian Americans demonstrates low use of mental health services (Akutsu, Tsuru, & Chu, 2004).

When research specifically looks at Cambodian Americans, however, a different picture emerges. In a study investigating barriers to mental health care utilization for U.S. Cambodian refugees, Wong et al. (2006) discussed the effects of structural barriers (e.g., high cost and language problems) and cultural barriers (e.g., bias against Western treatment and anticipated racial and ethnic discrimination). They noted little endorsement of cultural barriers, such as distrust of Western care and preference for alternative care. Instead, the findings indicated more structural barriers (e.g., high cost of services and language incompatibility with treatment providers). Akutsu et al. (2004) found that among Asian Americans, Southeast Asians (i.e., Cambodians) were most likely to show up for intake appointments. Furthermore, gender matching with an intake counselor reduced the likelihood for intake appearance. Other research indicated that when Cambodian Americans seek mental health services, when compared to other Asian American groups, they have the highest prioritized assignment to intake appointments because of their mental health needs (Akutsu et al., 2006).

Adding more support, Marshall et al. (2006) found that Cambodian refugees with mental health problems had high rates of seeking services for psychological problems from medical and mental health care providers. They suggested that one reason for the high rates is that many Cambodian refugees, by virtue of having been granted refugee status, have had more contact with social service agencies in the United States. In addition, the Cambodian refugee community has such a large mental health burden because of its sociopolitical history that these needs might just overwhelm any structural or cultural barriers to psychological health seeking.

PTSD is a salient issue for many Cambodian Americans who faced the traumas of the Cambodian Civil War, which included physical and psychological torture, the loss of family members, and persecution by one's own people who forced relocation to another country (Chung, 2001; Chung & Bemak, 2002; Lim, Heiby, Brislin, & Griffin, 2002). A 2005 study (Marshall et al., 2005) of 586 adults who lived in Cambodia during the Khmer Rouge reign found that all participants had been exposed to trauma before migration, noting that 99% experienced near-death because of starvation, 90% had a family member or friend murdered, and 70% reported exposure to violence after settlement in the United States. This study found that two decades after resettlement in the United States, 62% of the participants had high rates of PTSD. A study of Cambodian female refugees found that 90% of the participants had lost between 1 and 10 family members, that many of the deaths were witnessed, and that many of the women were widows because of the war (Rozee & van Boemel, 1989). In a study conducted by Kinzie et al. (1990), 92% of Cambodians receiving care at a psychiatric clinic currently suffers or previously suffered from PTSD. Furthermore, Cambodian youth who experienced traumas at a young age have shown PTSD over long periods of time (Abe, Zane, & Chun, 1994).

According to Kinzie and Fleck (1987), PTSD among Cambodian refugees is marked by one of two types of symptom clusters that are either intrusive or avoidant. Intrusive symptoms include reexperiencing trauma and having nightmares, daytime visions of past trauma, and hypersensitive startle response. Avoidant symptoms include numbing, withdrawal, and conscious avoidance of memories of the past. An additional consideration is the understanding that although a client of Cambodian descent may not have directly been exposed to trauma, it is highly likely that this same client would be exposed to family members experiencing a range of PTSD symptoms. Given the stresses associated with acculturation, it would be prudent for psychologists to be aware that PTSD symptoms may be exacerbated by acculturative stress, and vice versa.

For Cambodian Americans, anxiety is another salient issue due to the fear associated with anxiety-related symptoms. Excessive worry, changes in appetite, or difficulties sleeping are believed to deplete bodily energy, which may result in "weak heart," or *khsaoy beh doung*, which may manifest as palpitations. This heart weakness, in turn, can lead to fears that the heart will be hyperreactive to stimulus (e.g., noise), that simple tasks such as standing may overstrain the heart, and even that the heart may suddenly stop beating and result in death (Hinton, Pich, Safren, Pollack, & McNally, 2006).

Anxiety may also result in "wind attacks," or *kaeut khyâl*. Wind attacks manifest with symptoms not unlike those associated with panic attacks and occur when the flow of *khyâl*, a windlike substance that is believed to run alongside blood, is disrupted (Hinton et al., 2006). Sensation in the limbs (e.g., coldness, fatigue, and numbness) is believed to be the result of blockage of *khyâl* and blood and may elicit fears of death of the limb. The sensation of blood rushing in the ears and dizziness is believed to result from *khyâl* and blood rushing upward in the body through the head.

There is often a link between PTSD and panic disorder. Hinton, Ba, Peou, and Um (2000) found that 60% of a community sample of Cambodian refugees suffered from panic disorder. The authors noted that panic disorder may have gone unnoticed because of the existence of a culturally specific presentation of panic attacks. Orthostatic-induced episodes of dizziness panic lead to fears that death will occur. Furthermore, "sore neck" panic attacks stem from fears that the neck vessels will burst because of an increase in "wind and blood" pressure (Hinton, Um, & Ba, 2001). These types of concerns lead to an emphasis for panic attacks on the neck and head region (e.g., dizziness, blurred vision, headache, neck pain, etc.). Hinton et al. (2000) developed a culturally adapted panic assessment for Cambodians (the Cambodian Panic Disorder Survey) that is based on the SCID-panic module (Structured Clinical Interview for the DSM-IV).

Depression is also considered a significant concern for Cambodian Americans. Akutsu and Chu (2006), in a study of presenting problems among different Asian American groups, found that almost all Cambodian Americans in the sample (87%) reported depression with concurrent suicidality and somatic complaints. The reported rate of depression for Cambodian Americans was 25% to 40% higher than in other Asian American groups. Marshall et al. (2005) reported that 51% of his Cambodian refugee community participant sample met the criteria for major depression. Depression was associated with experiencing premigration trauma, being older in age, having poor English proficiency, being unemployed, being retired or disabled, and living in poverty. The theme of loss is especially poignant when considering the clinical issues presented by Cambodian Americans. In Cambodia, an individual's social support is often derived from a network of extended family and other community intimates. Under the Khmer Rouge, however, families were methodically separated and destroyed to further the regime's power over the masses.

During the early stages of psychotherapy, it is critical to have basic knowledge of Cambodian culture-specific cultural norms, values, and ideas to avoid ethnic stereotyping. This is especially meaningful when working with Cambodian Americans, whose cultural identities have been markedly distressed by the traumas wrought not only by the Khmer Rouge regime, but also through the migration experience and acculturation to life in the United States (Boehnlein et al., 1997). Psychologists who discount the experiences immigrant families have endured run the risk of overlooking and underutilizing valuable information that can contribute to a successful therapeutic experience (Chen & Park-Taylor, 2006). Furthermore, a lack of awareness can potentially exacerbate an already stressed family system and contribute to unsuccessful therapeutic outcomes. An awareness of the background from which many Cambodian Americans hail could facilitate the understanding of the unique acculturation issues related to the refugee experience and settlement in the United States. Given the unique features of traditional Cambodian culture and family structure, there are many acculturative tasks that Cambodian Americans may confront, especially as influenced by recent Cambodian history and the subsequent immigration experience (Boehnlein et al., 1995; Boehnlein et al., 1997; Chung, 2001). These events created shifts in traditional sex and generational roles that have become significant sources of conflict within the Cambodian family (Boehnlein et al., 1997). Furthermore, the traumas experienced by immigrants prior to arrival in the United States and the subsequent struggle to cope with these events also contribute to family conflict (Boehnlein et al., 1995; Chung, 2001).

The complexity of intergenerational conflict is highlighted with the understanding that the majority of Cambodian Americans (68%) were born overseas (U.S. Bureau of the Census, 2000); thus, many Cambodian Americans can trace their direct roots, cultural heritages, and traditions to their country of origin. These ideas may reflect a foundation in traditional Cambodian culture not shared by those born in the United States. Younger Cambodians are more apt to acquire the language, customs, and values of the host country. As a result, a reversal of generational roles often occurs in which Cambodian parents depend on their children to negotiate within the host society.

One of the difficulties for many Cambodian immigrants is that they entered the United States unprepared for the difficulties in navigating their new country. Many refugees were uneducated farmers, illiterate in their own language (Lynch, 1989), who came to the United States with no marketable skills and significant mental health concerns associated with trauma (Chan, 2004). Even today, the majority in this community speaks little to no English, live below the poverty level, and rely on public assistance (Marshall et al., 2005). A growing body of research documents the experience of Cambodian refugees and their settlement in the United States (Boehnlein et al., 1997; Chan, 2004; Chung, 2001; Keo, 2001; Marshall et al., 2005; Smith-Hefner, 1999). However, research that specifically addresses the process of acculturation and provides direction for evidence-based practice with Cambodian Americans is limited.

Pulled Between Two Worlds: The Case of Sam

The following is the case of Samang (Sam), whom I (MEC) worked with in individual counseling for 12 sessions over a 4-month period. The sessions took place at a university counseling center in Southern California. At the time of our work together, Sam was a 23-year-old, heterosexual, one-and-a-half-generation Cambodian American who was completing his third year in school as a business major. He identified as a Buddhist. On appearance, Sam did not look all that different from the other students I saw at this racially diverse campus; he was of average attractiveness and somewhat athletic. What seemed to set Sam apart from his peers was a particular seriousness and intensity about him—he was dressed in business casual attire that was mostly black, and his facial expression and nonverbal body language communicated a sense of focus and responsibility. Sam lived at home with his parents and five siblings who ranged in age from 9 to 20. He was self-referred to the counseling center.

The Beginning: Coming Together

We were fewer than 5 minutes into the first session, and Sam was nervous. Yet, he was not just nervous, as he seemed scared and his forehead was dripping sweat. Being in the room was anxiety provoking for Sam, and the only way to address this was to allow him to reveal what was so distressing. I stopped talking and asked, "So what brings you in to talk with me?" Sam spent the next 10 minutes telling me how great everything was in his life and how he was doing fine. He was doing well in school (better than most of the others in my business classes), he had been dating his girlfriend (Chaya) for 3 years (she is very beautiful!), he felt physically fit (I go to the gym every day), and he was on track to be successful in life. I got the sense he was putting up a strong front to retain a sense of pride in my presence, and so I commented on his success in life as a way to convey that I could see the strengths that he possessed (Kiselica, Englar-Carlson, & Fisher, 2006).

Sam looked away and said that he was feeling pretty "stressed out" as of late. School was demanding, Chaya wanted more from him in terms of time, he had not been to the gym in 4 weeks, and most of his time was consumed by his job of consulting with businesses in the local Cambodian community. His sleep patterns were erratic, his head and neck ached, and he noted that his "body just does not feel right." He did not have much of a social life (I don't really have any friends, but then again there is no time for them anyway). Sam rattled off his concerns with no emotion in his face. I asked Sam about living at home and being the eldest male child, and he said in a serious tone that he had a very important role in his family, noting "I basically take care of everyone in the house." Sam's father and mother spoke little to no English, which meant that for most of his life, Sam had served as the translator and conduit to the outside world for his parents. In addition, Sam helped his younger siblings with their schoolwork, and he was the one who communicated with school officials and teachers. Sam ended talking about his family by saying, "Nobody seems to do anything, so I end up doing it all for everyone. I don't really have a choice; it is what I am supposed to do."

At this point in the session, I summarized what I had been hearing and inquired about his mood, energy, and motivation over the past month. Sam noted feeling tired and down over the past month, but that he was too busy to worry about it. With a flurry, Sam commented, "I might be a little down and stressed, but that is not why I am here." Sheepishly and with some hesitation, he went on, "I did something wrong, and I need to talk with someone about it." Sam revealed that a couple of weeks ago he had gone alone to a topless bar. He had felt guilty and shameful about his actions, believing in some way he had a crossed a line that he should not have. Sam did not know what to do and questioned if he should tell his girlfriend that he had gone. I was a little surprised that this action caused so much strain, yet I listened to Sam struggle with his guilt and shame and to his self-degrading comments related to his visit. As our time was winding down, Sam asked if I had ever been to a topless bar. This direct question seemed important. My clinical experience with men has taught me that as some clients reveal perceived weaknesses or shameful acts, they are often helped by seeing me respond honestly to questions that may require some self-disclosure. Furthermore, this often feels like one of the first tests of the psychotherapy relationship, to see if I will take risks in the room alongside the client (Kiselica, 1999). It seemed like an early barometer to gauge if there was anything real about the real psychotherapy relationship (Gelso & Hayes, 1998).

Trying to remain nonjudgmental, I commented that on occasion I had, but that generally it was not the type of place I went. Sam listened to me and with obvious relief said, "So you have been there and you understand what I mean—it is really not the type of place I wanted to go either, but there I was." It felt like we had just built the beginning of a therapeutic bridge—Sam felt that I understood him. As we ended the session, I used action empathy (Pollack, 1998) to talk about ways that we could accomplish some short-term tangible goals of reducing his stress, increasing his mood, and getting him back into a routine of exercise as a way of stabilizing his life. Sam said that he wanted to come back next week.

Over the next two sessions, Sam examined some of his internal conflict between his motivation and desire to go back to the topless bar and his own sense of morality about what was appropriate. He was struggling to retain a sense of harmony in his life. Sam remained more cognitive in his speech, and I noted a variety of ways he kept his inner core and emotions protected.

I sensed some curiosity and desire about sex (e.g., though not a virgin, Sam had not had sexual intercourse with Chaya) and his own sexuality (e.g., "what is normal for me?" questions), but that seemed incomplete. We explored more about his relationship with Chaya, and Sam, after saying repeatedly that everything was fine, slowly revealed his dissatisfaction in the relationship. They had been dating for 2 years, and Sam felt pressure from her, her family, and his family around an expectation that they marry. Sam said it was a Cambodian thing, but it meant that he would feel responsible for everyone in both families. Chaya was also of Cambodian descent, was 3 years younger than Sam, and was not employed or in school. Sam revealed that initially he was attracted to her beauty, and he later admitted surprise that he could attract someone like Chaya. Over the past 2 years, however, Sam sensed they were different people going in different directions. Sam felt trapped in the relationship, and after repeated denials, he clearly stated that he wanted out. Like most other people in Sam's life, Chaya seemed dependent on Sam for many things. He provided spending money and took care of her by driving her places and making sure she was healthy, and he seemed to be a bigger part of her future than she was in his. As Sam talked about Chaya, I noticed the return of anxiety and exasperation in his face and posture. He felt tied to her by a series of personal and cultural knots. Family honor, even though no promises of marriage had occurred, was at stake. Furthermore, Sam's own notions of male responsibility for Chaya and his own personal desire not to upset or hurt her were intertwined.

By the end of the third session, Sam appeared ready to trust me enough to reveal a mixture of emotions and internal states. He felt some relief at being able to reveal for the first time that he was unhappy and wanted to end his relationship. Up until that moment, it seemed like the connection between Sam's emotional inexpressiveness and his psychological distress was linked with his conflicted ideas about his own emotional-related values and the conflict between these values and those of important people in his life (Wong & Rochlen, 2005). Now that his emotions were revealed, Sam commented that he felt a "huge weight" being lifted. Yet at the same time, Sam seemed to sense a new source of building anxiety and pressure: Because he had publicly revealed this to me, I was bound to ask him more about it, and he would ultimately have to make some choices about what he wanted to do. Drawing on the existential psychology of Yalom (1980), we talked about how decisions and choices not made often lead to feelings of anxiety and depression. We framed Sam's visiting the topless bar as an example of his anxiety and desire to create some change in his relationship.

Regardless of whether Sam had wanted to go the topless bar, going to the bar had set a process in motion that had him battling significant questions about his relationship and the type of life he could and wanted to lead.

Sam and I formulated a treatment plan to address his mood. In line with the notion that clinical decisions should be made in collaboration with the client (APA, 2006), I wanted to provide Sam with different options of treatment recommendations. Also, because I detected that Sam would agree to anything I suggested, I wanted Sam to have ownership of the treatment plan and the option to say "no." Because exercise has been associated with a decline in anxiety and depression (Biddle, Fox, & Boutcher, 2000; Dunn, Trivedi, & O'Neal, 2001; Tkachuk & Martin, 1999), and because Sam previously enjoyed consistent exercise, we developed a plan of getting Sam back to the gym every other day as a way to reduce some tension and build back his exercise routine. Sam agreed to cut the caffeine in his diet over time (he reported a sizeable increase in his daily caffeine intake from 2-3x to 6-7x daily over the past 6 weeks). We talked about the option for a psychiatric evaluation, yet Sam displayed some of his self-determinism by saying that he wanted to work on this in counseling first before considering that option.

The Middle Sessions: I Am So Alone

By the fourth session, Sam and I had developed a good therapy relationship. Sam seemed more relaxed with me, he smiled more and was lowering some of his intensity to reveal a more exposed and vulnerable side of his personality. Verbally speaking about emotions was a struggle, but his nonverbal behavior revealed his emotional state, and he was open to allowing me to use his nonverbal cues as an opportunity to probe a bit deeper. Sam often felt stuck and frustrated about expressing himself to others, and he noted growing up in a home where emotions were not expressed. We used a culturally adapted version of the Gender Role Conflict Checklist (O'Neil, 1988) with an emphasis on restricted emotionality and the influence of his cultural upbringing (e.g., emphasizing Cambodian culture and being male). Sam revealed more conflict around controlling his emotions in the presence of others rather than having any difficulty identifying his emotions. Sam needed a healthy way of understanding how, when, and to whom emotions can be expressed or withheld (Wong & Rochlen, 2005). To address this, we used a stoplight metaphor (i.e., developing an internal evaluation of with whom, what time, and what types of emotions are green-lighted as OK, red-lighted as restricted, and yellow-lighted as proceeding with caution or confusion)

(Englar-Carlson, 2006) to help Sam talk about the aspects of his emotional world and how he experiences the expression of emotions in his life.

During the fourth session Sam revealed, "I lied about why I came here. I did not go to a topless bar. I actually went to one of those massage parlors and ended up having sex with a woman there. I have done it since then, the last time was a few weeks ago." As Sam said this, his face bowed, and I felt a sense of shame from him about the act and about not being honest with me. I validated the importance of being honest in our counseling relationship, and at the same time I worked to reduce the shame he already felt. I asked how it felt to tell me about this, and Sam replied that he feared I would be angry with him, but that it seemed that I was not. He further commented on the huge relief he felt to finally tell someone about his secret. Sam said that he had privately vowed to not tell anyone about these visits, but that something changed over the past month. He felt listened to by me, and he was beginning to understand why he went to the massage parlor and thought that it had something to do with his relationship with Chaya. At this moment, Sam demonstrated the power of personal insight, which has been identified as a common factor in successful psychotherapy (Wampold, Imel, Bhati, & Johnson-Jennings, 2007).

For the remainder of the session we talked about his guilt and fears about getting a sexually transmitted disease. He had worn a condom during intercourse, and he planned to visit the campus clinic for testing. While in the office, I made an appointment for Sam to see one of the physicians on the men's health team at the clinic who could help educate Sam on sexual health and test for sexually transmitted diseases. Though a little unsure about this referral, Sam knew he could use more information about sex. Sam commented that he liked that I personally had helped him with the appointment and that I was sending him to someone whom I trusted. In a sense, Sam felt that I was treating him in a "special way," and that was a rare feeling for him, particularly because just moments before he wondered if I would still "like" him for not being honest.

Over the next few sessions, we focused on some pragmatic goals around his mood. Sam was going to the gym again every other day and felt good about that accomplishment. He went to the men's health clinic, and his test results were negative, and he liked the doctor he met. Revealing his visit to the massage parlor had lessened some of the guilt he was feeling, but his mood was still mildly depressed, and he continued to feel overwhelmed. He seemed to still be struggling between resigning himself to his relationship with Chaya and finding a way out of it. Throughout all of this, he still kept up his daily responsibility of looking out for all of his family members, developing his business, and studying for school. Like many other men, Sam had developed the outward appearance of looking successful and busy while masking his internal struggles and mood. Whereas other men often cope with their stress and depression with drugs and alcohol, Sam rarely drank and never used drugs. Instead, he plunged into his perceived responsibilities and duties. I was worried that counseling was his only outlet and one of the few times he had social contact with other men outside of his family. I shared my concern that Sam's propensity to suffer in silence and pour himself into work was a tried-and-true way that many men across all cultures have used to be unhappy for the rest of their life. Although not trying to judge him, I made this observation with a hopeful invitation: "We could create a different outcome for you?" Sam smiled and said, "OK, let's try something."

Sam vacillated about his need for friendships and social contact, going from "I don't need friendships because I am too busy" to "I wish there were people to hang out with to blow off steam." The former was more pronounced, yet this seemed more associated with his lack of confidence in making friends and his fear of rejection. We looked at some places where Sam could begin to meet other students and increase his confidence in making connections. As a business student with a high GPA, Sam was eligible for the business honor society. This group had social functions, but also worked on networking skills, organized a mentoring program for first-year undergraduates in business, and even had intramural sports teams and shared workout times. Previously, Sam had rejected invitations to join, but now we explored how this could be of help to him both socially and in terms of his career path. Sam did attend the next membership meeting and soon found himself among his peers having a good time. He liked that among this group, it seemed that nobody wanted anything from him and that he did not feel a sense of responsibility to anyone. Interestingly, over the next year, Sam became more involved in the honor society to the point where he was put in charge of the mentoring program, yet he reframed his contribution as wanting to help others rather than feeling compelled to be responsible for them.

During the sixth session, Sam provided a brief history of his family and his role in it. Sam was short for Samang, which in Khmer meant lucky or fortunate, and Sam told me the origin of his name. Before the Khmer Rouge, his father was an educator, and thus he was an immediate target of the Khmer Rouge's reforms to rid Cambodia of Western influences. His father was publicly beaten and tortured and was to be executed, but somehow his father and mother escaped to a rural labor camp. At the camp they lived in abhorrent conditions and worked endlessly. To survive they had to disguise their identities. While in the labor camp, his mother became pregnant, and they planned an escape to a refugee camp in neighboring Thailand. During their escape, they became separated, and Sam's mother walked the remaining way alone; at this stage she was 6 months pregnant. In the refugee camp, his parents were reunited, and Samang was born. After a year in the camp, they came to the United States.

Sam commented that he obviously did not know who his parents were before the Khmer Rouge, but older relatives and friends have commented on how his parents, particularly his father, are not the same people today. Sam's father, though he lived in the home, seemed to have little contact with the family. He spent most of his day reading and doing some odd jobs in the community, but he was uninvolved with his children. He was withdrawn and unavailable, and Sam craved some attention from and contact with his father. He tried to engage him and become closer, but his father appeared unable or uninterested in meeting Sam's needs for closeness in a father–son relationship. Sam's mother, on the other hand, was quite involved with the children, but in an almost helpless manner, as she spent most of her time getting Sam to do things for his siblings. Upon reflection, Sam added that he knew his parents were survivors of things not talked about, yet it seemed like most of who they were had died. Sam stated his parents had been depressed most of his life and that they both had never really recovered from the events of 25 years ago, and yet Sam retained a sense of family pride and honor for his parents (especially his mother because she had walked more than 100 miles while 6 months pregnant) because they were survivors. In a sense, Sam's overinvolvement with his family and siblings seemed to counterbalance his parents' underinvolvement.

Speaking about his own relationship with his parents and family, Sam added, "My parents really do not push me to do anything outside of the family; the fact that I am in college and doing well is all because of my motivation. I am not recognized for doing anything except being a dedicated son. Nobody knows what I go through and what it takes each day to set foot on campus." We explored the immense pressure Sam felt from family obligation and honor and the conflicts he experienced as he found himself gravitating toward a future less restrained by cultural and familial expectations and norms. Sam observed, "My struggles have built up to the point where my problem with Chaya seems indicative of my major problem in life—always living between two worlds."

Over the next two sessions, we explored more about his role in the family. Initially, Sam was focused on finding ways to lessen his connection to his family and his Cambodian culture. He was conflicted over his level of enculturation (e.g., the degree to which one endorses Asian values such as a collectivist world view, filial piety, conformity to norms, family recognition) (Liu & Iwamoto, 2006) and his desire for acculturation. Over the past year, Sam developed strategies ("losing" his cell phone so he could not be reached, overscheduling his school life, purposely driving in rush hour traffic) to escape his house and find ways to distance himself from his family and Chaya. He wanted his life to be more like the world he was exposed to in college—one that seemed dominated by autonomy and individuality. Sam felt free at school because there were no external expectations on him. He blended into the student body and could be whomever he wanted to be. As we parsed out what he gained from his current life and relationship, a new awareness crystallized for Sam. He did not want to date Chaya anymore, and he understood how his level of enculturation kept him in the relationship because he feared embarrassing his family in the Cambodian community. I encouraged Sam to consider ways he could honor his family and culture while being true to his own feelings. In a light bulb moment, Sam understood that his relationship with Chaya was not the same as his relationship with his family. He had been displacing his frustration with his relationship on his family and culture, blaming them for making him stuck in the relationship. When he separated his relationship from his family, Sam began to become more aware of the role he played within his family and the positive aspects it had on him and his identity.

For years, Sam had essentially served as the head of the household, as his responsibilities ranged from economic provision, caretaking for his mother and siblings, and making sure everyone was OK. Though stressful and tiring, Sam took pride in the accomplishments of his siblings at school (they were all doing well academically), as he felt a sense of contribution. Though saddened that his parents, especially his father, did not recognize his talents and accomplishments, Sam considered how he served as role models for his siblings and extended family. Among these family members, it was known that Sam was the first person to go to college and that Sam was the go-to person for any help. Sam and I talked about how he had really only been looking for signs of validation from his parents, yet all the while others around him were impressed and looked up to him. As we began to reframe aspects of his family role, Sam could see how his contribution served a central role in the social well-being and welfare of his family, and that was something that Sam could honor and be proud of. This is where Sam gained his sense of social interest in life (Carlson et al., 2006).

Some Resolution and an Ending to Remember

As we moved toward the end of our work together, we focused on Sam's ending his relationship with Chaya. Sam was feeling better about himself, and he had gained some self-confidence and awareness about his life direction. Out of respect for his parents and considering the impact on his family, Sam spoke with his mother and father about his decision to end the relationship with Chaya. Sam sensed disappointment from his parents, but he felt strongly about this decision and on the next day spoke with Chaya. In session with me, Sam admitted breaking up with Chaya was difficult because he felt responsible. She was upset, and Sam felt sad for closing a chapter in his life. Our session after the break up was a reversal into acute stress management and support for Sam. By the next week, Sam spoke more with Chaya, and she seemed better. They talked about their hopes and ambitions, and in a sense the ending of the relationship had provided a window for each of them to communicate honestly about their own needs. The result of that conversation seemed to clearly point out how they were going in very different directions and wanted different lives. Sam was proud that he was able to clearly communicate his needs and emotions to Chaya. It was the first time he had done that.

Our last session was focused on saying good-bye and cementing the changes Sam had made. In line with Prochaska and Norcross (2007), we talked about relapse prevention and ways to maintain the changes in his life. I worked to reinforce all that Sam did in psychotherapy to make his life better, in effect highlighting his significant contribution to his positive outcome (Hubble et al., 1999). The client's own capacity for healing is the most potent common factor in psychotherapy (Tallman & Bohart, 1999), and I wanted Sam to celebrate his being the star of our work together. Sam commented on feeling more free and owning some pride about his family role. He learned to attain some autonomy and individuality while retaining his place in the family. His mood had elevated, and he had regular exercise and sleep patterns. Some of the energy he had poured into his relationship was now being put into the business honor society group. Sam found that as others accepted him, he started to exercise with some of the male members, and though it was still anxiety provoking, Sam was feeling connected.

In terms of relapse prevention, Sam had a greater sense of self-efficacy about creating change in his life.

From outward appearances, the man who sat across from me during our last session was not the same man from the first session. We had developed a strong therapy relationship, and we talked about the sadness in saying good-bye. We ended with a handshake, and then Sam was gone. I found our ending a little anticlimactic and rushed, and with some disappointment about what was left unfinished, I sat down to finish my clinical notes and close the case file. Ten minutes later, there was a knock on my door, and Sam poked his head into the office. He came in and quickly said, "I walked away and felt upset that I was not able to tell you how important this, and you, have been to me. Our time together meant the world to me—thank you." With that he offered another handshake, which turned into a heartfelt hug of thanks. Sam again said thank you, and then with a smile of accomplishment and a nod of his head, he went on his way.

Case Conceptualization

Although many Cambodian Americans have resided in the United States for over 30 years, acculturation remains a salient issue, especially when intergenerational conflicts with family members born and raised in the United States come to the forefront. The case of Sam is an example of a young man whose life course has been marked by the sociopolitical history of his parents and the legacy it left for his family. When Sam came to counseling, he was at the crux of an acculturation process that had been building for many years. Within his family, Sam was the obedient first born and oldest male child who was driven by the need to maintain family honor and harmony. Yet outside of his family, and particularly at the university, Sam was pulled by what he saw in his peers: autonomy and freedom to make choices without being bound by family or cultural expectations. Sam wanted the freedom to chart his own path, which meant the ability to choose his dating partner. Feeling unable to have that choice, Sam seemed to lash out at what he perceived was holding him back—his family and cultural obligations. From my perspective, his experience of depression and even his visit to the massage parlor could be seen as symptoms of his anxiety around making a significant decision or, in his case, his perceived inability to make that decision.

On presentation, Sam appeared discouraged, and he struggled to meet the many demands in his life. Like many men I have worked with, Sam was uncertain about being in psychotherapy, yet he was keenly aware that things were not right. Using person-centered and male-sensitive approaches, I conveyed genuine, action empathy and validated Sam and his concerns. Rather than forcing Sam to reveal his inner world, I worked with Sam to develop an honest relationship with me where he felt that I was invested in him and that he had something to gain. By using recommendations that are in line with building the therapeutic alliance with men (Addis & Mahalik, 2003; Englar-Carlson, 2006; Good, Thomson, & Brathwaite, 2005), I found that the early clarification of the psychotherapy process, the establishment of objective goals, and the encouragement of the help-seeking process for Sam created a respectful, genuine, and hopeful therapeutic setting.

Over his life, Sam had learned to hide his vulnerabilities and restrict his emotional world to avoid shame and ridicule and to be accepted not only as a man, but also as a Cambodian man. Furthermore, this led Sam to having some difficulties creating and maintaining intimate relationships with others that required self-disclosure and emotional expressiveness. It is widely recognized that at the core of any effective psychotherapy experience is an intimate therapeutic relationship signified by trust, empathy, and positive regard. Furthermore, the quality of the therapeutic alliance has been noted as the single best predictor of therapeutic outcome (Bachelor & Horvath, 1999; Messer & Wampold, 2002). My main focus with Sam was on creating a collaborative and caring psychotherapy relationship that would allow for both individual–therapist effects and the client's variables to emerge (APA, 2006; Clarkin & Levy, 2004).

In terms of working with Asian American men, and in Sam's case a Cambodian American man, I was clearly aware of the influence of Cambodian culture, masculinity, and acculturation. Park (2006) pointed out some of the difficulties working with Asian men in psychotherapy. He noted that the field of Western psychology often values and encourages what may be considered by some cultures as nonmasculine processes (e.g., emotional awareness, admission for assistance), and thus psychotherapy may be viewed with caution (Atkinson & Gim, 1989; Atkinson, Whitely, & Gim, 1990; Lee & Saul, 1987). For Asian American men, a crucial consideration is the value on not disgracing the family; in other words, do not lose face (Park, 2006). Face is a consistent and salient variable in Asian American help-seeking preferences and attitudes (Zane & Yeh, 2002) and refers to a social and relational construct. Face's influence on help-seeking behavior (Liu, 2002; Liu & Chang, 2007; Park, 2006) is well documented, and Sam's own sweat and anxiety revealed how hard it was to open up. With Sam, I found that a key to understanding his world view was to understand how shame and saving face influenced his expression of emotions and what he wanted from me in return. At the time, that meant responding to his revealing of shameful experiences (going to the topless bar and massage parlor, admitting to not being honest, talking about the problems with his family) by validating the courage to be honest or caring enough to try to make a difference. By honoring his own process of making sense of his world, working to withhold judgment, and showing sensitivity to his cultural needs, I tried to help Sam not lose face in a potentially shameful setting (psychotherapy office) and act (requesting and obtaining psychological services, admitting acts he was ashamed of). Ultimately, our work together was about rebuilding face to where Sam could take pride in his family and his role in his family.

Additional Clinical Considerations

Future directions with Sam would include maintaining and strengthening the changes he had made. A crucial aspect of relapse prevention is maintaining the ability to ask for assistance and coming back for a booster session when the client is slipping back from previous gains (Prochaska & Norcross, 2007). For Sam, I was encouraged by his involvement with the business honor society and the opportunities for him to feel a part of something (i.e., the mentoring program). For Sam, like many first-generation college students, graduation and the transition into the workforce are significant events. Sam could benefit from time with a career counselor to help understand the social capital (Liu, 2001) required to advance educationally or vocationally and how to create social contacts that facilitate advancement, as well as to gain knowledge about how to work within social systems. Finally, I believe Sam could do additional work on his relationship with his father because it appeared as a significant source of sadness and unmet expectations.

Identification of Author's Personal Dimensions of Diversity and World View

In terms of my own personal dimensions, my being White and male were both quite present in the room. I got the sense that Sam did not have contact with men outside of his family and that the opportunities to speak closely with White men who appeared near his own age were also limited. In that regard, I represented and took advantage of privileges that Sam craved, namely, the ability to make decisions and choices that were not bound by strong cultural ties of collectivism and filial piety. In many ways, independence and autonomy represent privileges that have allowed me to navigate educational and vocational paths in different regions of the United States to the point where I have not lived within a time zone of my immediate family in over 20 years. I am sure that interpersonally I conveyed confidence and independence to Sam at a time when he was questioning his own right to such values and qualities.

More apparent to me was seeing how Sam and I engaged in the room as men. In my own family, I have an adopted younger brother and sister of Korean descent, and because of that, I have a keen interest in understanding Asian American masculinity, but also a secondary objective of understanding more about what my brother experiences as a man. In my work with Sam, I felt constant pulls to protect him and be as much of a mentor as I was a therapist. For many psychotherapists, a blending of a counselor and mentor role is not uncommon, as mentoring relationships are a culturally congruent style of relating for many Asian American men (Liu, 2003; Park, 2006). From the first session, I really liked Sam for who he was and also the man he wanted to be. He worked very hard at being a responsible and respectable person, and it was not very hard for me to have empathy and compassion for him. My desire to see Sam in a favorable light could also have been distorted by seeing him as if he were my younger brother and wanting him to be healthier and more capable than he was at the time.

Therapeutic Recommendations

1. Recognize, acknowledge, and gently affirm the difficulty that men have entering and being in counseling. Men are less likely than women to seek help for both mental health and physical health concerns (Addis & Mahalik, 2003). Men's relative reluctance to seek professional help stands in stark contrast to the range and severity of the problems affecting them. It has been well documented that men initially experience going to therapy as extremely difficult, as something to avoid at any cost, and usually as the last resort (Rabinowitz & Cochran, 2002). Men often believe they are being coerced into therapy (by a spouse, employer, or the law) and present with a great deal of resentment. Often, men

experience going to therapy with shame and fear (Park, 2006) because asking for help implies weakness and a failure to be self-sufficient.

2. Help the client save "masculine face." It is important for psychotherapists to communicate their genuine respect for their male client coming into therapy. Reflecting and contextualizing coming to therapy as a brave, courageous, and honorable behavior are congruent with traditional male socialization (Liu & Chang, 2007; Park, 2006). For many men, acceptance as a man is needed before they can progress with treatment.

3. Educate male clients up front about the process of therapy. Most male clients don't know how the therapy process works and worry the psychotherapist will be judgmental or discover their weaknesses. Look to check out his assumptions of what will be expected of him as a client and clarify your role as the psychotherapist. Look to explain how one practices psychotherapy. Men perceive therapy as a place where they will need to become emotional, yet some men often don't feel ready or equipped to do what they believe they will be asked to do in a traditional therapy setting. Find out goals he has for the sessions, and develop an initial plan to address them.

4. Be patient. Male clients often present a unique challenge for the psychotherapist (Englar-Carlson & Stevens, 2006). Men are often socialized to fear core components of the therapeutic process: the admission of the need for help, the language of feelings, the disclosure of vulnerability, and the admission of dependency needs. Male clients' discomfort with the developing intimacy of a psychotherapy relationship can manifest as early termination, anger at the psychotherapist, unproductive intellectualizing, and other forms of resistance. It is important to be patient and understanding of the walls men have erected if they are to be let inside. Men may slam their emotional doors and leave therapy if confrontation is used too early (Rabinowitz & Cochran, 2002). Many men often need to start therapy slow and resist sharing intimate personal details and feelings up front. Rituals of initial engagement through more traditional masculine means (small talk, good-natured humor, handshakes, etc.) are often needed.

5. Use a therapy language and approach that is congruent with your client's gender role identity. Masculinity-sensitive counseling interventions and therapeutic style are critical to the engagement and ultimate success of psychotherapy with male clients. Male clients may want to be treated in ways that feel congruent with their masculine socialization. This can be accomplished by listening carefully, projecting warmth without

appearing overly sympathetic, and tailoring the clinical work to the male client. This can mean substituting other words for psychotherapy (e.g., consultation, meeting, or discussion), using less jargon, being more active as psychotherapist, and matching one's relational style to the client's.

6. Be genuine and real. Modeling self-disclosure is another practice that can strengthen the relationship between the psychotherapist and the male client and assist in revealing personal matters (Kiselica, Englar-Carlson, & Horne, 2008). Male clients often trust and are more engaged in treatment when they experience their psychologist as a real human being. The Latino concept of *personalismo* (Paniagua, 2005), in which male clients become more oriented toward people and warmth, seems to apply here. Many male clients want to be treated as people, not as problems to be dealt with or fixed. When psychotherapists share something about who they are, they can go a long way toward showing clients that they are important. Furthermore, they can model openness and appropriate self-disclosure.

7. Understand a social justice or advocacy perspective. Because men historically and currently exercise considerable privilege and power across almost all domains in society, it may be easy to overlook, discredit, or not acknowledge the pain and injustice that many groups of men experience. The reality is that many individual men do not feel empowered in their life, and large groups of men (e.g., African American boys and young men, teenage fathers, blue-collar males, undocumented immigrant males, noncustodial fathers, etc.) (Franklin, 1999; Kiselica & Woodford, 2007) are marginalized within greater society. In that sense, psychotherapists need to be reminded that even though men and male privilege are powerful, not all men feel privileged or experience power in the same manner. Helping clients gain a voice and advocating for their traditionally ignored needs can empower some marginalized male clients to reclaim a self-image of being a visible and capable person who has a voice.

8. A final thought about psychotherapy with men is that one of the main things psychotherapists can do is begin to consider and appreciate the unique concerns, needs, and difficulties that men experience in life that are brought and reenacted in the clinical setting. When psychotherapists are gender aware, supportive, and male affirming in their approach, men can have the opportunity to tell their story and make sense of what is chaotic, distilling, and conflicting. For many men, safe spaces such as this are rarely found. The hope and promise of effective

therapy with men is that a male client can learn that asking for help will not kill or weaken him, understand that his own history has impacted his current life situations, gain the ability to open up with others, learn to value the importance of relationships, experience that vulnerability is a form of strength, and ultimately gain awareness of how to get to know himself (Englar-Carlson, 2009).

Conclusion

Despite the dramatic repercussions of the political upheaval of Cambodia and the subsequent immigration waves of refugees to the United States, relatively little is known about the acculturation of Cambodian Americans and implications for counseling this specific population. Whereas some scholarly research has identified the mental health concerns of this population, there has been little research to guide clinical practice. The purpose of the case of Sam was to demonstrate the complexities associated with acculturation and the intersection of multiple identities (cultural, gender) and how that can impact one's mental health. The clinical work in this case was guided by culturally adapted traditional theories of practice and a gender-sensitive and culturally competent approach that honored and recognized the salient cultural issues of Sam. The positive outcome of this case was supported by many common factors of successful outcome, including instilling hope and expectancy in the client; using a validating, supportive, and culturally sensitive therapeutic relationship; highlighting and using the strengths of Sam; and using specific interventions to target his clinical needs.

Discussion Questions

1. What steps can a psychotherapist take to build rapport with a male client of a different cultural background?
2. In what ways can a psychotherapist with more contemporary American values reconcile a situation in which his or her cultural values clash with those of a client with a more traditional Eastern background? What are the possible consequences of this psychotherapist trying to change or impose one's values on the client?
3. How can a female psychotherapist increase her effectiveness in helping a male client address issues related to culture and masculinity?

4. In what ways can the experiences of repeated trauma, either directly experienced or experienced by family members, influence the experience of a Cambodian American in psychotherapy? How might a psychotherapist overcome these challenges?

5. What types of issues related to acculturation occur in a multigenerational Cambodian American family? How does acculturative stress manifest in the case of Sam?

Cultural References

Becker, E. (1998). *When the war was over: Cambodia and the Khmer Rouge revolution.* New York: Public Affairs Books.

Boehnlein, J. K., Leung, P. K., & Kinzie, J. D. (1997). Cambodian American families. In E. Lee (Ed.), *Working with Asian Americans: A guide for clinicians* (pp. 37–45). New York: Guilford.

Chan, S. (2004). *Survivors: Cambodian refugees in the United States.* Champaign: University of Illinois Press.

Joffé, R. (Director), & Puttnam, B. (Producer). (1984). *The killing fields* [Motion picture]. United Kingdom: Enigma.

McKenzie-Pollock, L. (2005). Cambodian families. In M. McGoldrick, J. Giordano, & N. Garcia-Preto (Eds.), *Ethnicity and family therapy* (pp. 290–301). New York: Guilford.

Smith-Hefner, J. N. (1999). *Khmer American: Identity and moral education in a diasporic community.* Berkeley: University of California Press.

Web Sites of Interest

Cambodian American Resource Agency: http://www.caraweb.org/

Khmer Institute: http://www.khmerinstitute.org

Cambodian Information Center: http://www.cambodia.org

EthnoMed: Cambodian Cultural Profile: http://ethnomed.org/ethnomed/cultures/cambodian/camb_cp.html

References

Abe, J. S., Zane, N. W., & Chun, K. (1994). Differential responses to trauma: Migration-related discriminants of post-traumatic stress among Southeast Asian refugees. *Journal of Community Psychology, 22,* 121–135.

Abreau, J. M., Ramirez, E., Kim, B. S. K., & Haddy, C. (2003). Automatic activation of yellow peril Asian American stereotypes: Effects on social impression formation. *Journal of Social Psychology, 143*, 691–706.

Addis, M. E., & Mahalik, J. R. (2003). Men, masculinity, and the contexts of help-seeking. *American Psychologist, 58*, 5–14.

Akutsu, P., & Chu, J. (2006). Clinical problems that initiate professional help-seeking behaviors from Asian Americans. *Professional Psychology: Research and Practice, 37*(4), 407–415.

Akutsu, P., Tsuru, G., & Chu, J. (2004). Predictors of nonattendance of intake appointments among five Asian American client groups. *Journal of Consulting and Clinical Psychology, 72*(5), 891–896.

Akutsu, P., Tsuru, G., & Chu, J. (2006). Prioritized assignment to intake appointments for Asian Americans at an ethnic-specific mental health program. *Journal of Consulting and Clinical Psychology, 74*(6), 1108–1115.

American Psychological Association. (2003). Guidelines on multicultural education, training, research, practice, and organizational change for psychologists. *American Psychologist, 58*, 377–402.

American Psychological Association. (2006). Evidence-Based Practice in Psychology. *American Psychologist, 61*, 271–285.

American Psychological Association. (2007). Guidelines for psychological practice with girls and women. *American Psychologist, 62*, 949–979.

Atkinson, D. R., Bui, U., & Mori, S. (2001). Multiculturally sensitive empirically supported treatments: An oxymoron? In J. G. Ponterotto, J. M. Casas, L. A. Suzuki, & C. M. Alexander (Eds.), *Handbook of multicultural counseling* (2nd ed., pp. 542–574). Thousand Oaks, CA: Sage.

Atkinson, D. R., & Gim, R. H. (1989). Asian-American cultural identity and attitudes toward mental health services. *Journal of Counseling Psychology, 36*, 209–212.

Atkinson, D. R., Whitely, S., & Gim, R. H. (1990). Asian American acculturation and preference for help providers. *Journal of College Student Development, 31*, 155–161.

Bachelor, A., & Horvath, A. (1999). The therapeutic relationship. In M. Hubble, B. Duncan, & S. Miller (Eds.), *The heart and soul of change* (pp. 133–178). Washington, DC: American Psychological Association.

Bernal, G., & Scharrón-del-Río, M. R. (2001). Are empirically supported treatments valid for ethnic minorities? Toward an alternative approach for treatment research. *Cultural Diversity and Ethnic Minority Psychology, 7*, 328–342.

Biddle, S. J. H., Fox, K. R., & Boutcher, S. H. (Eds.). (2000). *Physical activity and psychological well-being*. London: Taylor & Francis.

Boehnlein, J. K., Leung, P. K., & Kinzie, J. D. (1997). Cambodian American families. In E. Lee (Ed.), *Working with Asian Americans: A guide for clinicians* (pp. 37–45). New York: Guilford.

Boehnlein, J. K., Tran, H. T., Riley, C., Vu, K., Tan, S., & Leung, P. K. (1995). A comparative study of family functioning among Vietnamese and Cambodian refugees. *Journal of Nervous and Mental Disease, 183*(12), 768–773.

Bordin, E. S. (1994). Theory and research on the therapeutic working alliance: New directions. In A. Horvath & L. Greenberg (Eds.), *The working alliance: Theory, research, and practice* (pp. 13–37). New York: Wiley.

Brooks, G. R., & Good, G. E. (Eds.). (2001). *The new handbook of psychotherapy and counseling with men: A comprehensive guide to settings, problems, and treatment approaches* (Vols. 1 & 2). San Francisco: Jossey-Bass.

Bugental, J. F. T. (1978). *Psychotherapy and process.* New York: Random House.

Carlson, J., Watts, M., & Maniacci, M. (2006). *Adlerian psychotherapy.* Washington, DC: APA Books.

Chae, M. H. (2001). Acculturation conflicts among Asian Americans: Implications for practice. *The New Jersey Journal of Professional Counseling, 56,* 24–30.

Chan, S. (2004). *Survivors: Cambodian refugees in the United States.* Champaign: University of Illinois Press.

Chen, A. S. (1999). Lives at the center of the periphery, lives at the periphery of the center: Chinese American masculinities and bargaining with hegemony. *Gender and Society, 13,* 584–607.

Chen, E. C., & Park-Taylor, J. (2006). The intersection of racism and immigration: Implications for educational and counseling practice. In M. Constantine & D. W. Sue (Eds.), *Addressing racism: Facilitating cultural competence in mental health and educational settings* (pp. 43–64). Hoboken, NJ: John Wiley & Sons.

Chung, R. (2001). Psychosocial adjustment of Cambodian refugee women: Implications for mental health counseling. *Journal of Mental Health Counseling, 23,* 115–126.

Chung, R., & Bemak, F. (2002). Revisiting the California Southeast Asian Mental Health Needs Assessment data: An examination of refugee ethnic and gender differences. *Journal of Counseling and Development, 80,* 111–119.

Clarkin, J. F., & Levy, K. N. (2004). The influence of client variables on psychotherapy. In M. J. Lambert (Ed.), *Handbook of psychotherapy and behavior change* (5th ed., pp. 194–226). New York: Wiley.

Cochran, S. V. (2005). Evidence-based assessment with men. *Journal of Clinical Psychology, 6,* 649–660.

Dinkmeyer, D. C., McKay, G. D., & Dinkmeyer, D. C., Jr. (1997). *The parent's handbook.* Circle Pines, MN: American Guidance Service.

Dunn, A. L., Trivedi, M. H., & O'Neal, H. A. (2001). Physical activity dose-response effects on outcomes of depression and anxiety. *Medicine and Science in Sports and Exercise, 3,* S587–S597.

Englar-Carlson, M. (2006). Masculine norms and the therapy process. In M. Englar-Carlson & M. Stevens (Eds.), *In the room with men: A casebook of therapeutic change* (pp. 13–47). Washington, DC: American Psychological Association.

Englar-Carlson, M. (2009). Men and masculinity: Cultural, contextual, and clinical considerations. In C. Ellis & J. Carlson (Eds.), *Cross cultural awareness and social justice in counseling* (pp. 89–120). New York: Routledge.

Englar-Carlson, M., & Stevens, M. (Eds.). (2006). *In the room with men: A casebook of therapeutic change.* Washington, DC: American Psychological Association.

Franklin, A. J. (1999). Invisibility syndrome and racial identity development in psychotherapy and counseling African American men. *The Counseling Psychologist, 27,* 761–793.

Gelso, C. J., & Hayes, J. A. (1998). *The psychotherapy relationship: Theory, research, and practice.* New York: Wiley.

Good, G. E., Thomson, D. A., & Brathwaite, A. (2005). Men and therapy: Critical concepts, theoretical frameworks, and research recommendations. *Journal of Clinical Psychology, 6,* 699–711.

Hinton, D., Ba, P., Peou, S., & Um, K. (2000). Panic disorder among Cambodian refugees attending a psychiatric clinic: Prevalence and subtypes. General *Hospital Psychiatry, 22*(6), 437–444.

Hinton, D., Hsia, C., Um, K., & Otto, M. W. (2003). Anger-associated panic attacks in Cambodian refugees with PTSD: A multiple baseline examination of clinical data. *Behaviour Research and Therapy, 41*, 647–654.

Hinton, D. E., Pich, V., Safren, S. A., Pollack, M. H., & McNally, R. J. (2006). Anxiety sensitivity among Cambodian refugees with panic disorder: A factor analytic investigation. *Journal of Anxiety Disorders, 20*, 281–295.

Hinton, D., Um, K., & Ba, P. (2001). A unique panic-disorder presentation among Khmer refugees: The sore-neck syndrome. *Culture, Medicine and Psychiatry, 25*(3), 297–316.

Hubble, M. A., Duncan, B. L., & Miller, S. D. (1999). *The heart and soul of change: What works in therapy.* Washington, DC: American Psychological Association.

Keo, S. (2001). *Child-rearing and discipline among Cambodian Americans* (Master's thesis, Department of Social Work, California State University, Long Beach). Retrieved April 26, 2004, from http://www.khmerinstitute.org

Kim, B. S. K., Atkinson, D. R., & Umemoto, D. (2001). Asian cultural values and counseling process: Current knowledge and directions for future research. *The Counseling Psychologist, 29*, 570–603.

Kim, B. S. K., Atkinson, D. R., & Yang, P. H. (1999). The Asian Values Scale: Development, factor analysis, validation, and reliability. *Journal of Counseling Psychology, 46*, 342–352.

Kinzie, J., David, J., Boehnlein, P., Leung, L., Moore, L., Riley, C., et al. (1990). The prevalence of posttraumatic stress disorder and its clinical significance among Southeast Asian refugees. *American Journal of Psychiatry, 147*, 913–917.

Kinzie, J. D., & Fleck, J. (1987). Psychotherapy with severely traumatized refugees. *American Journal of Psychotherapy, 41*(1), 82–94.

Kiselica, M. S. (1999). Counseling teenage fathers. In A. M. Horne & M. S. Kiselica (Eds.), *Handbook of counseling boys and adolescent males: A practitioner's guide* (pp. 179–198). Thousand Oaks, CA: Sage.

Kiselica, M. S., Englar-Carlson, M., & Fisher, M. (2006, August). A positive psychology framework for building upon male strengths. In M. S. Kiselica (Chair), *Toward a positive psychology of boys, men, and masculinity.* Symposium presented at the Annual Convention of the American Psychological Association, New Orleans, LA.

Kiselica, M. S., Englar-Carlson, M., & Horne, A. M. (Eds.). (2008). *Counseling troubled boys: A guidebook for professionals.* New York: Routledge.

Kiselica, M. S., & Woodford, M. S. (2007). Promoting healthy male development: A social justice perspective. In C. Lee (Ed.), *Counseling for social justice* (pp. 111–135). Alexandria, VA: American Counseling Association.

Kurlantzick, J. (2000). Letter from the killing fields: Cambodia now. *Washington Quarterly, 23*(3), 21–26.

Lay, S. (2001). *Remembering the Cambodian tragedy.* Retrieved March 1, 2005, from http://www.khmerinstitute.org

Lee, D. B., & Saul, T. T. (1987). Counseling Asian men. In M. Scher, M. Stevens, G. Good, & G. A. Eichenfield (Eds.), *Handbook of counseling and psychotherapy with men* (pp. 180–191). Thousand Oaks, CA: Sage.

Levant, R., & Pollack, W. S. (Eds.). (1995). *The new psychology of men*. New York: Basic.

Levant, R. F., & Silverstein, L. S. (2005). Gender is neglected in both evidence based practices and "treatment as usual." In J. C. Norcross, L. E. Beutler, & R. F. Levant. (Eds.), *Evidence based practice in mental health: Debate and dialogue on the fundamental questions* (pp. 338–345). Washington, DC: APA Books.

Lim, K. V., Heiby, E., Brislin, R. B., & Griffin, B. (2002). The development of the Khmer acculturation scale. *International Journal of Intercultural Relations, 26*, 653–678.

Liu, W. M. (2001). Expanding our understanding of multiculturalism: Developing a social class world view model. In D. B. Pope-Davis & H. L. K Coleman (Eds.), *The intersection of race, class, and gender in counseling psychology* (pp. 127–170). Thousand Oaks, CA: Sage.

Liu, W. M. (2002). Exploring the lives of Asian American men: Racial identity, male role norms, gender role conflict, and prejudicial attitudes. *Psychology of Men and Masculinity, 3*, 107–118.

Liu, W. M. (2003). Mentoring Asian American men. *The Society for the Psychological Student of Men and Masculinity Newsletter, 8*. Retrieved on January 28, 2008, from http://www.apa.org/divisions/div51/Newsletter/Spring03bulletin.htm

Liu, W. M. (2005). The study of men and masculinity as an important multicultural competency consideration. *Journal of Clinical Psychology, 6*, 685–697.

Liu, W. M., & Chang, T. (2007). Asian American masculinities. In F. T. L. Leong, A. Ebero, L. Kinoshita, A. G. Arpana, & L. H. Yang (Eds.), *Handbook of Asian American psychology* (2nd ed., pp. 197–211). Thousand Oaks, CA: Sage.

Liu, W. M., & Iwamoto, D. K. (2006). Asian American gender role conflict: The role of Asian values, self-esteem, and psychological distress. *Psychology of Men and Masculinity, 7*, 153–164.

Lynch, J. F. (1989). *Border Khmer: A demographic study of the residents of Site 2, Site B, and Site 8*. Bangkok, Thailand: Ford Foundation.

Marshall, G. N., Berthold, M., Schell, T. L., Elliot, M. N., Chun, C., & Hambarsoomians, K. (2006). Rates and correlates of seeking mental health services among Cambodian refugees. *American Journal of Public Health, 96*, 1829–1835.

Marshall, G. N., Schell, T. L., Elliot, M. N., Berthold, S. M., & Chun, C. (2005). Mental health of Cambodian refugees 2 decades after resettlement in the United States. *Journal of the American Medical Association, 294*, 571.

McKenzie-Pollock, L. (2005). Cambodian families. In M. McGoldrick, J. Giordano, & N. Garcia-Preto (Eds.), *Ethnicity and family therapy* (pp. 290–301). New York: Guilford.

Mellinger, T., & Liu, W. M. (2006). Men's issues in doctoral training: A survey of counseling psychology programs. *Professional Psychology: Research and Practice, 37*, 196–204.

Messer, S. B., & Wampold, B. E. (2002). Let's face the facts: Common factors are more potent than specific therapy ingredients. *Clinical Psychology: Science and Practice, 9*, 21–25.

Nishio, K., & Bilmes, M. (1987). Psychotherapy with Southeast Asian American clients. *Professional Psychology: Research and Practice, 18*, 342–346.

Norcross, J. C. (2001). Purposes, processes, and products of the Task Force on Empirically Supported Therapy Relationships. *Psychotherapy, 38*, 345–356.

Okazaki, S., & Hall, G. C. H. (2002). *Asian American psychology: The science of lives in context.* Washington, DC: American Psychological Association.

O'Neil, J. M. (1988). *The Gender Role Conflict Checklist.* Storrs: School of Family Studies, University of Connecticut.

Paniagua, F. A. (2005). *Assessing and treating culturally diverse clients: A practical guide* (2nd ed.). Thousand Oaks, CA: Sage.

Park, S. (2006). Facing fear without losing face: Working with Asian American men. In M. Englar-Carlson & M. A. Stevens (Eds.), *In the room with men: A casebook of therapeutic change* (pp. 151–173). Washington, DC: American Psychological Association.

Peang-Meth, A. (1991). Understanding the Khmer: Sociological-cultural observations. *Asian Survey, 31*(5), 442–455.

Pollack, W. S. (1998). *Real boys: Rescuing our sons from the myths of boyhood.* New York: Random House.

Pollack, W. S., & Levant, R. F. (1998). *New psychotherapy for men.* New York: Wiley.

Prochaska, J. O., & Norcross, J. C. (2007). *Systems of psychotherapy: A transtheoretical approach* (6th ed.). Belmont, CA: Thompson.

Rabinowitz, F. E., & Cochran, S. V. (2002). *Deepening psychotherapy with men.* Washington, DC: American Psychological Association.

Root, M. P. (1998). Facilitating psychotherapy with Asian American clients. In D. R. Atkinson, G. Morten, & D. W. Sue (Eds.), *Counseling American minorities* (pp. 214–234). Boston: McGraw-Hill.

Rousseau, C., Drapeau, A., & Rahimi, S. (2003). The complexity of trauma response: A 4-year follow-up of adolescent Cambodian refugees. *Child Abuse and Neglect, 27*(11), 1277–1290.

Rozee, P. D., & van Boemel, G. (1989). The psychological effects of war trauma and abuse on older Cambodian refugee women. *Women and Therapy, 8,* 23–50.

Scher, M. (2001). Male therapist, male client: Reflections on critical dynamics. In G. Brooks & G. Good (Eds.), *The handbook of counseling and psychotherapy approaches for men* (pp. 719–733). San Francisco: Jossey-Bass.

Smith-Hefner, J. N. (1999). *Khmer American: Identity and moral education in a diasporic community.* Berkeley: University of California Press.

Stevens, M. A. (2006). Paul's journey to calmness: From sweat to tears. In M. Englar-Carlson & M. Stevens (Eds.), *In the room with men: A casebook of therapeutic change* (pp. 51–68). Washington, DC: American Psychological Association.

Tallman, K., & Bohart, A. C. (1999). The client as a common factor: Clients as self-healers. In M. A. Hubble, B. L. Duncan, & S. D. Miller (Eds.), *The heart and soul of change: What works in therapy* (pp. 91–132). Washington, DC: APA Books.

Tkachuk, G. A., & Martin, G. L. (1999). Exercise therapy for patients with psychiatric disorders: Research and clinical implications. *Professional Psychology: Research and Practice, 30,* 275–282.

U.S. Bureau of the Census. (2000). *Fact sheet for race, ethnic, or ancestry group.* Retrieved on October 5, 2006, from http://factfinder.census.gov

U.S. Committee for Refugees. (1992). *Refugee reports* (Vol. 13). Washington, DC: U.S. Committee for Refugees, American Council for Nationality Service.

U.S. Department of Health and Human Services. (2001). *Mental health: Culture, race, and ethnicity; A supplement to mental health. A report of the surgeon general.* Retrieved on May 28, 2007, from http://mentalhealth.samhsa.gov/cre/ch5_need_for_mental_health_care.asp

Wampold, B. E. (2001). *The great psychotherapy debate: Models, methods, and findings.* Mahwah, NJ: Lawrence Erlbaum.

Wampold, B., Imel, Z., Bhati, K., & Johnson-Jennings, M. (2007). Insight as a common factor. In L. G. Castonguay & C. E. Hill, *Insight in psychotherapy* (pp. 119–139). Washington, DC: American Psychological Association.

Whaley, A. L., & Davis, K. E. (2007). Cultural competence and evidence-based practice: A complementary perspective. *American Psychologist, 62,* 563–574.

Wong, E. C., Marshall, G. N., Schell, T. L., Elliott, M. N., Hambarsoomians, K., Chun, C., et al. (2006). Barriers to mental health care utilization for U.S. Cambodian refugees. *Journal of Consulting and Clinical Psychology, 74*(6), 1116–1120.

Wong, J. Y., & Rochlen, A. B. (2005). Demystifying men's emotional behavior: New directions and implications for counseling and research. *Psychology of Men and Masculinity, 6,* 62–72.

Xiong, Z. B., Eliason, P. A., Detzner, D. F., & Cleveland, M. J. (2005). Southeast Asian immigrants' perceptions of good adolescents and good parents. *Journal of Psychology, 139,* 159–175.

Yalom, I. D. (1980). *Existential psychotherapy.* New York: Basic Books.

Zane, N., & Yeh, M. (2002). The use of culturally-based variables in assessment: Studies on loss of face. In K. S. Kurasaki & S. Okazaki (Eds.), *Asian American mental health: Assessment theories and methods* (pp. 123–138). New York: Kluwer Academic/Plenum Publishers.

9

Psychotherapy With a 17-Year-Old Iranian American Female
Therapeutic Guidelines

Maryam Sayyedi

Contents

This chapter will provide an evidence-based approach to psychotherapy with the Iranian American youth. The evidence presented here is grounded in my clinical experiences with this population and formulated based on the resiliency factors identified by Cicchetti and Rogosch (2002). The influences of cultural underpinnings are discussed in relation to the development of the "universal healing conditions" (i.e., a healing relationship, instilling hope in the healing process, rationale for healing, and rituals for healing) as identified and discussed by Fisher, Jome, and Atkinson (1998). Interpersonal psychotherapy (IP), the cognitive-behavioral therapy (CBT), psychodynamic therapy, pharmacotherapy, and psychoeducation compose the empirically based evidence of my integrative approach to psychotherapy with the Iranian American adolescents and their families. The integration of those empirically based therapies infused with cultural sensitivity provides the "healing rationale" for my work with this population. The guidelines I have provided here are limited to my clinical experience and evidence I have gathered in working with the Iranian American population for the past 6 years, as well as my own immigration experiences as an adolescent, my training and education as a clinical psychologist, and finally my own lived experiences as an Iranian American mother who has raised two adolescents in the United States.

Psychotherapy With Iranian American Adolescents: Uncharted Territory

The studies on Iranian Americans and their mental health needs are scarce and scattered across different disciplines (i.e., psychiatry, psychology, and counseling). These studies provide brief and stereotyped overviews of the culture, address mental health needs of older Iranian American immigrants without attention to intragroup diversity (Emami, Benner, & Ekman, 2001; Emami, Benner, Lipson, & Ekman, 2000; Ghaffarian, 1998; McConatha, Stoller, & Oboudiat, 2001; Pliskin, 1992; Rouhparvar, 2001; Torres, 2001), tackle the adjustment of young refugee children in the Netherlands and Sweden (Almqvist & Broberg, 1999; Hodes, 2002), or explore the relationship between acculturation stress and maladjustment in the adult population of Iranian immigrants in the Netherlands and Australia (Badal, 2001; Famili, 1997; Ostovar, 1997). None, however, provides evidence-based psychotherapy guidelines for working with the first generation of the immigrant Iranian adolescents and their families.

The studies on the developmental psychopathology also have neglected the children and adolescents of more recent immigrants to the United States. The cross-cultural studies of the psychopathology in childhood and adolescence have focused on the epidemiology of major diagnostic categories within the four primary minority groups in the United States (i.e., Asian Americans, African Americans, Hispanic Americans, and Native Americans) and have neglected other ethnic backgrounds (Choi, 2002; French, Seidman, Allen, & Aber, 2006). With an increasing number of ethnic minority adolescents in the United States, and in the anticipation of their population surpassing those of the majority culture, cross-cultural studies should act as a "door keeper" in research on the emotional adjustment of children and adolescents within the more recent enclaves of immigrants to the United States (Schneider, 1998).

The universality of the developmental process has been further challenged by the recognition of the historical and political context within which the development unfolds, particularly during the stormy phase of adolescence. The ongoing involvement of the United States in the Middle East, coupled with the permanent scars of the 9/11 tragedy, have exacerbated the acculturation stress and complicated the process of ethnic identity development for Middle Eastern American youth (Kishishian, 2000; Moradi & Talal Hassan, 2004). Unfortunately, studies addressing the level of adjustment and emotional hardship of this population are nonexistent.

Middle Eastern youth are underserved and misunderstood. Even worse, they are under a cloud of national suspicions and paranoia, and they are struggling to find their rightful place among other ethnic minority youth in the United States. Dwairy (2006) highlighted the challenges that Muslim Arab American youth face within the current historical context, as a subculture of Middle Eastern youth, and they are struggling to develop a positive sense of self and a positive group-esteem post-9/11. The poor success of immigrants in acculturating and accepting the values of the host culture has been positively associated with the negative attitude of the host culture toward ethnic minorities or subcultures (Nesdale & Mak, 2000).

Ethnic identity development as a part of social identity development is a critical facet of the adolescent's development and adjustment. When the adolescent's group is the dominant majority, it relieves the adolescent from struggling to modify his or her social identity; however, when the adolescent is from a devalued group membership, he or she experiences a great deal of stress negotiating an adaptive social identity (French et al., 2006). The stress of such negotiation further compromises the psychologically vulnerable adolescents and results in clinical manifestations of myriad disorders and severe adjustment problems.

Until culturally innovative therapeutic solutions are rendered by the scientific and/or professional community, culturally informed evidence-based psychotherapies are all we have in meeting the mental heath needs of the more recently immigrated population in the United States. Furthermore, accepting the universality of the common therapeutic factors or the "universal healing conditions" has helped me in organizing my clinical experiences across cultures and may lower one's anxiety in approaching the less known cultures in the United States.

What becomes pertinent is to develop an awareness of how those cultures may form a healing context (i.e., the psychotherapy relationship), what their expectations are of the healing process (i.e., expectation of the therapist and the psychotherapy), and what healing rationale (i.e., theories) and interventions (i.e., treatments) will be acceptable to them. In accordance with the American Psychological Association (APA) guidelines for Evidence-Based Practice in Psychology (EBPP) (APA, 2002), this chapter provides a systemic overview of my clinical experiences for the treatment of a mood disorder in an adolescent Iranian American female. My experiences (i.e., the evidence) rendered here are based on 15 years of clinical experience and training as a child clinical psychologist, 6 years of research and clinical experience working with the first and second generations of the Iranian Americans in Southern California, and finally my lived experiences as an Iranian American who immigrated to the United States at 17, and later as a mother who had raised two adolescents in the United States. The guidelines presented here are for ways of establishing culturally sensitive common healing factors in working with Iranian American adolescents and their parents. They are merely suggestions grounded in my strong appreciation for the level of intragroup diversity among this population.

Cultural Context

First-Generation Iranian Immigrants in the United States

According to the U.S. Census of 2002, there are approximately 330,000 Iranian Americans residing primarily in the United States, with the largest enclaves residing in Washington, D.C. and California. The estimated number of passports held by the Iranian Interest Section in Washington, D.C., however, was 900,000 within the same period. The discrepancy in estimations is possibly due to the Iranians' reluctance to participate actively in the U.S. Census because of distrust of the system. The census on Iranians in California has been somewhat more accurate as Iranians have become involved in the state government and have to use the census to gain political grounds as an ethnic minority. The Iranian enclave in California is largely concentrated in the Los Angeles and Beverly Hills congressional districts. Totaling 159,016 persons, this population is larger than the Iranian American population of 20 other U.S. states combined. Iranian Americans compose 0.469% of California's general population. When compared to California's sizeable Hispanic/Latino population (32.4%), persons of Iranian descent often go undetected as an ethnic minority (Fata & Rafii, 2003; Mostashari & Khodamhosseni, 2004).

Psychotherapy with Iranian Americans is, however, the quintessential implementation of multiculturalism (Sayyedi, 2004), demanding the therapist to go beyond ethnic stereotypes and generalities to understand the client and his or her struggles. Iranian Americans are unique in comprising many subcultures and in demonstrating vast variations in levels of acculturation. Their intragroup diversity stems from the ethnocultural complexity of Iran, variations in history of immigration to the United States, prominence and saliency of socioeconomic status prior to and after immigration, urbanization experiences prior to immigration, educational history, religious affiliations, gender discourse, and finally the individual's developmental history (Badal, 2001; Bozorgmehr, 1997).

Based on my observations and experiences, it appears that at least for the Iranian enclave in California, most facets of the culture have been fluid and malleable along a traditional–modern continuum that interacts with the generation and gender factors. However, there are aspects of the culture that resisted change. Iranians in the United States have been recognized for their high achievements in different fields of medicine, engineering, and other sciences; their pride and nationalistic fervor manifested in myriad cultural centers and devotion to engage in cultural events; and, on a less positive note, their strivings to maintain a social facade of affluence distinguish as elitist. Unfortunately, however, the scientific and business accolades have masked the psychological hardship and maladjustments of the population; thus, the Iranian Americans' need for mental health services has gone unrecognized and unexplored (Sayyedi, 2004).

Shared Cultural Values and Intragroup Diversity

The striving toward modernization, the pre-Islamic revolution of 1979, and the impact of globalization forces postrevolution have softened the sharp edges of the traditional values among the secular, upper-middle class, and more educated Iranians in Iran and abroad (Hojat et al., 1999; Hojat et al., 2000; Moallem, 2001; Wright, 2000). Iranians are more individualistic and competitive as a society as compared to more collectivistic societies of other Asians. However, similar to other traditional (collectivistic) societies and other Middle Eastern societies, most Iranian families value the harmony within an established patriarchy, the avoidance of open conflict, the unconditional respect and deference to parents, the indirect and figurative communication to maintain social hierarchy and family harmony, and fatalism (i.e., belief in destiny) (Daneshpour, 1998; Shokouhi-Behnam, Chambliss, & Caruso, 1997).

In the Middle Eastern societies, self-development and definition are relational and not autonomous given the collectivistic origin of the culture (Dwairy, 2006). However, among Iranians, the strict adherence to interrelatedness versus striving for individuality varies across gender, socioeconomic stratums, level of education, and their extent to which one has adopted the modern, postindustrialized values of the West. There is some evidence suggesting that, in general, female Iranian immigrants acculturate at a faster rate and begin to undermine the patriarchal and sexist traditional cultural values (Darvishpour, 2002). Males, on the other hand, acculturate faster in pursuing individualistic goals at the workplace while adhering to traditional values in their relationships with their spouse and children (Hojat et al., 1999; Moghissi, 1999).

The parenting values and behaviors also vary dramatically across immigrant Iranian families. Similar to all parents, Iranian parents are conscientious in meeting their children's needs for comfort, safety, and success. In return, however, the parents expect the children's absolute loyalty to the parents even after the child has established a family of his or her own. In my experience working with Iranian American families in California, I have come to realize that the extent to which a family maintains the traditional values is inversely associated with its appreciation for the children's individual and differentiation, and it varies dramatically across families. Families, however, in general emphasize interrelatedness, and the individuation process is supported only with respect to the child's academic or career pursuits. On the same note, the child's poor performance in academic accomplishments shames the family and often becomes a source of conflict between parents and their children, which is similar to other Middle Eastern families (Dwairy, 2006; Jambunathan, Burts, & Pierce, 2000).

In my personal and clinical experience, I have learned that Iranian parents are traditionally overprotective and rely on shaming or emotional control to discipline or ensure compliance. Those families that are more educated and modern have espoused a moderate stance in demanding deference and unconditionally support their adolescent's independent pursuit of happiness, even if it is not consistent with the family's expectations. Within this former group, perhaps as an exaggerated reaction to their own experiences with their own overbearing parents, some have become overindulging in their parenting style.

The adolescents of the former group often tend to become maladjusted, similar to the majority of adolescents who are overindulged. They often present with myriad clinical problems, such as addictions, conduct disorders, and school failures. The parents' lax and overindulging stance seems to leave those adolescents with marginalized ethnic identity and no meaningful structure, and they are often self-absorbed, entitled, antisocial, and engaged in self-destructive behaviors.

From the mid-1990s to now, the more educated Iranian American parents have become interested in improving their parenting skills to better meet the developmental needs of their children and their adolescents, who have rapidly acculturated and, thus, are not responsive to traditional means of parenting. They are attending parenting classes spearheaded by Iranian American psychologists, social workers, and marriage and family therapists and are learning to rely on the basics of behavioral modification techniques, such as implementing the schedule of reinforcements and using time-outs or loss of privileges to shape their children's behaviors (Sayyedi, 2004). The variations in parenting styles among subcultures of Middle Eastern Americans have been recognized among Arab and Muslim Americans as well (Dwairy, 2006).

Psychotherapy With Iranian American Adolescents: An Integrative Model

Previous studies have suggested guidelines for therapy with first-generation adult Arab immigrants, Muslims, and Iranians, emphasizing short-term, directive, and solution-focused treatment (Al-Krenawi & Graham, 2000; Ghaffarian, 1998). I have adopted the resiliency model of the developmental psychopathology to guide my clinical work with children and adolescents across cultures. This strength-based and bio-psycho-social model has been promoted by the studies of Cicchetti and Rogosch (2002) on resiliency and its relationship with manifestation of psychopathology in childhood. Their studies verified the importance of a small set of global factors related to resilience in childhood. These include the following: (a) the presence and accessibility of competent and caring adults in the child's family and community, (b) cognitive and self-regulating skills, and (c) positive views of self and one's motivation to be effective in the environment.

In my clinical work with adolescents in general, regardless of their ethnic background, I have adopted the aforementioned resiliency factors as a therapeutic paradigm that guides my clinical efforts and focus. However, my sensitivity to and awareness of the client's culture have shaped my efforts in establishing the healing relationship, facilitating healing expectations on the part of the client and his or her family, and allowing for the healing rationale, which is based primarily on my Western training as a clinical psychologist, to be adopted and accepted by the client and his or her family. I have been true to my training and clinical experiences in integrating a theoretically based and research-supported rationale. I have integrated the IP and CBT as empirically based treatments of mood disorders across the life span (Akiskal, 2005; Bleiberg & Markowitz, 2007; Parker, 2004) with my cultural understanding in choreographing the healing rituals. The case study presented here provides a unique opportunity to learn about the common and specific issues in the treatment of a female Iranian American adolescent presenting with bipolar II disorder, the most recent episode being a mixed state of an agitated and explosive major depression.

Treatment Implications

The adaptive functioning of the family and the level of family adjustment is the first component of the resiliency identified by the developmental psychopathology (Cicchetti & Rogsch, 2002; Patterson, 2002). Without adaptive functioning and adjustment of the parents and their unconditional support, attempts to ameliorate the adolescent's maladjustment therapeutic will not be as efficacious. Thus, it is pertinent that the parents' competency be assessed and, when needed, improved, and that they be involved in conjoint or collateral sessions with the adolescent to address cultural miscommunications, misunderstandings, and misperceptions while repairing and healing the emotional and relational ruptures.

However, in my experience working with first-generation Iranian American families, implementing a family system approach should be done with caution. I have come to realize that open communication may threaten the family harmony, relatedness, and power differentials for more traditional families. However, given the level of heterogeneity within the Iranian American community and different levels of acculturation among the immigrant families, there are families that may respond positively to a systemic family therapy approach to treatment. In the case discussed here, I used family sessions to facilitate open communication of feelings to alleviate misunderstandings and to shrink the acculturation gap between a single mother and her children. However, such open communication of feelings may not be appropriate for other families.

In family sessions in general and in the case presented here, I have the family members identify the buttons that they push in each other in starting conflicts and arguments to make them more conscious of their own role in the conflicts. Many Iranian parents are not quite aware how their indirect communications in the form of culturally condoned and subtle forms of sarcasm or double-meaning remarks push their adolescent's buttons and frustrate them. Similarly, the Iranian adolescents who end up in my office are often oblivious to cultural demand for their deference and respectful (i.e., *Ba Adab*) communication; thus, their irritated reactions (rolling their eyes or stomping away from a scene of an argument) often push their parents' buttons.

The culturally accepted form of communication in Iranian American families maintains the power differentials between the parent and the child; there is a formal way (i.e., *Rasmi*) to address the parents and the more friendly (i.e., *Doostaneh*) and informal way. Traditional families may expect the formal way of communication from their adolescent, yet because of language barriers, some adolescents fail to communicate appropriately, and the parents misinterpret the casual style of communication of their adolescents marked with English phrases and lingoes as disrespect. I had to ensure that the adolescent client could communicate with her parents in a culturally respectful and acceptable manner, and for her parents to realize that it is the nature of adolescence to question all demands and argue for autonomy. At times, I had to choreograph the family encounters to ensure meaningful communication. For the family presented here, this was a must, as the adolescent client was physically explosive and at risk to harm her mother when she was irritated or angered by her.

I played an active role in facilitating a respectful communication of feelings and expectations among the family members by avoiding direct confrontation of the parents, and I have worked hard at times to deflect the adolescent's verbal attacks by coaching the adolescent prior to the family session. In the case presented here, such coaching was crucial as the parent–child hierarchical boundaries were broken down given that the client was physically and verbally abusive toward her mother. Because of domestic violence, I had to ensure the safety of all members in session and after session. Thus, we did not start the family sessions until the client's explosive behaviors were ameliorated and addressed.

In coaching the adolescent client or educating the family regarding effective communication, I have found it invaluable to teach them the rules of active listening, such as reflecting other's feelings and using "I statements." Particularly for the family presented here, without such training the time would have been wasted in verbal altercations and blaming games, albeit I was not able to completely prevent such interactions.

Although learning active listening skills and developing the ability to validate others' feelings are not unique to working with Iranian American families, they are crucial components of therapy with this population. The use of I statements implies that one needs to accept and take responsibility for one's feelings, thoughts, and behaviors. Declaring one's feelings and thoughts by implementing "I" as a symbolic manifestation of an "independent" self is somewhat complicated in traditional Iranian families. For some families such a sense of self is not only foreign, buy also highly threatening to maintaining the hierarchical structure. In some other families, however, such expression of self have been welcomed. Those families have realized and adopted readily how such expressions strengthen their adolescent's sense of self and esteem.

Another obstacle in communication has been the level of the parents' openness to share their private feelings or thoughts given that the cultural mandates preclude open communication that may leave the older adults vulnerable to their children's scrutiny. Those parents tend to minimize or disguise their unwanted negative feelings in front of the therapist and may resort to sarcasm as a way of communicating those feelings. It is the therapist's role to assess the family's style of communication and the viability of exploring the emotional domain of the family. For the client and her family who are presented here, open and direct communication was encouraged only after the mother's and client's safety were ensured. The open communication of feelings in the family session presented here provided the opportunity for the mother to realize that her sarcastic or double-meaning communications were hurtful and damaged the relationship.

The culture also mandates and expects that the adolescent's devotion first and foremost be toward the family's well-being and maintaining the family's good name. The adolescent's level of maturity is measured by how helpful she can be with her immediate and extended family. The more responsibility the adolescent accepts toward doing well in school and helping others in the family, the more respect and trust will be bestowed upon her, not just by the parents, but by the community at large. The client presented here was burdened by all that responsibility and expectation, and her role was exaggerated by her having to be her mother's liaison in all official and financial interactions in the larger community.

The challenge for Iranian American adolescents has been that their parents compare their level of devotion to the family with the level of devotion the parents have had toward their own parents (i.e., the grandparents). The parents who were raised in the old country and in a traditional Iranian society might not have had the opportunity to solely pursue their own interests or desires. Now, those same parents, as a reaction to their early experiences, may have gone out of their way to provide all kinds of opportunities for their adolescent to pursue his or her own desires in the new country. Such parents in my experience have become hypersensitive to the adolescent declining the parental requests to run errands or do something for the family. They tend to misperceive the adolescent's developmental need to spend more time with their peers as the adolescent being selfish and not caring for the family.

Although parent–adolescent conflicts over the extent of the adolescent's participation in doing chores around the house are common across cultures, the extent of the devotion to one's family in Iranian American families may appear somewhat exaggerated from a Eurocentric world view. In my experience with some Iranian families, I have noted a direct relationship between the parents' need for help to navigate and survive in the larger society and their expectation for the adolescent's devotion to the family. It appears that for those families, the adolescent's attempts for independence tends to be misperceived as the abandonment of the parents and compromising their survival in the host culture.

In the case presented here, the mother had to realize that her daughter's pursuit of an independent life would not threaten the family's precarious existence away from the homeland, but it would rather allow her to better acculturate and succeed in the host culture. The mother, similar to many Iranian parents, also had to be reassured that a bicultural ethnic identity allows for the best of both cultures to be integrated and benefits both the adolescent's and the family's adjustment in the host culture.

I have also noticed that Iranian American parents are more willing to reconsider their parenting practices when they learn how their parenting practices may influence the adolescent's ability to assert his or her rights in the modern, individualistic, and competitive culture of the United States or any other technologically advanced, individualistic, and competitive society. Educating the parents regarding adaptive parenting practices and adolescent development has been a crucial component of my work with all parents across cultures. However, with Iranian parents, it is the quality of the therapeutic relationship with the therapist that encourages change in their parenting practices. It has been my experience that they also appreciate the scientific rationale even if the science is primarily influenced by an Eurocentric world view or based on experiences of the adolescents of the majority culture.

The history of each family and the parents' earlier developmental experiences further complicate the parents' level of competency in caring for an adolescent in the United States, and in some situations may call for encouraging the parents to seek their own individual therapy. The mother presented in this case had to be encouraged to seek therapy for her chronic adjustment depression that compromised her parenting role of being emotionally supportive of her daughter who was suffering from a severe mood disorder.

Parenting competence and presence of family support are the first component of resiliency in the Cicchetti and Rogosch (2002) model. However, the second component of that model focuses on the adolescent client. The adolescent client who presents with psychopathology or a clinical manifestation of a disorder will need individualized therapeutic interventions and discourse to develop adaptive coping and self-regulating skills. The individual therapy composes the second component of the resiliency model I have adopted in my clinical work with children and adolescents across cultures (Cicchetti & Rogosch, 2002).

Most of the adolescents I have had the privilege of working with in a therapeutic context present with depression secondary to experiencing multiple losses and role disputes, as well as harboring a depressive attributional style. In my experience working with those adolescents, my approach is twofold. First, I establish a healing context and relationship, and then I educate them regarding the rationale and rituals necessary for healing.

For my adolescent clients to become motivated to actively participate in therapy and to be willing to modify their own behaviors or learn new skills, I have realized that they need to feel understood and strong about the collaborative nature of the relationship. It is in their experiencing feelings of validation and understanding that the healing relationship will germinate and instill hope in the adolescent client about the healing practice of psychotherapy.

The healing rationale and rituals have to be integrative and multimodal to address the complexity of the experiences of Iranian immigrant adolescents. Chucking off all their issues and problems to the acculturation process undermines and limits therapeutic assessment and discourse; thus, it would be important to help the adolescent to distinguish between the cultural misunderstanding and not taking responsibility for poor choices. The therapeutic relationship provides an opportunity for an adaptive process of individuation and differentiation to unfold. But other healing practices are needed to provide the adolescent client with skills to ameliorate mood problems or coping failures.

I found the integration of the psychodynamic (developmental), IP, CBT, psychoeducation, and pharmacotherapy provided a comprehensive rationale and the therapeutic means to meet the aforementioned goals. The adolescent client develops insight about how severe and multiple losses, role transitions, and disputes have impacted their life.

In my experience with those families who are not familiar with the concept of psychotherapy as practiced in the United States, I have found that providing them with empirically based information regarding the nature of the problems has been crucial to positive psychotherapy outcome. Iranian Americans are quite skeptical in their approaches to any ideology or practice, within or outside their culture, but they appreciate acquisition of objective scientific knowledge in any domain of experience. Those with religious fervor, however, tend to be more fatalistic and consider the divine will as part of the healing experience, contrary to the stereotype that they do not consider the divine intervention as the sufficient practice.

Psychoeducation also plays a role in bridging the gap between the healing world views. The more contemporary Iranian world view regarding health and mental health is based on a stress-diathesis model. Modern and traditional Iranians alike have come to believe that severe stress and the lack of a healthy lifestyle (i.e., healthy eating and exercising, as well as the presence of good company and friends) are the culprits behind all medical and mental catastrophes. They are very responsive to a bio-psycho-social perspective; however, their belief in the importance of a healthy lifestyle often precludes their adherence to pharmacotherapy.

My approach in those cases that pharmacotherapy is called for to ensure the client's and family's safety or to be more efficient in symptom amelioration has been to educate the family regarding the temporary nature of pharmacotherapy while the client is learning more enduring practices to diminish the unwanted behaviors or symptoms.

I devote at least a session or two to directly develop and enhance the common therapeutic factors or to set the stage for the therapeutic rituals and practices that follow. In those sessions, I addressed the parents' expectations of the therapist, the therapist's expectations of the parents, the nature of their involvement in therapy, the therapeutic boundaries of the adolescent, how the therapist will maintain such boundaries, the nature of therapy, and how the treatment addresses the developmental challenges facing the adolescent.

Finally, education and orientation also help to diminish the parental fear of being negatively judged as the sole cause of all the adolescent's problems. It reassures them that they will be involved in treatment while the adolescent's boundaries and rights to privacy are maintained. More important, it invites the parents and the adolescent into a collaborative therapeutic relationship with the therapist.

Finally, as an attempt to address the third component of the resiliency model, meaning mobilizing support of the adolescent's larger environment, I have found myself somewhat bewildered given the negative political atmosphere toward the Middle East. The best I have been able to manage is to help them abandon their marginalized status by consciously becoming more involved in their social environment by educating peers and others regarding their own experiences, but patiently. I encourage them to focus on developing a supportive social network of like-minded peers but to also engage with those peers, whose prejudice is based on ignorance rather than on racism or malice. They are encouraged to become a model and a symbol of what is good about their culture to challenge the negative stereotypes. They learn that withdrawal from the community and a lack of a social network jeopardize their health and adjustment in the long run. My accounts of my experiences with both cultures, when I first arrived in the United States at the age of 17 amidst the Iranian Islamic Revolution, followed by the hostage crisis, open a unique window to the acculturation process across the generational divide that exists between me (the therapist) and the adolescent client. My self-disclosures are limited, however, to only those experiences that I might have in common with the adolescent client. Upon and within the first few years of my immigration to the United States as an adolescent, I also had similar experiences of culture shock, alienation, and a sense of a deep loss, as I had left all my friends and family behind. The exploration and discussions around cultural issues validate and normalize the adolescent's feelings of being misunderstood by the parents, as well as the host culture. It also provides a window to the world of the parents who belong to the author's generation and their struggle in developing and maintaining an ethnic identity during the politically unfavorable times.

Case Study

The client's identifying information including name, demographics, and family information have been changed to protect her confidentiality. If there is any resemblance or similarity with someone you may know, it is purely accidental and by chance.

An Iranian American primary care physician referred Sima, a 17-year-old Iranian American female, to this therapist for individual therapy. The family doctor had diagnosed Sima as severely depressed and had prescribed 150 mg of Bupropion SR (Wellbutrin SR) once a day to stabilize Sima's erratic outbursts and to improve her irritable depressed mood.

Four months prior to seeking help, Sima had manifested problems with agitated and labile mood, becoming withdrawn, refusing to take showers, and missing many school days because of headaches and stomach aches. She became violent in response to her mother's insistence to get out of her room, go to school, do schoolwork, or run errands and do chores. Any demands on her were resisted and responded to with her acting aggressively or screaming profanities to be left alone. Sima was failing in two classes, had withdrawn from family and friends, and was severely anhedonic. Her mother became tearful when she explained that Sima used to be an excellent student during her freshman and sophomore years and now was going to fail high school.

Sima's developmental history was remarkable, as she was precocious and had accelerated in reaching the developmental milestones. However, Sima had a long history of difficulties with being edgy, hyper, and moody with an erratic sleep pattern. Her mother and Sima reported that at times she would seem rested without sleeping, and at other times, she would not want to get out of bed. She had always excelled in school, particularly in writing and language arts, until her senior year. The mother admitted that although Sima had always been rebellious and somewhat unruly, she had never been disrespectful or violent, as she had been recently. Sima's mother attributed Sima's problems to her association with and subsequent rejection by her maladjusted peers. Her mother believed that her peers were poor role models for Sima; she referred to them as "the out-of-control White American kids."

Sima's family psychiatric history was remarkable for a long line of moody and explosive people on her father's side. Her father and paternal aunt were on antidepressants or some form of mood stabilizers, and her father was on a low dose of antipsychotic medication risperidone (Risperdal) while under the care of a psychiatrist in Iran. Sima's parents had divorced prior to her mother and the children immigrating to the United States. Her father refused to leave Iran and remarried shortly after Sima, her mother, and brother left Iran. Upon arrival to the United States, Sima and her family stayed with Sima's maternal uncle for almost a year before they were granted asylum. They fled Iran illegally in the mid-1990s and experienced an ordeal having to travel through treacherous terrain separating Turkey and Iran. Her mother reported during the interview that she had not yet recovered physically and emotionally from the hardship of that experience.

Initial Sessions: Establishing the Therapeutic Relationship and the Orientation to Psychotherapy

The initial sessions primarily were devoted to orienting them to psychotherapy, addressing their expectations and the limits of confidentiality, and establishing a common ground for healing expectations and rituals while establishing a healing relationship.

However, I was in for a surprise. Sima's rudeness and aggression toward her mother even during the first intake session was culturally unfamiliar to me given my own very formal and respectful experiences with my own mother. Furthermore, I was somewhat stunned to learn that Sima hit her mother or pulled her hair when she was experiencing rage. Until then I naively believed that violence in Iranian families either was manifested by a husband aggressing against his wife or was in the form of corporal punishment of the children by the parents.

My first therapeutic encounter with an Iranian American family was grounding my work in multiculturalism and the understanding of intragroup diversity among Iranian Americans abroad. It also challenged the universalistic paradigm of the medical model, under which I had completed my education and training in the United States. Sima was refusing to take her medication, and her mother was unwilling to hospitalize her. A lot had to happen before I was able to engage this adolescent and her family in the therapeutic discourse and interventions or healing practices that I knew at the time.

The behaviors of Sima's mother were culturally familiar, however, as she expected me to admonish her daughter for her disrespectful behavior and to help Sima get over her illness so that she could finish high school. She hoped for a direct and authoritarian intervention on my part to defend her and her parental rights for unconditional deference.

In orienting the mother to the process of therapy, although I related to her woes as a mother, being an Iranian mother myself, as a clinician I had to declare my alliance with Sima. I managed the maneuver apologetically, as would be as expected culturally. I politely declined the mother's demands for acting as her agent to teach Sima a lesson in compliance. I helped her understand that for Sima to respond to my therapeutic interventions, she needed to have a warm, caring, and safe relationship with me. In a separate session, without Sima, I further explained the importance of maintaining Sima's privacy and my inability to share the content of the sessions with the mother, but again I was apologetic rather than confrontational. I blamed the Western guidelines mandating such rights and explained the ways that such a process was going to help Sima benefit from upcoming interventions addressing her unruly behaviors. I also informed her regarding the importance of her feedback and involvement. On the basis of the developmental model that I was implementing, the mother's full involvement in therapy was crucial. She had to be empowered as a parent to weather the adolescence storm and to help Sima overcome her severe agitated depression.

In the individual sessions that I had with Sima's mother, I gave her ample time to tell her story, her immigration woes, and her challenges of raising Sima and her brother single-handedly in the United States. The individual meetings with the mother also helped in assessing her level of adjustment and the need for referral to her own individual therapy. I used those meetings to educate her regarding the therapy process, my role in that process, her role in therapy with Sima, and the nature of the developmental challenges that Sima was facing.

Sima's mother cried throughout the sessions when she related her history and gave an account of all the losses she endured in bringing her children to safety in the United States. It soon became evident that she had been depressed all her married life and prior to her arrival in the United States, and that she would benefit from seeking therapy for herself. She agreed to seek help and see her primary care physician for possible antidepressants. Such session outcomes and interactions have been quite common in my experiences with single-mother families or families that had an ordeal in immigrating to the United States. It has been harder to persuade fathers of intact families to seek psychotherapy, albeit males are receptive of pharmacotherapy and referral to primary care physicians.

When Sima came for her individual sessions, she seemed relaxed, less guarded, and spoke in English with only a few Farsi intrusions; she only related her mother's laments or sarcasms in Farsi. She started by reporting that it was her mother who had cultural issues and was unable to adapt to her new life in the United States. Sima indicated that her mother was "too Iranian" in that she did not allow Sima to have the same freedoms that her White American peers have. Sima wanted to be able to dress like her peers (i.e., more revealing and sexually provocative) and to have a boyfriend and a later curfew. Her mother wanted her home no later than 9 p.m., and any discussion about a boyfriend resulted in a serious fight or argument. Whenever she broke curfew, her mother tattled to Sima's older brother (age 23), who also lived with them but was rarely at home. He would scold Sima or threaten that he would embarrass her in front of her friends by showing up to take her home should she be late or pass her curfew. Sima cried while expressing her frustration with her mother and brother, saying she could not wait to go to college and live in a dorm away from them.

In my initial sessions with Sima, my focus was on establishing a meaningful and nurturing therapeutic relationship, without which other therapeutic interventions or treatment would have been impossible. Sima's concerns and frustrations were validated and normalized to help her realize that she was not going to be alone in her struggles anymore, as it was my role to be there for her, understand her, validate her, and help her communicate her needs better.

In emphasizing and establishing a collaborative therapeutic relationship, I also had Sima ask me any questions that would help her develop a trusting relationship with me. I have learned that by becoming more transparent as a therapist, young Iranian American clients become less anxious and more able to relate more openly. My transparency is the first experience that challenges the negative schemas they have regarding the two-faced nature of all social interactions and adults in their culture. Sima, like most of my adolescent clients, wanted to know about my immigration history. Self-disclosure regarding my immigration history and acculturation has become a constant in therapy with Iranian American adolescents, who seem to be suspicious of Iranian American therapists or psychologists, as they are Iranian adults, whom they have come to perceive as judgmental and two-faced.

Furthermore, Sima knew that I spoke with her mother in the previous session and would continue to see her a few more times to complete history taking and assessment of the family situation, and she was concerned about her mother's influence on me. Given the importance of deference to parents in the Iranian culture, her mother's close friends and extended family scolded Sima frequently regarding her outbursts or acting-out behaviors. In Sima's mind, the therapist was yet another adult Iranian female who was going to tell her what to do and scold her for her disrespectful behaviors. I addressed her concerns directly by explaining my role and by demonstrating that our relationship was different from her relationships with other Iranian adults in her life. Focusing on the common therapeutic factors of establishing a healing relationship, healing expectations, and healing rituals was crucial before Sima and I could engage in discussing the course of therapy, the treatment plan, or the rationale for healing.

Once a trusting relationship developed through active listening and implementing unconditional positive regard and acceptance, Sima shared a dark secret in that she had entertained suicidal thoughts, but was worried about her mother and her mother's inability to survive without her in the United States. She then reassured the therapist that she would never do it and that she believed that suicide was a selfish act. She agreed to a no-suicide contract and accepted my pager number so she could contact me any time she found herself overwhelmed with such thoughts.

Once Sima realized that I not only would not judge or scold her, but also, contrary to her mother and other female adults in her life, would be able to handle the intensity of her distress, she began to explore her feelings regarding all her losses: the loss of a luxurious lifestyle in Iran, the loss of old friends, the divorce of her parents just before immigration, the trauma of fleeing Iran through dangerous and rough terrains, and the stress of seeking asylum in the United States. She was quite disappointed that after all the hardship she and her family endured, she lived in a "dumpy one-bedroom apartment" and had to work to pay for all her expenses. The adolescents from her affluent socioeconomic status in Iran did not have to work. She also had learned through phone conversations with her cousins in Iran that they were partying and dating under the watchful eyes of the Islamic Republic guards, who, following the 1979 revolution, severely punished coed activities.

She also felt safe enough to complain and express frustrations with her depressive symptoms, such as being tired all the time, wanting to sleep most of the time, having problems concentrating in school, being absentminded and no longer interested in activities that used to make her happy, and not wanting to be with her friends anymore. She believed they were spoiled and ignorant, and they annoyed her. She believed that since 9/11, some of her friends had been tacitly discriminating against her by telling crude jokes about Middle Easterners. She was frustrated with her friends' ignorance regarding the Middle East and not distinguishing different nationalities of the Middle East. She was baffled that her friends confused Arabs and Iranians and in spite of the media coverage, they still did not know that the terrorists who were responsible for the 9/11 tragedy were Arabs and not Iranians. She also reported that she had been very depressed and irritable once before, when she was in eighth grade, but this time she felt worse.

In response to the question about whether she had experiences of elevated, exceptionally happy moods or up periods, she indicated that for very short periods in the past, off and on, she had been hyper and overly talkative, shopped more than usual, completed school projects ahead of schedule, became very creative and wrote poems, became quite confident, and did not need much sleep. She expressed worries regarding her outbursts, losing her mind like her paternal aunt in Iran, or becoming as violent as her father. She reported that she was not taking her medication because she was not crazy like her father or aunt. It was evident that educating her regarding her agitated depression or possible bipolar II diagnosis was premature, as she feared the stigma of mental illness, and she was not taking comfort in accepting a sick role as predicted by the IP model.

It was also evident that her mood problems were more severe than an adjustment reaction to acculturative stress or an exaggerated manifestation of the adolescence storming. The diagnosis of a bipolar II disorder with the latest episode being a mixed state of labile and agitated depression better accounted for her symptoms manifestation and the severity of her educational and social impairments. The pharmacotherapy that her mother sought earlier and prior to seeking therapy seemed appropriate, but a psychiatric referral for reevaluation and possible refinement of the pharmacotherapy with a mood stabilizer became necessary.

Her second individual session, however, focused on stopping her aggression toward her mother and ended with an agreement that she would refrain from aggressing against her mother or damaging household items. She agreed to retreat to her bedroom and stay there until she was calmed down. She also learned in session the relaxation response of deep breathing, guided imagery, and use of self-calming statements. With her permission, her mother was called and informed of the no-aggression contract, and the mother's collaboration in completing the behavioral contract was solicited over the phone. Her mother acknowledged that she followed Sima around the apartment relent-lessly, hoping to talk her into submission. According to Sima, her mother would retreat and act helpless and wounded only after Sima attacked her to get her to stop following her around and talking incessantly. On the phone, the mother agreed to let Sima retreat to her bedroom to calm down and not to follow her. I had to reach an agreement with Sima's mother over the phone as Sima refused to bring her to therapy. Having parents accompany the ado-lescents and wait in the waiting room will make them readily available to the therapist should there be a need for involving them, however, it was Sima's wish not to have her mother waiting for her in the waiting room, and she wanted to come to therapy on her own.

Middle Phase: Implementing the Healing Rituals and Interventions to Ameliorate Symptoms

Once Sima's more immediate needs for understanding, unconditional regard, and validation were addressed and her aggression was partially contained, the therapy had to focus on the other common therapeutic factors to engage her more actively in those interventions necessary for ameliorating her mood disorder and improving her level of adjustment.

The middle phase of our therapy together focused on further assessment and amelioration of the stressors with an eye on finding the most opportune moment to address pharmacotherapy. Sima's agitated mood state and severe depression debilitated her in many domains of functioning, particularly in academic performance, and she was risking failing high school. It was imper-ative to consider pharmacotherapy to regulate her mood more efficiently, as her high school graduation was at risk because of her missing school and not turning in her assignments. The stabilization of her mood and improvement of her concentration became the most salient therapeutic goals. In the second session, she was not ready to hear about her illness, but the opportunity arose in a subsequent session when she complained about being on the edge; expe-riencing anhedonia, hopelessness, tearfulness, depressed mood, poor sleep, and general fatigue; and not being able to concentrate or do schoolwork. Her complaining about her cognitive and somatic aspects of her depression provided the opportunity to address another component of the common therapeutic factor, which is to share a healing rationale and solicit the client's belief in that rationale. I educated her about the bio-psych-social treatment of depression. She felt hopeful once she realized that the medication was a temporary solution that would help her to sleep better, to feel less on the edge or irritable, to concentrate so she could do better at school, and to be able to graduate with her peers. Once her vegetative signs of depression were under control, she would then have more energy and time to develop cognitive and behavioral ways of overcoming her vulnerability to mood destabilization and depression.

Per Sima's and her mother's authorization, I was able to coordinate care with an Iranian psychiatrist, who increased her Wellbutrin to 450 mg and added 4 mg of risperidone at bedtime. Given her bipolar II diagnosis, it was also relevant to lower the chances for possible manifestation of a manic episode by having her on a low dose of the antipsychotic medication risperidone.

Sima was also educated regarding the premises of CBT and became interested in cognitive restructuring and modifying irrational processing. She learned how her irrational processing of information (i.e., minimizing the positives and exaggerating the negatives, doing all-or-nothing thinking) and her depressive attributional style left her vulnerable to feeling hopeless and enraged when she felt rejected or controlled. Sima gained insight regarding her insecure ambivalent attachment and the compromised self–other schemas influenced by her early experiences with domestic violence in her family.

She actively participated in anger management as she worried that she may treat her future partner or children violently. In analyzing her outbursts, she realized that she responded aggressively partially because of her poor impulse control and irritability and partially as a desperate attempt to regain control, as her mother left her alone only after she raged or attacked her. The early experiences of her father controlling her mother by aggression also left its imprint on her young mind. Her mother's retreating in response to her aggression further reinforced her outbursts and maintained her aggressions toward her.

Sima was a bright and verbal adolescent who enjoyed learning about her own psychology. She became interested in the notion of thoughts influencing one's way of feeling and behaving. It was through challenging her own negative automatic thoughts centered on fear of rejection and loss of control that she began to move toward a more positive sense of self and ethnic identity. She also learned how to use coping statements (i.e., self-assuring thoughts) to regulate her intense emotions. She began to take her mother's comments and reactions less personally and more objectively to differentiate between her own emotional state and her mother's state of crisis. Concurrently, as she adhered to pharmacotherapy, her mood became stabilized and her outbursts became less frequent, providing her with more opportunity to have adaptive and less aggressive communications with her mother as well as her peers. She also began to attend school regularly, as she was able to sleep better and be more rested in the mornings to attend school.

In those sessions, Sima also brought up her weekly stressors associated with her role transition and role dispute postimmigration; those issues were identified and addressed based on the rationale provided by IP. The primary premises of IP are consistent with the stressors that most Iranian immigrant families have experienced upon and following immigration.

Given her mother's lack of English proficiency and a driver's license, Sima spent most of her free time taking her mother to appointments, shopping malls, and Iranian cultural events or family events. However, she indicated that her mother called her "selfish" or "too Americanized" when she wanted time to herself or to be with her peers. She expressed frustration with her mother while yearning for her acceptance and support. I provided emotional support, reflections, and validations not only to strengthen the therapeutic alliance but also to help her process her unwanted and ambivalent feelings toward her mother.

Amidst what seemed like a selfless lifestyle, Sima had managed to have a boyfriend. However, her brother had intercepted a phone call from her boyfriend and threatened to teach her boyfriend a lesson, thus, abruptly ending the relationship a few months prior to the onset of her depression. It became evident that the loss of the boyfriend was perhaps the last straw that finally broke down her defenses and resulted in the onset of her depression and the subsequent violent outbursts.

In subsequent individual sessions with Sima, she explored and discussed at length her relationship with her brother and the nature of his role transition, which was to act as her father since they immigrated to the United States. However, he was only 6 years older than Sima. According to Sima, her brother became controlling and emotionally distant from her in his new role as the father figure. Sima missed the time they had in Iran, where he was a brother to her, and they had fun playing card games or watching their favorite TV shows together. To reestablish and mobilize the brother's support for Sima while healing their relationship, I recommended a family session. The family sessions began after Sima's mood was stabilized and her aggressive outbursts were diminished.

The family sessions were also the opportunity to engage her brother and mother in therapy to address deeper grief issues. A few sessions were devoted to exploring, reframing, validating, and normalizing Sima's fears and anxiety regarding the family encounter. She mentioned that her mother maintained a social facade of wellness by never admitting to any flaws and that she was not genuine with people, including the therapist. Sima believed that her mother would agree with the therapist's recommendations, but once they were home, she would not follow up with the recommendations and resort to her own maladaptive ways of parenting.

Sima had to be educated about the cultural sanctions regarding social decorum and not communicating unwanted thoughts or feelings or confronting authority to maintain social harmony, acceptance, and relatedness. Such an education was therapeutic, as it helped her to take a perspective and to realize why her mother was so obsessed about having the community's respect, influencing what others thought of her and her family, and maintaining a facade of adjustment and affluence.

Final Phase of Treatment: Resolving Grief, Addressing the Role Disputes, Healing the Family, and Facilitating Positive Ethnic Identity Development

The family session was to assist Sima and her family to communicate their feelings openly yet respectfully to negotiate needs and desires adaptively across the acculturation divide. The family session was also a way of reaching some form of equilibrium in the acculturation process of this family. Family sessions always began by setting ground rules for respectful communication and active listening.

For this family, given that Sima's rage and aggression had broken down the traditional and hierarchical structure of the family, open communication was not a threat to disturbing the family's harmony or structure. Furthermore, their immigration history and their history of family dysfunction prior to immigration necessitated open communication of feelings but with safeguards in place to discourage violent reprisals after sessions. The family session was going to provide an opportunity for airing years of stifled or mangled feelings. The family needed to air all those feelings, process them, and find meaning for their collective experiences in order to heal and reconnect. The goal was to promote interrelatedness and teach them the communication skills necessary to maintain relatedness while opening space for individuation and differentiation of both Sima and perhaps even her brother.

In our first family session, as I had feared, the client's mother became uncomfortable. She announced that she was not sure about open communication of feelings because she did not want to hurt her children's feelings. In response, both the client and her brother rolled their eyes and dropped their heads, trying to hide their smirking. I had an opportunity to comment on the process, but that was too threatening given that this was the beginning of the first family session, and my attention to their disrespect toward their mother would have shamed the mother. I focused on modeling active listening and empathy instead, so I said to her, "It is very hard on Iranian single mothers to raise successful and happy children in the United States, where so many things can go wrong." The mother nodded in agreement and became tearful while maintaining eye contact with the therapist, ignoring her children's behavior.

Sima reminded her mother that it was not that easy on them either and that they never wanted to hurt her when they did their own things or expressed their dissatisfaction with their life. The brother remained quiet despite Sima's attempt to engage him by using the pronouns we and they (establishing that her brother was on Sima's side). Being the only male in the room, he remained guarded, and I had to be more active in involving him; I started by inquiring about his thoughts and not his feelings, a less threatening focus. He shrugged and indicated that this type of communication went on at home but would never get anywhere. He believed that his sister was rebelling and acting "too American," referring to her wanting to have a boyfriend at age 17. He stated that he used to be a teenage boy so he knew how the mind of a teenage boy worked: "Boys don't want relationships you know!" He also believed that their mother was too lenient when his sister was in junior high school. He believed that if his mother had set limits then and did not spoil her like a "Persian Princess," she would not have so many problems. Sima became irritated and yelled at her brother, asking how many "Persian Princesses" did he know who worked, went to school, and took care of their mother's needs. The mother became tearful and indignantly apologized for being such a burden, and Sima snapped at her for making her feel guilty.

I ignored the mother's sympathy-seeking remarks to encourage more supportive communication between the siblings in an attempt to restructure the family. I shared my surprise regarding the brother's traditional views of dating and double standards regarding social freedom for his sister. Sima's brother stated that his mother demanded and expected him to protect his sister's honor and good name in the community. He added that if it were up to him, whom he believed was acculturated and not traditional, he would let Sima learn her lesson the hard way. He believed that his mother was overprotective of Sima. He stated that Sima needs to be responsible for her own actions to become successful in the United States. He also added that their mother did a lot for them by protecting them from an abusive father. He believed, however, that in the United States, he and Sima were working hard to support their mother but were left to feel that she was "disappointed" and "never happy." The mother cried and said that she was proud of them and that her sadness or disappointments were not their fault.

Sima went on describing to the therapist that her mother compared Sima and her brother to their cousins or with the other teens of family friends, only to shame them into submission or to do more for her. I had similar arguments with my mother, and I know every one of my friends have had similar experiences where they were compared to other children who were sources of pride for other parents. Such shared experiences stem from parents' reliance on emotional control and shaming as tools of parenting in the traditional Iranian culture, and my role as a cultural attaché was being tested during that session.

In most family sessions, I become a cultural attaché, going back and forth between the warring parties and helping them gain perspective of each other's culture. Contrary to the mother's earlier premonition, the open communication coupled with my cultural explanations and openness to explore the traditional wisdoms brought them emotionally closer to each other and modified their misperceptions and misattributions. I helped the mother to understand the challenges that her children were facing in the host culture and their stress associated with wanting to fit in and thus to acculturate. I also needed to challenge and ameliorate her cultural paranoia regarding White American adolescents' overindulging in sex and drugs. I helped her understand that the majority of adolescents were not acting out or in trouble. I explained the nature of mutual respect and how the mother and the brother should provide Sima with appropriate options as opposed to mandates or orders.

Over time and by practicing in sessions, the mother and Sima's brother realized that some arguments and discussions facilitated the adolescent's development of an identity and were not necessarily disrespectful. I also helped Sima and her brother to understand that what their mother did was rooted in her culture of origin and her own developmental experiences with authoritarian parents.

Conclusion and Additional Clinical Considerations

The other issues that were addressed in therapy were Sima's worries regarding her future and her ambivalence about leaving home to establish her own life. She badly wanted to have independence, but she felt guilty for not being there for her mother. Sima learned to identify and to challenge her misattributions that left her conflict avoidant with her peers and overly aggressive with her mother. She began to take an active stance toward her genetic vulnerability to mood disorders by adhering to pharmacotherapy, which ameliorated her agitation, irritability, low motivation, depressed mood, fatigue, and sleep problems.

Two more collateral sessions with her mother, and in absence of her brother, facilitated their understanding of a shared predicament as Iranian females, which brought them closer together. Sima's mother also sought pharmacotherapy and responded positively to a low dose of antidepressants. As the mother's mood improved, she was able to choose her battles with Sima more wisely. She also attended some parenting seminars provided by the Iranian American marriage and family therapists in her community.

Sima's grades improved, and she graduated that year after she negotiated a plan with her school counselor to complete some of her failed credits that summer in a local junior college. When we terminated our therapeutic relationship, her mother was asking the client's aunt to give her rides to the mall or to run her errands to allow the client to be with her friends more. Sima and I have stayed in touch from time to time.

Conceptualization

Sima's symptom manifestation and her history of presenting problems met the diagnostic criteria for a bipolar II disorder with the most recent episode being a major depressive episode, moderate to severe with no psychotic features. Her recent depression was precipitated by the stress of losing her boyfriend and experiencing discrimination by her peers at her high school following the 9/11 tragedy. Sima's early history revealed genetic and biological vulnerabilities to the development of severe mood disorders, and her early developmental history was also consistent with manifestation of mood dysregulation. Psychologically, however, her insecure-ambivalent attachment influenced by her early experiences of an unsafe environment (i.e., domestic violence) further compromised her coping ability and thus put her at risk for experiences of psychopathology in response to overwhelming stress. Socially, the chronic social stressors resulting from immigration and the loss of her family support because of role dispute and role transitions postimmigration further diminished her resiliency and coping ability. Finally, the presence of multiple acute stressors (i.e., loss of her boyfriend, rejection by peers) over-whelmed her vulnerable state and broke down her coping ability, resulting in manifestation of an agitated depression.

The strong nature of my collaborative therapeutic relationship provided Sima with a strong adult support to not be afraid of facing her problems. Her understanding of my role and her hope in my ability to help her motivated her to engage in the therapeutic interventions and come to believe in the rationale for how her problems could be solved. In addition to the relationship that developed over time, the time I spent on orienting and educating her and her mother regarding my ways of working in therapy paved the way for develop-ment of healing expectations in the process and in my role in that process. The healing interventions and practices were not unique to the culture but were responsive and effective in addressing the presenting symptoms and issues by remaining sensitive to the culture. My emphasizing the education compo-nent and keeping them informed about the rationale for my interventions and orientation to therapy furthered their trust in the process and willingness to engage in the rituals of psychotherapy and its more formal interventions.

Identification of Author's Personal Dimensions of Diversity

I was 17 when I left Iran in the midst of its 1979 revolution, the very revo-lution that inspired Robin Wright (2000) to write a book that she titled *The Last Great Revolution: Turmoil and Transformation in Iran*. Twenty-five years later, as a licensed clinical psychologist, I was sitting across from an Iranian mother and her 17-year-old daughter in a relationship crisis due to the daughter's erratic mood swings and violent outbursts.

My personal dimension of diversity has been evolving as I am developing in my clinical and personal life. The case presented here grounded my work in multiculturalism, but since then I have had many other healing experiences with teenage Iranians and their families that further enriched my clinical expertise in this area.

As an Iranian American mother of two (second-generation) Iranian American children (i.e., 16-year-old daughter and 23-year-old son) and as a first-generation Iranian American female who immigrated to the United States at age 17, I had a few ways through which I was able to relate to and culturally connect with Sima (the client presented here). My world view as a bicultural clinician, however, goes beyond the limits of my ethnicity and gender. I have come to acknowledge the universality of common therapeutic factors and to realize the centrality of relationships in all human experience, particularly the healing experiences.

In discussion of what constitutes maladjustment or pathology, I am acutely aware of the influence of privilege at multiple levels of discourse, as in how a society may privilege one rationale of healing over another and, at another level, how my own privileges influence my adherence to particular rationales for therapy or healing practices. I am more comfortable practicing in empirically grounded interventions and ways of conceptualizing my client's struggles. However, I have also benefited from my own lived experiences as I had struggled with similar developmental and cultural issues discussed in the case presented in trying to negotiate a bicultural ethnic identity of my own.

The issues of my differentiation and individuation from my mother, who also raised me single-handedly, to some extent were similar to the struggles of many of my female clients from diverse cultural backgrounds. I have come to realize that such developmentally based processes and challenges in mother–daughter relationships are present across cultures and may even be universal. I have also realized that across cultures, the developmental history and early interpersonal experiences play an important role in adjustment and one's adaptation to stressful situations later in life. Finally, I have come to realize that, perhaps contrary to the assertion of multiculturalism, culture influences the developmental process to the extent that it dictates the nature and intensity of relationships with one's parents and the larger community.

I believe in pluralism and diversity, as I have lived it and practiced it, but not to the extent that I would disregard or minimize our shared experiences as members of the human race. In my lived experiences and clinical observations, the distinctions between collectivism, individualism, or traditional and modern stances, which I presented here, are somewhat arbitrary or academic and their influence appears to be even more limited when it comes to psychotherapy per se.

The development of a collaborative and meaningful therapeutic relationship lies, however, at the core of any therapeutic discourse or healing experience with any client of any background or cultural persuasion. The other common therapeutic factors such as a rationale for therapy and particular therapeutic rituals or interventions may vary from therapist to therapist based on their training and their world view. Thus, the guidelines provided here are primarily focused on establishing a healing relationship and one's role as a healer. The guidelines here should be practiced combined with curiosity and flexibility in order not to encourage stereotyping.

General Therapeutic Guidelines for All Clinicians

Although cultural understanding is crucial in establishing a strong therapeutic relationship, when working with adolescents, it may not be wise to rely on them to educate you regarding the culture of the parents. Reliance on less biased sources for becoming familiar with the culture is necessary. The adolescent client may try to reap the benefits of the cultural gap by manipulating the therapist to focus on the cultural differences to the extent that the adolescents' individual shortcomings, deficits or conflicts, and problems may go unrecognized or undermined.

For the parents to trust the therapist's role as a healer, they need to overcome their cultural paranoia regarding the noncultural therapists. Sharing one's lived and personal experiences with any of the Middle Eastern cultures will be helpful, whereas specific knowledge of the Iranian American culture will be necessary for therapy with this population. Some meaningful experiences are to participate in cultural events, find Iranian American friends, eat at Iranian restaurants, read about Iranians' history and current politics, and read novels or biographies written about or by Iranian Americans. Iranian Americans, at this time in the political history of the United States, have become hypersensitive to the larger society's level of acceptance or appreciation of their culture. Some families have expressed annoyance with having to educate the therapists regarding the general cultural values and the level of intragroup diversity in acculturation, and many resent the fact that they are readily stereotyped as Moslems or mistaken as Arabs.

The extent and quality of greeting and engagement during the first contact are important for contacts in general and the professional healing contacts in particular. It allows the parents, the adolescent, and the therapist to assess each other's openness to participate and receive a healing relationship. Greetings are always formal yet warm and inviting, and the amount of time dedicated to the meeting should be flexible. Parents are addressed by their surname not first names, particularly when they are older than the therapist. The adolescent client, however, receives a shorter and less formal greeting to be more consistent with the adolescent's more acculturated stance (i.e., Western culture is perceived as informal).

Other issues pertinent to the development of trust and collaboration in therapy have to do with time management. It is imperative to allocate ample time for the first session assessment. It would be best if two intakes are scheduled: one for the parents to provide history of presenting problems and other relevant information, and one for the adolescent client. Should the family come together, there has to be ample time for seeing the parents separately. The parents may be hesitant to discuss all their issues in front of the adolescent client. The assessment should allow the parents to detail their hardship and struggles with their adolescent and, if need be, their own immigration history or possibly their own individual struggles with depression or anxiety. There should be enough time for the adolescent to feel heard as well and not to leave the intake session with the impression that the therapist will be an agent of the parents.

In most traditional cultures, the concept of time is relative and fluid rather than discrete and limited. On the basis of such a culturally engrained concept of time, Iranian American parents measure the therapist's level of care and interest in them by how much time they get with the therapist. The families often are late for appointments, which is yet another cultural glitch concerning the relativity of time in the culture that needs to be addressed once some relationship has developed. The discussion of such limitations should be conducted in a warm and friendly manner, with the therapist taking an apologetic tone. The therapist behaves as if it is truly beyond his or her control to extend the time as much as he or she may want to. Directly confronting the client, interpreting the lateness, or going over time and trying to strictly keep a 50-minute session may be perceived as lack of care for the client. I would like to recommend a 90- to 120-minute intake and 60- to 75-minute therapy sessions with parents, depending on their level of acculturation, education, and professional background. The more educated, professional, or acculturated the family, the easier the time management or setting of time boundaries. The time with the adolescent, however, can be shorter and consistent with the standard intake and therapy time, as the adolescent is more accustomed to Western concepts of time.

The first session usually focuses on assessing and obtaining the informed consent, with emphasis on educating the parents about therapy in general and more specifically about the therapeutic boundaries of the adolescent client. The general expectation of most Iranian American parents in therapy has been to be closely involved, and they expect the therapist to keep them abreast of the adolescent's progress, almost on a session-by-session basis. The notion of respecting the adolescent's privacy (i.e., maintaining confidentiality) has been a sensitive issue and requires at least a session to initiate the parents to the therapy process. The therapist needs to take some time in the initial session to educate the parents regarding the importance of confidentiality in providing a safe therapeutic environment for the adolescent. The initiation of the parents and their orientation to the psychotherapy process somewhat preclude the common misunderstandings inherent in all cross-cultural communications. The therapist will save time in not having to return multiple phone calls from the parents, who inadvertently want to dictate the focus of therapy when they are not well informed about the process and rationale of the therapy.

Although all parents have to be assured of their participation in the therapy process, there is variation among families in the extent to which they may want to micromanage the therapeutic process or the therapist's role. Some families are more controlling and intrusive than others. Such need for control appears to emanate from the parents' heightened anxiety associated with a perceived loss of control over their adolescent. Parents are leery of mainstream therapists, whose respect for the adolescent's individual rights results in excluding the parents from the therapy process and, thus, inadvertently encourages the adolescent's rejection of the family. *It is imperative to be mindful of the parents' level of anxiety and attempt to ameliorate that by providing general information about adolescence as well as about how the therapist is planning to help the adolescent client and the family.*

Self-disclosure is another important boundary issue across cultures. For highly acculturated and educated Iranian families, the expectation for the therapist's transparency might be limited to learning about the therapist's level of education and training. For more traditional and less acculturated families, the therapist's willingness to share aspects of his or her own life validates or normalizes the family's expectations for a close relationship with the therapist. The perception of the therapist as a family friend or even as an adopted member of the family (e.g., sister) is common, particularly with more traditional families. *Be willing to disclose your cultural experiences or lived experiences that validate the family members and put them at ease with regard to not being perceived by you as maladjusted or deviant.* The disclosure is to lower the power differential and enhance the perception of friendliness while maintaining the focus of the therapy on the family or the adolescent.

Culturally, the form of communication among first-generation Iranian Americans is more figurative and indirect. *Be familiar and patient with indirect and figurative forms of communication, at least to explore problems and to provide a context to validate and normalize the family's feelings. It is ironic, however, that the parents expect direct communication regarding interventions and solutions and appreciate any scientific evidence you provide to support your arguments and explanations.*

Iranian parents measure the therapist's level of competency based on the amount of information they receive about the psychology of their adolescents. *Educate the parents regarding the developmental challenges that characterize the immigrant adolescent's development in the United States. Also, educate them regarding the nature of adjustment reaction or symptom manifestations.* The stress of acculturation in adolescence, the importance of biculturalism in adjustment, and success in the United States are some of the topics often discussed in educating Iranian American parents. The education also allows the therapist to develop a positive therapeutic relationship with the parents and to establish his or her role as a consulting expert to the family. Such education enhances the family's belief in the rationale for therapy.

The adolescent client, however, prefers direct forms of communication rather than figurative ones and in fact is often frustrated with the parents' indirect communication. Help parents realize the communication styles across cultures; thus, reframe the problems secondary to miscommunications.

Establish your role as a cultural attaché with Iranian American adolescent clients by expanding the definition of culture beyond ethnicity to demonstrate the influence of multiculturalism in everyone's life. Your adolescent client needs to respect his or her own culture, that of the therapist, and those of his or her parents. The therapist may navigate the differences and similarities between his or her own culture, those of the adolescent, and the adolescent's parents to highlight the importance of culture above and beyond ethnicity. The therapist may act as a cultural attaché to help the parents understand the individuation process characterizing the self-development in modern, competitive societies while acknowledging the parents' world view.

Furthermore, the therapist may help the adolescent to develop an understanding of the cultural expectations of his or her parents. In Iranian culture, the child's level of maturity is measured by his or her ability to care for others as opposed to being responsible only for him- or herself. Help the adolescent to understand and respect such traditional values and to attain individual freedom via demonstrating his or her care for the well-being of the family. Have the parents identify what they believe to be responsible acts of caring for the family, and be able to negotiate with them with the adolescent's adjustment and development in mind.

Conclusions

Although the distinction between the modern (individualistic) society and the traditional (collectivistic) society has been drawn sharply in the present discussion, such a distinction in fact has been somewhat arbitrary but salient and necessary for organizing my observations. The adherence to strictly individualistic pursuits has never meant the abandonment or negation of the universal need for interrelatedness and the importance of relationship between family members or the members of a society. It is my strong belief that all human experiences unfold within the context of human relationships, and the quality of such relationships are expressed in the individual's level of adjustment and functioning in all human societies and across cultures. The emphasis on distinguishing traditional value systems from a modern value system is to emphasize that cultures may differ based only on their development across a time continuum. They are different only to the extent that they adapted to different levels of technological and thus economical advances across our collective history. Furthermore, all modern societies of today at some point in their history valued the traditional views that they may now find foreign.

The cultural nuances highlighted here are to facilitate the development of a strong therapeutic relationship and a healing experience in which the family and the adolescent come to trust and accept the healer and his or her practices. On the basis of my understanding of the universality of the common therapeutic factors as discussed by Fisher et al. (1998), I have integrated empirically based Western therapies with my clinical experiences (evidence based) to provide a model for psychotherapy with a female Iranian American adolescent client who presented with a severe depression and a history of bipolar II disorder. To be mindful of the high level of intragroup diversity among the Iranian enclaves abroad and to preclude stereotyping, I have increased my sensitivity toward the cultural uniqueness of each family, as if each family and each client is a unique window to the culture.

Finally, let us not forget that all therapeutic (healing) experiences in one form or another are contextual, interpretive, reflexive, and fluid, making it improbable to be able to account for all the nuances of the psychotherapy process and its efficacy, particularly within those populations that are newcomers to the field of psychotherapy. It is with those understandings that I have provided guidelines for therapy with Iranian American adolescents who present in therapy with myriad difficulties of affect, mood, and family issues.

Discussion Questions

1. Have you had contact with the Middle Eastern population within any context? How do your experiences lend themselves to cultural issues delineated here, and how have they been different?
2. What has been the role of popular media in your understanding of and willingness to work with the population of Middle Eastern immigrants in the United States? In your experience, what have you noted as distinctions or intragroup diversity among Middle Easterners in general or with Iranian Americans in particular?
3. What do you know about shared values of Middle Easterners in general and Iranian Americans in particular?
4. What aspects of the case presented here are you able to relate to based on your culture?
5. What are the unique aspects of the case presented here that allow for an integration of Western psychotherapy? What is the author's rationale for utilizing the Western psychotherapy approaches? What are the shortcomings and problems with her approach?

Cultural Resources

Dumas, F. (2003). *Funny in Farsi*. New York: Random House Trade Paperbacks.
Guppy, S. (2004). *The blindfold horse memories of a Persian childhood*. London: I. B. Tauris.
Nafisi, A. (2003). *Reading Lolita in Tehran*. New York: Random House.

References

Akiskal, H. S. (2005). The dark side of bipolarity: Detecting bipolar depression in its pleomorphic expressions. *Journal of Affective Disorders, 84*, 107–115.
Al-Krenawi, A., & Graham, J. R. (2000). Culturally sensitive social work practice with Arab clients in mental health settings. *Health and Social Work, 25*(1), 9–27.
Almqvist, K., & Broberg, A. G. (1999). Mental health and social adjustment in young refugee children 3 1/2 years after their arrival in Sweden. *Journal of the American Academy of Child and Adolescent Psychiatry, 38*(6), 723–730.
American Psychological Association. (2002). Criteria for evaluating treatment guidelines. *American Psychologist, 57*, 1052–1059.

Badal, A. (2001). A qualitative case study of the psychosocial effects of acculturative stress and forced displacement of Assyrian-Iranian refugees living in the United States. *Dissertation Abstracts International, 61*, 12B.

Bleiberg, K. L., & Markowitz, J. C. (2007). Interpersonal psychotherapy and depression. In C. Freeman & M. Power (Eds.), *Handbook of evidence-based psychotherapies: A guide for research and practice* (pp. 41–60). London: England: John Wiley & Sons.

Bozorgmehr, M. (1997). Internal ethnicity: Iranians in LA. *Sociological Perspective, 40*(3), 387–409.

Choi, H. (2002). Understanding adolescent depression in ethnocultural context. *Advances in Nursing Science, 25*(2), 71–85.

Cicchetti, D., & Rogosch, F. (2002). A developmental psychopathology perspective on adolescence. *Journal of Consulting and Clinical Psychology, 70*(1), 6–20.

Daneshpour, M. (1998). Muslim families and family therapy. *Journal of Marital and Family Therapy, 24*, 355–390.

Darvishpour, M. (2002). Immigrant women challenge the role of men: How the changing power relationship within Iranian families in Sweden intensifies family conflicts after immigration. *Journal of Comparative Family Studies, 33*, 270–296.

Dwairy, M. (2006). *Counseling and psychotherapy with Arabs and Muslims: A culturally sensitive approach.* New York: Teachers College Press.

Emami, A., Benner, P., & Ekman, S. L. (2001). A sociocultural health model for late in life immigrants. *Journal of Transcultural Nursing, 12*, 15–24.

Emami, A., Benner, P. E., Lipson, J. G., & Ekman, S. L. (2000). Health as continuity and balance in life. *Western Journal of Nursing Research, 22*, 812–825.

Famili, A. C. (1997). The relationship among acculturation, acculturative stress and coping processes in Iranian immigrants. *Dissertation Abstracts International, 58*, 3B.

Fata, S., & Rafii, R. (2003). *Strength in numbers: The relative concentration of Iranian Americans across the United States.* Iran Census Report: National Iranian American Council. Retrieved from http://web.niacouncil.org

Fischer, A. R., Jome, L. M., & Atkinson, D. R. (1998). Reconceptualizing multicultural counseling: Universal healing conditions in a culturally specific context. *Journal of Counseling Psychology, 26*, 525–588.

French, S. E., Seidman, E., Allen, L., & Aber, J. L. (2006). The development of ethnic identity during adolescence. *Developmental Psychology, 42*(1), 1–10.

Ghaffarian, S. (1998). The acculturation of Iranian immigrants in the United States and the implications for mental health. *Journal of Social Psychology, 138*, 645–655.

Hodes, M. (2002). Three key issues for young refugees' mental health. *Transcultural Psychiatry, 39*(2), 196–213.

Hojat, M., Shapurian, R., Nayerahmadi, H., Fouroughi, D., Nayerahmadi, H., Farzaneh, M., Shafieyan, M., & Parsi, M. (2000). Gender differences in traditional attitudes toward marriage and the family: An empirical study of Iranian immigrants in the United States. *Journal of Family Issues, 21*(4), 419–434.

Hojat, M., Shapurian, R., Nayerahmadi, H., Fouroughi, D., Nayerahmadi, H., Farzaneh, M., Shafieyan, M., Parsi, M., & Azizi, M. (1999). Premarital sexual, child rearing, and family attitudes of Iranian men and women in the United States and in Iran. Journal of Psychology, 133, 19–33.

Jambunathan, S., Burts, D. C., & Pierce, S. (2000). Comparisons of parenting attitudes among five ethnic groups in the United States. *Journal of Comparative Family Studies, 31*(4), 395–408.

Kishishian, F. (2000). Acculturation, communication, and the U.S. mass media: The experience of an Iranian immigrant. *Howard Journal of Communications, 11*, 93–106.

McConatha, J. T., Stoller, P., & Oboudiat, F. (2001). Reflections of older Iranian women: Adapting to life in the United States. *Journal of Aging Studies, 15*, 369–381.

Moallem, M. (2001). Middle Eastern studies, feminism and globalization. *Signs, 26*, 1265–1268.

Moghissi, H. (1999). Away from home: Iranian women, displacement cultural resistance and change. *Journal of Comparative Family Studies, 30*, 207–224.

Moradi, B., & Talal Hassan, N. (2004). Arab American persons' reported experiences of discrimination and mental health: The mediating role of personal control. *Journal of Counseling Psychology, 51*, 418–428.

Mostashari, A., & Khodamhosseini, A. (2004). *An overview of socioeconomic characteristics of the Iranian-American community based on the 2000 U.S. Census.* Iranian Studies Group at MIT. Retrieved from http://web.mit.edu/isg/

Nesdale, D., & Mak, A. S. (2000). Immigrant acculturation attitudes and host country identification. *Journal of Community and Applied Social Psychology, 10*, 483–495.

Ostovar, R. (1997). Predictors of acculturation among Iranian immigrant adults living in the United States. *Dissertation Abstracts International, 58*, 3B.

Parker, G. (2004). Highlighting bipolar II disorder. *Canadian Journal of Psychiatry, 49*(12), 791–793.

Patterson, J. M. (2002). Understanding family resilience. *Journal of Clinical Psychology, 58*, 233–246.

Pliskin, K. L. (1992). Dysphoria and somatization in Iranian culture. *Western Journal of Medicine, 157*, 295–301.

Rouhparvar, A. (2001). Acculturation, gender, and age as related to somatization in Iranians. *Dissertation Abstracts International, 61*, 8B.

Sayyedi, M. (2004, November/December). Psychotherapy with Iranian-Americans: The quintessential implementation of multiculturalism. *The California Psychologist, 37*, 12–13.

Schneider, B. H. (1998). Cross-cultural comparison as doorkeeper in research on the social and emotional adjustment of children and adolescents. *Developmental Psychology, 34*, 793–797.

Shokouhi-Behnam, S., Chambliss, C. A., & Caruso, K. A. (1997). Cross-cultural applicability of contextual family therapy: Iranian and American college students' perceptions of familial and peer relationships. *Psychological Reports, 80*, 691–694.

Torres, S. (2001). Understanding of successful aging in the context of migration: The case of Iranian immigrants in Sweden. *Aging and Society, 21*, 333–355.

Wright, R. (2000). *The last great revolution: Turmoil and transformation in Iran.* New York: Vintage Books.

10

Clinical Competency and Culturally Diverse Clients With Disabilities
The Case of Linda

Jennifer Gibson

Contents

Introduction

The case study of Linda examines the challenges of a Latina with cerebral palsy, providing an introduction into clinical competency and culturally diverse clients with disabilities. This case will highlight Linda's coming to terms with the end of her marriage, single parenthood, and her struggles with identity development as a Latina with a disability. Historically, persons with disabilities have been viewed primarily as "disabled" and not inclusive of having other identities. However, this population spans across every ethnicity, gender, sexual orientation, and age (Gibson, 2006). Approximately one of every five Americans has a disability, composing nearly 20% of our nation's population (Waldrop & Stern, 2003). Yet, disability competency education and training within psychology have been limited (Olkin, 2002). Linda's case study will raise awareness for the need of disability clinical competency by assessing the impact of disability while considering how other individual characteristics, including ethnicity, gender, and age, intersect and influence her mental health.

Evidence-Based Practice in Psychology has been defined by the American Psychological Association (APA) Presidential Task Force on Evidence-Based Practice as "the integration of the best available research with clinical expertise in the context of the patient characteristics, culture, and preferences" (APA, 2006). The greatest challenges society and mental health professions face are "making the 'invisible' visible" and ensuring that education and training of mental health professionals must incorporate issues of race and culture (Sue et al., 2007). The APA (2003) Multicultural Guidelines state, "All individuals exist in social, political, historical, and economic contexts, and psychologists are increasingly called upon to understand the influence of these contexts on individuals' behavior" (p. 377). Yet, empirical research and clinical expertise with persons with disabilities have been limited. As this chapter explores the treatment of Linda, the union of disability-cultural competency, along with the formation of a strong therapeutic relationship, will provide an example of evidence-based treatment for culturally diverse clients with disabilities.

A reality therapy approach can provide a fundamental structure that produces a space where clients experience a nonjudgmental atmosphere in exploring key relationships in their life. For clients with disabilities, this treatment shifts the perspective from the overriding societal message that they are powerless to their discovering that they have control over their lives. They are responsible for and capable of fulfillment in however they choose to define it. This chapter explores disability and the delivery of competent clinical practices in providing care to this diverse population. The author will highlight relevant research, developmental models, and skill development that have been utilized in the treatment and conceptualization in the case of Linda.

Theoretical Orientation: Reality Therapy and Disability Affirmative Therapy

Reality therapy stresses that having unsatisfactory or nonexistent connections with people we need in our life is often the source of struggle (Glasser, 1965). The goal is to help clients reconnect. Reality therapy focuses on (a) emphasizing the clients' responsibility for their thoughts, feelings, and behaviors; (b) teaching clients to avoid harmful external control behaviors of criticizing, blaming, and/or complaining that destroy relationships; (c) providing a nonjudgmental and noncoercive environment to allow clients to examine how their behaviors impact their relationships; (d) instructing clients that excuses, legitimate or not, stand directly in their way of making connections with others; and (e) planning a specific course of action with clients to connect and reconnect them with people they need in their life (Glasser, 1965). Granted, no one has complete control over how others will treat him or her. However, individuals have power over how they perceive, think about, and react to the outside world. Clients with disabilities may resist having such control, believing that their locus of control is external because traditionally, they have experienced systematic institutional victimization from all aspects of society. This includes, but is not limited to, the medical profession, the educational system, and the workforce (Gibson, 2006). Yet, when consistently given the message of ultimately being responsible for their life, clients can discover freedom from the burdens that have been placed on them by society. The simple intervention of having clients select the day and time of sessions can begin their development of an internal locus of control. The focus of therapy with Linda was to begin an examination of life as a Latina with a disability while providing an environment that was accepting and nurturing. Goals for therapy included (a) providing opportunities for Linda to connect with her inner sense of self while challenging societal views of her identity (as a woman with a disability, Latina, mother, wife, and daughter) and (b) shifting her perceptions of powerlessness to that of self-confidence. Therapy centered on forming a mutually respectful relationship while incorporating interventions from reality therapy (responsibility for thoughts, feelings, and behaviors while learning to avoid harmful external control behaviors).

Disability affirmative therapy (Olkin, 1999) highlights frequent goals commonly shared by clients with varying disabilities, despite differences in their presenting problems, psychological makeup, and levels of development. The six-goal approach of disability affirmative therapy is to provide a framework for clinicians to conceptualize issues facing their clients. For example, Goal 1 assesses the client's perspective of disability: moral, medical, or minority/social. This offers insight into the client's dynamics and concerns, allowing the clinician to design therapeutic interventions that do not alienate the client while maximizing treatment.

Disability affirmative therapy coupled with reality therapy provides tools to build a foundation for providing psychological assessments, building therapeutic relationships, and developing clinical interventions for clients with disabilities.

Culturally Responsive Treatment Considerations: Disability Psychology

When working with clients with disabilities, clinicians must recognize the heterogeneity of this population. As previously mentioned, individuals with disabilities are from all facets of life. Moreover, they differ vastly among one another: lifelong disabilities versus acquired disabilities, type of disability (i.e., physical, sensory, learning, and psychological), and variation of level and impact of disability. With such diversity among persons with disabilities, membership in the disability community does not guarantee acceptance by other individuals with disabilities. Unlike people in other marginalized groups in society who take pride and celebrate their commonalities, people

TABLE 10.1
Disability Affirmative Therapy (Olkin, 1999)

Goal	Moral	Medical	Minority/Social
1. Models of disability: Facilitating client's perspective of the disability, maximizing the model's benefits, and minimizing its deficits	Is disability a test of faith or a punishment? Focus on finding meaning in the disability	Focus is on prevention and cures	Identify as part of minority group
2. Empowerment: Taking the lead in one's own disability	Empowerment is the active role in making decisions affecting all aspects of life, including health care, social management, and disclosure of disability.		
3. Values: In the "acceptance of disability"	Enlargement of the scope of values	Shift within the hierarchy of one's value system (e.g., athletic to creative)	
	The subordination of physique relative to other values	Usually affected by disability; shift lower in the hierarchy relative to other values	
	The containment of disability effects	Ensuring that values unaffected by the disability are not demoted in the hierarchy (by self or others)	
	A change in the process by which one assigns a value to a place on the hierarchy	Comparative value is replaced by asset value (e.g., walking = wheelchair riding; both represent mobility)	
4. Containing spread effects	Spread is the power of a single known characteristic to evoke other, unknown characteristics of a person. One way to contain spread is by viewing disability as a possession ("He has a disability") rather than as a characteristic ("He is physically disabled").		
5. Looking forward: Four levels of positive future events	Small pleasures that occur at least once a day Slightly larger events that occur at least once a week Monthly events Yearly events		
6. Developing a support network	One develops a social network of others who understand and accept the disability as a part of the totality of the valued person with a disability; it's done to get empathy but not pity.		

Note. From *What Psychotherapists Should Know About Disability*, by R. Olkin, 1999, New York: Guilford. Summarized with permission.

are not eager to become a member of the disability population. Families do not celebrate when a baby is born with a disability or when a relative acquires a disability. Children with disabilities mostly grow up with able-bodied family members who may attempt to understand their daily struggles, but fall short of fully grasping the experience of the child with a disability. This is not because of a lack of effort by family members, but attributed to not sharing the same life experience. Likewise, individuals with acquired disabilities initially may have family and friends rally around them. However, because of fears and an inability to relate to the individual's experience, there is a tendency of others to withdraw over time. This may explain why the divorce rates among persons who acquire a disability have been reported to be anywhere from 8% to 48% (Kreuter, 2000).

Those with a disability do not differ from others in striving for psychological well-being. However, the mental health of these individuals is often ignored (Vash & Crewe, 2003). In instances when mental health treatment has been sought, clinicians tend to focus on the disability and medical aspects of the person, depersonalizing the individual. Sadly, unbeknownst to the clinician, this can lead to the revictimization of the client (Gibson, 2006) and the likelihood that the client will not continue treatment. Many persons with disabilities have internalized society's perceptions of being just a medical diagnosis and have experiences of marginalization. Therefore, it is essential for clinicians to understand when establishing the initial therapeutic alliance that a client's presenting problem may not be attributed to the disability. These individuals are multidimensional and experience life and its struggles in the same manner as others. With this in mind, clinicians should not assume that the disability is, or should be, the focus of treatment. Disability is an added variable that necessitates a clinician's awareness and sensitivity. It should be noted, as with clients without disabilities, that clients with disabilities will seek a clinician based on the area of specialization, phobias, adjustment issues, and so on. This is why it is imperative that clinicians possess disability-related competence to provide services to all persons who could benefit from their expertise (Johnson-Greene, 2006). To minimize the revictimization of clients, disability clinical competent treatment is needed and includes (a) showing sensitivity toward the disability, (b) confronting one's own beliefs and disability-related stereotypes, and (c) having knowledge of the disability. Table 10.2 gives an introduction to the Disability Identity Development Model (Gibson, 2006). This model has been developed over two decades of working with clients with disabilities by noting the common characteristics, issues, and preferences they share. The combination

TABLE 10.2
Disability Identity Development Model (Gibson, 2006)

Stage 1: Passive awareness: First part of life 0–? Can continue into adulthood	Stage 2: Realization: Often occurs in adolescence/early adulthood	Stage 3: Acceptance: Adulthood
• Has no role model of disability	• Begins to see self as having a disability	• Shifts focus from "being different" in a negative light to embracing self
• Medical needs are met	• Has self-hate	
• Taught to deny social aspects of disability	• Has anger: Why me?	• Begins to view self as relevant; no more, no less than others
• Disability becomes silent member of family	• Is concerned with how others perceive self	
• Shows codependency/ "Good Boy–Good Girl"	• Is concerned with appearance	• Begins to incorporate others with disabilities into life
• Shies away from attention	• Has "Superman/Super Woman" complex	• Involves self in disability advocacy and activism
• Will not associate with others with disability		• Integrates self into majority (able-bodied) world

Note.   From "Disability and Clinical Competency: An Introduction," by J. Gibson, 2006, *The California Psychologist, 39*, pp. 6–10.

of this knowledge, along with the resources of existing multicultural identity models, have led to the development of this disability-specific model. The model is intended to facilitate understanding for persons with lifelong disabilities while increasing the ability to provide competent treatment to this underserved population.

As with other multicultural identity models of development, the Disability Identity Development Model promotes understanding of a client by giving insight into his or her possible perceptions and struggles. However, one should not assume that all clients with disabilities fit into a particular stage. Identity development of persons with disabilities can be fluid. Thus, a client may have reached Stage 3: Acceptance, but may revert to Stage 2: Realization when faced with job discrimination or lack of dating partners. The feelings of "Why me?" and anger can resurface, creating much frustration for the client because he or she may have thought that he or she was beyond such feelings.

Cultural Considerations

Disability

A historical perspective is required to understand how treatment for persons with disabilities has evolved. Social work history teaches us that the first institution, which was built for housing persons with mental retardation, mental illness, and terminal illness, was constructed in 1848 (U.S. Department of Transportation Federal Transit Administration, 2006). Institutionalization represents approximately a 100-year aberration in our history of the standard care provided to persons with disabilities. In addition, it was common for persons with physical disabilities, particularly children, to be labeled "mentally retarded" and placed into these institutions. Often because of the lack of cognitive stimulation in these institutions, these children developed cognitive delays, reinforcing the decision for institutionalizing them. As a result of these systemic structures, a vicious cycle of marginalization had been created.

The perspective that persons with disabilities should not be inclusive members of society was perpetuated under Hitler's rule during World War II. Hitler declared that it was the medical community's responsibility to stop further transmission of inferior genes, and he sanctioned medical experiments (Wallace & Weisman, 2000) using individuals with any known or perceived disability. In total, Hitler had nearly 1 million people with disabilities killed (Piastro, 1993). During this time in U.S. history, parents were encouraged to institutionalize their children with disabilities. They were convinced by the medical profession that this decision would be best for all concerned. The societal message was that persons with disabilities could not contribute anything beneficial to the greater mass and only drain their families and communities financially and emotionally. Therefore, institutionalization appeared as the only viable solution.

By the 1950s, parents were questioning the humanness of the institutionalization of their children, and they began to organize their efforts. They created the Association for Retarded Citizens (The Arc, 2006). As parents united, they began advocating for their children to remain with the family. The demand for social support systems began. President John F. Kennedy's Special Panel on Mental Retardation propelled these efforts in the early 1960s and revealed that horrible conditions existed in these institutions (Gibson, 2003). This began a shift in how our society viewed and cared for persons with disabilities.

Throughout the past five decades, society has been on the path of deinstitutionalization. During the transition of deinstitutionalization, health care for this population has been incorporated into the practice of local community physicians. Formal links between persons with disabilities and health care providers have generally not been sought. Though sociological data clearly reveal the psychological benefits of living in dwellings rather than in institutional settings (Rimmer, Braddock, & Marks, 1995), an analysis of the mental health of these individuals has been a missing link.

Toward the end of last century, the creation of the Americans With Disabilities Act of 1990 (ADA) continued the evolution of how individuals with disabilities are perceived in society. The ADA defines disability as a physical or mental impairment that substantially limits one or more major life activities (ADA, 1990). It protects individuals from discrimination in employment, transportation, public accommodations, government, and telecommunications. Those who have complied with this law have primarily focused on the implementation of physical accessibility. As our society moves forward in the 21st century, clinicians need to take an active role of going beyond just providing physical access to providing competent clinical care to clients with disabilities.

Latina/o Culture

There are approximately 35.3 million Latinas/os in the United States, with an expected increase to 97 million by 2050, representing nearly one fourth of the U.S. population (Office of the Surgeon General, 2001). There are many challenges to providing competent services to Latinas/os. One challenge is providing linguistically consistent care to clients whose primary language is Spanish (Brach & Fraser, 2000). Another potential barrier for many clinicians is that the Latina/o population is heterogeneous and complex, making it difficult to address this population in total without risking stereotyping (Bein, Torres, & Kurilla, 2000). The heterogeneity requires that therapists remain in learning mode when working with this population.

As with people in all populations, Latina Americans seek treatment for a variety issues, though awareness of some special characteristics should be noted and include the following: (a) Latinas are at a higher risk of living in poverty (Berenson, Breitkopf, & Wu, 2003), (b) there is evidence that Latinas are more often diagnosed with depression than Latinos (Rosen, Spencer, Tolman, Williams, & Jackson, 2003) (this statistic is shared among women from various ethnicities in the United States, with women being twice as likely to be diagnosed with depression as men) (Blazer, Kessler, McGonagle, & Swartz, 1994), and (c) many women, Latinas in particular, suffer from "functional somatic complaint syndrome" (physical symptomatology as a culturally sanctioned expression of conscious and unconscious emotional distress) (Cordero & Kurz, 2006). Thus, Latinas may exhibit headaches, stomach aches, and so on without the traditional symptoms of depression, thus often going untreated and, therefore, misunderstood and misdiagnosed.

Insight into a client's level of acculturation can facilitate a clinician's ability to provide competent treatment. When providing care to Latinas, clinicians should examine acculturation at both the individual level and the family level (Santana-Martin & Santana, 2005) to facilitate awareness of the individual's dynamics. The Racial/Cultural Identity Development Model (Atkinson, 2003) provides an understanding of the stages of acculturation for culturally diverse persons living in a White-dominant society (see Table 10.3). This table is only a summary of a more in-depth description of the model. For a more detailed description of the model, see Atkinson (2003).

Being aware of a client's stage of acculturation provides a window into the ways he or she navigates life. When providing treatment, clinicians, including those who are Latina/o, should consider that clients may be coming into the office with different values, customs, and expectations of their own. Racism and classism can occur within one's own culture. Therefore, it is important for clinicians to be aware of these prejudices and biases (Santana-Martin & Santana, 2005). In addition, when interacting with clients of Latino descent, clinicians should include the family when needed, provide respect, be personable, and be trustworthy (Santana-Martin & Santana, 2005). Treatment should be geared toward what is best for the client. Therefore, a predefined theoretical framework may be challenged, and flexibility may be necessary.

Disability and Latina Culture

Disability and Latina cultural aspects have been examined separately to highlight unique struggles that may provide insight into Linda. However, neither disability nor culture resides solely in a vacuum. An inclusive view must be utilized. In examining culturally diverse persons with disabilities, researchers have found that this population is more likely to have lower education, higher unemployment, and lower incomes (Block, Balcazar, & Keys, 2002). These factors only add to the complexity of providing competent treatment to an already heterogeneous population. In addition, culturally diverse clients with disabilities often experience simultaneous oppression within society, potentially belonging to two or more marginalized groups, depending on their multiple identifications (i.e., gender, sexual orientation, socioeconomic status, etc.). An individual can be an oppressor, be a member of the oppressed, or simultaneously be an oppressor and be oppressed, adding to his or her psychological stress. Furthermore, the individual is faced with having to choose which marginalized groups to align with in society, with uncertainty about being accepted by the group that he or she has selected.

TABLE 10.3
Racial/Cultural Identity Development Model (Atkinson, 2003)

Stage 1: Conformity	Stage 2: Dissonance	Stage 3: Resistance and immersion	Stage 4: Introspection	Stage 5: Synergistic
• Have preference for dominant cultural values over their own • Characteristics that most resemble White society are highly valued	• Denial diminishes, leads to questioning and challenging attitudes and beliefs of the conformity stage • Not all Latinos are the same	• Endorsement of minority-held beliefs and rejection of dominant values; rejects White culture	• Rejection of White culture is exhausting—cannot focus on understanding themselves • Struggle with allegiance with one's own minority group and personal autonomy	• Individual develops a balance between an appreciation for own cultural values and dominant cultural values • Both are advantageous

Note.   From *Counseling American Minorities: A Cross-Cultural Perspective* (6th ed.), by D. R. Atkinson, 2003, New York: McGraw-Hill.

Thus, it is conceivable that these individuals align with different groups at different moments in time while at other times finding themselves alienated, depending on the acceptance of others.

Whether the individual is Latina, older, gay, or has a disability, the experience of marginalization is similar: the pain of discrimination, the despair of broken dreams, and the oppression of poverty in a land of relative affluence (Fawcett et al., 1994). As the clinician peels back the layers of an individual, he or she finds that the layers are not easily definable or, for that matter, that he or she can't determine which layer is dominant over the others. In fact, the layers quickly become a goulash, creating the uniqueness of each individual. Thus, the identity of culturally diverse clients with disabilities is complex, creating challenging and exciting opportunities for clinicians.

Adding to the intricacies of each individual's identity and world view is the knowledge of how different cultures perceive disability. For example, many Mexican families have a Moral Model view of disability. Disability is seen as either an act of God or a punishment for something one has done (Santana-Martin & Santana, 2005). However, individuals with disabilities are often accepted by the Mexican culture and within their families as contributing members. While the case presented in this chapter is not a client from a Mexican family, the author believes there are some cultural concepts that are consistent among all Latina/o groups. Unlike the views held by many in majority dominant culture, the pressure is not for them to become more independent, but for them to be more functional within the family (Santana-Martin & Santana, 2005).

Culturally diverse clients with disabilities and their families who seek disability-related services may have little or no direction. Clinicians may be faced with the challenge of becoming a culture broker (Jezewski & Sotnik, 2005; Stone, 2005) throughout the course of treatment. Culture brokering essentially is a conflict-resolution and problem-solving model, highlighting the need to have knowledge, skills, sensitivity, and awareness of cross-cultural variables while taking an active role as a problem solver concerning disability-related matters. Connecting clients with information and resources can give the culture-broker clinician advocate status. Clinicians who hold traditional views of therapy may resist this role of being challenged to step outside their definition of treatment while discovering the benefits of culture brokering.

Whatever role clinicians hold, they may find themselves perplexed when treating culturally diverse clients with disabilities. Gallardo and Gibson (2005) created a model of skill development inclusive of both disability and cultural issues (see Table 10.4). This model assesses the fundamentals of connecting with clients, providing assessment, and setting goals for this population.

TABLE 10.4
Skill Development: Culturally Diverse Clients with Disabilities (Gallardo, 2005)

Issue: (What to do)	Connecting with client	Assessment	Setting goals
Skills: How to do it	• Use rituals—handshakes and so on • Self-disclose • Explore disability identity and cultural identity • Shift environmental context (traditional hour or process) • Use stories, videos, and so on (i.e., provide positive role models) • Educate client about counseling process and role of the counselor	• Use verbal and nonverbal cues • Use language usage or model of disability • Note spiritual and religious beliefs and values • Assess bi- or tricultural living • Assess cultural strength—generate multiple hypothesis • Use appropriate clinical instruments (e.g., Minnesota Multiphasic Personality Inventory) • Note acculturation status • Explore beliefs about health care	• View goals as positive outcomes • Use active/acceptance approach—empowerment • Use collaborative approach with client; assess socioeconomic status, level of education, and so on • Address immediate and concrete concerns first—depression • Use clear, specific, focused treatment plan; note small pleasures • Expand role to community activist and case management • Include family and support services

Note. From *Understanding the Therapeutic Needs of Culturally Diverse Individuals with Disabilities*, by M. E. Gallardo and J. Gibson, 2005, Framingham, MA: Microtraining and Multicultural Development (http://www.emicrotraining.com).

This model highlights an interactive and collaborative approach, providing a framework to build on. As the layers of a client begin to mount—societal attitudes, lower income, physical access, physical pain, the need to accommodate others without being accommodated—the need to deliver competent treatment to culturally diverse clients with disabilities becomes essential.

Treatment Implications

Although reality therapy can facilitate conceptualizing Linda's issues and assist with developing a treatment plan, the additional resources discussed throughout this chapter are required to appreciate her completely. Disability affirmative therapy (Olkin, 1999), Gibson's (2006) Disability Identity Development Model, and Atkinson's (2003) Racial/Cultural Identity Development Model provide constructs for understanding Linda's views of herself and the world. *Skill Development: Culturally Diverse Clients With Disabilities* (Gallardo & Gibson, 2005) provides a structure for clinicians to begin connecting with, assessing, and treating Linda.

Case Presentation

Linda was referred to me for individual therapy by another therapist who was providing family therapy to Linda and her 12-year-old daughter. Linda was a 35-year-old Puerto Rican mother with cerebral palsy. Upon meeting Linda, I noticed that she walked with a pronounced gait, using one cane for balance, and that she had a slur to her speech. Linda's dress and makeup were casual, with her hair looking as if it had been professionally styled. The presenting issue Linda was seeking guidance for was handling her daughter's sudden change in behavior at home and school. The referral for individual counseling threw Linda's reality off because she believed that she had her life under control. She began to uncover feelings that had been deeply buried. What transpired throughout her therapy included insights into how disability, ethnicity, and gender intersected and presented in her life. The counseling setting was in a community clinic that allows a maximum of six sessions per calendar year.

Sessions Analyses and Rationale for Interventions

Sessions 1 and 2: Laying a Foundation and Discovering Layers The first session Linda arrived 10 minutes late. She stated that she would need to leave the session 15 minutes early to pick up her daughter, Kim, from school. When I said that this did not leave much time for her first visit, she quickly became defensive, saying that it wasn't her fault and that she had made many promises to people that she must keep. Our focus then shifted when I asked why she came in for treatment. It was at this point she realized that I had a disability because her tone of voice went from anger to surprise. She said that she wasn't sure why she came in. She said that she was currently in family therapy with her daughter to help control her daughter's behavior. She explained that Kim's grades went from As to Cs within the past 6 months and that Kim had been challenging everything she does and says. After three sessions, the family therapist made the suggestion that she seek individual counseling. Following the recommendation, she called me from the three referrals given to her by the family therapist. Linda did not know why she was in my office, and her tone of voice was wavering on hostile. It readily became evident that Linda did not like to be questioned. I then said, as I attempted to connect with her, that she was here to help her daughter (Gallardo, 2005). She agreed, but could not see how individual treatment for herself could help her daughter. I proceeded to ask her what she wants for her daughter's life, and she quickly changed her tone from hostile to hopeful when she began talking about her daughter. She uncrossed her arms and leaned forward as her face brightened as she began to describe her daughter and the hopes for her future. Linda proceeded to talk about her daughter until she ended the session exactly 15 minutes early. I engaged with Linda throughout this time by nodding in agreement with what she was sharing, reflecting back to her that I understood her as a mother and wanted the best for her daughter. I asked if she would like to schedule another appointment. There was hesitation. However, she agreed to come in the following week. I asked if there would be a better day or time for her to attend a complete 50-minute session (Glasser, 1965). She appeared surprised that I would ask her what would be convenient for her. She requested a different time to meet for our next session. As she was leaving, I told her that I truly enjoyed meeting her and looked forward to seeing her again. She smiled and said that she would see me next week.

Linda arrived 10 minutes late for our second session. I greeted her with a smile, asking how she was doing. She smiled as she politely said fine and asked how I was doing. I asked how things were with her daughter because I knew she relaxed last week when she shared about Kim. As she began to speak, she leaned back in her chair, appearing to be more at ease. Linda reported that she had not received a call from Kim's school and was very happy about that. She stated that she had been sitting down with Kim each school night, making sure her homework is complete. I asked if they spend other time together. Linda leaned forward as she explained how they both enjoy sewing together with Linda's mom. She said the three of them try to meet at least twice a week to work on their separate projects. Linda added that her mom also uses these visits to teach Kim how to cook Puerto Rican food. I noticed that Linda rolled her eyes as she told me this. I asked why she rolled her eyes, and she said that her mom won't let go of Puerto Rico and doesn't want Kim to be held back because of the old ways. To explore her level of acculturation, I asked what she meant by being held back by the old ways (Atkinson, 2003). She explained how her mom has refused to learn English and relies on her own brothers to support her. Linda stated that her mother lives with one of her brothers and is the housekeeper and nanny to her grandchildren. Linda expressed frustration by shaking her head as she said that she could never live feeling obligated to anyone. I asked if she has ever felt obligated to anyone for anything. She let out a great big "YES" as she sighed and leaned back. She proceeded to tell me that throughout her entire life she felt obligated to explain her disability to everyone, including classmates, people at church, everyone, especially when people would tease or laugh at her. Linda said it took her until age 30 to let go of having to teach everyone about her disability. I smiled as I told her that I related to what she is saying. To validate Linda, I stated that she had been carrying a heavy load. She began to cry, struggling to talk. I told her that she did not have to speak and to allow herself to express her feelings. I told her that when I cry, I can't talk very well either (Gallardo, 2005). Linda laughed through her tears. I could tell that she felt understood by me because of my own experiences. She was quick to regain her composure, as if crying were not allowed. I asked if she had cerebral palsy. She nodded her head yes. I shared with her that I have cerebral palsy, self-disclosing to further our connection (Gallardo, 2005). I told her that she did not have to feel obligated to tell me about her disability, providing her with a choice and a sense of control (Glasser, 1965). She said that she did not feel obligated to talk to me about it. She went on to say that she was born not breathing with the umbilical cord wrapped around her neck. Linda continued to share in a matter-of-fact tone the chronological events of her childhood in regard to her disability, as if she had been programmed. It was evident that Linda had told this story many times. Our session went 15 minutes over, and I had to end it because I had another scheduled appointment. I thanked Linda for sharing her life with me. I asked if she would be available next week at the same time. She nodded yes as she apologized for keeping me late. I told her that I am responsible for my own behavior, modeling a sense of control and responsibility (Glasser, 1965). I said that I would see her next week.

Analysis of Sessions 1 and 2   The goal for the initial sessions was to establish a mutually respectful relationship with Linda, which is acknowledged as a crucial common factor across psychotherapies (Wampold, 2001). I was quickly met with defensiveness. To begin building a bridge and to diffuse her anger, I shifted attention away from her and brought focus to her daughter. I saw an open door to enter by discussing Kim. I wanted to create a safe environment for her to begin sharing about her own life experiences. At the time of the session, I was 6 months pregnant and showing, and I disclosed that I was pregnant in an attempt to facilitate a therapeutic connection (Gallardo & Gibson, 2005). Such disclosure can prove therapeutic when working with diverse cultures, and I believe it has an equal impact for clients with disabilities. My decision to self-disclose was with the client's best interest in mind as a way to build a stronger therapeutic connection.

It is important to address disability within the therapeutic relationship to the degree that a clinician would address other personal characteristics of a client, such as gender, ethnicity, and so on. However, the timing of when to address disability issues can be crucial and, if done at the wrong time, can have a negative impact on establishing the therapeutic alliance. Having completed a quick assessment of my initial moments with Linda, I could sense that if I had brought up disability, Linda may have responded with defensiveness (Gibson, 2006), creating a void in our therapeutic relationship. I did not want to risk this setback and possibly jeopardize Linda's interest in further therapy. For some individuals, discussing disability can be offensive early in a relationship because they may often experience "a lack of societal boundary" when being asked personal questions about their disability by strangers. This lack of social boundaries can leave them feeling as if they have been a victim of voyeurism. Thus, I approach the topic of disability with caution. It was evident that Linda was not ready to discuss her disability. We had planted the seeds of our relationship, and I knew an opportunity to discuss disability would present at an appropriate time.

The second session brought an opportunity to assess Linda's perception of disability (Olkin, 1999). My intent in doing so was to provide her a forum that gave her control over her experience with disability (Glasser, 1965) and to not perpetuate her feelings of obligation (Gibson, 2006). In addition, I chose to allow the session to go beyond the hour. The reason for this decision was twofold: (a) I wanted to be sensitive toward Linda and our relationship and did not want to impose our traditional culture of therapy time limits by cutting her short and rushing her (Santana-Martin & Santana, 2005), and (b) I was self-modeling personal responsibility for my behavior (Gallardo & Gibson, 2005). We continued laying our foundation of trust and understanding through this process and established a therapeutic connection in doing so.

Sessions 3 and 4: The Fountain of Relief   Linda arrived 5 minutes late for our third session. I greeted her with a smile, asking how her week had been. She began by apologizing for breaking down last week and saying she had felt embarrassed all week. I said that crying is healthy, and I explored her feelings of embarrassment, providing an opportunity for her to connect with her inner self (Storr, 1983). She said that she is aware that her face contorts more than most people's when she cries because of the cerebral palsy and that she is very uncomfortable crying in front of people. She assured me that she has no problem crying alone. I then asked her when the last time she had cried might have been. She became teary and told me last night. I asked if she felt comfortable talking to me about it, empowering her to make decisions regarding disability disclosure (Olkin, 1999). Linda proceeded to tell me about her relationship with Ray, her husband. They had been married for 14 years, but they separated 8 years ago when Kim was 4. Linda said that they are still legally married and that her family doesn't believe in divorce, stating, "You know ... the Catholic thing." She said that they dated for 9 months before they married. She recalls her family saying that she had better marry Ray if he should ever propose.

Her family never said that she "better take what she can get," but Linda believes that it was implied. She had not dated much before Ray, and her family would make comments about her becoming an old maid. She believed that her family assumed she would never have a man interested in her, especially to marry her because of her disability. I asked how she felt about that as a way to address her feelings of the family's acceptance of her disability (Olkin, 1999). She began to cry, saying, "I'm not less of a person. ... People think I am ... even my own family." I asked if she had loved Ray, and she said she did, but she found out that he was having an affair with an ex-girlfriend 2 years after Kim was born. She said that this was very hurtful, but that she had stayed with him for the baby and the family. She did not want her family to think that she was a loser. She kept his affair a secret, even from Ray. She initially found out about the affair when she saw Ray and his ex-girlfriend hugging and kissing in his parked car a few blocks from their house on her way to her family's house. She remembers pulling her car over to the side of the road and crying. Linda explained that for 2 years, she kept the affair a secret, guessing why Ray might be late, listening to his phone messages at work, and, at times, doubting if the affair actually existed. She did not share her feelings with anyone. She finally came to realize that she wanted more for herself and was tired of living a lie. She confronted Ray, and he admitted that he was having the affair. Linda said that it was a relief when it came out, and as a result their separation shortly followed. The difficult part was appearing to be a failure in her family's eyes. Linda knew she disappointed them, especially her mother. She said that she was crying last night because she was tired of trying to meet everyone's needs while setting her own needs aside. Ray did not come over as he said he would last night to spend time with Kim. Linda knew that Kim was disappointed, and she blamed herself for Ray's not being a better father.

I challenged Linda's perceptions of her ability to control Ray (Glasser, 1965). She responded by saying that she should have known that he was not a responsible person. I asked if she blamed herself for Ray's not being a better husband. She nodded her head yes as she began to sob. She cried during the remainder of the session as I sat quietly, occasionally making eye contact with her because I knew that she was not comfortable crying in front of others. I handed her the Kleenex box and gave her a reassuring smile. As she got up to leave, I asked if she was OK. She said that she was fine and that she would see me next week.

Linda arrived on time for our fourth session. I asked how she had been since the previous session, and she explained how she had "a good cry" after leaving last week and felt the best she had in a long time. I reflected that I was glad that she was able to get some of her emotions out rather than to continue to hold them in. Linda described how she had been taught as a child that crying was a sign of weakness. I said it is clear to me that she puts a lot of pressure on herself, as if she were a "Super Woman" (Gibson, 2006). She nodded, saying that she does get tired of feeling that she has to do better at everything than everyone else. I asked what she meant by "better." She said that from the time that she can remember, people, including family, would assume that she could not do something or would not have an interest in what others do. She then asked if I understood what she meant. I said that I understood. Linda then asked how I dealt with society and having a disability myself. I told her how I have ups and downs, like everyone else, and

I know that having a disability has created additional challenges. I disclosed that I had grown up feeling like I had to continuously prove myself to others, in an attempt to facilitate a further connection with Linda (Gallardo, 2005) while helping her to develop a social network of understanding, not pity (Olkin, 1999). Linda leaned forward saying, "Wow ... someone gets it!" She said that nobody has really understood her when it comes to being disabled, but she knew that I did. She then asked if this was my first baby. I told her yes and asked how motherhood has been for her because I knew I could learn from her as well. She said her daughter has been great and that society has been the only problem. She explained how some people would stare at her baby, with some people questioning how she could care for a child. She was surprised at how supportive her family had been and that Ray never questioned her ability to take care of Kim. I asked if she thought that some of her feelings of needing to prove herself have been placed on Kim. Linda's eyes grew big as she yelled out, "Oh, my God ... I want from her what I want from me!" She began to blame herself for putting pressure on Kim. I asked her if she thought Kim was a good kid. She said yes. I then commented that maybe she does have high expectations for Kim and for herself and that maybe it's time for her to take a look at how these expectations impact their lives. I did not want Linda to believe that she was a bad mom. In fact, I continued to say that I actually believe that she's a great mom who wants the best for her daughter. My motive was to increase Linda's consciousness of her personal value and worth (Storr, 1983). Linda began crying, saying that she hopes Kim doesn't hate her. She then told me she didn't want Kim learning Spanish, afraid that it would hold her back in society. To further explore her racial and disability identity development, I asked if she looked at knowing Spanish and having a disability in the same way (Atkinson, 2003; Gibson, 2006). She said that she had never thought of it that way, but that she sees how society does look down on both. I asked how it was for her growing up as a Latina. She corrected me, saying that her parents are from Puerto Rico but she was born here and is American. I apologized and asked her what it has been like for her growing up in a Puerto Rican family in America. She said that they speak only Spanish at home and that she would pretend that she didn't know Spanish outside of the house. This would anger her parents. In addition, she had only White friends in school. I asked how she made the decision to marry Ray, who is second-generation Puerto Rican. She said that her family encouraged her and Ray to marry and that she did not want to disgrace the family by marrying someone outside of their race and religion. She added that Ray came along and her family acted as if she had better jump on him before her chance at marriage got away. As the session came to a close, I reminded Linda of our 6-week limit at the clinic and that this was our fourth meeting. She sat back in her chair and said that she had forgotten about the limit. To increase her sense of control, I asked what she wanted to focus on for the last 2 weeks (Glasser, 1965). Linda asked if we could save 1 week in case she felt that she needed someone to talk to in the future and if she could bring her mom and daughter next week. She said that she would love for them to meet me, seeing that I have a disability and how I do fine in life. I laughed, saying that I have my issues but thanking her for thinking that I have my act together, thus empowering Linda to see that I am similar to her and that she can achieve her own goals and dreams (Olkin, 1999). She added that she thinks that her mom and daughter would gain insight into her disability if they came in. I said that they could come and asked if her mom knew English, fearful that my limited Spanish would not be sufficient to communicate effectively while displaying respect for her culture. She said that her mom knew enough English and smiled. I said that I would be happy to speak the limited Spanish I knew and that I would look forward to seeing the three of them next week.

Analysis of Sessions 3 and 4   The goal of the third session was to assess Linda's development as a Latina with a disability and provide space for her to connect with her inner self. I challenged her perception of being able to control others (Glasser, 1965), Ray in particular. We explored the internalized messages regarding disability given by her family and her fear of vulnerability (Gibson, 2006).

In the fourth session, our relationship tightened as we discussed our experiences with disability. I believed that at this point in treatment, my disclosure regarding disability was imperative (Gallardo & Gibson, 2005). I asked what motherhood had been like, hoping that Linda realized that she has knowledge and gifts to share with others (Olkin, 1999). It was powerful to see her make the connection that what she wanted for herself was being displaced onto Kim. I believed having her mother and Kim join us for our last session would enhance Linda's therapy experience, knowing that the inclusion of family can be highly valued within the Latino culture (Santana-Martin & Santana, 2005).

Session 5: Joining and Separating   Linda arrived 15 minutes late for her session as she walked in with her mom and Kim. She appeared somewhat nervous and began to apologize for being late. I gave her a look of understanding that said there was no need to apologize. She proceeded to introduce me to her mom, whom I greeted with "mucho gusto" to show respect for her culture (Santana-Martin & Santana, 2005). Linda's mom smiled warmly and shook my hand. I apologized for knowing limited Spanish and said that I hoped that we would be able to understand one another. She said that she could understand English OK, but had trouble saying words. With the intent of connecting with her, I said that I have a similar problem and that we'll work on it together and smiled, referring to my own speech that has been affected by cerebral palsy (Gallardo & Gibson, 2005). I was also very aware of being given "role model" status by Linda and wanted to meet her expectations. Everyone laughed. Kim was friendly, asking me when my baby was due. I said in 2 months. She then asked if I knew if it was a boy or girl. I told her no and that I wanted to be surprised. Linda sat back and appeared more relaxed. I asked Linda how she wanted to spend our time in session together (Glasser, 1965). Linda said that she wanted us to just visit. I offered everyone something to drink and cheese and crackers, with the intention of creating an inviting atmosphere for Linda and her family (Santana-Martin & Santana, 2005). I knew the three of them liked sewing, so I began our conversation by commenting on my own enjoyment in sewing and asked if they did, too. Linda's mom began telling me about how she loves to sew and is very happy that Linda and Kim like to sew. Kim began talking about how she loves going over to Grandma's house to sew and to eat. She talked about learning to cook different dishes from Grandma that her mom didn't know how to cook. They all laughed, though I could see that Linda was disappointed that Kim thought she wasn't a good cook, struggling with the "Super Woman Complex" (Gibson, 2006) of not being perfect. I asked Kim if there is anything that she likes that her mom cooks. Kim quickly said that her tacos are great, seemingly trying to please her mom. Linda told Kim that she didn't have to make her feel better by saying she makes good tacos. Kim seemed uncomfortable with the exchange. I said that I bet my baby will complain about my food, attempting to help Kim feel comfortable. They laughed, and Linda began to talk about how smart Kim is and how well she is doing in school. Kim's face brightened, and Kim began to talk about how her mom has been making sure her homework is done every night and how she quizzes her for upcoming tests. Kim said that after she is done with homework, she and her mom watch TV together. I said that it sounds like she enjoyed spending time with her mom. Kim said, "Definitely, my mom is cool most of the time." I asked what she meant by "most of the time." She said, "My mom is a mom who tells me to do my chores and stuff like that; you know, mom stuff." I smiled and said that my mom did that too. Linda's mom was mostly quiet throughout the session, though she was listening intently, smiling and nodding during our conversation. Through my observations, it was evident that Linda and Kim share a loving relationship. Kim mentioned that since they had been seeing their family counselor, she feels more comfortable telling her mom how she is feeling when she is "mad or sad." I asked Linda if she had noticed a change at home. "Definitely," she said, adding that they both have been changing how they talk with one another. As the session came to a close, I asked Linda if she would like to come in next week. She smiled and said that she was fine and would call me in the future. I thanked her for bringing her family in and told them how nice it was to have met them. Linda hugged me, as she began to cry softly. I told her that it had been an honor working with her, and I thanked her for giving me so many gifts that made my life richer (Santana-Martin & Santana, 2005). Kim gave me a hug, and Linda's mom embraced me, with tears in her eyes, saying, "Vaya con Dios."

Analysis of Session 5   Our last session provided a sense of community with Linda's mom and daughter joining us. I offered snacks and attempted speaking Spanish to facilitate an inclusive and friendly environment (Santana-Martin & Santana, 2005) for Linda's mom and Kim. I was aware of Linda's hopes of my being an example to both her mom and her daughter, and I had fears that I would not meet Linda's expectations. However, as the session came to a close, I sensed a deeper connection not only between Linda and her family, but between Linda and her inner self (Storr, 1983).

Case Conceptualization

Throughout our sessions, it was evident that Linda had begun to challenge herself and her world views. She had internalized life experiences that are shared among many women who are in their mid-30s. She wanted the best for her daughter while struggling with her daughter's onset of puberty. She was coming to terms with wanting and expecting more from her significant-other relationships, discovering that she deserves to have someone to love her without her sacrificing her needs and values. In addition, Linda had concerns for her parents, juggling her time between family of origin, Kim, and work. Linda was carrying many stresses that impacted her mental health, world view, and inner sense of self. As I reflected on my work with Linda, I became more aware that research provides an inadequate analysis of working disability into a therapeutic context. What became more salient in my work with Linda were the common therapeutic factors associated with all therapeutic encounters. The therapeutic–working alliance with the client, the belief in the therapeutic modality implemented, and my own personal characteristics accounted for more of the success I had with Linda in the short time we worked together (Wampold, 2001). It was clear that my willingness to meet Linda where she was at during that time was essential in building and maintaining a therapeutic alliance with her. The establishment of this therapeutic alliance provided a foundation for further exploration and the creation of a safe therapeutic context for Linda's self-disclosure and exploration in our sessions. Moreover, the use of reality therapy and disability affirmative therapy with Linda was beneficial, as it addressed the essence of her life experiences as well as my own personal development as a therapist and person with a disability.

In addition, Linda had the added stresses of being a Latina with a disability. She was struggling with her identity, and she exhibited the following characteristics related to Stage 2: Realization from Gibson's Disability Identity Development Model (2006):

- She had an awareness of having a disability and of the impact it has on her life.
- She was aware of the physical presentation of her hair, makeup, and dress.
- She was embarrassed to cry in front of others, fearing how she looks.
- She was concerned with how others perceive her.
- She strived to be the best at everything that she attempted—the "Super Woman Complex."
- She displaced feelings of inadequacy onto Kim, expecting perfection.

As Linda was experiencing life with a disability, interwoven within her psychological makeup were her world views as a second-generation Puerto Rican woman. According to the Racial/Cultural Identity Development Model (Atkinson, 2003), Linda exhibited the following characteristics in Stage 1: Conformity:

- She preferred to not speak Spanish.
- She did not want Kim speaking Spanish, believing that it will hold her back in society.
- She did not understand or value why her mom is living with her brother and his family.
- She was offended when I referred to her as a Latina. She responded with, "I am an American."

During the sessions it became evident that Linda's stage of acculturation seemed to be in conflict with her mother's stage of acculturation. This may have contributed additional stress to Linda's life. In working with Linda, it was important for me to allow her to take some control of our time together, to self-disclose personal qualities that enhanced our therapeutic alliance, and to use positive modeling as a way to empower Linda in continuing to move through her personal disability discourse. It will be important for Linda to continue this dialogue and to further engage in self-exploration as it relates to her connecting to Puerto Rican culture and to disability culture; being a woman, mother, and daughter; and combining these multiple dimensions of her identity within the context of the ever-changing social, cultural, and political contexts around her. Together, we only touched the surface of these issues, but we planted the seed of future exploration and personal growth.

Evidence-Based Practice in Psychology

As previously stated, empirical research and clinical expertise with persons with disabilities have been limited. The APA has identified less than 2% of its membership as individuals with disabilities (Olkin, 2002), which may contribute to the lack of research and evidence-based practice in disability competency. Furthermore, the number of specific courses on disability offered in graduate programs actually decreased from 24% in 1989 to 11% in 1990 (Olkin, 2002). Many graduate programs do only a cursory treatment of the issues involved with this population as part of their multicultural counseling course. The limited exposure to training opportunities may leave psychologists prone to biases and misconceptions about disability (Taliaferro, 2005). Leigh, Powers, Vash, and Nettles (2004) conducted a survey and found additional concerns that included a lack of knowledge, limited training in disability issues and services, and a lack of sensitivity in providing psychological services to clients with disabilities. These data illustrate the call for increased efforts and contributions to the field of disability competency in evidence-based practice. Section 2.01(b) of the APA Ethics Code (APA, 2002) supports the development of more research as a profession to develop disability-related competence. This is a step toward inclusion and knowledge of disability within the field. However, it has been difficult, at best, to achieve training related to disability. In 2005, the APA took another step that recognizes the need for evidence-based practices within the field to promote effectiveness of treatment, including "psychological assessment, case formulation, therapeutic relationship and intervention" (APA, 2005). However, this concept does not automatically lend insight to persons with disability or to ethnic individuals.

Empirical research examining disability has been minimal. Nevertheless, an extensive study of empirical research reviewing the self-concept of children with cerebral palsy compared with that of children without disability showed that adolescent females with cerebral palsy have a lower self-concept than females without disability in the domains of physical appearance, social acceptance, athletic competence, and scholastic competence (Shields, Murdoch, Loy, Dodd, & Taylor, 2006). There was insufficient evidence to conclude that children with cerebral palsy, in general, have a lower global self-concept compared with those without disability. In addition to limited research, empirical evidence has been limited in regard to assessment tools that can be used in therapy for persons with disabilities. Recent research using the Minnesota Multiphasic Personality Inventory in a large group of patients with chronic occupational spinal disorders found that these patients are 14 times more likely to be depressed or anxious (Gatchel, 2006), which emphasizes the need for evaluation and treatment for clinical depression prior to other interventions to maximize treatment outcomes. Further research is needed not only in the study of disability, but also to determine the reliability and validity of assessment instrumentation.

Additional Clinical Considerations

It is expected that Linda will continue self-exploration of her identity as a Latina with a disability. As she contemplates her relationship with Ray, she may question why she married and remains married to him. This may evoke the need for cultural sensitivity and competence in the realms of disability, religion, gender, and Latina culture. It will be important for her to continue to strengthen her ability to handle discrimination and preconceived ideations that others try to place on her. This strength will connect Linda with her inner sense of self while giving her freedom from others' preconceived constructs.

Identification of Author's Personal Dimensions of Diversity and World View

Working with Linda had a profound impact on me as a clinician and as a woman with a disability. We quickly developed a bond based on unspoken understandings. I believe that my disability challenged Linda to begin facing her issues related to her own disability. In turn, I was also challenged as a clinician. During our sessions, I would often notice that the empathy I typically experience with clients often became sympathy. This was especially true as we explored Linda's family's attitudes of her disability. The attitudes Linda shared were quite similar to those of my own family, and I was aware of the countertransference that was being stirred within me. This was especially true during our final session, knowing that Linda had expectations of my serving as a positive role model for her mom and daughter. I was nervous prior to meeting them, especially about meeting her mom. Like Linda, I could relate to wanting my mom (and family) to realize that I could be successful while having a disability.

I truly believe that my pregnancy also factored into our quick bonding. Linda knew that I understood motherhood. Her transference was motivation to stay in treatment. Linda provided much material given our limited amount of time together. We did not have sufficient time to explore her identity as a second-generation Latina with a disability, however, our relationship facilitated a seed of discovering that women with disabilities do share similar life experiences apart from the commonalities most women share. Working with Linda gave me several insights into myself as a woman and mother-to-be with a disability. I knew for the first time that there are other people in this world who do understand the struggles of having a disability. In fact, it was in working with Linda that I began exploring the identity development of persons with disabilities.

Therapeutic Recommendations and Guiding Principles for Interacting With Clients With Disabilities

1. Clients with disabilities are inclusive individuals and encompass many characteristics including ethnicity, gender, age, and so on that impact mental health.
2. Be sensitive to the possibility that the client may have experienced "a lack of societal boundary" regarding the disability. He or she may be offended if disability is addressed prior to other traits, characteristics, and so on. This can impede the development of a therapeutic alliance.

3. The client's disability should be addressed. However, do not assume that disability is or should be the presenting problem. The timing of when to address disability issues is also very important.

4. Use person-first language. Language empowers.

5. Be willing to be creative with the traditional clinical session or setting. For example, conduct a session by phone for a client who is reliant on others for transportation.

6. When meeting a person with a visual disability, always identify yourself and others who may be with you. When conversing in a group, remember to identify the person to whom you are speaking.

7. Remember that nonverbal cues are often altered by disability (e.g., visual disability).

8. Speak directly to the person rather than through a companion or sign language interpreter. Although the care provider may need to be included in a session or meeting at times, people with disabilities have the right to expect privacy and confidentiality and to participate in decision making regarding their mental health care.

9. Treat adults as adults. Address people who have disabilities by their first names only when extending the same familiarity to all others.

10. Listen attentively when you are speaking with a person who has difficulty speaking. Be patient and wait for the person to finish rather than correcting or speaking for the person. If necessary, ask short questions that require short answers, such as a nod or shake of the head. Never pretend to understand if you are having difficulty doing so. Instead, repeat what you have understood and allow the person to respond. The response will clue you in and guide your understanding.

Conclusions

Throughout this chapter, I have discussed clinical competency in regard to disability and culture. It needs to be noted that we cannot attribute the understanding of an individual based solely on the created constructs that we use as tools, and we cannot say that a certain characteristic is solely due to having a disability, another is due to ethnicity, and so on. Human beings are much more complex. The focus of this chapter has highlighted that each one of us is a unique human being. We each have our own subculture within the many cultures we belong to and live among. As healing professionals, we need to consider the whole person if we are to have a chance of providing competent care.

Discussion Questions

1. How and when should disability be addressed with a client with a disability?
2. Should clinicians be aware of medications clients may be prescribed because of disability-related issues? What are the medical implications, drug interactions, and effects on mood and behavior?
3. Can sessions be held in nontraditional meeting places, over the phone, and so forth to accommodate persons with disabilities?
4. How do you work with clients who require the presence of a personal attendant or a sign language interpreter with regard to the therapeutic relationship? What are the confidentiality issues?
5. How can you be respectful to persons of diverse cultures with disabilities while challenging their world views?

Cultural Resources

Suggestions for Further Reading

Goodley, D., & Lawthom, R. (2005). *Disability and psychology: Critical introductions and reflections.* New York: Palgrave Macmillan.

Olkin, R. (1999). *What psychotherapist should know about disability.* New York: Guilford.

Stone, J. H. (2005). *Culture and disability: Providing culturally competent services.* Thousand Oaks, CA: Sage.

Vash, C. L., & Crewe, N. M. (2003). *Psychology of disability* (2nd ed.). New York: Springer.

Suggestions for Viewing

Gallardo, M. E., & Gibson, J. (2005). *Understanding the therapeutic needs of culturally diverse individuals with disabilities.* Framingham, MA: Microtraining and Multicultural Development. (http://www.emicrotraining.com)

References

American Psychological Association. (2002). Ethical principles of psychologists and code of conduct. *American Psychologist, 57*(12), 1060–1073.

American Psychological Association. (2003). Guidelines on multicultural education, training, research, practice and organizational change for psychologists. *American Psychologist, 58*(5), 377–402.

American Psychological Association. (2005). *American Psychological Association statement: Policy statement on Evidence-Based Practice in Psychology.* Retrieved April 16, 2007, from http://www2.apa.org/practice/ebpstatement.pdf

American Psychological Association. (2006). Evidence-Based Practice in Psychology. *American Psychologist, 61*(4), 271–285.

Americans With Disabilities Act of 1990, 42 U.S.C.A § 12101 et seq.

Atkinson, D. R. (2003). *Counseling American minorities: A cross-cultural perspective* (6th ed.). New York: McGraw-Hill.

Bein, A., Torres, A., & Kurrilla, V. (2000). Service delivery issues in early termination of Latino clients. *Journal of Human Behavior in the Social Environment, 3*, 43–59.

Berenson, A., Breitkopf, C., & Wu, Z. (2003). Reproductive correlates of depressive symptoms among low-income women. *Obstetrics and Gynecology, 1002*, 1310–1317.

Blazer, D., Kessler, R., McGonagle, K., & Swartz, M. (1994, July). The prevalence of major depression in a national community sample: The national comorbidity survey. *American Journal of Psychiatry, 151*, 979–986.

Block, P., Balcazar, F., & Keys, C. B. (2002). Race, poverty and disability: Three strikes and you're out! Or are you? *Social Policy, 33*(1), 34–38.

Brach, C., & Fraser, I. (2000). Can cultural competency reduce racial and ethnic health disparities? A review and conceptual model. *Medical Care Research and Review, 57*, 181–217.

Cordero, A., & Kurz, B. (2006). Acculturation and the mental health of Latina women in the women, infant, and children program. *Affilia: Journal of Women and Social Work, 2*(1), 46–58.

Fawcett, S. B., White, G. W., Balcazar, F. E., Suarez-Balcazar, Y., Matthews, R. M., Paine Andrews, A., Seekins, T., & Smith, J. F. (1994). A contextual-behavioral model of empowerment: Case studies involving people with physical disabilities. *American Journal of Community Psychology, 22*(4), 471–496.

Gallardo, M. E., & Gibson, J. (2005). *Understanding the therapeutic needs of culturally diverse individuals with disabilities.* Framingham, MA: Microtraining and Multicultural Development. (http://www.emicrotraining.com)

Gatchel, R. J. (2006). MMPI Disability Profile: The least known, most useful screen for psychopathology in chronic occupational spinal disorders. *Spine, 31*(25), 2973–2978.

Gibson, J. (2003). Health care for patients with disabilities: An introduction. *Journal of Southern California Clinicians, 1*(1), 9–12.

Gibson, J. (2006). Disability and clinical competency: An introduction. *The California Psychologist, 39*, 6–10.

Glasser, W. (1965). *Reality therapy.* New York: HarperCollins.

Jezewski, M., & Sotnik, P. (2005). Disability service providers as culture brokers. In J. H. Stone (Eds.), *Culture and disability: Providing culturally competent services* (pp. 37–64). New York: State University of New York, Multicultural Aspects of Counseling Series 21.

Johnson-Greene, D. (2006). Ethics of testing and assessment of persons with disabilities: Moving towards disability-related competence. *American Psychological Association, Division 22 Newsletter, 33*(3), 12–13.

Kreuter, M. (2000). *Spinal cord injury and partner relationships.* Retrieved April 29, 2007, from http://www.nature.com/sc/journal/v38/n1/abs/3100933a.html

Leigh, L., Powers, L., Vash, C., & Nettles, R. (2004). Survey of psychological services to clients with disabilities. *Rehabilitation Psychology, 49*(1), 49–54.

Office of the Surgeon General. (2001). Culture, race and ethnicity. In *A supplement to mental health: A report of the Surgeon General*. Retrieved September 10, 2006, from http://www.surgeongeneral.gov/library/mentalhealth/cre/fact3.asp

Olkin, R. (1999). *What psychotherapists should know about disability*. New York: Guilford.

Olkin, R. (2002). Could you hold the door for me? Including disability in diversity. *Cultural Diversity and Ethnic Minority Psychology, 8*(2), 130–137.

Piastro, D. B. (1993). *Nazi legacies: Hate for disabled in modern Germany*. Newspaper Enterprise Association, 106.

Rimmer, J. H., Braddock, D., & Marks, B. (1995). Health characteristics and behaviors of adults with intellectual disabilities residing in three living arrangements. *Research in Developmental Disabilities, 16*, 489–499.

Rosen, D., Spencer, M., Tolman, R., Williams, D., & Jackson, J. (2003). Psychiatric disorders and substance dependency among unmarried low-income mothers. *Health and Social Work, 28*, 157–165.

Rotter, J. (1966). Generalized expectancies for internal versus external control of reinforcements. *Psychological Monographs, 80*, 1–28.

Santana-Martin, S., & Santana, F. O. (2005). An introduction to Mexican culture for service providers. In J. H. Stone (Ed.), *Culture and disability: Providing culturally competent services* (pp. 161–186). New York: State University of New York, Multicultural Aspects of Counseling Series 21.

Shields, N., Murdoch, A., Loy, Y., Dodd, K., & Taylor, N. (2006). *A systematic review of the self-concept of children with cerebral palsy compared with children without disability*. Retrieved May 1, 2007, from http://www.journals.cambridge.org/action/displayAbstract?fromPage=online&aid=375182#

Stone, J. H. (2005). *Culture and disability: Providing culturally competent services*. Thousand Oaks, CA: Sage.

Storr, A. (1983). *The essential Jung: Selected writings*. Introduced by Anthony Storr. Princeton, NJ: Princeton University Press.

Sue, D. W., Capodilupo, C. M., Torino, G. C., Bucceri, J. M., Holder, A. M. B., Nadal, K. L., & Esquilin, M. (2007). Racial microaggressions in everyday life: Implications for clinical practice. *American Psychologist, 62*(4), 271–286.

Taliaferro, G. (2005). Evidence-based practices and disability. *Rehabilitation Psychology News, 32*(4), 15.

The Arc. (2006). *The Arc—The first 50 years*. Retrieved September 13, 2006, from http://www.thearc.org/history/

U.S. Department of Transportation Federal Transit Administration. (2006). *Disability rights movement timeline*. Retrieved September 12, 2006, from http://www.fta.dot.gov/civilrights/ada/civil_rights_4064.html

Vash, C. L., & Crewe, N. M. (2003). *Psychology of disability* (2nd ed.). New York: Springer.

Waldrop, J., & Stern, S. M. (2003, March). *Disability status: Census 2000 brief*. Retrieved February 1, 2008, from http://www.census.gov/prod/2003pubs/c2kbr-17.pdf

Wallace, D. J., & Weisman, M. (2000). Should a war criminal be rewarded with eponymous distinction? The double life of Hans Reiter (1881–1969). *Journal of Clinical Rheumatology, 6*(1), 49–54.

Wampold, B. E. (2001). *The great psychotherapy debate: Models, methods, and findings*. Mahwah, NJ: Lawrence Erlbaum.

Conclusion

Evidence-Based Practice and Multiple Implications
Reflections and Future Directions

Miguel E. Gallardo and
Brian W. McNeill

Contents

What becomes clear as we examine the implications of integrating evidence-based practices in a culturally responsive way with diverse populations is the ongoing debate regarding the manner in which to incorporate these two distinct, yet complementary, perspectives (Sue & Sue, 2008; Whaley & Davis, 2007). As the contributors in this casebook examined the interplay of research, culture, and context, and we reflected on their implications, what is most salient to us are the modifications, or adaptations, that are needed to implement evidenced-based treatments within an Evidence-Based Practice in Psychology (EBPP) framework.

This casebook is representative of the more real-world therapeutic encounters that produce change through the process of deductive reasoning (Weston, Novotny, & Thompson-Brenner, 2005), and we concur that understanding and studying what clinicians do in therapy with their clients yield some of the most useful information about treatment efficacy. Kazdin (2008) argued that clinical work undoubtedly contributes to the scientific knowledge base. In addition, Lopez, Kopelowicz, and Canive (2002) advocated for a process model of cultural competence over a content model, emphasizing that a process model defends against the perpetuation of cultural stereotypes in therapy. Again, we can no longer examine Latinas/os or any other ethnic or cultural group from the perspective that to understand one implies that we understand all. What has been demonstrated throughout this casebook is that although, for example, a Mexican American client may have some consistent cultural patterns for living with other Mexican Americans, there are also very unique differences that determine one's context for living. The uniqueness within each individual reinforces the need to increase ethnic-specific research, taking into account issues such as class, gender, sexual orientation, and so on. More specifically, we are advocating for research that delves into the complexities of any culturally diverse group separate from research that examines the group as a homogenous entity.

In addition, this casebook is illustrative of the concept of dynamic sizing with clients, that is, each clinician's skill level in knowing when to generalize specific treatments methodologies while also customizing individualized treatments based on their client's specific characteristics, cultural values, and world views (Sue, 1998). Indeed, our research agendas have lacked a more in-depth understanding of the uniqueness within each culture, leaving students in training and clinicians without the needed skills to address culture-specific needs therapeutically. Contrary to ethnic-specific research and dynamic sizing is the implementation of empirically supported treatments (ESTs). ESTs focus on specific ingredients applied to specific problems under specific circumstances (American Psychological Association [APA], 2006). Although the application of ESTs has its role in the context of EBPP and as a component of the healing process (see Wampold, 2001b), ultimately, attempting to implement ESTs as is and apply them to clients with specific problems can be challenging at best, raising the issue of fidelity in the therapeutic setting. Fidelity can be described as a clinician's ability to take an EST and apply it in its purest form with no modifications. In reviewing the chapters of this casebook, it is clear that therapeutic fidelity may present some challenges in working with clients who have multiple identities and who live within multiple contexts. These challenges further reinforce the need to reexamine the perceived efficacy of ESTs and their role in the advancement of EBPP.

As noted in the introduction to this casebook, EBPP begins with the various contexts of the client's life and attempts to determine what research evidence exists that might facilitate change for clients. From this perspective, the importance of instituting flexibility in clinical applications and incorporating research evidence from multiple sources becomes essential. The cases in this book underscore the importance that therapists' desire to be culturally responsive supersedes their desire to be clinically competent. In essence, before we determine that all ESTs lack validity within a multicultural context, researchers and clinicians alike must shift their professional lens to one that is culturally responsive rather than narrowly define their lens by which traditional mainstream research and clinical interests take precedence. In making this shift, it is clear that our definition of clinical competence must expand to include cultural responsiveness. That is, to not include the core value of culture and context into our definition of clinical competence potentially creates unethical circumstances, misunderstandings, and unintentional violations by well-intentioned therapists. In addition, in negating culture from our discourse, we essentially limit the application of ESTs within real-world therapeutic encounters. Consequently, it is apparent that to address the needs of diverse communities, we need to continue to identify what works with whom and why, or we risk continuing to allow our ethical kaleidoscope to be colored only by our mainstream clinical view rather than to infuse the multicolored cultural lens that is necessary. This examination requires that we revisit, and possibly redefine, how we explain the notion of what is cultural and what constitutes culturally responsive practices in therapeutic settings. We believe that the authors, through their case examinations, have done an exemplary job of facilitating the intentionality by which we define and address cultural issues in therapy.

In accentuating the Fourth Force in Psychology, several bodies and authors within the fields of counseling and psychology have continued to advocate for a more in-depth understanding of cultural issues through the passage of sets of multicultural guidelines within the profession (APA, 2003; Arredondo et al., 1996; Lewis, Arnold, House, & Toporek, 2003; Sue, Arredondo, & McDavis, 1992). These guidelines call for a multicultural paradigm shift in the way that we research, train our students, and treat diverse communities. In addition, this paradigm shift implies that we understand the importance of responding to our clients in a culturally consistent and responsive manner, first and foremost. Cultural responsiveness means having the mindfulness and the appropriate skills to accurately assess, plan, and treat individuals within their own environmental and cultural contexts without pathologizing, blaming, or invalidating their experiences. It is not a concept that one arrives at, but more a process that is lifelong and ever evolving (Gallardo & Curry, 2008). What is salient in this definition is a call to personal action for clinicians and researchers to deepen their understanding of the manifestation of culture within clinical settings and to create a system of care that is consistent with, and reflects, the clients' world views. This paradigm shift requires that we seek to understand the notion of culture and cultural differences in therapy the same way we seek to understand psychiatric diagnosis or differences. This comparison is not to be confused with pathologizing culture or cultural differences, but more to highlight the indifference and apathy by which many clinicians and controlled laboratory trials in research seek to understand the multiple dimensions of culture therapeutically.

Hays (2001) described the essence of culture and therapy through her ADDRESSING framework by highlighting the multiple identities and group memberships that characterize individuals in treatment. As is evidenced in this volume, the ADDRESSING framework focuses on the cultural complexities that clinicians need to consider when working with multiculturally diverse communities. Hay's model includes Age and generational differences, Developmental or acquired Disabilities, Religion and spiritual orientation, Ethnicity, Socioeconomic status, Sexual Orientation, Indigenous heritage, National origin, and Gender. In addition, Hay's model, and the authors of this casebook, accentuated the need to examine culture beyond simply race and ethnicity. Specifically, we cannot mistake our desire to be culturally sensitive for cultural responsiveness in the therapeutic domain. A close examination of the chapters in this casebook demonstrates that we cannot narrowly define our clients, as this limits their capacity to change and our capacity to heal. The authors highlighted the importance of addressing the multiple identities of each client and community they treat. Hay's framework not only underscores the importance of addressing patients' characteristics, values, and context, but also underscores the importance of recognizing the utility of clinical expertise in the development of culturally responsive interventions.

One aspect of clinical expertise and experience includes the clinician's ability to continually self-reflect to assess and reassess his or her own cultural lens and world view within a therapeutic context (APA, 2006). The contributors described their own dimensions of personal identity as it relates to the delivery of culturally responsive services. Our hope is that students in training, as well as practicing therapists, strive to deepen their own understanding of how culture manifests intrapsychically and interpersonally. To understand culture, one must begin with one's own personal identity, as everyone possesses culture. As a profession, we have shifted our own internal thinking about the manifestation of culture and who "has" culture and who does not. Gone are the days where we implied that to have culture, one must be a representative from one of the four major ethnic groups studied (i.e., Latinos, American Indians, African Americans, Asians). The cases highlight the importance for all clinicians, regardless of race or ethnicity, to examine the manifestation of culture in their own life and to understand that to be effective in a culturally consistent manner, they do not have to remain a prisoner to any socialization patterns that may impede their ability to connect with and treat clients from multiculturally diverse backgrounds. Whether the readers of this casebook represent the mainstream Caucasian culture or a historically underrepresented group, their willingness to challenge their own cultural beliefs, to understand the manifestation of culture in their own lives, and to engage in a continual process of reexamination ultimately indicates their ability to treat those from diverse backgrounds different from their own. In essence, the color of one's skin may not ultimately be the best indicator of one's ability to successfully intervene with clients. Ultimately, when people engage in this reexamination process, they also uncover a deeper connection to their own ethnic identity while strengthening the cultural lens through which they view the world. The contributors make the case that although it is important to use a theoretical and empirically grounded framework, the healer's experiences and expertise in the process of therapy cannot be neglected.

As stated earlier, we believe that ESTs have their place in the development of culturally appropriate treatment methodologies. However, we also advocate for the expansion of perspectives in the development of culturally consistent and appropriate treatment methods for individuals representing multiple identities. The chapters in this casebook begin to challenge the issue of whether adapting generic ESTs makes sense. Hwang (2006) reported that the literature addressing the adaptation of treatments is varied and loosely used across studies, thereby creating a lack of clarity in designing and implementing the adaptation of treatments. This lack of clarity suggests that we need to better define what cultural adaptation means within the research domain. For example, Griner and Smith (2006) conducted a meta-analysis of 76 studies on culturally adapted interventions, finding that interventions targeted toward specific cultural groups were four times more effective than those applied to clients from a variety of cultural backgrounds. Specifically, the authors found that when clinicians provided treatment in the language of origin, if other than English, therapy was twice as effective as therapy conducted in English. The notion of beginning with the client's social, political, and cultural contexts to construct a treatment method appears to shed light on a very important area of further research and study that includes, but is not limited to, the expansion of perspectives in the development of culturally consistent and appropriate treatment methods for individuals representing multiple identities within our research methodologies and in the education and training of therapists and healers.

Future Directions in Research

Most recently, Kazdin (2008) highlighted that evidence might be narrowly defined within a research domain and that a gap needs to be bridged between research and practice. A serious concern in the process and outcome research is that the role of race, ethnicity, and culture is neglected (Hill & Williams, 2000). This lack of inclusion leaves us asking three very important questions: (a) Is therapy effective for nondominant racial and ethnic populations in the United States in comparison to therapy for Caucasian populations? (b) Are specific treatments equally effective across racial and ethnic groups in the United States? (c) How have race and ethnicity been incorporated in the research that has examined process and outcome within a therapeutic setting? As previously mentioned, future research directions need to further examine and increase our understanding of culturally competent treatment modalities with culture-specific populations. Kazdin (2008) stated that we need to improve our understanding of clinicians' decision-making skills, the types of variables clinicians consider in making decisions, and the ways clinicians reach any conclusions about treatment interventions. Kazdin further stated that clinicians are researchers in that they hypothesize about what particular treatment combinations or adaptations will work with particular clients. He suggested that we begin to codify the experiences of clinicians who practice as a way to inform research hypotheses. As a result, Kazdin advocated for direct collaborations between researchers and clinicians, as researchers would benefit clinicians more by attempting to understand why therapy works and/or how it produces change. Furthermore, Kazdin suggested that this is an area that has received the least amount of attention to date. The challenge as we move forward is that our real-world structure or format for designing and implementing a therapeutic domain becomes idiosyncratic to each clinician. As we forge ahead, it becomes necessary that we develop better formats or strategies for understanding the process of therapy with culturally diverse individuals as we attempt to better understand and expand our knowledge base of what works with whom. As the contributors to this casebook can testify, it was not an easy process to describe their work within an evidence-based practice template. The systematic measurement and investigation of understanding the complexities involved in working therapeutically, at times, seems insurmountable. We need to do a better job of defining evidence for good treatment and describing the process through which this evidence takes place, thereby increasing our ability to explain and, we hope, replicate efforts from one clinician to another. We have a big task ahead of us, and it demands that we become more intentional in our efforts to crystallize our work within a multicultural framework. This process also expands our possibilities in bridging the gap between research and practice. One way to begin to decrease this gap is through the incorporation of qualitative research.

Consequently, we need to advocate for the acceptance and inclusion of qualitative research methodologies in the examination of culture (Kazdin, 2008). Qualitative research methodologies allow for the understanding of the unique perspectives from the cultural group under study. This emic, or culture-specific, approach can be incredibly useful for areas that are not well understood or those that have been underexplored or neglected (Bernal, 2006). In addition, as noted by Morrow and Smith (2000), applied psychologists are trained in skills required to conduct qualitative investigations, as many of the same skills that underlie the counseling process are essential to qualitative interview procedures. Ancis (2004) also advocated for the design of interventions and programs from a bottom-up approach, as programs designed based on the needs of the cultural group studied potentially provide a more culturally inclusive and consistent method for diagnosing, assessing, and treating these populations. We believe that the incorporation of qualitative research methodologies can help us begin to understand what works with whom and why. These methods also allow for the inclusion of clinician's expertise and experiences in working with diverse clients, as we have attempted to capture in this casebook. Most important, Kazdin (2008) encouraged the inclusion of qualitative research methodologies as another way to begin to bridge the gap between research and practice. However, the foundations for these shifts in the way we examine cultural implications within the research and clinical domains begin in our education and training programs.

Future Directions in Training and Education

As we begin to create a paradigm shift in our training institutions, it is important that we become more intentional about incorporating qualitative research methodologies and EBPP in the curriculum. Bernal and

Scharron-del-Rio (2001) expressed concerns that teaching from a dogmatic perspective is an exclusive ideology and that implementing only ESTs in our work across cultures is another form of cultural imperialism. Thus, it becomes important that we increase our attention to EBPP and incorporate it into our training programs. We believe that when we begin to place more emphasis on the inclusion of culture and context within our training programs, we automatically integrate and include culture and context along the training and professional continuum. In essence, if we begin with culture and context at the outset, anything we do beyond this beginning point reflects this perspective and therefore also reflects a more real-world research mindset and clinical focus. We cannot falsely teach our students that cultural sensitivity is synonymous with being culturally responsive. Although it is important to understand overarching commonalities among diverse cultural groups, it is not enough, and in fact, it can often times be more detrimental than useful. We need to balance our education and training models with culture-individual-specific analyses to help students and trainees understand that understanding one is not the same as understanding all. Simultaneously, we also do not want our students to be deceived into thinking that they should not make attempts to understand the manifestation of culture on a global level as it relates to specific cultural groups. What has not changed is our responsibility as students and therapists to take it upon ourselves to do our own research as it applies to our clients. We need to help our students understand that there is a balance between understanding and being understood. Most important, we need to train our students to be methodological researchers within a therapeutic framework. To bridge the gap between research and practice, we believe a major emphasis of future training needs to focus on helping our students develop the ability to assess methodologically what they are doing in the room therapeutically, to know how they know what they are implementing is working, and to gauge their own barometer in therapy with clients. Increasing our attention in this area helps our students do a better job of translating clinical work into research. It is important that we facilitate the development of clinical researchers in our training programs who are equipped with the mind-set and skill set to not only work within a therapeutic domain, but also contribute within the research domain. In essence, we need to have a foundation for our work with culturally diverse clients while not assuming we know the person who sits before us.

Cultural immersion is another way to help students and trainees begin to balance what they think they know and what they do not know that they do not know. The chapters in this casebook also illustrate the need for our educational and training programs to extend from the classroom to the community. If we want our students to understand culture, they need to understand the "lived experience" of those they serve (Carter, 2005). Studying about culture in the classroom and learning about cognitive-behavioral methods alone do not adequately prepare our students to meet the demands of a demographically diverse population. It is imperative that students have an opportunity to experience culture from the lens of the communities they serve while simultaneously understanding the limitations of treatment models in their purest form. In addition, this pathway to understanding also allows the communities to participate in the development of treatment strategies and interventions that work from their own perspectives. Therefore, it is imperative that students and trainees have an opportunity to engage with diverse communities outside the classroom setting. This method of teaching is also important because it provides students with an opportunity to understand the systemic and sociocultural influences in their client's life. This is particularly important because students need to understand that expanding their role as provider may be necessary at times. We do not believe that one needs to discard his or her already existing clinical knowledge and skill set to treat diverse communities. However, we do understand that if we do not educate and teach future clinicians from culturally inclusive perspectives, we will continue to limit their capacity as providers and researchers. Thus, it is important that we begin to incorporate more diverse approaches to research, diagnosis, assessment, and intervention in our education and training programs.

Finally, within an EBPP perspective, the role of common factors, specifically training students in the skills required to form therapeutic alliances with clients, is paramount, as suggested by the research of Wampold (2001b). Stein and Lambert (1995) also documented that positive client outcome is related to therapist experience level. Stein and Lambert's meta-analysis also demonstrates that therapeutic outcome is facilitated by therapist-relationship factors and that such factors are enhanced by specific training. Consequently, we need to better expose students to the importance of these findings, which leads to a better appreciation of the role the therapeutic alliance maintains in the healing process as opposed to the premature application of specific ingredients in the form of ESTs. In addition, future research on the training process will need to focus on the skills needed to form alliances with diverse clientele and expressions of cultural empathy.

In Closing

The therapists represented in this casebook have provided a "window into the therapy room" and transferred their clinical experience and expertise onto the pages of this book. They have stated, from multiple perspectives, a case for providing more insight in the "how" of clinical work. In addition, they have made the case that further research is needed in the area of psychotherapy process and outcome and that there is a need for more direct collaborations between researchers and clinicians. We have attempted to make the case that clinical experience and expertise, culture, and context can, and should, inform and drive research hypotheses that more accurately reflect real-world life experiences and situations of clients with multiple identities who reside within multiple contexts. Furthermore, it is essential that we begin to teach and train our students to be better clinical researchers within a therapeutic domain and to incorporate culture-specific treatment modalities. Finally, we also argue that we need not "throw the baby out with the bath water," and that when we place our desire to be culturally responsive above all else, we will create research, training, and clinical agendas that reflect the global multicultural society in which we live and work.

References

American Psychological Association. (2003). Guidelines on multicultural education, training, research, practice, and organizational change for psychologists. *American Psychologist, 58*, 377–402.

American Psychological Association. (2006). Evidence-Based Practice in Psychology. *American Psychologist, 61*, 271–285.

Ancis, J. R. (2004). *Culturally responsive interventions: Innovative approaches to working with diverse populations.* New York: Brunner Routledge.

Arredondo, P., Toporek, R., Brown, S. P., Sanchez, J., Locke, D. C., & Stadler, H. (1996). Operationalization of the multicultural counseling competencies. *Journal of Multicultural Counseling and Development, 24*, 42–78.

Bernal, G. (2006). Intervention development and cultural adaptation research with diverse families. *Family Processes, 45*(2), 143–151.

Bernal, G., & Scharron del Río, M. (2001). Are empirically supported treatments valid for ethnic minorities? Toward an alternative approach for treatment research. *Cultural Diversity and Ethnic Minority Psychology, 7*, 328–342.

Carter, R. T. (Ed.). (2005). *Handbook of racial-cultural psychology and counseling: Training and practice* (Vol. 2). New York: John Wiley & Sons.

Gallardo, M. E., & Curry, S. (2008). Shifting perspectives: Culturally responsive interventions with Latino substance abusers. Manuscript submitted for publication.

Griner, D., & Smith, T. B. (2006). Culturally adapted mental health intervention: A meta-analytic review. *Psychotherapy: Theory, Research, Practice, Training, 43*(4), 531–548.

Hays, P. (2001). *Addressing cultural complexities in practice: A framework for clinicians and counselors.* Washington, DC: American Psychological Association.

Hill, C. E., & Williams, E. N. (2000). The process of individual therapy. In S. D. Brown & R. W. Lent (Eds.), *Handbook of counseling psychology* (3rd ed., pp. 670–710). New York: Wiley.

Hwang, W. (2006). The psychotherapy adaptation and modification framework: Application to Asian Americans. *American Psychologist, 61*(7), 702–715.

Kazdin, A. E. (2008). Evidence-based treatments and practice: New opportunities to bridge clinical research and practice, enhance the knowledge base, and improve patient care. *American Psychologist, 63*(3), 146–159.

Lewis, J., Arnold, M. S., House, R., & Toporek, R. L. (2003). *ACA advocacy competencies. Advocacy task force, American Counseling Association.* Retrieved June 11, 2008, from http://www.counseling.org/Resources/

Lopez, S. R., Kopelowicz, A., & Canive, J. M. (2002). Strategies in developing culturally congruent family interventions for schizophrenia: The case of Hispanics. In H. P. Lefley & D. L. Johnson (Eds.), *Family interventions in mental illness: International perspectives* (pp. 61–90). Westport, CT: Praeger Publishers.

Morrow, S. L., & Smith, M. L. (2000). Qualitative research for counseling psychology. In S. D. Brown & R. W. Lent (Eds.), *Handbook of counseling psychology* (3rd ed., pp. 199–232). New York: John Wiley & Sons.

Stein, D. M., & Lambert, M. J. (1995). Graduate training in psychotherapy: Are therapy outcomes enhanced? *Journal of Consulting and Clinical Psychology, 63,* 182–196.

Sue, D., & Sue, D. M. (2008). *Foundations of counseling and psychotherapy: Evidence-based practices for a diverse society.* New York: John Wiley & Sons.

Sue, D. W., Arredondo, P., & McDavis, R. J. (1992). Multicultural counseling competencies and standards: A call to the profession. *Journal of Multicultural Counseling and Development, 20*(2), 64–88.

Sue, S. (1998). In search of cultural competence in psychotherapy and counseling. *American Psychologist, 53,* 440–448.

Wampold, B. E. (2001a). Contextualizing psychotherapy as a healing practice: Culture, history, and methods. *Applied and Preventive Psychology, 10,* 69–86.

Wampold, B. E. (2001b). *The great psychotherapy debate: Models, methods, and findings.* Mahwah, NJ: Lawrence Erlbaum.

Weston, D., Novotny, C., & Thompson-Brenner, H. (2005). EBP ≠ EST: Reply to Crtis-Cristoph et al. (2005) and Weisz et al. (2005). *Psychological Bulletin, 131,* 427–433.

Whaley, A. L., & Davis, K. E. (2007). Cultural competence and evidence-based practice in mental health service: A complementary perspective. *American Psychologists, 62*(6), 563–574.

Afterword

Intersections of Multiple Identities
A Casebook of Evidence-Based Practices With Diverse Populations

Thomas A. Parham

Counseling Psychologist and Assistant Vice Chancellor,
Counseling and Health Services, University of California–Irvine

Traversing the highways of professional practice can be a lonely journey if one expects to find an abundance of signs illustrating culturally enriched counseling and clinical practice, academic instruction, or even training and supervision. In some respects, the loneliness is related to a few professional highways, where the void of culturally specific materials that have been unsuccessful at penetrating both the halls of academia and the corridors of mental health treatment agencies is quite pronounced. Indeed, the level of cultural sterility in some corners of the clinical and counseling professions is significant, even in this day and time.

In other respects, the loneliness has less to do with an absence of cultural information, for there are a few highways along the national landscape where culturally based theoretical orientations, assessment strategies, and treatment protocols have been the norm rather than the exception. The challenge here is not with the absence of relevant information per se, but rather with questions about the validity of the information presented and whether or not the absence of empirical validation renders the information less worthy of being applied to someone's counseling or clinical work or academic instruction. Well, Drs. Gallardo and McNeill have begun to answer those questions with this text titled *Intersections of Multiple Identities: A Casebook of Evidence-Based Practices With Diverse Populations*. They should be applauded for this contribution to the literature, for contained within the chapters of this text are some very important works and perspectives.

The salience of this text is underscored by several themes that run through-out the chapters. First, the authors of the various chapters take the time to define and explain the theoretical orientations that frame the assumptions they make about their intervention strategies. This is a critical element of the chapters specifically and the text generally, because all good counseling and clinical work should be anchored in theoretical assumptions that serve as a road map for intervention with specific client populations. Among the conceptual anchors that guide therapeutic interventions should be assump-tions about the nature of humanity, the etiology of client distress, how and why people change, the role and task of the clinician or counselor, and the expected therapeutic outcomes. Having this information should have helped you, the reader, connect up what might otherwise be a confusing road map of intervention.

Second, the authors of the various chapters discuss specific ways in which their approaches have been modified to accommodate an evidence-based focus in their work. This is an important addition given the struggle many counseling professionals face in whether and how to adapt a particular theoretical approach to a client population that is sufficiently different. Third, the chapter authors provide valuable case study materials that help bring to life the ways in which evidence-based practice is operationalized in their work. Remember, we just read case studies with several different clients representing an array of different cultural perspectives (African Americans, Latino/a Americans, Native Americans, Hawaiians, clients with disabilities, and those with issues involving their sexual orientation). Collectively, these three elements help to distinguish this text from many others in the field.

By themselves, these three elements would be enough to both sell many books and hail this effort as a tremendous success, but, there is more. Drs. Gallardo and McNeill have confronted the question of whether there is merit in applying this evidence-based practice perspective to work that is more culturally centered. This is no small feat, for there are many in the camps of cultural specificity who have questioned the utility of Western-based, Eurocentrically oriented approaches serving as models for anything cultural. In some respects, the authors of this text have challenged some of that resis-tance by taking the time to define what they mean by evidence and by broadening the scope of what counts as evidence to include more than just empirically supported treatments. This is a key element for those students and professionals who assume that evidence-based practice and empirically based treatments are overlapping synonymous terms. This text makes it clear that they are related, but not the same.

Reading this text has evoked memories of my days as a tenure-track academician, who, despite full-time faculty status, insisted on a joint clinical–counseling appointment in the counseling center before joining that institution. At that time, I reasoned that the clinical work would support my academic endeavors and help to keep my teaching sharp. Conversely, I believed that the academic instruction would shore up my knowledge base in theoretical orientations and enhance my counseling interventions. In a similar way, Evidence-Based Practice in Psychology (EBPP) helps to create a reciprocal exchange of benefit for both the instructor and the clinician.

In proposing this book, Drs. Gallardo and McNeill hoped that the text would help bridge the gap between practitioner self-awareness and knowledge and practice based on sound theory and techniques and have a broad appeal to master's- and doctoral-level students. This final product has certainly fit that bill and will definitely be an important resource for those students engaged in graduate study. However, after reading this text, I am convinced that this body of knowledge and information should and will have a broader appeal to a much wider audience, including doctoral-degreed professionals and even consumers, who deserve an opportunity to know about the efficacy of treatment approaches that they are subjected to. Having just finished this work yourself, I know you will agree that this information needs to be shared with the students and professionals whom you encounter. The only question is, how soon can you get started?

Your journey across the landscape of our profession has just become more crystallized, for you now have a new resource book that will better inform your travels through the corridors of academia and counseling and clinical practice. The challenge for you, however, is in determining how much risk you are willing to take, now that you have been informed. To see a broader possibility and potential for EBPP, are you willing to take the mental risks necessary to stretch your mind beyond what you have been previously taught or exposed to? Are you willing to take verbal risks, discussing this information with colleagues, students, supervisors, and supervisees? Finally, I ask if you are prepared to take behavioral risks and improvise on some of your own counseling or clinical practice supported by this storehouse of information. If you are, then I applaud you, for you will have fulfilled one of Dr. Gallardo's and Dr. McNeill's desires for contributing this text to our disciplines of psychology, counseling, and helping. This is more than just another contribution to the literature. It is a genuinely unique compendium of information that deserves the broadest coverage we can give it. Having read it, I am not just interested in knowing if you found it interesting and informative. I want to know if you now feel compelled to use it. I know I do, and I hope you do as well.

Subject Index

H

M

Author Index

A

T